Beta Sigma Phi
Home Sweet Home Cooking
Family Favorites

Beta Sigma Phi

Home Sweet Home Cooking

Family Favorites

Home Sweet Home

EDITORIAL STAFF

Managing Editor	Mary Jane Blount
Executive Editor	Debbie Seigenthaler
Project Managers	Georgia Brazil, Mary Cummings Shirley Edmondson, Maribel S. Wood
Editors	Linda Jones, Mary Wilson Jane Hinshaw, Christie Carlucci Debbie Van Mol, Nicky Beaulieu
Associate Editors	Carolyn King, Judy Jackson, Kay Kenerly, Ann Orendorff
Typographers	Pam Newsome, Sara Anglin Jessie Anglin, Walter Muncaster
Award Selection Judges	Bill Ross Mary Jane Blount Charlene Sproles
Test Kitchen	Charlene Sproles

Cover Photograph: Courtesy of the North American Blueberry Council;
Page 1: Courtesy of Borden, Inc.; Page 2: Courtesy of Pace Foods

© Favorite Recipes® Press, A Division of Heritage House, Inc. MCMLXIII
P.O. Box 305141, Nashville, Tennessee 37230

ISBN: 0-87197-376-6
Library of Congress Number: 93-71692

Manufactured in the United States of America
First Printing 1993

Recipes for photographs are on pages 210–211.

Contents

*Asterisk beside contributor name indicates submission of similar recipe.

Beta Sigma Phi

Linda Rostenberg

Dear Beta Sigma Phis:

When life moves a little too fast, and you're overdosing on too much work and too much fast food, there's a cure to that stressed-out feeling—a great home-cooked meal.

Now you don't have to run home to your mother to get one! Your thoughtful sorority sisters have sent you lots and lots of great cooking ideas, and we've compiled them in our newest Beta Sigma Phi cookbook, *Home Sweet Home Cooking: Family Favorites*.

As usual, we've awarded prizes in various food categories; these "best-of-the best" recipes are specially marked by a diamond symbol ❖ in the book. Just for fun, we've included some quick and easy craft projects, too.

For this, our silver anniversary year with Favorite Recipes® Press, we received so many great recipes that we decided to create a companion book, *Home Sweet Home Cooking: Company's Coming*. Either one or both make beautiful (and reasonably price!) gifts.

There really is no better present than a home-cooked meal. It's a gift of the heart and hands that tell those seated around your dinner table they're special. (They'll think you're pretty special, too!)

Yours in Beta Sigma Phi,

Linda Rostenberg
Beta Sigma Phi International
Executive Council

The Hobby Shop

There are so many things today that pull families apart—Dad and Mom work longer hours, the kids head off to the Mall. And on those rare nights when everyone *is* home, the Television turns us all into couch potatoes! What we need is something to bring families together away from the TV. In this chapter, we think you'll find something fun for everyone. From simple handmade barrettes to pretty stenciled recipe cards, there's a craft here to match everyone's interest and level of skill. Why not decide now to start working on next year's Christmas cards or ornaments? And while we're on the subject of Christmas, don't forget handmade gifts. So call your family together, turn off the TV, and get started on a hobby you can share.

Home Sweet Home

Kitten Barrette and Necklace

Delight the little kitten in your family with a gift of kitty cat jewelry. Purchased wooden hearts turned upside down become puffy cheeks and a pointed wisp of fur. Then, folded ribbon ears and your paintbrush make pretty kitties for a necklace and barrette.

MATERIALS

1 (2-inch wide) 1/8-inch thick wooden heart
3 (1-inch wide) 1/8-inch thick wooden hearts
Acrylic paint: White, Gray, Peach, Black, Gold, Blue
Paintbrushes: Medium flat, liner
Tracing paper
Graphite or carbon paper
Clear spray sealer
Scraps of 1/2-inch wide peach, gray, and white ribbon
Adhesive sealant (E-6000)
Dark peach embroidery floss
3/4 yard (1 1/2-inch wide) peach satin ribbon
Barrette back
3/4 yard (1/8-inch wide) peach satin ribbon
2 (1/4-inch diameter) gold beads
See Pattern

DIRECTIONS

☐ Paint large heart white and small hearts gray, white, and peach.

☐ Transfer patterns onto tracing paper. Place graphite or carbon paper between patterns and hearts.

☐ Trace over pattern to transfer image onto hearts.

☐ Paint as indicated. Let dry.

☐ Spray with sealer. Let dry.

☐ Make ears with 1/2-inch wide ribbon in coordinating colors. Glue to back of face.

□ Make embroidery floss bows and glue to fronts of ears, referring to illustration for placement.

□ Make a large bow from 1½-inch wide ribbon. Glue large kitty face to front of bow and back of barrette to back of bow.

□ Glue a kitten face onto ⅛-inch wide ribbon and string a gold bead next to it for necklace.

□ Repeat to attach remaining heart faces and bead.

Rhinestone Cowgirl Sweat Shirt

Your favorite little girl will always feel special wearing this colorful and jewel-studded sweat shirt. She'll be a hit wherever she may roam.

MATERIALS

White sweat shirt
Waxed paper
Gick Publishing Mini Iron-On Transfer Design: S-1 Rhinestone Cowgirl
Tulip® Paints: Ice Blue Pearl, Pink Pearl, Silver Glitter
Small paintbrush
Gick Publishing Nailheads (1 package each): #86-55, #86-68, #86-7
6 blue crystal rhinestones with sets
6 pink crystal rhinestones with sets
7 clear crystal rhinestones with sets
1 large pink rhinestone
1 package Gick Publishing 11mm pink star-shaped rhinestones
Rhinestone setter
5 inches (⅛-inch wide) clear rhinestone braid

DIRECTIONS

□ Wash, dry and press sweat shirt. Line sweat shirt with waxed paper to keep excess paint from soaking through to back.

□ Follow manufacturer's instructions for using iron-on transfer designs.

□ Refer to transfer for placement of paint. Let sweat shirt dry for 24 hours.

□ Refer to transfer for placement of nailheads, rhinestones and rhinestone braid.

Embossed Greeting Cards

If you do much stenciling, you probably have a collection of favorite designs stored away for future use. This year, give those old standards new life by making stunning embossed greeting cards. Whether you want to make up a batch of special cards for family and your closest friends, or create a surefire bestseller for the sorority bazaar, these cards will fill the bill.

MATERIALS

Pre-cut stencils
Blank note cards
Masking tape
Engraving tool or 1/2-inch sharpened dowel,
    sanded smooth

DIRECTIONS

☐ Position stencil on front of blank card and tape in place. Hold paper and stencil up to sunny window with stencil to glass. Press paper carefully into stencil cuts with engraving tool or sharpened dowel. Continue to emboss rest of design.

☐ Raised areas can be tinted with watercolor washes or lightly applied inks or dyes.

Molly Mop Doll

Despite Molly's humble beginnings, she is a doll sure to win the heart of any little girl. A fluffy string mop, available at craft stores, makes a cuddly friend just by tying a couple of bows and dressing her in a lacy bonnet.

MATERIALS

1   (10-inch) mop
14 inches string to match
1³/4 yards (¹/8-inch wide) blue satin ribbon
¹/4 yard print fabric
16¹/2 inches (1¹/4-inch) ecru lace

DIRECTIONS

☐ Define head by cinching end of mop with matching string.

☐ Gather 2 equal bunches of mop string for arms and bring to front of body.

☐ Tie arm sections tightly halfway between neck and bottom of doll with 18 inches of satin ribbon.

☐ Cut mop string 1¹/2 inches below bow to make hands.

☐ Cut a 6-by-16½-inch piece of fabric. Align raw edges. Sew lace to 1 long side of fabric. Press open.

☐ Fold long sides of fabric together with wrong sides facing. Sew along lace edge with a ⅛-inch seam. Sew another seam ¼ inch from first for ribbon casing.

☐ Sew a seam ¼ inch from fold for another casing.

☐ Insert a 30-inch piece of ribbon in casing on lace edge and a 12-inch piece of ribbon in casing on fold edge. Slip bonnet over head, and tighten gathers to fit.

☐ Tie ends of ribbon in casing on lace edge in a bow under doll's chin. Tie ribbon in back casing in bow at back of neck.

Decorative Bookmarks

These pretty bookmarks are perfect for your reader friends. Within minutes, you can decorate a wooden craft stick or a strip of satin ribbon. These are so easy that even a child can make them.

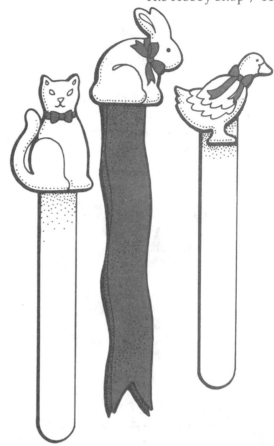

MATERIALS

14 inches (⅜-inch wide) satin ribbon
Pre-cut and pre-painted wooden craft decoration
Hot glue gun or white craft glue
6-inch wooden craft stick
Wood stain
Black marker

DIRECTIONS FOR RIBBON BOOKMARK

☐ Fold ribbon in half to make 7-inch bookmark. Glue ribbon together.

☐ Glue wooden craft decoration at folded edge.

☐ Trim ends of ribbon in V shape.

DIRECTIONS FOR WOODEN BOOKMARK

☐ Stain craft stick. Let dry.

☐ Glue wooden craft decoration to one end.

☐ Print name or message with black marker.

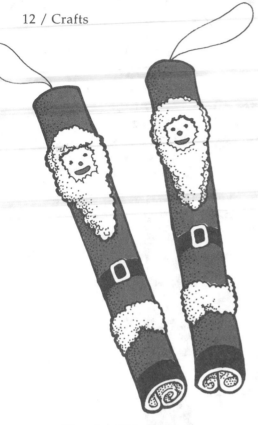

Santa Stick Ornament

Do you have a few spare cinnamon sticks? Pull them out, gather together your paints and make some wonderul Santa ornaments.

MATERIALS

Cinnamon stick
Acrylic paints: Dark Red, Beige, White, Black, Gold
Paintbrushes: small round, liner
Sand or cornmeal
5 inches thin gold cord
Hot glue gun

DIRECTIONS

☐ Paint entire stick with dark red paint. Let dry.

☐ Paint Santa's face beige approximately ¼ of the way down. Mix a dab of sand or cornmeal into some white paint, and paint cap fringe. Paint beard white. Paint black eyes, red nose and mouth with liner brush, referring to illustration for placement.

☐ Paint black belt below beard. Paint gold square

for buckle on center of belt.

☐ Paint fringe on bottom of jacket below belt with sand and white paint mixture. Paint end of cinnamon stick black for feet.

☐ Loop gold cord and glue inside stick for hanger.

Cinnamon Ornaments

What child can resist playing with dough? What Mom or Grand Mom can resist the delicious scent of cinnamon streaming from these ornaments? It's a perfect combination. Set aside time to make a bunch of these ornaments. You'll have all the ingredients for an afternoon of fun, and you'll have something more—memories to linger like the fragrance of cinnamon filling the air.

MATERIALS

1 cup (about 3.2 ounces) ground cinnamon
2 tablespoons ground allspice
1 cup applesauce
¼ cup craft glue
Cookie cutters

DIRECTIONS

☐ Combine cinnamon and allspice in glass bowl.

☐ Add applesauce and glue; mix well. Mixture will be stiff.

☐ Add water or additional cinnamon, if needed, to achieve a clay-like consistency.

☐ Roll out dough between sheets of waxed paper to ½-inch thickness.

☐ Remove top sheet of waxed paper. Cut with cookie cutters. Remove excess dough.

☐ Air dry on flat surface for a few days.

Festive Centerpiece

Fill a basket with an assortment of colorful peppers, vegetables, pine cones and candles for a special centerpiece any time of the year.

Bird Feeder Wreath

*Extend goodwill to the treetops with a wreath
that contains a birdseed holder. Begin with
a grapevine wreath and embellish with
natural materials you can cut from your own
yard or purchase from your local nursery—
fir, holly, magnolia, aucuba, nandina, and
ivy. Wire a small plastic-lined basket to the
wreath. Then surround the basket with wisteria
and honeysuckle vines, which are woven around
it to resemble a nest. Last, wire on a bright
red bow and a couple of artificial birds. For an
even easier version, fill a shallow basket
with seed, embellish the handle, and choose a
spot to hang it that will give you a
good view of the activity inside.*

Stained Glass Cookies

*Get out your rolling pen on the next rainy day
and make up a batch of stained glass cookies.
Why not take a batch to a sick friend, you'll
feel better for it and so will they.*

1   (14-ounce) can Eagle® Brand sweetened
    condensed milk
3/4 cup margarine, softened
2 eggs
1 tablespoon vanilla extract or 2 teaspoons almond
    or lemon extract
3½ cups all-purpose flour
1 tablespoon baking powder
½ teaspoon salt
¼ cup margarine
¼ cup water
½ cup baking cocoa
2 cups confectioners' sugar
1 teaspoon vanilla extract

☐ Combine first 4 ingredients in mixer bowl; beat until smooth. Add mixture of flour, baking powder and salt; mix well. Chill for 2 hours.

☐ Preheat oven to 350 degrees.

☐ Knead dough on floured surface until smooth.

☐ Cut dough into desired 3-inch shapes; cut out holes in center. Place on foil-lined cookie sheet. Fill centers with crushed hard candies. Bake for 6 to 8 minutes or until candy melts. Cool in pan for 5 minutes.

☐ Yield: 8 dozen.

Goodie Bag Tray

Simply spectacular—a tray filled with brown bags of special treats for a party nibbling center or a late night snack-attack.

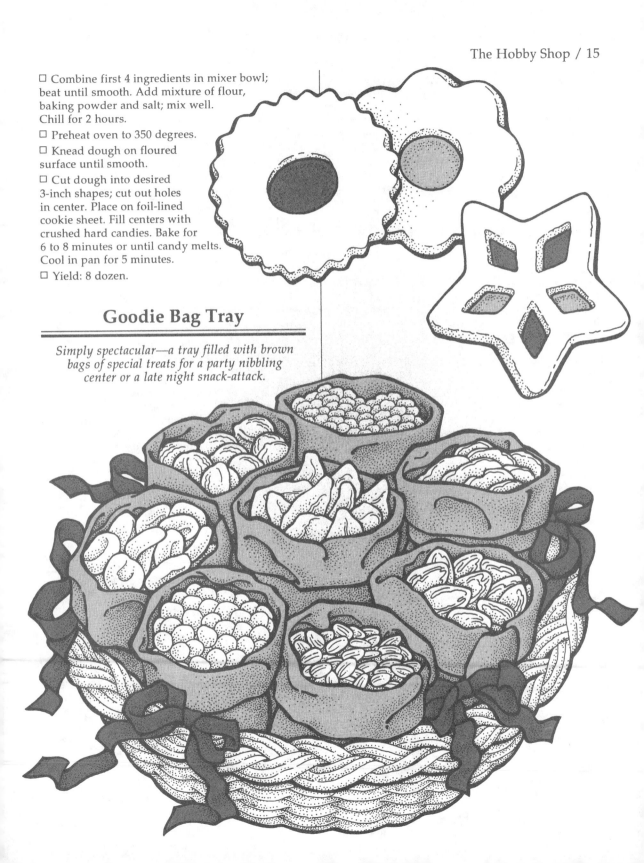

Stenciled Jar Covers and Recipe Cards

Everyone appreciates a gift from the kitchen, especially when the recipe is included. Spice up your culinary presents with decorative jar covers and matching recipe cards. You'll be the talk of the coffee klatch.

MATERIALS

Muslin, osnaburg, burlap, or other light-colored fabric scraps
Pinking shears
Floral stencils
Masking tape
Desired colors of stencil paint
Paper plate or saucer
Stenciling brushes: 3/8 inch to 1/2 inch in diameter, 1 brush for each color
Paper towels
Assorted ribbons and trims
Index cards

DIRECTIONS

☐ Cut circles to desired size to fit jar tops from fabric scraps using pinking shears.

☐ Place stencil in position and tape in place with masking tape.

☐ Review paint manufacturer's instructions. Place a small amount of paint on a paper plate or saucer.

☐ Dip tip of brush into paint. Wipe off excess on a paper towel until brush is "dry" and paint is light and smooth in appearance.

☐ Hold brush perpendicular to surface. Start at outside edge of cut-out area and work in clockwise motion from edge across design area.

☐ Reverse to counter-clockwise motion and continue building up color to desired shade.

☐ Clean stencils and brushes gently following paint manufacturer's directions and allow to air dry before using again.

☐ Decorate with ribbon and trim as desired.

☐ Stencil matching recipe cards.

Cookie Swap

Are you itching to have a party, but looking for something easy. Why not try an old-time cookie swap. Extend an invitation to your neighbors and extended family members. Ask each guest to bring 6 dozen cookies along with copies of their cookie recipe. On the day of the swap provide punch and let everyone sample a few of the creations. Let everyone spend some time enjoying one anothers company, and then divide the cookies among the guests. Everyone will leave with a wonderful assortment of homemade cookies and also warm feelings towards each other.

No-Rush Breakfast and Brunch

Experts tell us that breakfast is the most
important meal of the day, but during the week,
who has time for extensive preparations in the
morning? And who wants to spend a great deal
of time with breakfast on the weekend when
so many other activities are calling? That's why
it's important to have a ready supply of
breakfast and brunch menus that are good
tasting and good for you, but can be put
together with little fuss and bother. The recipes
in this chapter can all be prepared in a matter of
minutes for those hurry-up mornings or can be
made in advance and kept waiting in the
freezer. Save yourself some time on busy
mornings to come, and get started now on these
no-rush breakfast and brunch ideas.

Home Sweet Home

Easy Brunch

Fast and Easy Fruit Salad
Sausage Soufflé
Glazed Coffee Cake

This is an easy brunch because everything can be prepared ahead of time. I use it for family gatherings as well as for sorority rush parties.

Cathy Dreher, Theta Chi
Dodge City, Kansas

FAST AND EASY FRUIT SALAD

1 21-ounce can peach pie filling
1 8-ounce package frozen strawberries, thawed
1 8-ounce can pineapple tidbits, drained
2 large bananas, sliced

Combine all ingredients in bowl; mix well. Chill until serving time. Yield: 8 servings.

SAUSAGE SOUFFLÉ

1 pound bulk sausage
6 slices bread, cubed
1/4 cup shredded Cheddar cheese
1/2 teaspoon salt
1/4 teaspoon dry mustard
4 eggs
2 cups milk

Brown sausage in skillet, stirring until crumbly; drain. Add bread, cheese, salt and dry mustard; mix well. Beat eggs with milk in bowl. Add to sausage mixture; mix well. Spoon into greased 6-by-10-inch baking dish. Chill overnight. Preheat oven to 350 degrees. Bake casserole, covered, for 45 minutes. Bake, uncovered, for 15 minutes longer. Yield: 8 servings.

GLAZED COFFEE CAKE

1 2-layer package yellow cake mix
1 small package vanilla instant pudding mix
3/4 cup vegetable oil
3/4 cup water
4 eggs
1 teaspoon vanilla extract
1/4 cup sugar
2 teaspoons cinnamon
1/4 cup chopped pecans
1 cup confectioners' sugar
3 tablespoons milk
1/2 teaspoon vanilla extract

Preheat oven to 350 degrees. Combine cake mix, pudding mix, oil and water in mixer bowl; mix well. Add eggs 1 at a time, beating for 6 to 8 minutes. Beat in 1 teaspoon vanilla. Spoon 1/3 of the batter into greased and floured bundt pan. Mix sugar, cinnamon and pecans in small bowl. Layer pecan mixture and remaining batter 1/2 at a time in prepared pan. Bake for 45 minutes. Cool on wire rack for 8 minutes. Invert onto serving plate. Combine remaining ingredients in small bowl; mix well. Spoon over warm coffee cake. Yield: 12 servings.

Volunteers' Brunch

Champagne Mimosas
Link Sausages
Make-Ahead Mushrooms and Eggs
Sliced Oranges
Coffee Cake

See index for similar recipes.

This was the menu when a group gathered to taste different brunch and breakfast recipes. The group was composed of volunteers at the non-profit Garden Cafe, proceeds of which go to the Sacramento Children's Home. We have several common interests in that we all like to cook and experiment with food, and we enjoy knowing that the money realized is helping children who have been abused or are without homes.

Jo An Pidd, Laureate Beta Omega
Gold River, California

MAKE-AHEAD MUSHROOMS AND EGGS

1 10-ounce can cream of mushroom soup
3 tablespoons sherry or milk
1 1/2 cups each shredded Monterey Jack and Cheddar cheese
18 eggs
2 tablespoons milk
1 teaspoon parsley flakes
1/2 teaspoon dillweed
Salt and pepper to taste
4 ounces mushrooms, sliced
1/4 cup chopped green onions
1/4 cup butter or margarine
Paprika to taste

Preheat oven to 300 degrees. Heat soup and sherry in small saucepan over medium heat, stirring until smooth; set aside. Mix cheeses in small bowl. Beat eggs, milk, parsley flakes, dillweed, salt and pepper in medium bowl. Sauté mushrooms and green onions in butter in large skillet until onion is tender. Add egg mixture. Cook until eggs are soft-set, lifting

cooked portion to cook evenly. Layer eggs, soup mixture and cheese 1/2 at a time in 7-by-11-inch baking dish; sprinkle with paprika. Bake for 30 to 35 minutes or until bubbly. Let stand for about 10 minutes before serving. May chill overnight before baking and increase baking time to 1 hour.
Yield: 8 to 10 servings.

Summer Brunch

Egg and Sausage Bake
Fresh Fruit Platter
Caramel Rolls — Banana Bread
Honey-Raisin Bran Muffins
Coffee — Milk

See index for similar recipes.

During the summer months we live at a lake in northern Minnesota where we are blessed with the visits of family and friends. Because the morning meal is the send-off for the day of activities, I often prepare this menu, which allows me to spend time enjoying the morning and my guests. The breads can be made in advance and warmed at brunch time. For the fruit platter, I include fresh strawberries dipped into confectioners' sugar, seedless red and green grapes, quartered bananas and melon balls or chunks.

Kathryn Stoterau, Zeta Master
Mesa, Arizona

EGG AND SAUSAGE BAKE

2 pounds pork sausage	3/4 teaspoon dry
2 1/2 cups herb-seasoned	mustard
croutons	Salt and pepper to taste
2 cups shredded	1 10-ounce can cream
Cheddar cheese	of mushroom soup
8 eggs	1/2 cup milk
2 1/2 cups milk	

Brown sausage in skillet, stirring until crumbly; drain. Layer croutons, sausage and cheese evenly in greased 9-by-13-inch baking dish. Beat eggs with 2 1/2 cups milk, dry mustard, salt and pepper in mixer bowl. Pour over layers. Chill, covered, overnight. Preheat oven to 300 degrees. Spread mixture of soup and 1/2 cup milk over top of casserole. Bake for 1 1/2 hours. Let stand for 5 to 10 minutes before serving.
Yield: 12 servings.

CARAMEL ROLLS

2 envelopes dry yeast	1/4 cup butter or
2 cups warm water	margarine
1 teaspoon salt	1 cup packed light
1/3 cup sugar	brown sugar
6 1/2 cups all-purpose	2 tablespoons dark corn
flour	syrup
1/2 cup melted	Melted butter or
shortening or	margarine
margarine	Cinnamon
2 eggs	Light brown sugar

Dissolve yeast in warm water in large bowl. Add salt, sugar and 2 cups flour; beat for 2 minutes. Add shortening and eggs; mix well. Add remaining 4 1/2 cups flour; mix well. Let rest for 20 minutes. Combine 1/4 cup butter, 1 cup brown sugar and corn syrup in saucepan; heat until butter melts. Spread in baking pan. Roll dough on floured surface. Brush with melted butter; sprinkle with cinnamon and additional brown sugar. Roll up jelly-roll fashion. Cut into slices; arrange on caramel mixture in baking pan. Let rise for 1 hour. Preheat oven to 350 degrees. Bake for 20 to 30 minutes or until golden brown.
Yield: 2 dozen.

BANANA BREAD

1 tablespoon butter or	1 teaspoon baking
margarine, softened	powder
1 cup sugar	1/2 teaspoon salt
2 eggs	3 bananas, mashed
2 cups all-purpose flour	1/2 cup chopped nuts
3 tablespoons sour milk	(optional)
1 tablespoon baking	
soda	

Preheat oven to 350 degrees. Cream butter and sugar in mixer bowl until light and fluffy. Add next 6 ingredients; mix well. Stir in bananas and nuts. Spoon into greased loaf pan. Bake for 1 hour.
Yield: 12 servings.

HONEY-RAISIN BRAN MUFFINS

2 1/2 cups raisin	1 1/4 cups all-purpose
bran cereal	flour
1 cup milk	1 tablespoon baking
1/3 cup honey	powder
1 egg	1/4 teaspoon salt
3 tablespoons vegetable	
oil	

Preheat oven to 400 degrees. Combine cereal, milk and honey in large bowl. Let stand until cereal is softened. Beat in egg and oil. Add mixture of flour, baking powder and salt; mix just until moistened. Spoon into greased or paper-lined muffin cups. Bake for 18 to 20 minutes or until light brown.
Yield: 1 dozen.

Tropical Brunch for Twelve

Mimosas Hawaiian
Mexican Breakfast Burritos
Baked Cheddar Tomatoes
Jalapeño Cheese Grits
Citrus Salad Orange Cups
Quick Apple Pinwheel

I served this menu for a brunch for the Newcomers' Club in Mobile, Alabama.

Linda A. McConnell, Preceptor Iota Sigma
Dallas, Texas

MIMOSAS HAWAIIAN

1 12-ounce can apricot nectar	1 12-ounce can pineapple juice
1 6-ounce can frozen orange juice concentrate, thawed	3/4 cup water
	1 25-ounce bottle of dry Champagne, chilled

Combine fruit juices and water in pitcher; mix well. Chill in refrigerator. Stir in Champagne gently at serving time. Yield: 7 1/2 cups.

MEXICAN BREAKFAST BURRITOS

12 flour tortillas	1 1/2 cups taco sauce
16 eggs	1 cup plus 2 tablespoons shredded Cheddar cheese
2/3 cup water	
1/4 cup chopped green chilies	

Preheat oven to 350 degrees. Wrap tortillas in foil. Bake for 7 minutes; keep warm. Combine eggs, water, green chilies and 1/4 cup taco sauce in medium bowl; whisk until smooth. Spoon into large skillet sprayed with nonstick cooking spray. Cook over medium heat until set, stirring frequently. Spoon eggs onto tortillas; top eggs with 1 tablespoon taco sauce and 1 tablespoon cheese. Fold sides over and roll tortillas to enclose filling. Top servings with remaining taco sauce and cheese. Yield: 12 servings.

BAKED CHEDDAR TOMATOES

6 medium tomatoes	Garlic powder to taste
Seasoned salt to taste	1 cup shredded Cheddar cheese
Melted butter or margarine	

Preheat oven to 350 degrees. Cut tomatoes into halves crosswise. Place cut side up on work surface. Make 6 cuts across tops of tomatoes. Sprinkle with seasoned salt; drizzle with butter. Sprinkle with garlic powder and cheese. Place in 9-by-13-inch baking dish. Bake for 15 minutes or until tomatoes are heated through and cheese melts. Yield: 12 servings.

JALAPEÑO CHEESE GRITS

4 1/2 cups water	1/4 cup butter or margarine
1 teaspoon salt	
1 1/2 cups quick-cooking grits	2 4-ounce cans jalapeño pepper, seeded, chopped
4 cups shredded sharp Cheddar cheese	3 eggs, beaten

Preheat oven to 300 degrees. Bring water and salt to a boil in large saucepan. Stir in grits; reduce heat. Cook, covered, for 5 minutes, stirring occasionally. Stir in cheese and butter until melted. Add peppers. Stir a small amount of hot grits into eggs; stir eggs into hot grits. Spoon into greased 8-by-12-inch baking dish. Bake for 30 minutes. Yield: 12 servings.

CITRUS SALAD ORANGE CUPS

6 medium oranges	1 cup miniature marshmallows
1 banana, cut into halves, sliced	1 cup sour cream
1 apple, peeled, shredded	2 tablespoons honey
1/3 cup each green and red grape halves	Grapes

Cut oranges into halves crosswise. Remove and chop pulp, reserving cups. Combine pulp with banana, apple, grape halves and marshmallows in medium bowl. Mix sour cream and honey in small bowl. Add 3/4 cup mixture to fruit; mix gently. Scallop edges of orange cups with kitchen shears. Spoon fruit mixture into orange cups; top with remaining sour cream mixture. Garnish with grapes. Yield: 12 servings.

BAKED APPLE PINWHEEL

2 8-count cans crescent rolls	1 teaspoon grated lemon rind
2 medium apples, peeled, finely chopped	Nutmeg to taste
	Milk
2/3 cup raisins	2 tablespoons light brown sugar
1/4 cup sugar	

Preheat oven to 350 degrees. Separate roll dough into triangles. Arrange triangles into circle on baking sheet with points out, overlapping corners of wide edges slightly to form center of circle; press overlapping edges to seal. Combine apples, raisins, sugar, lemon rind and nutmeg in medium bowl; mix well. Spoon into ring toward center of pinwheel. Fold points of dough over filling and secure under center edge of circle. Brush with milk; sprinkle with brown sugar. Bake for 25 minutes or until golden brown. Yield: 12 servings.

Family Brunch

Carrot Soup
Ham and Veal Rolls
Cheese Grits
Fruit Salad
Hard Rolls
Snicker Bar Pie

See index for similar recipes.

This wholesome menu is sure to suit family members of all ages.

Brownie L. Penrod, Epsilon Nu
Ennis, Texas

CARROT SOUP

3/4 cup finely chopped onion	*2 tablespoons uncooked rice*
2 tablespoons margarine	*Salt and pepper to taste*
3 cups finely chopped carrots	*1/2 cup whipping cream*
4 cups canned chicken stock	*1 tablespoon margarine, softened*
2 tablespoons tomato paste	

Sauté onion in 2 tablespoons margarine in saucepan until tender but not brown. Add carrots. Sauté for several minutes. Stir in chicken stock, tomato paste, rice, salt and pepper. Simmer for 30 minutes. Process in several batches in blender until smooth. Combine batches in saucepan. Cook until heated through. Stir in cream and 1 tablespoon margarine; do not boil. May chill before adding cream and reheat to serve. Yield: 8 servings.

HAM AND VEAL ROLLS

2 pounds ground veal	*1 cup packed light brown sugar*
2 pounds ground ham	*1/2 cup cider vinegar*
2 1/2 cups graham cracker crumbs	*1/2 cup water*
1 1/2 cups milk	*1 teaspoon dry mustard*
2 10-ounce cans tomato soup	

Preheat oven to 250 degrees. Combine first 4 ingredients in bowl; mix well. Shape into small rolls the size of cocktail wieners; place in 9-by-13-inch baking pan lightly sprayed with nonstick cooking spray. Combine remaining ingredients in bowl. Spoon over rolls. Bake for 2 hours. Yield: 10 servings.

SNICKER BAR PIE

5 1 1/2-ounce Snickers candy bars, chopped	*1/3 cup creamy peanut butter*
1 baked 9-inch pie shell	*1/3 cup sour cream*
1/2 cup sugar	*2/3 cup miniature semisweet chocolate chips*
12 ounces cream cheese, softened	
2 eggs, beaten	*1 cup whipped topping*

Sprinkle candy in pie shell. Combine sugar, cream cheese, eggs, peanut butter and sour cream in medium bowl; mix well. Spread over candy. Chill for 1 hour. Mix chocolate chips with whipped topping in bowl. Spread over pie. Chill for 1 hour. Yield: 8 servings.

Danish Breakfast

Medisterpolse (Pork Sausage)
Aebleskiver (Pancake Balls)
Sugar — Jams — Jellies — Syrup
Orange Juice

See index for similar recipes.

We are Danish and serve this menu for family gatherings at Thanksgiving, Easter and Christmas as well as for friends on Saturday morning or Sunday after church. The children usually ask for this after a slumber party or prom or for a wedding breakfast.

Veltea Beck, Laureate Xi
Santa Barbara, California

AEBLESKIVER

5 egg whites	*2 cups milk*
2 1/2 cups baking mix	*5 egg yolks*
1/4 cup melted margarine	*Shortening*
1 tablespoon baking powder	

Beat egg whites in mixer bowl until stiff peaks form. Combine next 5 ingredients in mixer bowl; mix well. Fold in egg whites. Heat aebleskiver pan over medium heat. Add 1/4-inch shortening to each cup. Spoon batter into heated cups, filling to within 1/8 inch of top. Bake until bubbles rise to surface of batter. Turn aebleskiver 1/2 turn with long fork. Bake until golden brown on all sides, continuing to turn. Repeat with remaining batter, adding shortening before refilling cups. Yield: 6 to 8 servings.

Country Breakfast

Country Ham — Bacon
Scrambled Eggs
Fried Potatoes and Onions
Cooked Apples
Homemade Biscuits — Country Gravy
Butter — Jelly — Honey
Coffee — Juice

See index for similar recipes.

This is the type of breakfast I was raised on. It is not considered heart-smart nowadays, but it sure is "good eatin'" once in a while. We add grits on special occasions when treating friends to a real country breakfast. The important thing to remember is to take time to enjoy and savor the food and the company of friends and family.

Kim Thorn, Beta Sigma
Pollocksville, North Carolina

SCRAMBLED EGGS

6 eggs	1 tablespoon bacon
1/4 cup milk	drippings
Salt and pepper to taste	

Beat eggs with milk, salt and pepper in medium bowl. Heat bacon drippings in 10-inch skillet over medium-high heat. Add eggs. Cook until soft-set, stirring constantly. Yield: 4 servings.

FRIED POTATOES AND ONIONS

2 cups potato strips	1 large onion, cut into
Vegetable oil or bacon	wedges or strips
drippings for frying	Salt and pepper to taste

Fry potatoes in hot oil in large skillet until nearly tender. Add onion. Fry until tender. Season with salt and pepper. Serve immediately. Yield: 4 servings.

COOKED APPLES

5 or 6 Granny Smith	1/4 cup butter or
apples, peeled, sliced	margarine
1/4 cup water	1 teaspoon cinnamon
3 tablespoons sugar	

Cook apples in water in saucepan over medium-high heat for 10 minutes. Stir in sugar, butter and cinnamon. Cook until tender. Spoon into glass bowls. Yield: 4 servings.

HOMEMADE BISCUITS

1/3 cup shortening	3/4 cup milk or water
2 cups self-rising flour	

Preheat oven to 350 to 400 degrees. Cut shortening into flour in medium bowl until crumbly. Add milk; mix with hands. Roll 1/2 inch thick on floured surface. Cut with biscuit cutter; place in baking pan. Bake for 12 to 15 minutes or until golden brown. Yield: 1 dozen.

COUNTRY GRAVY

According to my mother-in-law, if your gravy turns out thin, it shows that you "ain't" got much money. If it is thick, you have all the money you need! That's probably why the measurements are all approximate.

2 tablespoons bacon	1 1/2 cups milk
drippings	Salt and pepper to taste
3 tablespoons	
all-purpose flour	

Heat bacon drippings in skillet until hot but not smoking. Stir in flour until smooth; mixture should have consistency of thin paste. Cook for several minutes. Stir in milk gradually. Cook until thickened, stirring constantly. Season with salt and pepper. Serve with hot biscuits. Yield: 4 servings.

Wood Stove Brunch

Fried Idaho Trout
Scrambled Eggs — Tortillas
Creole Sauce — Shredded Cheese
Fried Potatoes and Onions

See index for similar recipes.

We prepare this brunch for friends on a wonderful old wood stove with an oven and a warmer oven. It came from our home in the mountains in Big Bear City, California. It now stands on our porch in our home here in the California desert, but it brings back memories of the mountains. We dip the trout in a mixture of eggs and a small amount of milk, coat them with instant potato buds and fry them until golden brown. We arrange the brunch as a buffet. Each guest places a tortilla on his plate and layers potatoes, eggs, Creole sauce and cheese on it and rolls it up.

Gretta Lou Askey, Preceptor Kappa Upsilon
Marengo Valley, California

CREOLE SAUCE

1 cup chopped celery
1 cup chopped onion
1 cup chopped green bell
  pepper
1/4 cup butter or
  margarine
1/2 teaspoon minced
  garlic
1/2 teaspoon each basil,
  thyme, paprika, black
  pepper, white pepper
  and cayenne pepper

3/4 teaspoon oregano
2 bay leaves
1 cup chopped fresh
  tomato
1 10-ounce can chicken
  broth
1 8-ounce can tomato
  sauce
2 drops of Tabasco
  sauce

Sauté celery, onion and green pepper in butter in saucepan for 5 minutes. Add garlic and seasonings; mix well. Stir in remaining ingredients. Simmer for 20 minutes; discard bay leaves. Yield: 6 cups.

Holiday Breakfast

Good Morning Orange Juice
Breakfast Sausage
Mexican-Style Eggs
Fresh Fruit — Orange Muffins
Whipped Orange Butter
Zucchini Muffins

See index for similar recipes.

I serve this breakfast on Christmas morning after we open our gifts. I also served it to six special friends on New Year's Day and included an assortment of Christmas goodies as well. For the Good Morning Orange Juice, I mix equal parts of chilled orange juice and bubbly white wine and serve it in pretty glasses.

Lil Blasko, Preceptor Pi
Kindersley, Saskatchewan, Canada

MEXICAN-STYLE EGGS

12 eggs
1/4 cup water
Salt and pepper to taste
3 tablespoons melted
  butter or margarine
1 1/2 cups sliced fresh
  mushrooms
1/2 cup each chopped
  green and red bell
  pepper

1/2 cup chopped green
  onions
1/2 to 3/4 cup coarsely
  chopped zucchini
1/2 cup chopped tomato
3 tablespoons butter or
  margarine
8 to 16 ounces shredded
  mozzarella cheese
Salsa

Preheat oven to 150 degrees. Beat eggs with water, salt and pepper in medium bowl. Spoon into 3 tablespoons melted butter in heated large skillet. Cook until soft-set, stirring constantly. Spoon around edge of large ovenproof dish. Keep warm in oven. Sauté vegetables in 3 tablespoons butter in large skillet just until tender-crisp; season with salt and pepper. Spoon into center of eggs; sprinkle with cheese. Increase oven temperature to 300 degrees. Bake just until cheese melts. Serve with salsa. Yield: 6 servings.

ORANGE MUFFINS

1/2 cup butter or
  margarine, softened
1/2 cup sugar
1 egg
1/2 cup bran cereal
1/2 cup orange juice
1/4 cup milk
1/2 cup drained crushed
  pineapple

1 3/4 cups all-purpose
  flour
2 teaspoons baking
  powder
1/4 teaspoon each
  baking soda and salt
2 teaspoons grated
  orange rind (optional)
Whipped Orange Butter

Preheat oven to 350 degrees. Cream butter and sugar in mixer bowl until light and fluffy. Beat in egg. Mix cereal and orange juice in medium bowl. Add milk and pineapple; mix just until moistened. Add to creamed mixture; mix well. Beat in remaining ingredients. Spoon into greased muffin cups. Bake for 20 minutes. Serve with Whipped Orange Butter. Yield: 1 dozen.

WHIPPED ORANGE BUTTER

1/2 cup butter, softened
2 tablespoons thawed
  frozen orange juice
  concentrate

2 tablespoons
  confectioners' sugar
1 1/2 tablespoons finely
  grated orange rind

Combine all ingredients in food processor; process until smooth. Spoon into small serving dish. Chill until serving time. Yield: 1/2 cup.

ZUCCHINI MUFFINS

3 eggs
1 1/2 cups sugar
1 cup vegetable oil
2 cups grated zucchini
2 teaspoons vanilla
  extract
2 cups all-purpose flour
1/4 teaspoon baking
  powder

2 teaspoons baking soda
2 teaspoons cinnamon
1 teaspoon salt
1/4 cup bran
1/4 cup wheat germ
1 cup each raisins and
  chopped walnuts

Preheat oven to 350 degrees. Combine eggs, sugar and oil in large mixer bowl; beat until smooth. Stir in zucchini and vanilla. Add dry ingredients; mix until moistened. Stir in raisins and walnuts. Spoon into greased muffin cups. Bake for 15 to 20 minutes or until golden brown. Yield: 2 dozen.

Christmas Morning Brunch

Egg and Sausage Casserole
Hashed Brown Potatoes
Fruit Compote
Banana Muffins
Croissants
Orange Juice
Coffee

See index for similar recipes.

I have prepared this brunch every Christmas morning for five years. The guest list includes our parents, our four children, our three grandchildren and a Jewish friend of our daughter who likes to share our family and food. We enjoy watching the grandchildren open presents and then we sit down for brunch at 10:30. It is a joy to gather four generations to pray, eat and share good times.

Ann Frenzel, Mu Sigma
Plantation, Florida

EGG AND SAUSAGE CASSEROLE

1 1/2 pounds link sausage	2 3/4 cups milk
8 slices bread, cubed	1 10-ounce can cream
2 cups shredded	of mushroom soup
Cheddar cheese	3/4 tablespoon dry
4 eggs	mustard

Brown sausage in skillet; drain and cut into thirds. Layer bread, cheese and sausage in greased 9-by-13-inch baking dish. Beat eggs with 2 1/4 cups milk in mixer bowl. Pour over layers. Combine remaining 1/2 cup milk with soup and dry mustard in bowl; mix well. Spread over casserole. Chill, covered with foil, overnight. Place in cold oven; set oven temperature at 300 degrees. Bake for 1 1/2 hours. Serve immediately. Yield: 8 servings.

HASHED BROWN POTATOES

4 large potatoes	Butter or vegetable oil
1 tablespoon minced	
onion	

Preheat oven to 400 degrees. Bake potatoes for 1 hour. Cool to room temperature. Chill overnight. Chop unpeeled potatoes. Brown with onion in butter in skillet, stirring frequently. Yield: 8 servings.

FRUIT COMPOTE

1 16-ounce can each	1 teaspoon lemon juice
peach halves, pear	1 2 1/2-ounce package
halves, pineapple	sliced almonds, toasted
chunks, pitted sweet	12 soft coconut
dark cherries	macaroons, crumbled
and apricot halves	1/4 cup margarine, sliced
2 or 3 bananas, sliced	1/3 cup Amaretto

Preheat oven to 350 degrees. Drain canned fruits well. Combine with bananas and lemon juice in large bowl; mix gently. Reserve 1/3 of the almonds. Layer fruit, macaroons, margarine and remaining almonds 1/2 at a time in baking dish. Pour liqueur over layers. Bake for 30 minutes. Sprinkle with reserved almonds. Stir before serving. Yield: 12 to 16 servings.

Legacy Christmas Brunch

Smokehouse Quartet
Scrambled Egg Casserole
Marinated Mushrooms
Orange Blossom Salad
Blueberry Cream Muffins
Easy Strawberry Trifle
Coffee — Juice

See index for similar recipes.

When my friend Sally died, her husband passed her recipes on to me, so I feel that they are somewhat of a legacy from her. I have added some of the recipes on this menu, but the Smokehouse Quartet and Orange Blossom Salad are her recipes and I always include them in my annual Christmas Brunch. I always give a toast to Sally and know that she is with me in spirit.

Patsy Ruth Frye, Laureate Mu
Rapid City, South Dakota

SMOKEHOUSE QUARTET

6 sausage patties	2 apples, sliced
12 ounces smoked	3 tablespoons melted
sausage, cut into	margarine
chunks	1 teaspoon cinnamon
12 link sausages	1/4 teaspoon nutmeg
1 pound ham, cut into	1 tablespoon cornstarch
serving pieces	1 cup cranapple juice

Brown sausage patties, smoked sausage and sausage links in skillet, stirring frequently; drain. Combine with ham in chafing dish. Add apples to melted margarine in small skillet; sprinkle with cinnamon and nutmeg. Cook over medium heat until apples are tender, stirring occasionally. Remove apples to chafing dish. Stir cornstarch into drippings in skillet. Add cranapple juice. Cook over medium-high heat until thickened, stirring constantly. Pour into chafing dish. Yield: 12 servings.

SCRAMBLED EGG CASSEROLE

2¹/2 tablespoons all-purpose flour	3 tablespoons margarine
2 tablespoons melted margarine	12 eggs, beaten
2 cups milk	1 4-ounce can sliced mushrooms, drained
1/2 teaspoon salt	2¹/4 cups soft bread crumbs
1/8 teaspoon pepper	1/4 cup melted margarine
1 cup shredded American cheese	1/8 teaspoon paprika
1/4 cup chopped green onions	

Blend flour into 2 tablespoons melted margarine in saucepan. Cook for 1 minute. Add milk gradually. Cook over medium heat until thickened, stirring constantly. Add salt, pepper and cheese. Cook until cheese melts. Sauté green onions in 3 tablespoons margarine in skillet until tender. Add eggs. Cook over medium-high heat until soft-set, stirring frequently. Stir in mushrooms and cheese sauce. Spoon into 9-by-13-inch baking dish. Top with mixture of bread crumbs and 1/4 cup melted margarine; sprinkle with paprika. Chill, covered, overnight. Preheat oven to 350 degrees. Bake casserole for 30 minutes. Yield: 12 servings.

MARINATED MUSHROOMS

2 pounds mushrooms	1 16-ounce bottle of Caesar or Italian salad dressing
3 or 4 green onions, sliced	
1 2-ounce jar chopped pimento	

Cut large mushrooms into halves. Combine with remaining ingredients in serving bowl; mix gently. Marinate in refrigerator overnight. Yield: 12 to 14 servings.

Theresa Kossman, Delta Sigma, Spring, Texas, makes Mushrooms Divine by stuffing 1 pint washed fresh mushroom caps with a mixture of finely chopped stems that have been removed and 1 pound uncooked hot pork sausage. Place on two 9-by-13-inch baking pans. Sprinkle with 1 small bag shredded Parmesan cheese. Bake in preheated 375-degree oven for 30 minutes or until sausage is cooked.

ORANGE BLOSSOM SALAD

1 3-ounce package lemon gelatin	2 cups ginger ale or Champagne
1¹/2 cups boiling water	2 11-ounce cans mandarin oranges, drained
1/4 cup lemon juice	Green or red grape clusters
8 ounces cream cheese, softened	1 egg white, beaten
1 cup shredded Cheddar cheese	Sugar or flavored gelatin
1/2 cup chopped pecans	Lettuce leaves
1 16-ounce can pineapple chunks	
2 3-ounce packages orange gelatin	

Dissolve lemon gelatin in 1¹/2 cups boiling water in small saucepan. Stir in lemon juice. Add gradually to cream cheese in medium bowl, beating at medium speed until smooth. Chill until partially set. Fold in Cheddar cheese and pecans. Spoon into oiled 10-cup ring mold. Chill until almost set. Drain pineapple, reserving juice. Add enough water to reserved juice to measure 1¹/2 cups. Bring to a boil in small saucepan. Stir in orange gelatin until dissolved; remove from heat. Add ginger ale gradually. Chill until partially set. Fold in oranges and pineapple. Spoon over congealed layer. Chill for 8 hours to overnight. Brush grape clusters with egg white; sprinkle with sugar or flavored gelatin. Let stand on rack until dry. Unmold salad onto lettuce-lined serving plate; garnish with grapes. Yield: 12 to 14 servings.

BLUEBERRY CREAM MUFFINS

4 eggs	4 cups all-purpose flour
2 cups sugar	1 teaspoon baking soda
1 cup vegetable oil	1 teaspon salt
1 teaspoon vanilla extract	2 cups sour cream
2 teaspoons baking powder	2 cups fresh or frozen blueberries

Preheat oven to 400 degrees. Beat eggs in mixer bowl. Add sugar gradually, beating constantly. Beat in oil and vanilla gradually. Sift dry ingredients. Add to batter alternately with sour cream, mixing after each addition. Fold in blueberries. Spoon into greased muffin cups. Bake for 20 minutes. Yield: 24 muffins.

Elenrae Joyner, Kappa Theta, Shreveport, Louisiana, makes Grandma's Buttermilk Biscuits by melting 1¹/2 (rounded) teaspoons shortening in iron skillet. Mix 1¹/4 cups self-rising flour and 3/4 cup buttermilk in medium bowl. Pour melted shortening into batter, leaving just a coating of shortening in skillet; mix well. Roll dough into balls, using small amount of flour. Dip biscuits into shortening to coat sides. Place in greased iron skillet. Bake in preheated 450-degree oven for 10 to 15 minutes or until browned on top.

Easter Brunch

Champagne Mimosas
Cheesy Mushroomy Eggs
Canadian Bacon
Fresh Fruit
Almond Poppy Seed Muffins
Coffee

See index for similar recipes.

Eggs are always the basis for this breakfast at Easter and we all look forward to this dish. If good fresh fruit is not available, I supplement it with frozen or canned fruit. I mix Champagne and orange juice a pitcher at a time for the Mimosas. The Canadian bacon is baked on a rack in a baking pan at 350 to 400 degrees for 5 minutes. I like to grind my own coffee beans and usually select a bean with a subtle flavor for this brunch.

Candy Hicks, Sigma Lambda
Diamond Springs, California

CHEESY MUSHROOMY EGGS

8 ounces mushrooms	1/2 teaspoon salt
1/2 cup chopped onion	1 pound Cheddar
1/4 cup butter or	cheese, shredded
margarine	2 cups nonfat cottage
10 eggs	cheese
1/2 cup all-purpose flour	
1 teaspoon baking	
powder	

Preheat oven to 350 degrees. Sauté mushrooms and onion in margarine in skillet. Beat eggs in medium mixer bowl. Add remaining ingredients and sautéed vegetables; mix well. Spoon into greased 9-by-13-inch baking dish. Bake for 30 minutes or until set. Yield: 10 to 12 servings.

Debbie Clarke, Beta Omega, Gering, Nebraska, makes Svetek by mixing 3 beaten eggs, 3/4 cup milk and 1 cup all-purpose flour together in medium bowl. Fry in preheated lightly greased square electric skillet like large pancake until golden brown on both sides. Remove; cut into squares. Serve with melted butter and sugar.

ALMOND POPPY SEED MUFFINS

1/4 cup margarine,	2 cups all-purpose flour
melted	2 1/2 teaspoons baking
3/4 cup sugar	powder
2 eggs	1 cup milk
1 1/2 teaspoons almond	1 tablespoon
extract	poppy seed

Preheat oven to 400 degrees. Combine margarine, sugar, eggs and almond extract in large mixer bowl; beat until smooth. Add mixture of flour and baking powder alternately with milk, mixing until moistened after each addition. Stir in poppy seed. Spoon into paper-lined muffin cups, filling 2/3 full. Bake for 20 minutes or until golden brown. Yield: 12 servings.

Special Brunch

Mimosas
Swiss Bacon and Corn Quiche
Fresh Fruit
Orange Butter Coffee Cake
Coffee — Tea

See index for similar recipes.

I have served this lovely brunch many times for family and friends. The quiche, coffee cake and fruit can be prepared in advance and while the quiche is baking, I have time for relaxing with guests and enjoying a mimosa. The mimosas are made of equal parts of chilled Champagne and orange juice. I use cantaloupe and honeydew wedges with fresh orange and grapefruit sections for the fruit plate.

Carol Gentry, Preceptor Iota Pi
Redlands, California

SWISS BACON AND CORN QUICHE

8 ounces bacon,	1/2 cup finely chopped
crisp-fried, crumbled	onion
1 cup shredded Swiss	1/2 cup baking mix
cheese	2 cups milk
1 12-ounce can whole	4 eggs or egg substitute
kernel corn or	1/4 teaspoon each salt
Mexicorn, drained	and pepper

Preheat oven to 350 degrees. Spread bacon, cheese, corn and onion in greased 10-inch quiche or pie plate. Combine remaining ingredients in blender container; process for 1 minute. Pour into prepared plate. Bake for 50 to 55 minutes or until knife inserted in center comes out clean and top is golden brown. Let stand for 5 minutes before serving. Yield: 8 servings.

ORANGE BUTTER COFFEE CAKE

1 envelope dry yeast
1/4 cup sugar
1/4 cup 110-degree water
3 1/2 cups (about) all-purpose flour
1 teaspoon salt
1/2 cup sour cream
6 tablespoons butter or margarine
2 eggs
2 tablespoons melted butter or margarine
3/4 cup sugar
3/4 cup coconut
2 tablespoons grated orange rind
6 tablespoons sugar
1/4 cup sour cream
1 tablespoon orange juice
2 tablespoons butter or margarine
1/4 cup coconut

Dissolve yeast and 1 teaspoon of the 1/4 cup sugar in warm water. Let stand for 5 minutes. Mix remaining portion of the 1/4 cup sugar, 1 cup flour and salt in large bowl. Warm 1/2 cup sour cream and 6 tablespoons butter in small saucepan. Add to flour mixture with yeast; beat for 2 minutes. Add eggs and 1/2 cup flour; beat for 2 minutes. Add enough remaining flour to made a soft dough. Knead for 8 to 10 minutes or until smooth and elastic, kneading in additional flour as needed to prevent sticking. Place in greased bowl, turning to coat surface. Let rise in warm place for 1 to 1 1/2 hours or until doubled in bulk. Roll to 10-by-18-inch rectangle on floured surface. Brush with 2 tablespoons melted butter. Mix 3/4 cup sugar, 3/4 cup coconut and orange rind in small bowl. Sprinkle over dough. Roll dough from wide edge to enclose filling; seal edges. Place seam side down in greased 10-inch tube pan; press ends to seal. Let rise, loosely covered, for 1 hour. Preheat oven to 350 degrees. Bake coffee cake for 30 minutes. Bring 6 tablespoons sugar, 1/4 cup sour cream, orange juice and 2 tablespoons butter to a boil in small saucepan. Cook for 2 minutes, stirring constantly. Pour over coffee cake; sprinkle with 1/4 cup coconut. Yield: 16 servings.

Sue Knight, Preceptor Alpha Alpha, Forsyth, Georgia, makes Sour Cream and Butter Biscuits by mixing 1 cup melted butter, 8 ounces sour cream and 2 cups self-rising flour together in medium bowl. Spoon dough into well-greased muffin cups. Bake in preheated 400-degree oven for 12 to 14 minutes or until golden brown. May knead and cut dough with biscuit cutter if desired.

CARLETON PLACE QUICHE

12 slices bread, crusts trimmed
8 ounces Cheddar cheese, shredded
8 ounces Monterey Jack cheese, shredded
8 ounces bacon, chopped, crisp-fried
8 eggs, beaten
3 cups milk

Layer bread, cheeses and bacon, 1/2 at a time, in 9-by-13-inch casserole. Beat eggs and milk in bowl. Pour over layers. Chill for 12 hours. Preheat oven to 350 degrees. Bake for 1 hour. Yield: 6 servings.

*Sue Anne Burgess, Gamma Kappa
London, Ontario, Canada*

FAVORITE BRUNCH CASSEROLE

This recipe is a favorite for Christmas morning. Put it in the oven while opening gifts and breakfast is ready!

4 cups dried French bread cubes
2 cups shredded Cheddar cheese
10 eggs
1 quart milk
1 teaspoon dry mustard
1 teaspoon salt
1/4 teaspoon onion powder
Freshly ground pepper to taste
8 to 10 slices crisp-fried bacon, crumbled
1/2 cup sliced mushrooms
1/2 cup chopped, peeled tomatoes

Place bread cubes in greased 9-by-13-inch casserole. Sprinkle with cheese. Beat eggs, milk, mustard, salt, onion powder and pepper in large bowl. Pour evenly over bread cubes. Sprinkle with bacon, mushrooms and tomatoes. Chill, covered, overnight. Preheat oven to 325 degrees. Bake, uncovered, for 45 minutes to 1 hour or until knife inserted near center comes out clean. Yield: 8 to 10 servings.

*Sandra MacCoubrey, Phi Beta Beta
Cobourg, Ontario, Canada*

CRUSTLESS BACON QUICHE

8 slices bacon
3 eggs
1 1/2 cups milk
1/2 cup baking mix
1/2 cup melted butter or margarine
Pepper to taste
1 cup shredded Cheddar cheese

Preheat oven to 350 degrees. Fry bacon in skillet until crispy; drain and crumble. Combine eggs, milk, baking mix, butter and pepper in blender container. Process until smooth. Pour into buttered 9-inch glass pie plate. Sprinkle with bacon and cheese. Bake for 30 to 40 minutes or until knife inserted near center comes out clean. Let stand for 10 minutes before serving. Yield: 6 to 8 servings.

*Debby Waddle, Zeta
Kansas City, Missouri*

CHAMPAGNE BRUNCH CASSEROLE

3 tablespoons all-purpose flour	1 pound bacon, crisp-fried, crumbled
2 tablespoons melted butter or margarine	12 eggs, scrambled
2 cups low-fat milk	1 4-ounce can button mushrooms, drained
1/4 cup chopped green onions	Salt and pepper to taste
3 tablespoons butter or margarine	1/2 cup buttered bread crumbs
1 cup shredded Cheddar cheese	Paprika

Combine flour and 2 tablespoons melted butter in saucepan; mix well. Stir in milk. Cook over medium heat until mixture thickens, stirring constantly. Sauté green onions in 3 tablespoons butter in skillet. Add cheese, stirring until melted. Add crumbled bacon, eggs, mushrooms, salt and pepper; mix well. Pour into buttered 9-by-12-inch casserole. Top with buttered bread crumbs; sprinkle with paprika. Chill, covered, overnight. Preheat oven to 350 degrees. Bake for 30 minutes. Yield: 8 to 10 servings.

Betty Carmichael, Laureate Phi
Sun City West, Arizona

EGG-STRA BRUNCH CASSEROLE

I first enjoyed this dish with my college roommate and her family in New Jersey. We have been good friends for 35 years.

2 cups seasoned croutons	1/2 teaspoon prepared mustard
1 cup shredded natural Cheddar cheese	1/8 teaspoon onion powder
4 eggs	Pepper to taste
2 cups milk	4 slices bacon, crisp-fried, crumbled
1/2 teaspoon salt	

Preheat oven to 325 degrees. Toss croutons and cheese together in bowl. Spread evenly in greased 6-by-10-inch baking dish. Beat eggs, milk, salt, mustard, onion powder and pepper in bowl. Pour over crouton mixture. Sprinkle with crumbled bacon. Bake for 55 minutes to 1 hour or until knife inserted near center comes out clean. Yield: 9 servings.

Beverly S. Demers, Preceptor Alpha Beta
Colorado Springs, Colorado

LUSCIOUS QUICHE

8 ounces bacon, crisp-fried, crumbled	1/2 teaspoon salt
4 to 6 ounces fresh or canned mushrooms	Chopped onions to taste
3/4 cup shredded Cheddar cheese	1 1/2 cups milk
3/4 cup shredded mozzarella cheese	3/4 cup biscuit mix
	5 eggs

Preheat oven to 350 degrees. Combine bacon, mushrooms, cheeses, salt and onions in bowl; mix well. Spoon into greased 9-by-13-inch casserole. Process milk, biscuit mix and eggs in blender until smooth. Pour over cheese mixture. Bake for 30 minutes. Yield: 6 to 8 servings.

Betty Ross, Xi Zeta Kappa
Rock Rapids, Iowa

MAKE-AHEAD BACON 'N CHEDDAR STRATA

This make-ahead, minimum clean-up brunch entrée is a family favorite. Add warm muffins, fresh fruit salad and gather a gang!

16 slices bread, cubed	4 cups shredded Cheddar cheese
16 slices bacon, crisp-fried, crumbled	7 eggs
	3 cups milk
1/2 red bell pepper, finely chopped	1/2 teaspoon salt
3 green onions, finely chopped	1/2 teaspoon dry mustard
	1/4 teaspoon pepper

Layer bread, bacon, bell pepper, onions and cheese, 1/2 at a time, in greased 9-by-13-inch casserole. Beat eggs, milk, salt, mustard and pepper in bowl. Pour over layers. Chill, covered, for 3 hours to overnight. Preheat oven to 350 degrees. Bake, uncovered, for 50 minutes to 1 hour or until knife inserted near center comes out clean. Let stand for 5 minutes before serving. Yield: 10 servings.

Shereen Mazurek, Alpha Iota
Brockville, Ontario, Canada

SOUTH TEXAS STRATA

This is an easy breakfast when you have a houseful of company on a holiday morning.

9 slices white bread, crusts trimmed	6 eggs
3 tablespoons soft margarine	1/2 teaspoon salt
	3 cups milk
1 pound bacon, crumbled	1 4-ounce can chopped green chilies, drained
8 ounces sharp Cheddar cheese, shredded	2 eggs
	1/2 teaspoon chili powder or paprika

Spread bread with margarine; cut into 1 1/2-inch cubes. Place in greased 9-by-13-inch casserole. Sprinkle with crumbled bacon and cheese. Beat 6 eggs, salt and milk in bowl; stir in green chilies. Pour over cheese layer. Chill, covered, overnight. Preheat oven to 350 degrees. Beat remaining 2 eggs and chili powder in bowl. Pour over top layer. Bake for 1 hour. Yield: 8 to 10 servings.

Patricia Moore, Gamma Xi
Weslaco, Texas

MACARONI AND CHEESE QUICHE

1 7-ounce package elbow macaroni	1 small green bell pepper, finely chopped
6 to 8 slices bacon, crisp-fried, crumbled	4 egg yolks
2 cups shredded Cheddar cheese	2 cups milk
2 cups shredded Monterey Jack cheese	1 teaspoon salt
2 cups soft bread cubes	6 to 8 drops of hot pepper sauce
1 onion, finely chopped	4 egg whites
	Salsa

Preheat oven to 325 degrees. Cook macaroni using package directions; drain. Combine with next 6 ingredients in large bowl; mix gently. Beat egg yolks, milk, salt and hot pepper sauce in small bowl; pour over macaroni mixture. Beat egg whites in large mixer bowl until stiff peaks form. Fold in macaroni mixture gently. Spoon into buttered 12-inch quiche dish. Bake on center rack in oven for 1 hour. Serve with salsa. Yield: 12 servings.

Carole A. White, Epsilon Kappa
Tonawanda, New York

CHRISTMAS BREAKFAST

7 slices bread, crusts trimmed	3 cups milk
8 ounces Cheddar cheese, shredded	1/2 teaspoon salt
	1/4 teaspoon pepper
6 eggs	1 teaspoon dry mustard
	3 slices bacon, cut in half

Crumble bread; mix with cheese in bowl. Place in greased 7-by-12-inch shallow baking dish. Beat eggs, milk, salt, pepper and mustard in bowl. Pour over bread mixture. Arrange bacon slices on top. Chill, covered, overnight. Preheat oven to 350 degrees. Bake, uncovered, for 50 to 55 minutes or until knife inserted near center comes out clean.
Yield: 4 servings.

Frances C. Lorenz, Laureate Chi
Pottsville, Pennsylvania

SCRAMBLED EGG BRUNCH

2 tablespoons butter or margarine	18 eggs
2 tablespoons all-purpose flour	6 tablespoons nondairy creamer
1/4 cup nondairy creamer	1 teaspoon salt
1 cup boiling water	1/8 teaspoon pepper
3 tablespoons butter or margarine	3/4 cup hot water

Melt 2 tablespoons butter over medium heat in saucepan. Add flour, stirring until blended. Stir in 1/4 cup nondairy creamer and 1 cup boiling water. Cook over low heat until thickened, stirring constantly; remove from heat and cover. Melt 3 tablespoons butter in large skillet. Beat eggs, 6 tablespoons nondairy creamer, salt, pepper and hot water in bowl. Pour into skillet. Cook over very low heat until eggs are almost set. Do not overcook. Remove from heat. Stir in sauce. Pour into chafing dish and serve.
Yield: 12 servings.

Gerry Hurd, Preceptor Alpha Xi
Jacksonville, Florida

CHEESE DELIGHT

We always serve this on Christmas morning when all the children and grandchildren are with us to exchange gifts and love.

1 cup milk	1/4 cup butter or margarine
1 cup all-purpose flour	
2 cups cottage cheese	1/4 cup melted butter or margarine
16 ounces Monterey Jack cheese, shredded	Salsa
6 eggs, slightly beaten	

Preheat oven to 350 degrees. Combine first 6 ingredients in bowl; mix well. Pour melted butter in 9-by-13-inch baking dish. Add mixture. Bake for 40 minutes. Serve with salsa. Yield: 10 to 12 servings.

Joan Holt, Tau Eta
San Jacinto, California

BREAKFAST BONANZA

1 package all-ready pie pastry	1 4-ounce can mushrooms, drained
1 onion, chopped	1 cup shredded Cheddar cheese
1/2 of 8-ounce package frozen spinach, thawed, drained	8 eggs
	1/2 cup milk

Preheat oven to 350 degrees. Line 8-by-11-inch baking dish with pie pastry. Combine onion, spinach, mushrooms and cheese in bowl. Spread over pie pastry. Beat eggs with milk in bowl. Pour over vegetables. Bake, covered, for 40 minutes or until knife inserted near center comes out clean.
Yield: 8 to 10 servings.

Denise Bradley, Delta Omega
Windsor, Wisconsin

CHEESE SOUFFLÉ

8 slices bread, crusts trimmed, cubed	3 eggs
12 ounces sharp Cheddar cheese, shredded	2 cups milk

Layer bread cubes and cheese 1/2 at a time in buttered soufflé dish. Beat eggs and milk in bowl. Pour over layers. Chill, covered, overnight. Preheat oven to 350 degrees. Bake, uncovered, for 1 hour. Serve immediately. Yield: 6 to 8 servings.

Pat Matteo, Xi Epsilon Epsilon
Hazleton, Pennsylvania

BRUNCH BAKE SUPREME

1 to 2 tablespoons
    butter or margarine
6 slices bread, crusts
    trimmed
1 cup cubed Cheddar
    cheese
1/2 to 1 cup chopped
    onion
1/2 to 1 cup chopped
    green bell pepper
5 eggs
2 cups milk
1 1/2 teaspoons prepared
    mustard
1 teaspoon salt

Butter bread slices; cut into cubes. Place in buttered 2-quart baking dish. Cover with cheese, onion and green pepper. Beat eggs with milk, mustard and salt in bowl. Pour over bread cubes. Chill, covered, overnight. Preheat oven to 325 degrees. Bake, uncovered, for 1 hour or until knife inserted near center comes out clean. Yield: 6 servings.

Gloria Hayengs, Xi Gamma Omega
Granville, Illinois

EGG SOUFFLÉ

This recipe is great for a quick family meal or dressed up with salad and rolls for company brunch.

16 slices bread, crusts
    trimmed, cubed
8 ounces Swiss cheese,
    shredded
6 eggs
2 cups milk
1 teaspoon salt
1/2 cup melted butter
    or margarine

Layer bread cubes and cheese, 1/3 at a time, in greased 9-by-13-inch baking dish. Beat eggs, milk and salt in bowl. Pour over layers. Drizzle with butter. Chill, covered, for 12 hours. Preheat oven to 400 degrees. Bake, uncovered, for 45 minutes.
Yield: 6 to 8 servings.

Pat Cleland-Blinn, Preceptor Pi
Toledo, Ohio

MARY'S EGGS

I prepare this recipe the night before and bake the next morning for a great Christmas breakfast.

16 ounces Monterey
    Jack cheese, cubed
12 ounces cream cheese,
    cubed
1 cup cottage cheese
2 tablespoons melted
    butter or margarine
1/2 cup all-purpose flour
1 teaspoon baking
    powder
6 eggs
1 teaspoon sugar
1 teaspoon salt

Preheat oven to 350 degrees. Combine first 4 ingredients in bowl; set aside. Combine flour and baking powder in small bowl. Beat eggs, sugar and salt in medium bowl. Stir egg mixture into cheese mixture. Add dry ingredients, stirring until crumbly. Pour into greased 8-inch square baking dish. Bake for 40 minutes. Yield: 9 servings.

Donna Nasker, Lambda
Boise, Idaho

MAPLE BREAKFAST DELIGHT

8 slices bread, crusts
    trimmed, cubed
16 ounces cream
    cheese, cubed
12 eggs
2 cups milk
1/3 cup maple syrup

Line greased 9-by-13-inch baking dish with half the bread cubes, all the cream cheese and remaining bread cubes. Beat eggs, milk and syrup in bowl. Pour over layers. Chill, covered, overnight. Preheat oven to 375 degrees. Bake for 45 minutes. Let stand for 5 minutes before serving. Yield: 8 servings.

Trina M. Miller, Preceptor Beta Epsilon
Brocton, New York

SURPRISE NO-CRUST QUICHE

12 eggs
16 ounces Cheddar
    cheese, shredded
16 ounces Monterey
    Jack cheese, shredded
1 cup salsa

Preheat oven to 350 degrees. Combine all ingredients in large bowl; mix well. Pour into 9-by-11-inch baking dish. Bake for 35 to 40 minutes or until set in center. Yield: 12 servings.

Sharon Talley, Preceptor Zeta
Caldwell, Idaho

SOUTHWESTERN QUICHE

1 teaspoon chili powder
1 unbaked 9-inch
    pie shell
2 tablespoons water
3/4 cup shredded
    Cheddar cheese
1/2 cup shredded
    Monterey Jack cheese
3 eggs, slightly beaten
1 teaspoon salt
White pepper to taste
1 1/2 cups half and half
1 4-ounce can chopped
    green chilies
1 2-ounce can sliced
    black olives
2 tablespoons finely
    chopped green onion

Preheat oven to 350 degrees. Press chili powder into pie shell. Brush with water. Spread mixture of cheeses over bottom of pie shell. Mix eggs with remaining ingredients in bowl. Pour over cheese layer. Bake for 40 to 45 minutes or until set in center. Yield: 8 servings.

Teri Fleming
Oklahoma City, Oklahoma

Diane Evanovich, Xi Epsilon Kappa, Washington, Iowa, makes a Kangaroo by beating 2 eggs, 2 tablespoons chopped black olives and salt and pepper to taste with a fork in small bowl until well mixed. Melt 1 tablespoon butter in skillet over medium heat until butter begins to sizzle. Add egg mixture. Draw pancake turner across bottom of skillet as eggs begin to set, forming large soft curds. Cook until eggs are thickened but moist. Spoon into pita bread pocket. Top with 1 tablespoon chopped tomato, 1 teaspoon chopped green bell pepper and 2 tablespoons shredded Cheddar cheese.

LOW-FAT CHILIES RELLENOS

2 4-ounce cans
    chopped green chilies,
    drained
2 cups shredded low-fat
    Cheddar cheese
1 8-ounce carton
    frozen egg substitute,
    thawed

2 cups skim milk
1¹/4 cups baking mix
1 cup low-fat cottage
    cheese
¹/2 can cream-style corn

Preheat oven to 350 degrees. Place mixture of green chilies and Cheddar cheese in 3-quart baking dish coated with nonstick cooking spray. Set aside. Whisk egg substitute with milk and baking mix in bowl until smooth. Stir in cottage cheese and corn. Spoon into prepared pan. Bake for 45 minutes. May substitute 4 eggs for egg substitute. Yield: 8 servings.

Jessie R. Ballmer, Alpha Master
Riverside, California

DOROTHY'S EGGS

12 eggs, beaten
4 cups shredded sharp
    Cheddar cheese
2 4-ounce cans
    chopped green chilies,
    drained

2 17-ounce cans
    cream-style corn
1 tablespoon
    Worcestershire sauce
1 tablespoon salt

Preheat oven to 325 degrees. Combine eggs with remaining ingredients in large bowl; mix well. Pour into 9-by-13-inch baking dish. Bake for 1¹/4 hours or until firm. Yield: 12 servings.

Diane Flora, Laureate Zeta
Wheat Ridge, Colorado

GREEN CHILI-CHEESE BAKE

32 ounces shredded
    Cheddar cheese
2 4-ounce cans
    chopped green chilies

1 can mushrooms,
    drained
12 eggs, beaten

Preheat oven to 350 degrees. Spread half the cheese in greased 9-by-12-inch baking dish. Layer green chilies, mushrooms, remaining cheese and eggs over top. Bake for 45 minutes. Let stand for 10 to 15 minutes before serving. Yield: 8 to 10 servings.

Danette Russell, Xi Zeta Eta
St. John, Kansas

CHILI-EGG PUFF

10 eggs
¹/2 cup all-purpose flour
1 teaspoon baking
    powder
¹/2 teaspoon salt
    (optional)
2 cups low-fat small
    curd cottage cheese

16 ounces Monterey
    Jack cheese, shredded
¹/2 cup melted margarine
1 4-ounce can chopped
    green chilies

Preheat oven to 350 degrees. Beat eggs in mixer bowl. Add flour and next 5 ingredients; mix well. Stir in green chilies. Pour into 9-by-13-inch baking dish coated with nonstick cooking spray. Bake for 35 minutes or until firm in center.
Yield: 10 to 12 servings.

Lannette C. Gee, Delta Iota Upsilon
Santa Maria, California
*Penelope Neargarder, Preceptor Lambda Eta
San Jose, California
*Cheryl Amorelli, Xi Alpha Epsilon
Durango, Colorado

CONNI HADEN'S CHILI RELLENOS CASSEROLE

6 4-ounce cans
    chopped or whole
    green chilies
16 ounces Monterey
    Jack cheese, shredded

16 ounces longhorn
    cheese, shredded
1 teaspoon salt
12 eggs, separated
2 cups sour cream

Preheat oven to 350 degrees. Spread half the green chilies in greased 9-by-13-inch baking dish. Layer Monterey Jack cheese, remaining green chilies and longhorn cheese over top. Sprinkle with salt. Beat egg whites until stiff peaks form. Beat egg yolks in large bowl until thick and lemon-colored. Beat in sour cream. Fold in egg whites gently. Pour over layers in pan. Bake for 50 minutes to 1 hour or until lightly browned. Yield: 12 servings.

Sandra Helbert, Preceptor Beta Omega
Emporia, Kansas

CHILI RELLENOS CASSEROLE

Butter or margarine,
    softened
6 slices bread, crusts
    trimmed
2 cups shredded
    Cheddar cheese
2 cups shredded
    Monterey cheese
1 4-ounce can chopped
    green chilies

6 eggs
2 cups milk
2 teaspoons paprika
1 teaspoon oregano
¹/4 teaspoon garlic
    powder
¹/4 teaspoon dry
    mustard
2 teaspoons salt
¹/2 teaspoon pepper

Butter 1 side of bread slices. Place buttered side down in 7-by-11-inch baking dish. Top with mixture of cheeses. Arrange green chilies over top. Beat eggs until frothy. Add milk and remaining ingredients; mix well. Pour over layers in pan. Chill, covered, for 4 hours to overnight. Preheat oven to 325 degrees. Remove cover. Bake for 50 to 55 minutes or until lightly browned. Let stand for 10 minutes before serving. Yield: 6 servings.

Norma Wood, Preceptor Theta Mu
Austin, Texas
*Joy Warden, Xi Pi Nu
Chico, California

BANANA-FILLED OMELET

1 tablespoon butter or margarine	1/4 cup milk or half and half
2 bananas, sliced	2 tablespoons rum
2 tablespoons light brown sugar	2 tablespoons butter or margarine
4 eggs	

Melt 1 tablespoon butter in small skillet over medium heat. Add bananas and brown sugar. Cook for 2 to 3 minutes, stirring frequently. Set aside. Beat eggs with milk and rum in bowl. Melt remaining 2 tablespoons butter in nonstick skillet. Add egg mixture. Cook for 30 seconds without stirring. Lift edge as eggs set to allow uncooked egg to flow underneath. Cook until almost set. Spread half the cooked bananas over omelet. Cook until eggs are set. Place on serving plate, folding in half. Top with remaining bananas. Yield: 2 servings.

Kay Poling, Xi Eta Nu
College Station, Texas

GARDENER'S DELIGHT OMELET

1/2 cup shredded carrot	1 medium tomato, chopped
1/4 cup chopped green onions with tops	8 eggs
1/4 cup chopped green bell pepper	1/2 cup milk
2 tablespoons Italian salad dressing	1/2 teaspoon salt
1/2 cup chopped peeled cucumber	1 1/3 tablespoons oil
	1/4 cup alfalfa sprouts

Combine carrot, green onion, green pepper and salad dressing in small saucepan. Cook until vegetables are tender. Stir in cucumber and tomato. Remove from heat; keep warm. Beat eggs with milk and salt in bowl. Pour by 1/2 cupfuls into omelet pan with 1 tablespoon hot oil. Lift edge as eggs set to allow uncooked egg to flow underneath. Cook until set. Fill with 1/4 cup vegetable mixture; top with 1/4 of the sprouts. Fold over. Remove to warm plate. Repeat with remaining ingredients. Yield: 4 servings.

Minnie S. Wall
Glasgow, Montana

OVEN OMELET

The yummy taste makes it up to all the girls you have hauled out of bed at 6:00 a.m. for a kidnap breakfast in 30-degree weather!

1/4 cup butter or margarine	1 cup milk
18 eggs	2 teaspoons salt
1 cup sour cream	1/4 cup chopped green onion

Preheat oven to 325 degrees. Melt butter in 9-by-13-inch baking dish, spreading butter evenly. Beat eggs with sour cream, milk and salt in large bowl until smooth. Stir in onion. Pour into prepared baking dish. Bake for 35 minutes or until eggs are set. Yield: 6 to 8 servings.

Maureen Tatem, Xi Alpha Chi
Okotoks, Alberta, Canada

BRUNCH OMELET

1 10-ounce can cream of mushroom soup	8 ounces shredded Cheddar cheese
12 eggs, slightly beaten	1 4-ounce can sliced mushrooms
16 ounces bacon, crisp-fried, crumbled	

Preheat oven to 350 degrees. Spread soup evenly in 8-by-12-inch baking dish. Layer remaining ingredients over top. Bake for 1 hour and 15 minutes or until bubbly in center. Yield: 9 to 12 servings.

Ann Thiede, Pi Eta
Castalia, Ohio

BRUNCH CASSEROLE

16 slices white bread, crusts trimmed	1/4 cup chopped green bell pepper or 1/4 cup minced onion
8 thin slices Canadian bacon or ham	2 tablespoons Worcestershire sauce
8 slices American cheese	3 cups milk
6 eggs, beaten	1/2 cup butter or margarine, melted
1/2 teaspoon salt	
Pepper to taste	

Place 8 bread slices in 9-by-13-inch greased baking pan. Place 1 slice bacon and 1 slice cheese on each bread slice. Top with remaining bread slices. Combine next 6 ingredients in bowl; mix well. Pour mixture over bread. Refrigerate overnight. Preheat oven to 350 degrees. Drizzle butter over top. Bake for 1 hour. Yield: 12 to 15 servings.

Doris E. Galbraith, Xi Beta Mu
Crete, Nebraska

CRUSTLESS QUICHE

1/2 cup butter or margarine	2 cups small curd cottage cheese
1/2 cup all-purpose flour	1 teaspoon baking powder
6 eggs, well beaten	1 teaspoon salt
1 cup milk	1 teaspoon sugar
4 cups grated Monterey Jack cheese	1 pound crisp-fried bacon, sausage or ham
3 ounces cream cheese	

Preheat oven to 350 degrees. Melt butter in 1-quart saucepan. Stir in flour. Cook until smooth, stirring constantly. Stir in next 8 ingredients. Add bacon. Pour into well-greased 9-by-13-inch baking pan. Bake for 45 minutes. Yield: 12 servings.

Kay Harmon
Holyoke, Colorado

EASY HAM QUICHE

I've experimented with this recipe and my husband seems to think that I've gotten it right. He always laughs and says, "Real men do eat quiche."

1 unbaked 9-inch pie shell	1/2 cup milk
8 ounces cream cheese, softened	1/2 teaspoon dry mustard
5 eggs	1 cup chopped ham
	5 green onions, chopped

Preheat oven to 350 degrees. Line 9-inch quiche dish with pie shell. Perforate with fork. Combine cream cheese, eggs, milk and mustard in bowl; blend well. Spread ham and onions in quiche dish. Bake for about 5 minutes. Pour cream cheese mixture over ham and onions. Bake for 40 to 50 minutes or until set. May be refrigerated and microwaved later. Yield: 8 servings.

Karen Johnson, Pi Omega
Henderson, Texas

HAM FRITTATA

14 slices white bread, crusts trimmed, buttered	1 to 2 cups shredded Cheddar cheese
1 ham slice, cubed	7 eggs
	4 cups milk

Place 7 bread slices in 9-by-12-inch baking pan. Sprinkle ham and cheese over bread. Top with remaining bread slices. Beat eggs and milk in bowl. Pour over bread. Refrigerate, covered, overnight. Preheat oven to 350 degrees. Bake for 1 hour and 5 minutes or until center tests done. Yield: 8 servings.

Barbara Firor, Laureate Delta Nu
Santa Ana, California

HAM AND SAUSAGE OMELET

I served this at a very elegant brunch with muffins, orange juice, etc. It tastes good even as leftovers.

1 pound sausage	2 1/4 cups milk
8 slices bread, cubed	3/4 teaspoon dry mustard
1 1/2 cups shredded Cheddar cheese	1 10-ounce can cream of mushroom soup
2 cups cubed cooked ham	1/2 cup milk
12 eggs, beaten	

Brown sausage in skillet, stirring until crumbly; drain. Layer bread, cheese, sausage and ham in greased 9-by-12-inch baking dish. Combine eggs, milk and mustard in bowl; beat until lemon-colored. Pour over bread mixture. Refrigerate, covered, overnight. Preheat oven to 300 degrees. Combine soup and milk in bowl. Pour over bread mixture. Bake for 1 hour and 30 minutes. Yield: 9 to 12 servings.

Kathleen Pieper, Xi Alpha Rho
Grand Island, Nebraska

BAKED EGGS AND HAM

16 eggs, beaten	2 cups diced ham
3/4 cup sour cream	2 tablespoons melted butter or margarine
1 cup half and half	Salt and pepper to taste
1 1/2 cups shredded Cheddar cheese	

Preheat oven to 350 degrees. Combine all ingredients; beat well. Pour into greased 9-by-13-inch baking pan. Bake for 40 to 45 minutes or until set and top is golden. Yield: 10 to 12 servings.

Barbara Plummer, Delta Lambda
Poteau, Oklahoma

MARYBETH'S VALENTINE BRUNCH

A Beta sister and I combined 2 recipes on Valentine's Day and came up with this breakfast casserole.

12 eggs, beaten	1/2 teaspoon salt
4 green onions, sliced (optional)	Pepper to taste
3/4 cup sliced fresh mushrooms (optional)	1/4 teaspoon dillweed
1 cup diced ham	2 cups milk
2 tablespoons butter or margarine	2 cups shredded Swiss cheese
2 tablespoons all-purpose flour	2 cups rye bread cubes
	2 tablespoons melted margarine

Combine eggs, onions, mushrooms and ham in saucepan. Scramble until softly cooked. Set aside. Melt butter in saucepan. Blend in flour, salt, pepper and dillweed. Add milk, stirring constantly; cook until thickened. Stir in cheese. Fold in egg mixture. Pour into 9-by-13-inch greased baking dish. Toss bread and margarine together in bowl until bread is coated; sprinkle on top. Refrigerate overnight or until 30 minutes before baking. Preheat oven to 350 degrees. Bake for 30 minutes. Yield: 10 to 12 servings.

Jody Malsam, Xi Kappa
Coeur d'Alene, Idaho

EGG AND HAM MIX-UP

I use this recipe for Christmas and Easter mornings. It is simple and fast—I can enjoy the holiday activities.

6 slices whole wheat bread, cubed	1 teaspoon salt
6 eggs, slightly beaten	1 teaspoon dry mustard
1 cup shredded Cheddar cheese	1 1/2 cups cubed cooked ham
	2 cups milk

Combine all ingredients in 1 1/2-quart glass casserole. Refrigerate for 4 to 6 hours or overnight. Microwave on Medium-High for 12 to 14 minutes. Serve immediately. Yield: 6 servings.

Donna Branson, Laureate Zeta Epsilon
Ukiah, California

HAM AND CHEESE QUICHE

This is an easy dish to prepare for breakfast or brunch.

16 slices bread, crusts trimmed	**6 eggs**
1 pound ham, cubed	**1/2 teaspoon onion salt**
8 ounces Swiss cheese	**3 cups cornflakes, crushed**
8 ounces Cheddar cheese	**1/2 cup melted margarine**
3 cups milk	

Place 8 bread slices in 9-by-13-inch baking pan. Layer half the ham, half the cheese, remaining bread, remaining ham and remaining cheese. Combine milk, eggs and salt in bowl; mix well. Pour over layered mixture. Refrigerate overnight. Remove from refrigerator 30 minutes before baking. Preheat oven to 375 degrees. Combine cornflakes and margarine; sprinkle on top. Bake for 40 minutes. Yield: 12 servings.

Nancy Johnston, Preceptor Beta Epsilon
Marion, Iowa

THE CRESCENT QUOIT

When I hosted our meeting I served this dish and asked my sisters to help me give it a name so I could enter it in the contest. We had lots of ideas that night and calls kept coming. Most included the word ring. I looked up ring in the dictionary and came up with the title.

1/4 pound ham, cubed	**6 ounces Swiss or**
2 cups chopped fresh broccoli	**Monterey Jack cheese, cubed**
1 small onion, chopped	**1 teaspoon lemon juice**
1/2 cup chopped parsley	**2 cans crescent rolls**
2 tablespoons Dijon mustard	

Preheat oven to 350 degrees. Combine first 7 ingredients in bowl; mix well. Separate rolls into triangles. Arrange triangles in circle on greased round baking sheet with points out, overlapping corners of wide edges slightly to form center of circle; press overlapping edges to seal. Press chopped mixture into ring toward center of circle. Fold points of dough over filling to inside of circle and secure under center edge of circle. Bake for 20 minutes or until golden brown. Yield: 16 servings.

Lyn Patterson, Beta Omega
LaCygne, Kansas

SPINACH QUICHE

This was served at a 1987 Rush Brunch when I joined.

24 ounces cottage cheese	**1 10-ounce package**
2 cups diced ham	**frozen spinach,**
8 ounces shredded Colby cheese	**thawed, drained**
6 eggs	**1 teaspoon seasoned salt**
1/2 cup all-purpose flour	**1/2 cup melted margarine**

Preheat oven to 350 degrees. Combine all ingredients in large bowl; mix well. Pour into lightly greased 9-by-13-inch baking pan. Bake for 1 hour. Yield: 8 to 10 servings.

Karen Hagen, Alpha Tau
Detroit Lakes, Minnesota

EGGLESS BREAKFAST CASSEROLE

Its low cholesterol makes it great for heart patients.

9 slices bread, cubed	**2 cups plus 2**
1 pound cooked turkey or ham, cubed	**tablespoons egg substitute**
1 1/2 cups cheese, shredded	**3 cups skim milk**

Preheat oven to 375 degrees. Layer bread, turkey and cheese in greased 9-by-13-inch baking pan. Combine egg substitute and milk in bowl; mix well. Pour over layered mixture. Bake for 1 hour. May microwave on Medium-High for 15 minutes or until done. Yield: 12 servings.

Emilie M. Smith, Preceptor Gamma Theta
Arlington, Washington

COUNTRY CLUB EGGS

1 pound sausage	**1 1/2 cups shredded sharp**
8 eggs, slightly beaten	**Cheddar cheese**
6 slices bread, cubed	**1 teaspoon dry mustard**
1 teaspoon salt	

Brown sausage in skillet, stirring until crumbly; drain. Combine all ingredients in large bowl; mix well. Pour into 9-by-13-inch greased baking pan. Refrigerate for 12 hours. Preheat oven to 350 degrees. Bake for 45 minutes or until center tests done. Yield: 8 to 10 servings.

Joy McClellan, Xi Lambda Gamma
Sesser, Illinois

WEDDING BRUNCH

1 pound sausage	**6 eggs, beaten**
6 slices bread, crusts trimmed	**2 cups half and half**
1 1/2 cups shredded Longhorn cheese	**1 teaspoon salt**
	Salsa

Brown sausage in skillet, stirring until crumbly; drain. Layer bread, sausage and cheese in greased 9-by-13-inch baking pan. Combine eggs, half and half and salt in bowl; mix well. Pour over layered mixture. Refrigerate, covered, overnight. Remove from refrigerator 15 minutes before baking. Preheat oven to 350 degrees. Bake for 45 minutes or until set. Serve with salsa. Yield: 8 to 10 servings.

Barbara D. Williams, Xi Epsilon Beta
Edinburg, Virginia
*Jodie M. Mutchler, Chi Rho
Tampa, Florida

BREAKFAST CASSEROLE

1 pound sausage	*1 cup milk*
12 slices wheat or	*12 ounces shredded*
white bread,	*Cheddar cheese*
crusts trimmed	*Fresh fruit*
12 eggs, beaten	

Brown sausage in skillet, stirring until crumbly; drain. Place bread in greased 9-by-13-inch baking pan. Combine eggs and milk in bowl; mix well. Pour over bread. Add sausage. Top with cheese. Refrigerate overnight. Preheat oven to 375 degrees. Bake for 30 minutes. Serve with fresh fruit. Yield: 12 servings.

Lisa Grimsley, Xi Beta Pi
Boonville, Missouri

MIMI'S BREAKFAST EGGS

Sunday breakfast at my mother-in-law's is always a special occasion. The table is decorated with flowers, china and crystal. This delicious entrée is served with fruit salad and coffee cake.

1¹/2 cups sausage	*1 teaspoon salt*
16 slices white bread,	*¹/4 teaspoon dry*
crusts trimmed, cubed	*mustard*
10 ounces shredded	*6 tablespoons butter*
Cheddar cheese	*or margarine, melted*
8 eggs, beaten	*2 cups cornflakes, crushed*
2 cups milk	*2 tablespoons melted*
1¹/2 cups half and half	*butter or margarine*

Brown sausage in skillet; drain and crumble. Place half the bread in greased 9-by-13-inch baking pan. Add layers of cheese, sausage and remaining bread. Combine eggs, milk, half and half, salt, mustard and 6 tablespoons butter in large bowl; mix well. Pour over layered mixture. Combine cornflakes and 2 tablespoons butter in small bowl. Sprinkle over top. Refrigerate, covered, overnight. Remove from refrigerator 2 hours before baking. Preheat oven to 350 degrees. Bake for 1 hour. Serve immediately. Yield: 8 servings.

MaryEllen House, Xi Alpha Pi
Albuquerque, New Mexico

FAVORITE BREAKFAST CASSEROLE

This is my family's favorite breakfast dish.

1 pound pork sausage	*4 eggs*
10 slices bread, cubed	*2¹/2 cups milk*
12 ounces Cheddar or	*1 10-ounce can cream*
American cheese,	*of chicken soup*
sliced	*¹/2 cup milk*

Brown sausage in skillet, stirring until crumbly; drain. Layer bread, sausage and cheese in greased 9-by-13-inch baking pan. Combine eggs and 2¹/2 cups milk in bowl; mix well. Pour over layered mixture. Refrigerate, covered, overnight. Preheat oven to

350 degrees. Combine soup and ¹/2 cup milk in bowl. Pour over casserole. Bake, covered, for 30 minutes. Uncover; bake for 40 minutes longer. Yield: 10 to 12 servings.

Bernadette Kleinsmith, Preceptor Gamma Mu
DeWitt, Iowa

BRUNCH SAUSAGE SOUFFLÉ

1 pound sage sausage	*5 slices white bread,*
1¹/2 teaspoons salt	*cubed*
¹/4 teaspoon nutmeg	*4 ounces Swiss cheese,*
¹/8 teaspoon pepper	*shredded*
6 eggs, well beaten	*1 tablespoon diced*
1¹/2 cups milk	*pimento*

Brown sausage in large skillet; pour off drippings. Sprinkle salt, nutmeg and pepper over sausage; let cool. Combine eggs and milk in bowl; mix well. Fold in bread, cheese and pimento. Stir in sausage. Pour into greased 8-inch square casserole. Refrigerate, covered, overnight. Preheat oven to 325 degrees. Bake for 1 hour and 10 minutes. Let stand for 5 minutes before serving. Yield: 6 to 8 servings.

Suzi Hagamon, Xi Beta Kappa
Salmon, Idaho

JANICE'S BRUNCH CASSEROLE

Our chapter has served this at many of our Mother's Day brunches and always enjoyed it!

1¹/2 pounds sausage	*4 eggs, beaten*
6 slices bread, cubed	*2 cups milk*
1¹/2 cups Velveeta	*¹/4 teaspoon dry mustard*
cheese, cubed	*Salt to taste*

Brown sausage in skillet, stirring until crumbly; drain. Layer sausage, bread and cheese in greased 9-by-13-inch baking pan. Combine eggs, milk, mustard and salt in bowl; mix well. Pour over casserole. Refrigerate overnight. Preheat oven to 325 degrees. Bake for 55 minutes to 1 hour or until browned. Yield: 12 servings.

Michelle Ilsley, Mu Lambda
Fairfax, Missouri

SAUSAGE AND EGG CASSEROLE

2 pounds sausage	*4 eggs, beaten*
1 10-ounce can cream	*³/4 cup shredded*
of mushroom soup	*Cheddar cheese*
8 slices bread, torn in	*1 cup milk*
pieces	*1 cup evaporated milk*

Brown sausage in skillet, stirring until crumbly; drain. Combine all ingredients in large bowl; mix well. Pour into greased 9-by-13-inch baking pan. Refrigerate overnight. Preheat oven to 325 degrees. Bake for 1 hour. Yield: 8 servings.

Dolores Sandusky, Laureate Alpha Epsilon
Tucson, Arizona

BREAKFAST QUICHE

I use this recipe during the holidays because it can be prepared ahead of time and popped into the oven. It allows me more time to spend with my family plus everyone loves it!

1 pound sausage
3 slices white bread, crumbled
12 eggs, beaten
1 teaspoon dry mustard
1 10-ounce can cream of mushroom soup
3/4 cup milk
10 ounces shredded Cheddar cheese

Brown sausage in skillet, stirring until crumbly; drain. Preheat oven to 350 degrees. Layer bread and sausage in greased 9-by-13-inch baking pan. Combine next 4 ingredients in bowl; beat well. Pour over sausage. Bake for 35 to 40 minutes or until eggs are set. Sprinkle cheese on top. Bake until cheese melts. Yield: 12 servings.

Jane Teuton, Preceptor Chi
Tallahassee, Florida

EGG CASSEROLE

I always fix this casserole on Christmas Eve. While it cooks on Christmas morning, our family enjoys opening gifts. It is wonderful with sparkling grape juice.

1/4 cup margarine
16 eggs
1/4 teaspoon salt
1 cup evaporated milk
6 slices bacon, diced
1/4 cup margarine
1/2 cup all-purpose flour
1 quart milk
1/4 pound smoked sausage, diced
1 8-ounce can mushroom pieces and stems, drained
Pepper to taste

Melt 1/4 cup margarine in heavy skillet. Combine eggs, salt and evaporated milk in bowl; beat well. Pour into skillet; scramble until softly cooked. Set aside. Sauté bacon in saucepan. Add 1/4 cup margarine, stirring until melted. Stir in flour, cooking over medium heat until bubbly. Add milk slowly, stirring until mixture begins to thicken. Add sausage, stirring carefully. Add mushrooms and pepper. Pour half the sauce into greased 9-by-13-inch casserole. Add eggs. Top with remaining sauce. Refrigerate, covered, overnight. Preheat oven to 300 degrees. Bake, covered, for 1 hour. Yield: 12 servings.

Christy Stratton, Lambda
Excelsior Springs, Missouri

WIFE SAVER BREAKFAST

This is a great recipe for a sorority brunch.

1 pound link sausage
6 slices white bread, crusts trimmed, cubed
1 cup shredded Cheddar cheese
4 eggs, well beaten
1 teaspoon salt
1/2 teaspoon dry mustard
2 cups milk

Brown sausage in skillet; drain and cut into bite-sized pieces. Layer sausage, bread and cheese in greased 2 1/2-quart baking dish. Combine eggs, salt, mustard and milk in bowl; mix well. Pour over layered mixture. Refrigerate, covered, overnight. Preheat oven to 350 degrees. Bake, uncovered, for 1 hour to 1 hour and 30 minutes or until set. Yield: 6 to 8 servings.

Roselee Soyka, Preceptor Delta Rho
Caledon East, Ontario, Canada

BREAKFAST CASSEROLE

Mom made this for Easter and Christmas breakfasts. She prepared it ahead and everyone was able to enjoy.

1 1/2 pounds link sausage, cut into 1/2-inch pieces
8 slices bread, torn into pieces
2 cups shredded sharp cheese
4 eggs, beaten
2 1/4 cups milk
3/4 teaspoon dry mustard
1 10-ounce can cream of mushroom soup
1/2 cup milk

Brown sausage; drain. Layer bread, cheese and sausage in greased 9-by-13-inch baking dish. Combine eggs, 2 1/4 cups milk and mustard in bowl; beat well. Pour over layered mixture. Refrigerate, covered, overnight. Preheat oven to 300 degrees. Combine soup and 1/2 cup milk in bowl; mix well. Pour over casserole. Bake for 1 hour and 30 minutes. Yield: 6 servings.

Beverly Raze, Preceptor Alpha Nu
Fruitland, Idaho
*Lori Murray, Xi Epsilon Xi
New Hampton, Iowa
*Millicent Thompson, Beta Omega
Savannah, Missouri

BUFFET BREAKFAST

I had a house full of people for Christmas morning. so I made this the night before. I just put this in to bake when we got up. When gifts were opened, we were ready to eat. I served fruit and sweet rolls with it.

2 pounds pork sausage
4 eggs, beaten
3/4 teaspoon dry mustard
2 1/2 cups milk
1 10-ounce can cream of mushroom soup
1 can mushrooms, drained
2 1/2 cups herbed croutons
2 cups shredded medium Cheddar cheese

Brown sausage in skillet, stirring until crumbly; drain. Combine eggs, mustard and milk in large bowl; mix well. Add remaining ingredients; mix well. Pour into greased 9-by-13-inch baking pan. Refrigerate, covered, overnight. Preheat oven to 350 degrees. Bake for 1 hour. Yield: 10 to 12 servings.

Betty Schluter, Preceptor
Beaumont, Texas

TEXAS QUICHE

1 pound sausage
8 ounces chopped
green chilies
1 small can
evaporated milk
6 eggs, beaten
1 pound Monterey Jack
cheese, shredded
1 pound Cheddar
cheese, shredded

Brown sausage in skillet, stirring until crumbly; drain. Preheat oven to 350 degrees. Layer chilies and sausage in greased 9-by-13-inch baking pan. Combine milk, eggs and cheeses in bowl; mix well. Spread over top of layered mixture. Bake for 40 minutes. May serve hot or cold. Yield: 12 servings.

Maxine Moran, Laureate Alpha Alpha
Maryville, Missouri

OVERNIGHT EGGS 'N CHILIES

I serve this every Christmas morning, and my family loves it!

12 ounces pork sausage
4 cups shredded
Monterey Jack
cheese
2 tablespoons
all-purpose flour
3 4-ounce cans whole
green chilies
2 cups shredded
Cheddar cheese
12 eggs, beaten
1 cup milk

Brown sausage in skillet; drain and crumble. Toss Monterey Jack cheese and flour together in bowl. Sprinkle into ungreased 4-quart baking dish. Slice chilies open to lie flat; remove seeds. Layer chilies, Cheddar cheese and sausage over cheese mixture. Combine eggs and milk in bowl; mix well. Pour over casserole. Refrigerate, covered, for up to 24 hours. Preheat oven to 350 degrees. Bake, uncovered, for 45 minutes or until mixture is puffed and egg custard is set. Serve immediately. Yield: 12 servings.

JoAnne Bell, Laureate Zeta Kappa
Colusa, California

ONE PAN BRUNCH

This recipe has been in our family for years. It is served at many family as well as many sorority get-togethers.

1 pound kielbasa,
browned, sliced
8 to 10 eggs, beaten
2 cups milk
1 teaspoon salt
6 slices bread, torn in
pieces
1 cup shredded Cheddar
cheese

Combine all ingredients in large bowl; mix well. Pour into greased 9-by-13-inch baking pan. Refrigerate, covered, overnight. Preheat oven to 350 degrees. Bake for 45 minutes or until set. Fat and calories can be reduced by using turkey kielbasa, egg substitute, skim milk, calorie reduced bread and calorie reduced cheese. Yield: 12 to 16 servings.

Velma G. Sherwood, Xi Eta
Bel Air, Maryland

MICRO BREAKFAST CASSEROLE

This is my husband's favorite breakfast next to biscuits and gravy.

1 pound sausage
1 14-ounce can
mushrooms, drained
1 to 2 tablespoons
parsley flakes
2 to 3 tablespoons
Parmesan cheese
1/8 teaspoon pepper
1/2 teaspoon onion
powder
1/4 teaspoon garlic
powder
6 eggs, beaten
1/3 cup milk
1 cup shredded Cheddar
cheese

Brown sausage in skillet; drain and crumble. Layer sausage, mushrooms, parsley, Parmesan cheese and seasonings in greased 2-quart glass casserole. Combine eggs and milk in bowl; mix well. Pour over layered mixture. Microwave on High for 4 to 6 minutes or until firm, stirring and turning every 2 minutes. Add Cheddar cheese. Microwave for 45 to 50 seconds longer or until cheese melts.
Yield: 6 servings.

Linda L. Harmon, Xi Delta Lambda
Gig Harbor, Washington

SAUSAGE AND EGGS

1 pound sausage
6 eggs, separated
2 cups grated Cheddar
cheese
1 cup grated Swiss or
mozzarella cheese
2 cups sour cream
1 4-ounce can chopped
green chilies
(optional)

Preheat oven to 350 degrees. Brown sausage in skillet; drain and crumble. Beat egg whites in mixer bowl until stiff peaks form; set aside. Beat egg yolks in mixer bowl. Add cheeses, 1 cup sour cream, sausage and chilies; mix well. Fold into stiffly beaten egg whites. Pour into greased 11-by-14-inch baking pan. Bake for 40 minutes. Let set for 5 to 7 minutes. Spread 1 cup sour cream on top. Yield: 12 servings.

Iva Lou Miller, Nu Delta
Clinton, Iowa

BISCUIT PIZZA

1 10-count can biscuits
1 pound sausage
5 eggs
1/2 cup milk
1/2 teaspoon salt
1/4 teaspoon pepper
1/4 cup shredded
Cheddar cheese

Preheat oven to 350 degrees. Brown sausage in skillet; drain and crumble. Press biscuits over bottom and up side of pizza pan. Spread sausage over dough. Beat eggs in bowl until thick. Add milk, salt and pepper; mix well. Pour over sausage. Sprinkle with cheese. Bake for 30 to 40 minutes or until golden brown. Yield: 6 to 8 servings.

Kathy Borthwick, Mu Phi
Beeler, Kansas

BREAKFAST PIZZA

1 pound sausage	5 eggs
1 8-count can crescent rolls	1/4 cup milk
	1/2 teaspoon salt
1 cup frozen loose-pack hashed brown potatoes, thawed	1/8 teaspoon pepper
	2 tablespoons grated Parmesan cheese
1 cup shredded sharp Cheddar cheese	

Preheat oven to 375 degrees. Brown sausage in skillet, stirring until crumbly; drain. Unroll crescent rolls. Arrange triangles with points toward center in pizza pan, sealing edges. Layer sausage, potatoes and cheese over dough. Beat eggs, milk, salt and pepper in bowl. Pour over layers. Sprinkle with Parmesan cheese. Bake for 25 to 30 minutes or until done. Yield: 6 to 8 servings.

Linda Melick, Preceptor Alpha Nu
Shelby, Ohio
*Lorraine Duchene, Xi Lambda Sigma
Royalton, Illinois
*Judy Agnew
Grinnell, Iowa

CORNED BEEF BRUNCH BAKE

I served this at one of our brunches. It was really enjoyed.

1/2 cup chopped onion	12 ounces corned beef, sliced into 6 equal portions
1/2 cup finely chopped celery	
	4 ounces shredded Cheddar cheese
1/2 cup chopped green bell pepper	3 eggs, beaten
2 tablespoons butter or margarine	11/2 cups milk
	1 teaspoon salt
12 slices white bread	Dash of pepper

Sauté onion, celery and green pepper in butter in skillet until tender. Arrange 6 bread slices in lightly greased 9-by-13-inch baking dish. Place 1 corned beef slice on each bread slice. Spoon equal amount onion mixture on corned beef slices. Sprinkle with cheese. Top with remaining bread. Combine eggs, milk, salt and pepper in bowl; mix well. Pour over bread. Bake for 40 minutes. Yield: 8 to 12 servings.

Nancy Smith, Preceptor Omicron
Gaithersburg, Maryland

EASY HAMBURGER QUICHE

1/2 pound ground beef	11/2 cups shredded Cheddar cheese
1/2 cup mayonnaise	
1/2 cup milk	1/3 cup sliced green onions
2 eggs	
1 tablespoon cornstarch	Dash of pepper
	1 unbaked 9-inch pie shell

Preheat oven to 350 degrees. Brown ground beef in skillet, stirring until crumbly; drain. Combine next 4 ingredients in mixer bowl; blend until smooth. Stir in ground beef, cheese, onions and pepper. Pour into pie shell. Bake for 35 to 40 minutes or until golden brown on top and knife inserted near center comes out clean. Yield: 6 to 8 servings.

Martha M. Robertson, Laureate Sigma
Glenns Ferry, Idaho

QUICK AND EASY STROGANOFF

This is a one-pan, quick clean-up recipe and is great as a brunch menu served over biscuits!

1 pound lean ground beef	Dash of pepper
1 small onion, chopped	1 8-ounce can mushrooms, drained
1/4 cup butter or margarine	
	1 10-ounce can cream of chicken soup
2 tablespoons (about) all-purpose flour	
	1 cup low-fat sour cream
1 teaspoon garlic powder	

Brown ground beef and onion in skillet. Stir in butter, flour, garlic powder and pepper. Add mushrooms and soup; mix well. Simmer for 10 minutes. Add sour cream. May serve over egg noodles, toast or biscuits if desired. Yield: 4 to 6 servings.

Colleen "Coke" Aafedt, Alpha Master
Williston, North Dakota

DRIED BEEF BRUNCH CASSEROLE

2 5-ounce jars dried beef, cut up	1/2 cup all-purpose flour
	3/4 cup evaporated milk
1/2 cup diced onion	12 eggs
1/2 cup diced green bell pepper	1/4 teaspoon salt
	1/8 teaspoon pepper
1 4-ounce can mushroom pieces, drained	6 tablespoons margarine
	3 slices bacon, crisp-fried, crumbled
1/2 cup margarine	4 ounces shredded sharp cheese
4 cups milk	

Preheat oven to 275 degrees. Sauté beef, onion, green pepper and mushrooms in 1/2 cup margarine in saucepan. Combine milk and flour in bowl; stir until smooth. Add to beef mixture, stirring until thick and smooth. Remove from heat. Combine evaporated milk, eggs, salt and pepper in large bowl; mix well. Melt 6 tablespoons margarine in skillet. Add eggs; scramble until softly cooked. Layer half the sauce, half the eggs, remaining sauce and remaining eggs in greased 9-by-13-inch baking dish. Cover with foil. Bake for 30 minutes. Uncover; sprinkle bacon and cheese over top. Bake until cheese melts slightly. Yield: 10 to 12 servings.

June Armbruster, Laureate Beta Iota
Ocala, Florida

HOT CHICKEN SALAD

4 cups chopped cooked chicken	1 10-ounce can cream of chicken soup
1 small jar diced pimentos, drained	2 tablespoons lemon juice
2 cups chopped celery	2/3 cup chopped toasted almonds
1/2 cup finely chopped green onion	1 cup shredded Cheddar cheese
4 hard-cooked eggs, chopped	1 1/2 cups crushed potato chips
3/4 cup mayonnaise	

Combine first 8 ingredients in large bowl; mix well. Pour into greased 9-by-13-inch baking pan. Refrigerate, covered, until ready to bake. Preheat oven to 375 degrees. Top with almonds, cheese and potato chips. Bake for 30 minutes. Yield: 8 servings.

Maria Broome, Xi Tau
Biloxi, Mississippi

HOT CHICKEN SOUFFLÉ

12 slices white bread, cubed	4 eggs
4 cups chopped cooked chicken or turkey	1 3/4 cups milk
1 cup minced onion	1 3/4 cups chicken broth
1 cup chopped celery	2 10-ounce cans cream of celery soup
1 cup mayonnaise	1 cup shredded sharp Cheddar cheese
1 teaspoon salt	or 1 10-ounce can cheese soup
1/2 teaspoon pepper	

Place 1/3 bread in greased 9-by-13-inch baking pan. Combine next 6 ingredients in bowl; mix well. Spoon over bread. Add remaining bread. Combine eggs and milk in bowl; mix well. Pour over bread. Refrigerate for 2 hours or overnight. Combine broth and soup in bowl; mix well. Spoon over top. Bake for 45 minutes. Sprinkle with cheese. Bake for 15 minutes longer. Let set before serving. Yield: 12 servings.

Sue Benson, Omicron
Albert Lea, Minnesota

SWISS AND CHICKEN CASSEROLE

4 cups chopped cooked chicken	1/2 cup milk
2 cups sliced celery	1/4 cup chopped onion
2 cups croutons	1 teaspoon salt
2 cups shredded natural Swiss cheese	1/8 teaspoon pepper
1 cup mayonnaise-type salad dressing	1/4 cup chopped walnuts, toasted

Preheat oven to 350 degrees. Combine first 9 ingredients in large bowl; mix well. Spoon into greased 2-quart casserole. Sprinkle walnuts over top. Bake for 40 minutes. Yield: 6 servings.

Edna Virene, Preceptor Kappa Eta
Upland, California

BREAKFAST BURRITOS

1 pound sausage	4 eggs, beaten
1/4 cup chopped onion	6 large soft tortilla shells
1/4 cup chopped green bell pepper	Picante sauce to taste
1 1/2 cups frozen Southern-style hashed brown potatoes	Sour cream to taste
	1/2 cup shredded Cheddar cheese

Brown sausage in skillet; drain and crumble. Add onion and green pepper. Cook to desired doneness. Add potatoes; cook for 6 to 8 minutes or until tender. Add eggs; cook until eggs are scrambled. Spoon into shells. Top with picante sauce, sour cream and cheese. Yield: 6 servings.

Cathy Koppin, Iota Delta
Oskaloosa, Iowa

SAUSAGE BARS

This is a husband pleaser and great on snow skiing trips because of quick preparation.

1 pound sausage	1 cup shredded mild Cheddar cheese
3 cups milk	Picante sauce
2 cups baking mix	
6 eggs	

Preheat oven to 400 degrees. Brown sausage in skillet; drain. Crumble sausage into greased 8-by-12-inch baking pan. Combine milk, baking mix and eggs in mixer bowl. Mix 1 minute with electric mixer. Pour over sausage. Top with cheese. Bake for 35 to 40 minutes or until done. Serve with picante sauce. Yield: 6 servings.

Robyn Wright, Alpha Zeta
Early, Texas

SAUSAGE SQUARES

This recipe can be made ahead of time. When ready to serve, sprinkle with water, cover with plastic wrap and reheat in the microwave.

1 pound bulk hot sausage	1 1/2 teaspoons salt
1/2 cup chopped onion	2 tablespoons parsley
1/2 to 3/4 cup grated Parmesan cheese	2 cups baking mix
1 egg, beaten	2/3 cup milk
1/4 teaspoon hot sauce	1/4 cup mayonnaise
	1 cup shredded Swiss cheese

Preheat oven to 400 degrees. Cook sausage and onion in skillet over low heat until sausage is browned; drain. Combine remaining ingredients in large bowl; mix well. Add sausage and onion; mix well. Pour into greased 9-by-13-inch baking dish. Bake for 25 to 30 minutes or until done. Let cool; cut into squares. Yield: 10 to 12 servings.

Mary Jo Rollins, Preceptor Laureate Gamma Theta
Pearland, Texas

BREAKFAST SAUSAGE CAKE

This is great left over—just slice and reheat it in the microwave. It keeps up to 1 week in the refrigerator.

1¹/2 pounds sausage
2 10-count cans butter-
   flavored biscuits
2 pounds Velveeta
   cheese, cubed

Preheat oven to 350 degrees. Brown sausage in skillet, stirring until crumbly; drain. Separate biscuits; cut into halves. Layer half the biscuits, half the sausage and half the cheese in greased bundt pan. Repeat layers. Bake for 30 minutes or until done. Remove from pan to serving plate. Slice and serve. Yield: 12 servings.

Lee Wilson-Knott, Preceptor Kappa Rho
Temple, Texas

SWEET AND SOUR SAUSAGES

1 pound beef or pork
   breakfast sausage
¹/2 cup catsup
¹/2 cup water
¹/4 cup vinegar
¹/4 cup packed light
   brown sugar
¹/2 teaspoon
   Worcestershire sauce
1 tablespoon soy sauce
2 teaspoons cornstarch

Preheat oven to 350 degrees. Brown sausage in skillet; drain. Crumble sausage into greased 9-by-13-inch baking pan. Combine remaining ingredients in bowl; mix well. Pour over sausage. Bake for 1 hour, stirring occasionally. May serve with rice if desired. Yield: 4 servings.

Brenda Pasishnik, Lambda
Yorkton, Saskatchewan, Canada

SAUSAGE-APPLE SAUTÉ

1 pound smoked
   sausage or kielbasa,
   cut into ¹/2-inch slices
2 medium onions,
   thinly sliced
2 apples, cored, thinly
   sliced
2 tablespoons
   margarine

Sauté sausage, onion and apples in margarine in large skillet until onion and apple slices are tender, stirring constantly. May serve with scrambled eggs, hashed brown potatoes and cantaloupe slices if desired. Yield: 6 servings.

Jean J. Dooly, Preceptor Lambda Alpha
Vallejo, California

RICE AND SAUSAGE CASSEROLE

This was served at a chapter "Favorite Recipe" program.

1 cup uncooked rice
2 chicken bouillon cubes
1 pound hot pork
   sausage
1 soup can water
2 10-ounce cans cream
   of mushroom soup
2 teaspoons dry onion
¹/4 cup slivered almonds
1 cup grated cheese

Preheat oven to 350 degrees. Cook rice according to package directions, adding bouillon cubes to water. Brown sausage in skillet; drain and crumble. Combine rice, sausage and next 4 ingredients in large bowl; mix well. Pour into greased 9-by-11-inch casserole. Top with cheese. Bake for 30 minutes. Yield: 6 servings.

Ruby Richardson, Preceptor Beta Nu
Oklahoma City, Oklahoma

❖ BRUNCH FOR A BUNCH

My sorority sisters live for this recipe, even the Yankees who don't eat grits.

2 pounds bulk sausage
1 6-serving package
   quick grits
¹/2 cup butter or
   margarine
4 cups shredded medium
   Cheddar cheese
Salt and pepper to taste
2 eggs, fried

Preheat oven to 350 degrees. Brown sausage in skillet, stirring until crumbly; drain. Prepare grits according to package directions. Stir in butter and 2 cups cheese. Remove from heat. Add sausage, salt and pepper; stir until well mixed. Pour into greased 3-quart baking dish. Sprinkle remaining cheese on top. Bake for 10 to 15 minutes or until cheese has melted. Garnish with eggs. Yield: 12 to 15 servings.

Sue B. Fulcher, Xi Alpha Mu
Fayetteville, North Carolina

SAUSAGE AND GRITS CASSEROLE

This can be adapted for low-fat diets by substituting turkey sausage, fat-free cheese and egg substitute.

1 pound pork sausage
3 cups hot cooked grits
2¹/2 cups shredded
   Cheddar cheese
3 tablespoons butter or
   margarine
3 eggs, beaten
1¹/2 cups milk
Pimento strips
Parsley

Preheat oven to 350 degrees. Brown sausage in skillet; drain. Crumble sausage into lightly greased 9-by-13-inch baking dish. Combine hot grits, cheese and butter in bowl; stir until cheese and butter are melted. Combine eggs and milk in bowl; mix well. Stir in grits mixture until well blended. Pour over sausage. Bake for 1 hour. Garnish with pimento strips and parsley. Yield: 15 servings.

Sharon Johnson, Mu Epsilon
Jefferson City, Missouri

CHEESE GRITS

2 quarts water
¹/2 cup butter or
   margarine
3 to 5 teaspoons
   seasoned salt
Garlic powder to taste
2 cups uncooked grits
8 to 10 ounces sharp
   cheese, shredded
2 eggs, well beaten

Preheat oven to 350 degrees. Combine water, butter and seasonings in saucepan; bring to a boil. Stir in grits; cook over low heat until done. Stir in cheese. Fold in eggs. Pour into greased 9-by-13-inch baking dish. Bake for 45 minutes to 1 hour or until lightly browned. Yield: 8 to 10 servings.

Gwynne Stover, Rho
Waynesboro, Virginia

GRITS CHEESE SOUFFLÉ

This is a great brunch for Sunday or "come as you are" breakfast for sorority sisters.

1 cup cold cooked grits	3 egg yolks, well beaten
1¹/2 cups hot milk	3 egg whites, stiffly
Salt to taste	beaten
Dash of paprika	
1 cup grated Cheddar	
cheese	

Preheat oven to 350 degrees. Combine grits and milk in bowl; beat until smooth. Add salt, paprika and cheese; mix well. Stir in egg yolks. Fold in egg whites. Pour into greased 2-quart casserole. Bake for 30 minutes. Serve immediately. Yield: 8 servings.

Helen Spacek, Xi Alpha Lambda
Warner Robins, Georgia

DENVER POTATO PIE

6 eggs	1 cup shredded Swiss
¹/2 teaspoon onion	cheese
powder	¹/2 cup chopped ham
¹/2 teaspoon thyme	¹/2 cup chopped green
¹/4 teaspoon salt	bell pepper
¹/8 teaspoon pepper	1 tomato, thinly sliced
3 cups hashed brown	
potatoes	

Preheat oven to 350 degrees. Combine eggs and seasonings in large bowl; mix well. Stir in potatoes and next 3 ingredients. Spoon into greased 10-inch pie plate. Bake for 40 to 45 minutes or until center is set. Garnish with tomato. Yield: 8 servings.

Pamela G. Wallberg, Beta Tau
Albany, Oregon

ALL-IN-ONE BREAKFAST

I needed a recipe low in fat and cholesterol. Great for people who don't like the taste of egg substitute.

5 tablespoons light	1 carton frozen egg
margarine	substitute, thawed
2 cups thinly sliced	³/4 cup low-fat shredded
peeled potatoes	Cheddar cheese
1 small onion, chopped	Salt and pepper to taste
5 slices turkey bacon,	Toast
crisp-fried, crumbled	Fresh fruit

Melt margarine in large nonstick skillet over medium-high heat. Add potatoes and onion. Sauté for 10 minutes or until potatoes are golden brown and tender. Stir in bacon. Add egg substitute. Stir until almost set. Sprinkle cheese over top. Cook, covered, until cheese melts. Add salt and pepper. Serve immediately with toast and fresh fruit. Yield: 4 or 5 servings.

Shirley Carnine, Preceptor Xi
Hamden, Connecticut

HASHED BROWN BRUNCH CASSEROLE

2 pounds link sausage	2¹/2 cups milk
or 1 to 2 cups	¹/2 teaspoon each salt
chopped ham	and pepper
2¹/2 cups herb-seasoned	1 10-ounce can cream
croutons	of mushroom soup
1¹/2 cups shredded	¹/2 cup milk
Cheddar cheese	16 to 32 ounces hashed
4 eggs	brown potatoes
³/4 teaspoon dry	1 cup shredded Cheddar
mustard	cheese

Brown sausage in skillet, turning frequently; drain. Spread croutons in 9-by-13-inch baking dish. Layer 1¹/2 cups cheese and sausage over top. Mix eggs with dry mustard, 2¹/2 cups milk, salt and pepper in bowl. Pour over sausage. Chill overnight. Preheat oven to 325 degrees. Mix soup with ¹/2 cup milk in bowl. Pour over casserole. Top with potatoes; sprinkle with 1 cup cheese. Bake for 1¹/2 hours. Yield: 8 to 10 servings.

Ann White, Xi Zeta Mu
Long Grove, Iowa

HASHED BROWN BREAKFAST CASSEROLE

1 pound sausage	1 cup Southern-style
²/3 cup milk	hashed brown
1 10-ounce can cream	potatoes, thawed
of chicken soup	²/3 cup bread crumbs
4 eggs, slightly beaten	³/4 cup shredded mild
1 cup chopped Velveeta	Cheddar cheese
cheese	

Preheat oven to 350 degrees. Brown sausage in skillet, stirring until crumbly; drain. Combine milk, soup, eggs, Velveeta, sausage and potatoes in bowl; mix well. Spoon into greased 9-by-13-inch baking dish. Sprinkle with bread crumbs and Cheddar cheese. Bake, covered, for 20 minutes. Remove cover. Bake for 10 to 20 minutes longer or until set in center. Let stand for 5 to 10 minutes before serving. May refrigerate overnight before baking; increase baking time 5 to 10 minutes. Yield: 6 to 8 servings.

Linda Ridlon, Eta Mu
DeQueen, Arkansas

POTATO SCRAMBLE

16 ounces sliced bacon,
  chopped
1/2 cup butter or
  margarine
5 or 6 potatoes,
  chopped

1 small onion, chopped
1/2 to 1 cup chopped
  green bell pepper
5 eggs, beaten

Fry bacon in skillet until almost crisp; drain. Remove bacon. Melt butter in same skillet. Add potatoes, onion and green pepper. Sauté until potatoes are of desired tenderness. Add eggs and bacon. Cook until eggs are soft-set, stirring constantly.
Yield: 4 to 5 servings.

Doris E. Edmonds, Alpha Tau
Clarksville, Tennessee

SAUSAGE SKILLET

1 pound sausage
2 green onions, chopped
2 large unpeeled
  potatoes, chopped
1 4-ounce can green
  chilies
1/2 cup sliced
  mushrooms

3 small zucchini, sliced
1 teaspoon ground
  cumin
1 teaspoon dried basil
  leaves
Salt and pepper to taste

Brown sausage in skillet, stirring until crumbly. Remove sausage; drain most of drippings. Sauté onions for several minutes in same skillet. Add sausage, potatoes and remaining ingredients. Cook over medium-low heat until potatoes are browned and tender, turning frequently. Cover for last 5 to 10 minutes of cooking time. Yield: 4 to 6 servings.

Lori Lemm, Tau Eta
Hemet, California

FRITTATA

3/4 to 1 cup country
  sausage
2 cups thinly sliced
  potatoes
2 tablespoons olive oil
1 green bell pepper,
  sliced into thin strips

2 green onions, chopped
Salt and pepper to taste
6 eggs
1 tablespoon milk
3/4 cup shredded
  Cheddar cheese

Preheat oven to 350 degrees. Brown sausage in skillet, stirring until crumbly; drain. Sauté potatoes in olive oil in large ovenproof skillet until lightly browned. Add green pepper and green onions. Sauté for 2 to 3 minutes longer. Stir in sausage, salt and pepper. Beat eggs and milk together in small bowl; add to mixture. Sprinkle with cheese. Cook until eggs begin to set on bottom. Remove from heat. Bake for 15 to 20 minutes or until eggs are set.
Yield: 6 servings.

Alice Marie Null, Laureate Alpha Beta
Princeton, Indiana

HOT POTATO CASSEROLE

9 unpeeled potatoes
1 10-ounce can cream
  of chicken soup
1 10-ounce can cream
  of celery soup
2 cups sour cream

1 1/2 to 2 cups shredded
  Cheddar cheese
1/2 cup butter or
  margarine, cut into
  8 pieces

Preheat oven to 350 degrees. Cook potatoes with water to cover in large saucepan until tender; drain. Peel and chop potatoes. Mix soups, sour cream and cheese in large bowl. Stir in potatoes. Spoon into 9-by-13-inch baking dish. Press butter pieces into top. Bake for 45 minutes. Yield: 12 to 14 servings.

Cherryl B. Patten, Preceptor Alpha Xi
Bellingham, Washington

SPICED POTATOES

1/2 cup chopped onion
1/2 cup chopped green
  bell pepper
3 cloves of garlic,
  minced
1/2 cup butter or
  margarine
3 or 4 unpeeled
  potatoes, thinly sliced

1 cup water
1 teaspoon onion
  powder
1 teaspoon paprika
1 teaspoon garlic salt
1 teaspoon cayenne
  pepper
1 teaspoon black pepper

Sauté onion, green pepper and garlic in half the butter in large skillet. Place potatoes on top of sautéed mixture. Add remaining butter. Pour water over top. Stir in onion powder and remaining ingredients. Cook over medium heat for 20 minutes or until potatoes are tender. Yield: 6 to 8 servings.

Tracy Hine, Alpha Omega
Ventura, California

UNSTUFFED POTATOES

If time allows, prepare this recipe and chill it overnight before baking. I serve it Christmas morning with baked ham, yule kakka, and home-made chunky applesauce.

3 cups shredded cooked
  potatoes
2 1/2 cups sour cream
1 bunch green onions,
  chopped
1 cup shredded sharp
  Cheddar cheese

1 1/2 teaspoons salt
1/2 teaspoon pepper
1/2 cup shredded sharp
  Cheddar cheese

Preheat oven to 350 degrees. Combine potatoes with next 5 ingredients in large bowl; mix well. Spoon into greased 9-by-11-inch baking dish. Sprinkle with 1/2 cup cheese. Bake for 35 to 45 minutes or until lightly browned. Yield: 12 servings.

Carolie Larson, Xi Delta Lambda
Gig Harbor, Washington

OVERNIGHT COFFEE CAKE

*1 package frozen
cloverleaf roll dough
1/2 cup melted butter or
margarine
1/2 cup packed light
brown sugar*

*1 4-ounce package
vanilla instant
pudding mix
1/2 cup chopped pecans*

Separate each roll into 3 pieces. Place in buttered bundt pan. Pour melted butter over dough. Mix brown sugar, pudding mix and pecans in bowl. Sprinkle over all. Let stand to rise overnight. Preheat oven to 350 degrees. Bake for 20 to 30 minutes or until browned. Invert onto serving plate. Yield: 8 servings.

*Cylesta Peters, Xi Zeta Rho
Goddard, Kansas*

SWEDISH COFFEE CAKE

This is a favorite to be shared early in the morning with neighbors and friends.

*1/2 cup butter or
margarine
2 teaspoons water
1 cup all-purpose flour
1/2 cup butter or
margarine
1 cup water
1 cup all-purpose flour*

*1 teaspoon vanilla
extract
3 eggs
1 cup chopped pecans
Maraschino cherries
1 1/2 cups confectioners'
sugar
2 teaspoons water*

Preheat oven to 425 degrees. Combine 1/2 cup butter with 2 teaspoons water in saucepan. Cook until butter is melted. Add 1 cup flour. Beat with wire whisk until smooth. Shape into firm ball. Place on foil-lined baking sheet. Flatten to 1/4-inch thick; smooth with fingers. Bring remaining 1/2 cup butter and 1 cup water to a boil in saucepan. Remove from heat. Beat in remaining 1 cup flour and vanilla. Beat in eggs 1 at a time. Spread over first layer. Bake for 20 to 25 minutes or until browned. Cake will rise as it bakes and fall as it cools. Top with pecans and cherries. Mix confectioners' sugar and remaining 2 teaspoons water in bowl. Drizzle over coffee cake. Yield: 24 to 30 servings.

*Lynn Lenker, Xi Eta Lambda
Lena, Illinois*

FEATHERY SPICE COFFEE CAKE

I serve this every Christmas with broiled grapefruit.

*1 cup all-purpose flour
1/2 cup sugar
1/2 teaspoon salt
1 teaspoon cinnamon
1 tablespoon baking
powder*

*1 egg
1/2 cup milk
1/4 cup salad oil
1 tablespoon dark
brown sugar
2 teaspoons cinnamon*

Preheat oven to 400 degrees. Sift flour, sugar, salt, 1 teaspoon cinnamon and baking powder together in bowl. Combine eggs, milk and oil in bowl; beat well. Stir into flour mixture. Spread in nonstick 9-inch square cake pan. Sprinkle with brown sugar and 2 teaspoons cinnamon. Bake for 15 minutes. May add raisins or chopped nuts to batter if desired. Yield: 8 to 10 servings.

*Marcell Weaver, Laureate Lambda
Roy, Utah*

GOOEY ALMOND CAKE

This is wonderful with your morning coffee. Using aluminum foil makes cleanup a snap!

*3/4 cup melted margarine
1 1/2 cups sugar
2 eggs
1/8 teaspoon salt
2 teaspoons almond
extract
1/2 teaspoon vanilla
extract*

*1 1/2 cups all-purpose
flour
2 teaspoons sugar
2 tablespoons sliced
almonds*

Preheat oven to 350 degrees. Line an 8- or 9-inch cast-iron skillet with foil. Mix melted margarine and 1 1/2 cups sugar in bowl. Beat in eggs 1 at a time. Stir in salt and extracts. Add flour gradually; mix well. Pour into skillet. Sprinkle with remaining 2 teaspoons sugar and almonds. Bake for 35 to 40 minutes or until cake is golden brown and tests done. Yield: 6 to 10 servings.

*Gail Hefner, Kappa Kappa
Meriden, Kansas*

SOUR CREAM COFFEE CAKE

I take this coffee cake to bereaved families. It's so quick to warm and serve on their day of sorrow.

*1 3/4 cups all-purpose
flour
1 teaspoon baking
powder
1/4 teaspoon salt
1 cup margarine,
softened
2 cups sugar*

*2 eggs
1 cup sour cream
1 1/2 teaspoons vanilla
extract
1 tablespoon cinnamon
3 tablespoons light
brown sugar
1/2 cup chopped pecans*

Preheat oven to 350 degrees. Sift flour, baking powder and salt together in bowl. Cream margarine, sugar and eggs in mixer bowl until light and fluffy. Fold in sour cream and vanilla. Add flour mixture gradually, beating well after each addition. Mix cinnamon, brown sugar and pecans in bowl. Layer batter and pecan mixture 1/2 at a time in greased 9-inch springform pan. Shake pan gently to settle batter. Bake for 1 hour. Let cool completely in pan. Yield: 16 servings.

*Eleanore L. Powers, Laureate Beta Theta
Bowling Green, Ohio*

EASY SOUR CREAM COFFEE CAKE

This is a recipe that I make often to take to work in the morning, serve at committee meetings, or take to convention for our morning wake-up.

1 cup chopped pecans	1/8 teaspoon salt
2 cups sifted	1 cup margarine
all-purpose flour	1/2 tablespoon baking
1 cup sugar	soda
1 cup packed light	2 eggs
brown sugar	1 cup sour cream
1 teaspoon cinnamon	

Preheat oven to 350 degrees. Sprinkle pecans in buttered 9-by-13-inch cake pan. Combine flour, sugar, brown sugar, cinnamon and salt in bowl. Cut in margarine until crumbly. Reserve half the crumb mixture. Add baking soda and eggs to remaining crumb mixture; mix well. Stir in sour cream. Pour over pecans. Sprinkle with reserved crumb mixture. Bake for 35 minutes. Yield: 20 servings.

Sharon Ingram, Preceptor Epsilon Theta
St. Petersburg, Florida

COFFEE CAKE

This coffee cake freezes very well.

1 cup sour cream	1 cup sugar
1 teaspoon baking soda	2 eggs, beaten
1 1/2 cups all-purpose	1/2 cup packed light
flour	brown sugar
1 1/2 teaspoons baking	1/2 cup chopped walnuts
powder	2 teaspoons cinnamon
1/4 teaspoon salt	
1/2 cup butter or	
margarine, softened	

Preheat oven to 350 degrees. Mix sour cream and baking soda in bowl; set aside. Sift flour, baking powder and salt together. Cream butter and sugar in mixer bowl until light and fluffy. Beat in eggs. Add flour mixture gradually, beating well after each addition. Stir in sour cream mixture. Mix brown sugar, walnuts and cinnamon in small bowl. Layer batter and brown sugar mixture 1/2 at a time in ungreased 9-inch square cake pan. Bake for 35 to 40 minutes or until browned. Yield: 16 servings.

Jean Rudy, Laureate Epsilon
Yorkton, Saskatchewan, Canada

BLUEBERRY COFFEE CAKE

2 cups all-purpose flour	2 cups blueberries
2 teaspoons baking	1/4 cup all-purpose flour
powder	1/2 cup sugar
1/2 teaspoon salt	1/3 cup all-purpose flour
3/4 cup sugar	1/2 teaspoon cinnamon
1/4 cup shortening	1/4 cup butter or
1 egg	margarine, softened
1/2 cup milk	1/2 cup chopped nuts

Preheat oven to 350 degrees. Sift 2 cups flour, baking powder and salt together in bowl. Cream 3/4 cup sugar and shortening in mixer bowl until light and fluffy. Stir in egg and milk. Add flour mixture gradually, beating well after each addition. Sprinkle blueberries with 1/4 cup flour, stirring gently until lightly coated; fold into batter. Pour into buttered 7-by-11-inch cake pan. Combine 1/2 cup sugar, 1/3 cup flour, cinnamon and butter in bowl; mix well. Stir in nuts. Sprinkle over batter. Bake for 45 to 50 minutes or until cake tests done. Yield: 10 servings.

Dorothy D. Laughlin, Laureate Beta Theta
Tacoma, Washington
*Karen Taylor, Preceptor Phi
Sioux Falls, South Dakota

BLUEBERRY STREUSEL COFFEE CAKE

This is a wonderful coffee cake for a morning coffee or brunch. It smells delicious as people are arriving.

1 cup sifted	1 cup blueberries,
all-purpose flour	drained
1 1/2 teaspoons	1 tablespoon lemon
baking powder	juice
1/2 teaspoon salt	1/3 cup sugar
1/3 cup sugar	1/4 cup all-purpose flour
1 egg	1/8 teaspoon salt
1/2 cup milk	1/4 teaspoon cinnamon
1/3 cup vegetable	2 tablespoons vegetable
oil	oil

Preheat oven to 375 degrees. Sift 1 cup flour, baking powder, 1/2 teaspoon salt and 1/3 cup sugar together. Beat egg in bowl. Stir in milk and 1/3 cup oil. Add flour mixture gradually, beating well after each addition. Pour into nonstick 8-inch square cake pan. Mix blueberries and lemon juice. Arrange over batter. Combine remaining 1/3 cup sugar, 1/4 cup flour, 1/8 teaspoon salt and cinnamon in bowl; mix well. Stir in 2 tablespoons oil. Spread over fruit. Bake for 40 minutes. Yield: 16 servings.

Rose Marie Olsen, Zeta Master
Colorado Springs, Colorado

MARY KAY'S COFFEE CAKE

Mary Kay Plumb served this coffee cake at brunches in her charming Victorian home in San Francisco. I submit this recipe in her memory.

2 cups baking mix	1/2 cup confectioners'
1 teaspoon cinnamon	sugar
1 egg	1 tablespoon butter or
2 tablespoons melted	margarine, softened
butter or margarine	1 tablespoon grated
3/4 cup sour cream	orange rind
1 16-ounce can	1 tablespoon orange
blueberries, rinsed,	juice
drained	1/3 cup chopped walnuts
1/2 cup chopped walnuts	

Preheat oven to 400 degrees. Combine baking mix, cinnamon, egg, melted butter and sour cream in bowl; mix well. Fold in blueberries and 1/2 cup walnuts. Pour into greased 8-inch square cake pan. Bake for 30 minutes. Combine confectioners' sugar and butter in bowl; mix well. Stir in orange rind, orange juice and 1/3 cup walnuts. Spread over warm cake. Yield: 6 servings.

Marilyn A. Adkins, Psi Chi
Mountain View, California

BANANA COFFEE CAKE

My family has always enjoyed this cake, hot out of the oven or cold after school.

3/4 cup melted butter or margarine	1 teaspoon vanilla extract
2 eggs	1/2 cup melted butter or margarine
5 tablespoons milk	
3 bananas, mashed	1 cup chopped nuts
1 1/2 cups sugar	2/3 cup packed light brown sugar
2 cups all-purpose flour	
1/2 teaspoon baking soda	

Preheat oven to 350 degrees. Combine first 8 ingredients in bowl; mix well. Pour into greased 9-by-13-inch baking pan. Combine remaining ingredients in bowl; mix well. Spoon over batter. Bake for 35 to 40 minutes or until cake tests done. Topping will bubble but will absorb into cake as cake cools. May drizzle with favorite icing.
Yield: 15 to 20 servings.

Alma Meyer, Preceptor Beta Delta
Calmar, Iowa

GERMAN BEER COFFEE CAKE

This has been a favorite recipe in my family for years. My German grandmother made it at least once a week.

3 cups all-purpose flour	1 cup butter or margarine, softened
2 teaspoons baking soda	
1 teaspoon cinnamon	2 cups packed dark brown sugar
1/2 teaspoon allspice	
1/2 teaspoon cloves	2 eggs
2 cups chopped dates	2 cups beer
1 cup chopped nuts	

Preheat oven to 350 degrees. Sift flour, baking soda, cinnamon, allspice and cloves together. Mix dates and nuts in bowl. Stir in a small amount of flour mixture to coat. Cream butter and brown sugar in mixer bowl until light and fluffy. Add eggs 1 at a time, beating well after each addition. Add flour mixture and beer alternately to creamed mixture, beating well after each addition. Stir in dates and nuts. Spoon into greased and floured bundt pan. Bake for 1 hour and 15 minutes. Yield: 14 servings.

Norma J. Boyer, Preceptor Beta Iota
Colorado Springs, Colorado

HEATH BRUNCH COFFEE CAKE

1/2 cup butter or margarine	1 egg
1 cup packed light brown sugar	1 teaspoon baking soda
	1 teaspoon vanilla extract
2 cups all-purpose flour	6 Heath bars, crushed
1/2 cup sugar	1/4 cup chopped walnuts or pecans
1 cup buttermilk	

Preheat oven to 350 degrees. Combine butter, brown sugar, flour and sugar in bowl; mix well. Reserve 1/2 cup mixture. Add buttermilk, egg, baking soda and vanilla to remaining mixture; mix well. Pour into greased and floured 9-by-13-inch baking pan. Combine reserved mixture, candy and walnuts in bowl. Sprinkle over batter. Bake for 30 minutes.
Yield: 12 to 15 servings.

Marilyn Peterson, Preceptor Alpha
Gulfport, Mississippi

COCONUT PINEAPPLE COFFEE CAKE

Although this is a brunch recipe, it is always my request for my birthday. It is great warm.

1 14-ounce package wild blueberry muffin mix	1/3 cup margarine, softened
	1/3 cup packed light brown sugar
1 8-ounce can crushed pineapple, drained	1/2 cup flaked coconut

Preheat oven to 400 degrees. Prepare muffin mix according to package directions. Stir in pineapple. Pour into greased 9-inch square cake pan. Mix margarine, brown sugar and coconut in bowl. Spoon evenly over batter. Bake for 25 to 30 minutes or until golden brown. Yield: 9 servings.

Pat McAtee, Xi Alpha Pi
Carrollton, Missouri

QUICK MINCEMEAT COFFEE CAKE

1/2 cup margarine, softened	1 cup milk
	1 teaspoon vanilla extract
1 cup sugar	
2 eggs	1 cup mincemeat
2 cups all-purpose flour	1/4 teaspoon baking soda
2 teaspoons baking powder	3 tablespoons margarine, softened
1/2 teaspoon salt	1/2 cup chopped walnuts

Preheat oven to 350 degrees. Cream 1/2 cup margarine and sugar in mixer bowl until light and fluffy. Add next 6 ingredients; beat well. Combine remaining ingredients in bowl; mix well. Layer half the batter, mincemeat mixture and remaining batter in nonstick 9-inch springform pan. Bake for 45 minutes to 1 hour or until cake tests done.
Yield: 12 to 14 servings.

Susan Geddes, Xi Zeta
Yorkton, Saskatchewan, Canada

APPLE COFFEE CAKE

1 cup margarine, softened	1/2 teaspoon salt
1 cup sugar	1 teaspoon baking soda
1 cup packed light brown sugar	1 teaspoon cinnamon
2 eggs	1 cup buttermilk or sour milk
2 1/2 cups all-purpose flour	2 cups chopped apples
1 1/4 teaspoons baking powder	1/2 cup sugar
	1 teaspoon cinnamon
	1/2 cup chopped nuts

Preheat oven to 300 degrees. Cream margarine, 1 cup sugar, brown sugar and eggs in mixer bowl until light and fluffy. Add next 6 ingredients; mix well. Stir in apples. Pour into greased 9-by-13-inch baking pan. Mix remaining ingredients in bowl. Sprinkle over batter. Bake for 1 hour and 15 minutes. Yield: 15 to 18 servings.

Dana Farmer, Xi Gamma Alpha
Dubuque, Iowa

DESSERT COFFEE CAKE

I have used this for several rush breakfasts and gotten new members with it.

1 1/2 cups all-purpose flour	1/2 cup milk
1/2 teaspoon salt	1/2 cup packed light brown sugar
1 1/2 teaspoons baking powder	1 tablespoon all-purpose flour
1/2 cup shortening	1/4 cup melted butter or margarine
1/2 cup sugar	1/2 cup chopped nuts
1/2 teaspoon vanilla extract	1/2 cup chopped dates
1 egg	

Preheat oven to 350 degrees. Sift 1 1/2 cups flour, salt and baking powder together. Cream shortening, sugar and vanilla in mixer bowl until light and fluffy. Beat in egg. Add flour mixture and milk alternately to creamed mixture, beating well after each addition. Combine remaining ingredients in bowl; mix well. Layer half the batter, brown sugar mixture and remaining batter in greased 9-inch square cake pan. Bake for 45 minutes. Yield: 8 to 12 servings.

Edyth M. Schuyler, Laureate Alpha Xi
Lakewood, Colorado

CRANBERRY-NUT COFFEE CAKE

2 cups baking mix	2/3 cup whole cranberry sauce
2 tablespoons sugar	1 cup confectioners' sugar
1 egg	1/2 teaspoon vanilla extract
2/3 cup water or milk	1 tablespoon (about) water
1/4 cup packed light brown sugar	
1/2 cup chopped walnuts	
1/4 teaspoon cinnamon	

Preheat oven to 400 degrees. Combine baking mix, sugar, egg and 2/3 cup water in mixer bowl. Beat vigorously for 30 seconds. Spread in greased 9-inch square cake pan. Mix brown sugar, walnuts and cinnamon in bowl. Sprinkle over batter. Spread cranberry sauce over all. Bake for 20 to 25 minutes or until cake tests done. Combine confectioners' sugar, vanilla and remaining 1 tablespoon water in bowl; beat until of spreading consistency. Spread over warm cake. Yield: 9 servings.

Mariette Selavka, Xi Kappa
North Franklin, Connecticut

BUTTE, MONTANA RHUBARB COFFEE CAKE

This delicious family recipe can be made a day ahead and reheated in the microwave.

2 cups all-purpose flour	1 cup sour cream
1 teaspoon baking soda	1/2 cup chopped nuts
1 1/2 cups packed light brown sugar	1 1/2 cups chopped fresh or frozen rhubarb
1/2 cup shortening	1/2 cup sugar
1 teaspoon vanilla extract	1 tablespoon cinnamon
1 egg	1 tablespoon butter or margarine

Preheat oven to 350 degrees. Sift flour and baking soda together. Cream brown sugar and shortening in mixer bowl until light and fluffy. Add vanilla, egg and sour cream; beat well. Stir in flour mixture. Add nuts and rhubarb; mix well. Pour into greased 9-by-13-inch baking pan. Mix sugar, cinnamon and butter in bowl. Sprinkle over batter. Bake for 30 to 40 minutes or until cake tests done. Yield: 9 servings.

Nadine Leffelman, Gamma Psi
Paris, Illinois

COFFEE CAKE WITH CRUNCH

1/2 cup packed light brown sugar	3/4 cup vegetable oil
1 1/2 cups chopped nuts	4 eggs
1 teaspoon cinnamon	1/2 cup sugar
1/4 teaspoon salt	1 cup sour cream
1 2-layer package white cake mix	

Preheat oven to 350 degrees. Combine brown sugar, nuts, cinnamon and salt in bowl; mix well. Combine remaining ingredients in mixer bowl. Beat at medium speed for 5 minutes. Layer cake mix mixture and brown sugar mixture alternately in greased and floured tube pan, ending with brown sugar mixture. Bake for 1 hour. Cool in pan for 10 minutes. Invert onto wire rack to cool completely. Yield: 12 to 14 servings.

Darlene Mowry, Preceptor Beta Sigma
Magalia, California

STREUSEL COFFEE CAKE

This is always a hit for carry-in dinners or brunch.

1/4 cup packed light
  brown sugar
2 teaspoons cinnamon
1/4 cup chopped nuts
3/4 cup vegetable oil
3/4 cup water
1 2-layer package
  yellow cake mix

1 4-ounce package
  vanilla instant
  pudding mix
4 eggs
1 teaspoon vanilla
  extract
1 teaspoon butter
  extract

Preheat oven to 350 degrees. Mix brown sugar, cinnamon and nuts in bowl. Combine oil, water, cake mix and pudding mix in mixer bowl; beat well. Add eggs 1 at a time, beating well after each addition. Stir in extracts. Layer batter and streusel alternately in greased and floured tube pan. Bake for 45 minutes. Cool in pan for 15 to 20 minutes. Invert onto serving plate. May drizzle with favorite glaze or frosting. Yield: 16 servings.

Mercedes Lager, Epsilon Alpha
Guilford, Missouri

BUTTERSCOTCH COFFEE CAKE

1 2-layer package
  yellow cake mix
1 4-serving can
  butterscotch pudding

2 eggs
1/2 cup sugar
2 cups butterscotch
  chips

Preheat oven to 350 degrees. Combine cake mix, pudding and eggs in mixer bowl; beat for 2 minutes. Spread in greased 9-by-13-inch cake pan. Sprinkle with mixture of sugar and chips. Bake for 35 minutes. Yield: 15 servings.

Betty Atton, Delta Master
Mansfield, Ohio

CRANBERRY YOGURT COFFEE CAKE

I sampled this at the Ocean Spray kitchen at Cranberry World Visitors' Center in Plymouth, Massachusetts—a most delicious cake.

1 2-layer package
  yellow cake mix
1 4-ounce package
  vanilla instant
  pudding mix
4 eggs

1 cup plain yogurt
1/4 cup vegetable oil
1 16-ounce can whole
  cranberry sauce
1/2 cup chopped nuts

Preheat oven to 350 degrees. Combine first 5 ingredients in mixer bowl. Beat at high speed for 3 minutes. Spread 2/3 of the batter in greased and lightly floured 9-by-13-inch cake pan. Spoon cranberry sauce evenly over batter. Spread remaining batter over cranberry sauce. Sprinkle with nuts. Bake for 55 minutes to 1 hour or until cake tests done. Cool on wire rack for 35 minutes. Yield: 20 servings.

Doris A. Slaughter, Beta Master
Daytona Beach, Florida

SPICED APPLE MUFFINS

2 cups sifted
  all-purpose flour
1/2 cup sugar
2 1/2 teaspoons baking
  powder
1/2 teaspoon salt
1 egg
1 cup milk

1/4 cup melted butter
  or margarine
1 cup chopped apple
1/4 cup sugar
1/4 cup melted butter or
  margarine
1/4 teaspoon cinnamon

Preheat oven to 375 degrees. Sift flour, 1/2 cup sugar, baking powder and salt together. Combine egg, milk and 1/4 cup melted butter in bowl; mix well. Add flour mixture, stirring just until mixed. Stir in apple. Fill greased muffin cups 1/2 full with batter. Combine remaining ingredients in bowl; mix well. Sprinkle over muffins. Bake for 25 minutes. Yield: 12 servings.

Susan Rand, Xi Eta
Omaha, Nebraska

BLUEBERRY BUTTERMILK MUFFINS

These are wonderful to enjoy with friends over coffee or tea!

2 cups sifted
  all-purpose flour
1/2 cup sugar
1 teaspoon salt
1/4 teaspoon baking
  soda
2 1/4 teaspoons baking
  powder

1/4 cup melted butter
  or margarine
1 egg, slightly beaten
1 cup buttermilk
1 cup blueberries
1 to 2 tablespoons
  sugar

Preheat oven to 400 degrees. Combine first 8 ingredients in bowl; mix just until moistened. Stir in blueberries. Spoon into greased muffin cups. Sprinkle with a small amount of sugar. Bake for 20 to 25 minutes or until muffins test done. Yield: 12 servings.

Joyce Alder, Laureate Psi
Challis, Idaho

BANANA YOGURT MUFFINS

1 1/2 cups all-purpose
  flour
1/2 cup wheat germ
1/3 cup sugar
2 teaspoons baking
  powder
1 teaspoon baking soda

1/2 teaspoon salt
1 cup mashed bananas
1/2 to 2/3 cup plain
  yogurt
1/4 cup melted
  shortening
1 egg

Preheat oven to 400 degrees. Sift first 6 ingredients together in bowl. Combine bananas, yogurt, shortening and egg in bowl; mix well with fork. Stir into flour mixture. Fill greased muffin cups 2/3 full with batter. Bake for 20 minutes. Yield: 14 servings.

Patty Massullo, Pi Zeta
Lecanto, Florida

BANANA POPPY SEED MUFFINS

2 bananas, mashed
1 egg
1/2 cup sugar
1/4 cup vegetable oil
1/2 cup milk
1 tablespoon poppy seed

1 1/2 cups all-purpose
flour
2 teaspoons baking
powder
1/2 teaspoon salt
1/2 teaspoon baking soda

Preheat oven to 400 degrees. Combine all ingredients in large bowl; mix well. Spoon into greased muffin cups. Bake for 20 minutes. Yield: 12 servings.

Sarah Morra, Phi
Moscow, Idaho

SIX-WEEK BRAN MUFFINS

15 ounces Raisin Bran
cereal
3 cups sugar
5 cups all-purpose flour
5 teaspoons baking
soda
2 teaspoons salt

4 eggs, beaten
1/2 cup shortening,
melted
1/2 cup melted butter or
margarine
1 quart buttermilk

Preheat oven to 400 degrees. Combine cereal, sugar, flour, baking soda and salt in large bowl; mix well. Add eggs, shortening, butter and buttermilk; mix well. Fill greased muffin cups 2/3 full. Bake for 15 to 20 minutes or until test done. Batter can be stored in covered container in refrigerator for up to 6 weeks. Yield: 24 muffins.

Judi M. Craig, Theta Nu
Batesville, Indiana
*Jane Fruendt, Omicron Nu
Hoyt, Kansas

PERPETUAL BRAN MUFFINS

2 cups boiling water
4 cups bran
5 cups all-purpose flour
5 teaspoons baking soda
1 teaspoon salt

1 cup shortening
2 1/2 cups sugar
4 eggs, beaten
1 quart buttermilk

Combine boiling water and bran in large bowl; set aside. Sift flour, baking soda and salt together in bowl. Cream shortening and sugar in mixer bowl until light and fluffy. Beat in eggs and buttermilk. Add flour mixture gradually, beating well after each addition. Store in tightly covered container in refrigerator for up to 6 weeks, using as needed. Preheat oven to 350 degrees. Fill greased or paper-lined muffin cups 1/2 to 2/3 full with batter. Bake for 20 minutes or until golden brown.
Yield: 10 to 12 dozen muffins.

June Thompsett, Xi Gamma Nu
Richardson, Texas
*Barbara Gribble, Laureate Nu
Fresno, California

APPLE-ORANGE BRAN MUFFINS

2 cups Raisin Bran
cereal
3/4 cup milk
1 egg, beaten
1/4 cup margarine,
softened
1 apple, peeled, grated
1 orange with rind,
grated

1 cup all-purpose flour
2 1/2 teaspoons baking
powder
1/2 teaspoon salt
1 1/2 teaspoons cinnamon
6 tablespoons sugar

Preheat oven to 400 degrees. Combine cereal, milk, egg and margarine in bowl; mix well. Stir in apple and orange. Add remaining ingredients all at once; mix just until moistened. Pour into paper-lined muffin cups. Bake for 25 minutes. Yield: 12 servings.

Lucy Bean, Laureate Beta Pi
Redmond, Washington

HIGH-FIBER LOW-FAT BRAN MUFFINS

1 1/4 cups whole wheat
flour
1/2 cup sugar
1/2 teaspoon salt
1 tablespoon baking
powder

2 cups All-Bran extra
fiber cereal
1 1/4 cups milk
1 egg or 2 egg whites
1/4 cup applesauce

Preheat oven to 400 degrees. Sift flour, sugar, salt and baking powder together. Mix cereal and milk in bowl. Stir into flour mixture. Add egg and applesauce; mix well. Spoon into muffin cups coated with nonstick cooking spray. Bake for 20 minutes. May add 1 grated apple to batter if desired.
Yield: 12 servings

Gail Shaver, Preceptor Beta Epsilon
Needles, California

CHEESE MUFFINS

My grandmother used to make these from an old "Clabber Girl" baking powder recipe—when baking powder sold for 10 cents a can!

2 cups all-purpose flour
1 teaspoon salt
4 teaspoons baking
powder
2 eggs, beaten
1 teaspoon paprika

3/4 cup milk
3/4 cup shredded
Cheddar or Colby
cheese
1/4 cup melted
shortening

Preheat oven to 425 degrees. Sift flour, salt and baking powder together. Combine 2 tablespoons beaten eggs with paprika; set aside. Mix remaining eggs with milk in bowl. Add cheese, shortening and flour mixture; mix well. Pour into greased muffin cups. Brush with paprika mixture. Bake for 20 to 25 minutes or until muffins test done.
Yield: 12 to 15 servings.

Dorothy A. Majors, Laureate Phi
Ponca City, Oklahoma

COTTAGE CHEESE MUFFINS

1/3 cup sugar	1 teaspoon grated
3 tablespoons	lemon rind
margarine, softened	1 egg
1/2 cup cream-style	13/4 cups baking mix
cottage cheese	1/2 cup milk

Preheat oven to 400 degrees. Cream sugar and margarine in mixer bowl until light and fluffy. Beat in cottage cheese and lemon rind. Add egg; beat well. Stir in baking mix and milk just until moistened. Fill greased muffin cups 3/4 full with batter. Bake for 20 minutes. Yield: 12 servings.

Colleen Hughes, Lambda Delta
Lake Zurich, Illinois

BREAKFAST MUFFINS

11/2 cups whole wheat	2 teaspoons cinnamon
flour	1 teaspoon salt
11/2 cups oats	3 eggs, slightly beaten
1 cup all-purpose flour	1 8-ounce can crushed
2/3 cup sugar	pineapple
1/3 cup wheat germ	2 cups mashed bananas
2 teaspoons baking soda	1/2 cup vegetable oil

Preheat oven to 350 degrees. Combine whole wheat flour with next 7 ingredients in large bowl. Make a well in center. Add eggs, pineapple, bananas and oil to well. Stir just until moistened. Spoon into greased and floured muffin cups. Bake for 20 minutes. Yield: 24 servings.

Joan Vaughn, Xi Kappa Mu
Keystone Heights, Florida

JAM MUFFINS

31/2 cups all-purpose	4 eggs
flour	2/3 cup melted butter
1 cup sugar	or margarine
8 teaspoons baking	11/3 cups milk
powder	4 tablespoons jam
1 teaspoon salt	

Preheat oven to 400 degrees. Sift flour, sugar, baking powder and salt together. Combine eggs, melted butter and milk in bowl; beat well. Stir in flour mixture; mix just until moistened. Fill greased muffin cups 1/2 full with batter. Add 1 teaspoon jam to each muffin cup. Add remaining batter. Bake for 17 to 20 minutes or until browned. Yield: 12 servings.

Pam Spencer, Gamma Phi
Pitt Meadows, British Columbia, Canada

Carol Moyer, Delta Sigma, Waverly, Missouri, makes Fruit-Flavored Syrup by mixing 3 ounces fruit-flavored gelatin, 1/2 cup sugar and 2 tablespoons cornstarch in small saucepan. Stir in 1 cup water. Heat until thickened. Use diet gelatin and omit sugar for calorie-reduced syrup.

PECAN-RAISIN MUFFINS

13/4 cups all-purpose	1/3 cup margarine
flour	1/2 cup chopped pecans
1/4 cup sugar	1/3 cup raisins
1 tablespoon baking	1 egg
powder	3/4 cup milk
3/4 teaspoon salt	

Preheat oven to 400 degrees. Sift flour, sugar, baking powder and salt together. Cut in margarine until mixture resembles coarse meal. Stir in pecans and raisins. Beat egg with milk in bowl. Add to flour mixture, stirring just until moistened. Fill nonstick muffin cups 3/4 full with batter. Bake for 15 to 20 minutes or until muffins test done. Yield: 12 servings.

Lucille Caskey, Zeta Master
Colorado Springs, Colorado

SPICE MUFFINS

2 cups all-purpose flour	1/2 cup margarine,
1 teaspoon cinnamon	softened
1/2 teaspoon allspice	1 cup sugar
1/2 teaspoon nutmeg	1 egg
1/2 teaspoon salt	1 cup applesauce
1 teaspoon baking soda	1 cup raisins
2 tablespoons hot water	1/2 cup nuts

Preheat oven to 350 degrees. Sift flour with next 4 ingredients. Dissolve baking soda in hot water in bowl. Cream margarine and sugar in bowl until light and fluffy. Add egg and applesauce; mix well. Add dry ingredients, raisins, nuts and baking soda mixture in order listed, stirring well after each addition. Spoon into muffin cups coated with nonstick cooking spray. Bake for 15 to 20 minutes or until muffins test done. Yield: 12 servings.

Leesa Lile, Xi Alpha Epsilon
Durango, Colorado

PEANUT BUTTER MUFFINS

2 cups all-purpose flour	1/2 cup packed light
1 tablespoon baking	brown sugar
powder	1/4 cup vegetable oil
1/4 teaspoon salt	1 cup bran cereal
1 egg	2 cups chopped
11/2 cups milk	bananas
1/2 cup chunky peanut	
butter	

Preheat oven to 400 degrees. Sift flour, baking powder and salt together. Combine egg with next 4 ingredients in bowl; mix well. Stir in bran cereal. Let stand for 5 minutes. Add bananas and dry ingredients, stirring just until moistened. Spoon into muffin cups. Bake for 20 minutes. Yield: 16 servings.

Carolyn Towle, Delta Lambda
Port Roberts, Washington

BLUEBERRY MUFFINS

2 cups baking mix	1 egg
1/4 cup sugar	1 to 2 cups fresh or
1/2 teaspoon cinnamon	frozen blueberries
1 cup sour cream	2 tablespoons sugar

Preheat oven to 425 degrees. Combine baking mix, 1/4 cup sugar and cinnamon in bowl; mix well. Make a well in center of mixture. Add sour cream and egg; stir with fork. Fold in blueberries gently. Spoon 1/4 cup batter into each of 12 paper-lined muffin cups. Sprinkle with remaining sugar. Bake for 20 minutes. Yield: 12 serving.

Terry Malott, Pi Eta
Castalia, Ohio

REFRIGERATOR MUFFINS

2 cups all-purpose flour	1 cup packed light
Salt to taste	brown sugar
1/2 teaspoon baking soda	1 cup milk
1/2 cup shortening	1/2 cup nuts
1 egg	

Blend flour, salt and baking soda. Cream shortening, egg and sugar in bowl until light and fluffy. Add dry ingredients and milk alternately to creamed mixture, beating well after each addition. Stir in nuts. Chill for 24 hours or longer. Preheat oven to 375 degrees. Spoon batter into muffin cups. Bake for 20 minutes. Yield: 12 servings.

Elsie Louise Rosenbaum
Ponca City, Oklahoma

OAT BRAN MUFFINS

2 1/2 cups oat bran	3/4 cup milk
1/2 cup raisins	1/2 cup maple syrup or
1 tablespoon baking	honey
powder	2 tablespoons vegetable
1/2 teaspoon salt	oil
2 eggs	

Combine oat bran with next 3 ingredients in bowl; mix well. Beat eggs with milk, syrup and oil in large bowl. Add oat bran mixture; stir just until moistened. Bake for 12 to 15 minutes or until muffins test done. Yield: 12 servings.

Jackie Ayers, Alpha Tau
Columbus, Indiana

CRANBERRY MUFFINS

These muffins were served on my mother's 100th birthday in San Antonio, Texas. A number of my son's college friends flew down from Pennsylvania because they had never seen a 100-year-old person!

1 cup cranberries, cut	3/4 teaspoon baking soda
into halves	1 egg
3/4 cup sugar	3/4 cup milk
2 cups all-purpose flour	1/4 cup melted margarine

Preheat oven to 400 degrees. Combine cranberries and 1/2 cup sugar in bowl. Combine 1/4 cup sugar with flour and baking soda in large bowl; make well in center of mixture. Mix egg, milk and margarine in bowl. Add to well in dry ingredients; stir just until moistened. Fold in cranberry mixture gently. Fill muffin cups 3/4 full. Bake for 20 minutes. Yield: 16 servings.

Kay L. Roberts, Xi Epsilon Epsilon
Freeland, Pennsylvania

BREAKFAST-IN-A-MUFFIN

1 cup buttermilk	1 cup all-purpose flour
1 cup quick-cooking	1 teaspoon baking
oats	powder
1 egg	1/2 teaspoon baking soda
1/2 cup packed light	1/8 teaspoon salt
brown sugar	1/2 cup raisins and/or
1/2 cup vegetable oil	1/2 cup chopped nuts

Preheat oven to 400 degrees. Combine buttermilk and oats in bowl. Let stand for 30 minutes. Combine egg and remaining ingredients in large bowl. Add buttermilk mixture; stir just until moistened. Spoon into greased muffin cups. Bake for 15 to 20 minutes or until muffins test done. Yield: 12 servings.

Nancy Carole Davis, Beta Omega
Savannah, Missouri

ORANGE MARMALADE MUFFINS

2 cups all-purpose flour	1/4 cup orange
1 cup sugar	marmalade
3/4 teaspoon baking	1 tablespoon melted
powder	butter or margarine
2 eggs, beaten	1 1/2 teaspoons vanilla
1 cup sour cream	extract

Preheat oven to 400 degrees. Combine flour, sugar and baking powder in large bowl. Make a well in center of mixture. Mix eggs with remaining ingredients in bowl. Add to well in dry ingredients; stir just until moistened. Fill greased muffin cups 2/3 full. Bake for 20 to 25 minutes or until muffins test done. Yield: 12 servings.

JoAnn L. Moller, Omega Tau
Jackson, Missouri

ALL-IN-ONE BREAKFAST MUFFINS

1 3/4 cups all-purpose	1/3 cup vegetable oil
flour	8 ounces bacon,
1 cup quick-cooking	crisp-fried, crumbled
oats	1/2 cup shredded
1/4 cup sugar	Cheddar cheese
2 teaspoons baking	1/3 cup finely chopped
powder	green bell pepper
1/4 teaspoon salt	1/3 cup finely chopped
1 egg, slightly beaten	onion
1 cup milk	

Preheat oven to 400 degrees. Combine flour with next 4 ingredients in large bowl. Mix eggs, milk and oil in small bowl. Add to dry ingredients; stir just until moistened. Fold in bacon and remaining ingredients gently. Fill greased muffin cups 2/3 full. Bake for 15 to 18 minutes or until golden brown. Yield: 12 servings.

Frances Sullivan, Xi Omega Pi
Ovilla, Texas

CINNAMON ROLLS

1 envelope dry yeast	1/2 cup sugar
1/4 cup very warm water	2 teaspoons cinnamon
1/2 cup melted butter or	Butter
margarine	Applesauce
1 cup milk	Raisins
2 eggs	Confectioners' sugar
1 teaspoon salt	1 teaspoon vanilla
1/2 cup sugar	extract
4 cups all-purpose flour, sifted	

Dissolve yeast in water. Pour into 4-quart bowl. Combine 1/2 cup butter and milk in saucepan; heat until warm, stirring until well mixed. Beat eggs in small mixer bowl. Add milk mixture; beat until well blended. Add to yeast. Add salt and 1/2 cup sugar; mix well. Gradually add 2 cups flour; mix well. Add 2 cups flour; mix until well blended. Cover bowl; set aside in warm place. Allow dough to rise for 1 1/2 to 2 hours or until doubled in bulk. Place half dough on floured surface. Roll to 16-inch square. Combine 1/2 cup sugar and cinnamon in small bowl; mix well. Sprinkle half cinnamon-sugar mixture over dough. Top with glumps of butter, applesauce and raisins so each roll contains some of each when cut. Roll dough, bottom to top, to enclose filling and create what appears to be a long tube; cut into 12 equal sized single rolls. Place on ungreased cookie sheet with cut side up; let rise until doubled in bulk. Repeat procedure for other half of dough. Preheat oven to 325 degrees. Bake for 20 minutes or until browned. May want to add 2 tablespoons more flour to dry mixture for high altitude. Pour confectioners' sugar into bowl. Add vanilla and enough water to make desired consistency. Spread over warm rolls. Yield: 24 rolls.

Kathy Schneyer, Xi Alpha Epsilon
Durango, Colorado

BUBBLE BREAD

1/2 cup chopped nuts	1 teaspoon cinnamon
1 28-count package	1 package vanilla
frozen rolls	pudding mix
3/4 cup packed light	6 tablespoons
brown sugar	margarine, diced

Place nuts in bottom of greased bundt pan. Layer frozen rolls over nuts. Combine brown sugar, cinnamon and pudding mix in bowl. Sprinkle over rolls. Top with margarine. Let unthaw and rise for 4 to 6 hours or overnight. Preheat oven to 350 degrees. Bake for 30 minutes. Immediately invert onto serving plate. Yield: 28 rolls.

Michelle Parker, Xi Beta Xi
Manhattan, Kansas

ANITA'S BREAKFAST ROLLS

A good friend gave me this recipe when I had unexpected relatives coming to visit overnight.

2 loaves frozen bread	1 teaspoon cinnamon
dough	1 teaspoon vanilla
1/2 cup butter	extraact
1 cup packed light	1/3 cup cream
brown sugar	

Thaw dough in refrigerator overnight. Cut into 1/2-inch pieces. Place in greased 9-by-13-inch baking pan. Let rise for 1 hour. Preheat oven to 350 degrees. Combine remaining ingredients in saucepan; bring to a boil, cooking until sugar is dissolved. Pour over dough. Bake for 20 to 25 minutes or until done. Immediately invert onto serving plate. Yield: 12 servings.

Gerry Brunton, Epsilon Zeta
Rolla, Missouri

❖ CAKE MIX STICKY ROLLS

1 2-layer package	1 cup walnuts or pecans
yellow cake mix	1/2 cup maple syrup
2 envelopes dry yeast	Butter, softened
5 cups all-purpose flour	1/2 cup sugar
2 1/2 cups hot water	4 teaspoons cinnamon
1 cup melted margarine	1 cup raisins
1 cup packed light	
brown sugar	

Combine cake mix, yeast, flour and water in large bowl; mix to form dough. Let rise until doubled in bulk. Combine margarine, brown sugar, walnuts and maple syrup in bowl. Spread in two 9 or 10-inch baking pans. Heat in 350-degree oven until mixture is caramelized; cool. Divide dough into 2 portions. Roll each portion into 9-by-18-inch rectangle on floured surface. Spread with softened butter; sprinkle with sugar, cinnamon and raisins. Roll each portion from long side to enclose filling; press edges and ends to seal. Cut rolls into 1-inch slices; arrange in prepared baking pans. Let rise until doubled in bulk. Preheat oven to 350 degrees. Bake rolls for 15 minutes. Invert immediately onto serving plates. Yield: 30 servings.

Patricia A. McCourry, Preceptor Gamma Theta
Canton, Ohio

CREAMY CARAMEL-PECAN ROLLS

1¹/4 cups sifted
confectioners' sugar
¹/2 cup whipping cream
1 cup coarsely chopped
pecans
2 14- to 16-ounce
loaves frozen sweet
or white bread
dough, thawed

3 tablespoons melted
margarine or butter
¹/2 cup packed light
brown sugar
1 tablespoon ground
cinnamon
³/4 cup light or dark
raisins (optional)

Combine confectioners' sugar and whipping cream in small bowl. Divide evenly between two 9-inch round baking pans. Sprinkle with pecans. Roll each loaf of dough on lightly floured surface into 8-by-12-inch rectangle. Brush with margarine. Combine brown sugar and cinnamon in small bowl. Sprinkle over rectangles. Top with raisins. Roll up rectangles jelly roll-style to enclose filling, starting from 12-inch side. Pinch edges to seal. Cut each roll into 10 to 12 slices. Place slices, cut side down, on top of mixture in baking pans. Cover with towel. Let rise in warm place for 30 minutes or until doubled in bulk. Preheat oven to 375 degrees. Bake rolls, uncovered, for 20 to 25 minutes or until golden brown. May cover rolls with foil last 10 minutes of baking to prevent over browning if desired. Cool in pan on wire rack for 5 minutes. Invert onto serving plate. Unbaked rolls can be refrigerated covered with oiled waxed paper and then plastic wrap for 2 to 24 hours. Let chilled rolls stand, covered, for 20 minutes at room temperature before baking. Add 5 minutes to baking time. Yield: 20 to 24 servings.

Jackie Morgan, Laureate Beta Epsilon
Port Angeles, Washington

MONKEY PULL-APART CINNAMON BREAD

4 cans biscuits
³/4 cup butter or
margarine
³/4 cup sugar
1 cup light brown sugar
(not packed)

2 teaspoons cinnamon
³/4 cup sugar
1 teaspoon cinnamon
Pecan pieces

Preheat oven to 350 degrees. Cut each biscuit into quarters. Combine butter, brown sugar and 2 teaspoons cinnamon in saucepan; heat until sugar melts. Combine sugar and 1 teaspoon cinnamon in paper bag. Shake biscuit pieces in sugar mixture. Place in well-greased bundt pan alternately with pecan pieces. Sprinkle remaining sugar mixture in bag over top. Pour hot sugar mixture over biscuits. Bake for 30 minutes or until browned. Yield: 24 servings.

Jennifer Willis, Mu Omega
Tahlequah, Oklahoma

MAPLE CREAMS

1 cup packed light
brown sugar
¹/2 cup chopped nuts
¹/3 cup maple syrup
¹/4 cup melted
margarine or butter
8 ounces cream cheese,
softened

¹/4 cup confectioners'
sugar
2 tablespoons
margarine, softened
¹/2 cup coconut
2 10-count cans flaky
biscuits

Preheat oven to 350 degrees. Combine brown sugar, nuts, syrup and ¹/4 cup margarine in bowl. Spread evenly in ungreased 9-by-13-inch baking pan. Combine cream cheese, confectioners' sugar and 2 tablespoons margarine in small bowl; blend until smooth. Stir in coconut. Separate biscuits. Roll each biscuit on lightly floured surface into 4-inch circle. Spoon 1 tablespoon cream cheese mixture down center of each circle to within ¹/4 inch of edge. Fold sides of dough over filling, overlapping to form finger-shaped rolls. Arrange rolls, seam side down, in 2 rows over brown sugar mixture. Bake for 25 to 30 minutes or until lightly browned. Cool 3 to 5 minutes; invert onto foil. Yield: 20 rolls.

Carol Zack, Preceptor Gamma Rho
Martinton, Illinois

TASTY AND BIG CINNAMON ROLLS

Instead of getting this recipe passed down to me, I passed it to my mother and grandmother who can't stop talking about it.

2 tablespoons dry yeast
2 cups warm water
1 cup sugar
4 eggs
¹/2 cup margarine
2 teaspoons salt
7 cups all-purpose or
whole wheat flour
2 tablespoons melted
butter

1 cup packed light
brown sugar
2 tablespoons cinnamon
¹/2 cup sugar
1 cup raisins
1 cup chopped nuts
1 cup melted margarine
1 1-pound package
light brown sugar

Dissolve yeast in water with ¹/2 cup sugar in large bowl. Add ¹/2 cup sugar, eggs, ¹/2 cup margarine, salt and flour; beat well. Let rise, covered, for 2 hours. Roll dough out on lightly floured surface. Brush with butter. Sprinkle next 5 ingredients over dough. Roll up jelly-roll fashion; cut into 1-inch thick slices. Combine 1 cup melted margarine and 1 pound brown sugar in bowl; stir until dissolved. Pour, dividing equally, into two 10-inch cake pans. Place rolls on top. Let rise until doubled in bulk. Preheat oven to 350 degrees. Bake for 30 minutes. Yield: 12 rolls.

Kim Normand, Xi Kappa
Coeur d'Alene, Idaho

FLORENTINE CRESCENTS

1 package frozen chopped spinach	3 to 4 slices crisp-fried bacon, crumbled
1 6-ounce package Cheddar cheese	2 10-count cans crescent rolls
2 teaspoons bread crumbs	

Preheat oven to 375 degrees. Thaw spinach; drain well. Combine spinach, cheese, bread crumbs and bacon in saucepan. Heat until cheese is melted. Separate rolls into triangles. Cut each triangle into 2 smaller triangles. Place spinach mixture on each triangle; roll up. Place on greased 11-by-13-inch cookie sheet. Bake for 10 to 13 minutes or until brown. Yield: 32 crescents.

Sara Chimeno, Preceptor Lambda Sigma
Beaumont, Texas

CHEESE ROLLS

2 8-count cans crescent rolls	3/4 cup sugar
16 ounces cream cheese	1 teaspoon lemon juice
1 egg	1 teaspoon vanilla extract
1 egg, separated	Confectioners' sugar

Preheat oven to 375 degrees. Roll 1 package rolls into 9-by-13-inch rectangle. Place in greased 9-by-13-inch baking pan. Combine cream cheese, egg, egg yolk, sugar, lemon juice and vanilla in mixer bowl; beat well. Spread over dough. Roll out remaining package rolls into 9-by-13-inch rectangle. Place on top cream cheese mixture. Beat egg white slightly in small bowl; brush on top. Bake for 25 minutes. Sprinkle with confectioners' sugar. Yield: 18 servings.

Carolyn Burnett, Preceptor Epsilon Epsilon
Belvidere, Illinois

DANISH BREAKFAST TREATS

These are great for a brunch, coffee or afternoon tea.

1/2 cup butter or margarine	18 ounces orange marmalade or apricot preserves
1 cup sugar	
2 egg yolks	3/4 cup chopped pecans
2 cups all-purpose flour	

Preheat oven to 325 degrees. Cream butter and sugar in mixer bowl. Add egg yolks; mix well. Mix in flour with fork until pastry consistency. Set aside 1/4 cup mixture. Press remaining mixture into greased 10-by-15-inch cookie sheet. Spread marmalade over pastry. Sprinkle with pecans. Sprinkle reserved pastry mix over pecans. Bake for 30 minutes or until lightly browned. Let cool for 5 to 10 minutes. Cut into squares. May be frozen. Yield: 60 squares.

R. Gene Farley, Laureate Gamma Iota
Tallahassee, Florida

STRAWBERRY BARS

3/4 cup butter, softened	2 egg yolks
1 cup sugar	2 cups self-rising flour
1 teaspoon vanilla extract	1 cup chopped pecans
	1/2 cup strawberry jam

Preheat oven to 325 degrees. Cream butter in mixer bowl with electric mixer. Add sugar gradually, beating until light and fluffy. Add vanilla and egg yolks; beat well. Stir in flour and pecans gradually. Pat half of dough evenly into greased 9-inch square baking pan. Spread jam over dough. Drop remaining dough by tablespoonfuls over jam; spread evenly. Bake for 1 hour. Let cool; cut into bars. Yield: 24 bars.

Gwen Beaver, Zeta Phi
Wingate, North Carolina

GRANDMA'S APPLE FRITTERS

This recipe was my grandmother's and has been our Christmas morning breakfast for three generations now! We always made a game of deciding what animal or object each fritter resembled.

Vegetable oil for frying	2 teaspoons baking soda
2 eggs, well beaten	2 or 3 tart apples, peeled, cored
3/4 cup milk	
2 cups all-purpose flour	2 cups sugar
1 teaspoon salt	1 cup water

Preheat fat in deep-fryer to 375 degrees. Combine eggs and milk in bowl; mix well. Sift flour, salt and baking soda together in bowl. Add egg mixture, stirring vigorously for a few minutes. Slice thin small pieces of apples into batter; stir to coat. Drop by heaping teaspoonfuls into hot fat. Fritters turn over by themselves when golden brown. Combine sugar and water in saucepan; heat to boiling. Serve fritters in cereal bowls with warm syrup. Yield: 12 servings.

Jackie Hanson, Chi Beta Nu
Ankeny, Iowa

"BEST-EVER" BANANA BREAD

1 cup butter or margarine	4 eggs, well beaten
2 cups sugar	2 1/2 cups all-purpose flour
3 cups mashed ripe bananas	2 teaspoons baking soda
	1 teaspoon salt

Preheat oven to 350 degrees. Cream butter and sugar in mixer bowl until light and fluffy. Add bananas and eggs; beat until well mixed. Sift remaining ingredients 3 times in bowl. Blend into banana mixture. Do not overmix. Pour into 2 greased loaf pans. Bake for 45 minutes to 1 hour or until tests done. Let cool in pans on rack for 10 minutes. Freezes well wrapped in foil. Yield: 12 servings.

Linda Stucchi, Xi Delta Zeta
Mississauga, Ontario, Canada

BANANA CAKE

4 tablespoons sour
 cream
1 teaspoon baking soda
1 cup sugar
1/2 cup margarine
2 eggs

1 teaspoon vanilla
 extract
1 1/4 cups all-purpose
 flour
1 cup mashed bananas

Preheat oven to 350 degrees. Combine sour cream and baking soda in glass cup; mix well. Cream sugar and margarine in bowl. Add eggs and vanilla; mix well. Add sour cream mixture; mix well. Add flour alternately with bananas; mix well. Pour into 5-by-9-inch loaf pan lined with waxed paper. Bake for 45 to 55 minutes or until cake tests done. Yield: 12 servings.

Margo Annunziello, Xi Theta
Nelson, British Columbia, Canada

DROP DOUGHNUTS

This was my mother's recipe. I grew up eating these little "sweeties." I like them a little soft in center.

Vegetable oil for frying
1 cup sugar
Dash of salt
3 teaspoons baking
 powder
3 cups all-purpose
 flour

Dash of nutmeg
2 eggs
1 cup milk
1 teaspoon vanilla
 extract
Confectioners' sugar

Preheat oil in skillet or deep-fryer. Combine next 5 ingredients in bowl; mix well. Combine eggs, milk and vanilla in bowl; mix well. Stir into dry ingredients. Drop batter by spoonfuls into hot oil. Cook until golden brown. Drain on paper towels. Roll in confectioners' sugar. Yield: 6 servings.

LaRue Robinson, Laureate Alpha Upsilon
Garden City, Kansas

FUNNEL CAKE

This is a special treat our family enjoys on special mornings. We use an assembly-style production.

1 to 1 1/2 cups vegetable
 oil
2 eggs, beaten
1 1/2 cups milk
2 cups all-purpose
 flour

1 teaspoon vanilla
 extract
1/2 teaspoon salt
Confectioners' sugar

Preheat oil in 8-inch skillet to 360 degrees. Combine remaining ingredients in mixer bowl; beat until fluffy. Drizzle 1/2 cup batter into heated oil using a spiral motion. Cook 2 to 3 minutes or until edges are brown. Turn over; cook for 2 minutes longer. Drain on paper towel. Sprinkle with confectioners' sugar. Yield: 12 servings.

Jean Stonewall, Xi Epsilon Beta
Marshalltown, Iowa

BAKED FRENCH TOAST

8 slices thick white
 bread, cubed
16 ounces reduced-
 calorie cream cheese,
 cubed

12 eggs
2 cups milk
Maple syrup
Fresh fruit

Preheat oven to 375 degrees. Place half the bread in bottom of greased 9-by-13-inch baking pan. Spread cream cheese over bread. Add remaining bread. Combine eggs, milk and 1/3 cup syrup in mixer bowl; beat well. Pour over layered mixture. Bake for 45 minutes. Serve with additional maple syrup and fresh fruit such as blackberries, strawberries and blueberries. Yield: 8 servings.

Sharon A. Dunham, Zeta Nu
Monroeville, Alabama

STUFFED FRENCH TOAST

1 1-pound loaf
 unsliced French bread,
 cubed
8 ounces cream cheese
8 eggs

2 1/2 cups milk
6 tablespoons butter or
 margarine, melted
1/4 cup maple syrup
Apple Cider Syrup

Place half the bread in greased 9-by-13-inch baking pan. Place cream cheese in blender container; beat well. Spread over bread. Top with remaining bread. Combine eggs, milk, butter and maple syrup in blender container; blend well. Pour over bread. Press layers slightly down with spatula. Cover with plastic wrap. Refrigerate for 2 to 24 hours. Preheat oven to 325 degrees. Bake for 35 to 40 minutes or until done. Spread Apple Cider Syrup over top. Let stand for 10 minutes before serving. Yield: 8 servings.

APPLE CIDER SYRUP

1/2 cup sugar
4 teaspoons cornstarch
1/2 teaspoon cinnamon

1 cup apple juice
1 tablespoon lemon juice
2 tablespoons butter

Combine sugar, cornstarch and cinnamon in small saucepan. Stir in apple juice and lemon juice. Cook over medium heat, stirring constantly, until thickened. Cook for 2 minutes longer. Add butter. Remove from heat. Yield: 1 1/2 cups.

Amy Mueller, Mu Epsilon
Jefferson City, Missouri

MAKE-AHEAD FRENCH TOAST

3 eggs
3/4 cup milk
1 tablespoon sugar
1/2 teaspoon vanilla
 extract

6 English muffins,
 split into halves
Melted butter or
 margarine

Combine eggs, milk, sugar and vanilla in bowl; mix until well blended. Place muffin halves on greased 9-by-13-inch rimmed baking sheet. Pour egg mixture gradually over muffins, turning to coat both sides. Let stand for 5 minutes or until all liquid is absorbed. Place, uncovered, in freezer until frozen. Store in freezer bag in freezer. To bake, preheat oven to 425 degrees. Remove desired number of muffins from freezer. Brush each side with melted margarine. Place, face side down, on greased 9-by-13-inch rimmed baking pan. Bake for 10 minutes. Turn slices over; bake for 5 minutes longer. Yield: 6 servings.

Trena Woods, Xi Delta Rho
Post, Texas

LOW-FAT STUFFED FRENCH TOAST

This is low-calorie low-fat version of a family favorite.

8 slices calorie-reduced bread, cubed	16 ounces egg substitute
15 ounces calorie-reduced ricotta cheese	1/3 cup calorie reduced syrup
	2 cups skim milk

Place half the bread in greased 8-inch square baking pan. Add cheese. Top with remaining bread. Combine egg substitute, syrup and milk in bowl; mix well. Pour over bread. Refrigerate, covered with plastic wrap, overnight. Preheat oven to 375 degrees. Bake for 45 minutes. Let cool for 15 minutes. Cut into 8 squares. May serve with fresh fruit and syrup if desired. Yield: 8 servings.

Susan R. Page, Xi Kappa Mu
Melrose, Florida

CINNAMON FRENCH TOAST

6 eggs	1 tablespoon sugar
1/2 cup milk	1 to 2 teaspoons cinnamon
1 teaspoon vanilla extract	8 slices day-old bread

Preheat griddle on medium heat. Combine first 5 ingredients in shallow bowl; mix well. Dip bread slices into mixture, coating both sides. Cook on griddle turning until both sides are golden brown. Yield: 4 servings.

JoAnn Hartley, Alpha Iota
Coral Springs, Florida

OVERNIGHT CARAMEL FRENCH TOAST

1 cup packed light brown sugar	6 eggs, beaten
1/2 cup butter	1 1/2 cups milk
2 tablespoons light corn syrup	1 teaspoon vanilla extract
12 slices sandwich bread	1/4 teaspoon salt

Combine brown sugar, butter and corn syrup in small saucepan; cook over medium heat until thickened, stirring constantly. Pour into greased 9-by-13-inch baking dish. Place 6 slices bread on top syrup

mixture. Top with remaining bread. Combine eggs, milk, vanilla and salt in bowl; stir until blended. Pour over bread. Refrigerate, covered, for 8 hours. Preheat oven to 350 degrees. Bake, uncovered, for 40 to 45 minutes or until done. Serve immediately. Yield: 12 servings.

Kimberly Beach, Zeta
Overland Park, Kansas
*Ann Terfehr
Fairmont, Minnesota

HIGHLAND HOTCAKES

We make these ahead of time for outdoor brunches. Add meat and fruit for a complete breakfast.

3/4 cup oats	2 eggs, beaten
1 1/2 cups milk	1/4 cup melted or liquid shortening
1 1/4 cups sifted all-purpose flour	Syrup or jam
2 tablespoons sugar	
1 tablespoon baking powder	

Preheat griddle. Combine oats and milk in bowl; let stand for 5 minutes. Sift flour, sugar and baking powder together in bowl. Add to oat mixture alternately with eggs and shortening, stirring only until combined. Pour about 1/4 cup batter onto hot lightly greased griddle for each hotcake. Turn over when top side bubbles. Serve with syrup. Yield: 8 servings.

Patti Loree, Preceptor Gamma Mu
Bloomfield Hills, Michigan

APPLE PANCAKES

I serve these to my visiting family for breakfast and even put whipped cream on them. It is wonderful!

2 tablespoons butter or margarine	1/2 teaspoon baking powder
1/4 cup sugar	2 egg yolks
2 teaspoons cinnamon	1/3 cup milk
3 apples, peeled, sliced	4 egg whites
1/3 cup all-purpose flour	1/3 cup sugar

Preheat oven to 400 degrees. Place 1 tablespoon butter in each of two 9-inch pie plates. Melt in oven for about 2 minutes. Combine 1/4 cup sugar and cinnamon in bowl; sprinkle over butter in pie plates. Bake for 2 minutes. Arrange apples over mixture. Bake for 10 minutes. Combine flour, baking powder, egg yolks and milk in bowl; mix well. Beat egg whites in mixer bowl until soft peaks form. Add 1/3 cup sugar gradually, beating until stiff. Fold into batter. Spoon batter over apples. Bake for 15 to 20 minutes or until lightly browned. Loosen edges with knife; place on serving plates. Yield: 2 pancakes.

Noella LaCouvee, Laureate Omicron
Port Alberni, British Columbia, Canada

BANANA PANCAKES

6 eggs	Pinch of salt
1 cup all-purpose flour	2 tablespoons
1 cup milk	confectioners' sugar
3 tablespoons melted	1/4 teaspoon cinnamon
butter or margarine	2 bananas, thinly sliced

Preheat oven to 450 degrees. Beat eggs slightly in large mixer bowl. Stir in flour. Add milk, butter and salt; mix well. Pour batter into well-greased 9-by-13-inch baking pan. Bake for 15 to 20 minutes or until puffed. Sprinkle with confectioners' sugar and cinnamon. Cut into pieces. Add banana slices. Yield: 12 pancakes.

Joan Hayn, Beta Master
San Diego, California

BANANA CINNAMON PANCAKES

2/3 cup whole wheat	2 tablespoons honey
flour	1 egg, beaten
1 1/2 teaspoons baking	1/2 cup milk
powder	1 tablespoon vegetable
2 medium bananas,	oil
mashed	Cinnamon

Preheat large skillet over medium heat. Sift flour and baking powder into bowl. Combine bananas, honey, egg, milk and oil in bowl; mix well. Add dry ingredients, stirring until moistened. Ladle batter onto lightly greased hot skillet. Sprinkle each pancake with cinnamon just before turning. Cook until lightly browned. Yield: 2 to 4 servings.

Ann Wayne, Lambda Delta
Barrington, Illinois

PUFFED PANCAKE WITH STRAWBERRIES

When city cousins come to visit in the country, we serve this delicious pancake for brunch.

6 eggs	Confectioners' sugar
1 cup milk	2 10-ounce packages
1/4 cup orange juice	frozen strawberries
1/2 cup sugar	in syrup
1 cup all-purpose flour	2 tablespoons orange
1/4 teaspoon salt	juice
1/2 cup butter or	
margarine	

Preheat oven to 400 degrees. Combine first 6 ingredients in bowl; mix until blended. Melt butter in 9-by-13-inch baking dish in oven until it sizzles. Do not let brown. Pour batter into hot dish; bake for 20 minutes or until puffed and browned. Sprinkle with confectioners' sugar. Combine strawberries and orange juice in saucepan. Heat until hot. Serve warm over pancake. Yield: 6 to 8 servings.

Gaynel Gering, Xi Delta Chi
Ritzville, Washington

SATURDAY MORNIN' PANCAKES

Every Saturday morning my mom cooked pancakes. When my son became insulin dependent at age 3, I made this "low-fat" by using skim milk, vanilla yogurt instead of sour cream, and added wheat germ. It is still a family favorite!

2 1/2 cups complete	1 1/2 cups milk
pancake mix	1/2 cup applesauce
2 to 3 tablespoons	2 tablespoons sour
wheat germ (optional)	cream
1 teaspoon cinnamon	1 teaspoon vanilla
1/2 teaspoon nutmeg	extract
1 teaspoon baking	
powder	

Preheat griddle to 400 degrees. Combine first 5 ingredients in large bowl; mix well. Combine remaining ingredients in bowl; mix well. Add to dry ingredients, stirring gently. Ladle batter onto hot griddle. Turn when top side bubbles; cook until lightly browned. Yield: 16 to 18 pancakes.

Pat Borowski, Delta Gamma
Lakewood, New York

SOUR DOUGH OVERNIGHT PANCAKES

When children come home for holidays, everyone, especially grandchildren, says, "We are having the famous pancakes, aren't we?" They are light and delicious.

3 eggs, beaten	1 tablespoon baking
2 cups buttermilk	powder
1/2 cup evaporated milk	1 tablespoon baking
2 tablespoons salad oil	soda
1 tablespoon dry yeast	1 tablespoon sugar
2 cups all-purpose flour	1/2 teaspoon salt

Combine eggs, buttermilk, milk and oil in large bowl; mix well. Combine yeast and 1 cup flour in small bowl; mix well. Sift together remaining 1 cup flour and remaining ingredients in bowl. Add yeast mixture; mix well. Stir in egg mixture. Refrigerate batter overnight or up to 1 week. Preheat electric skillet to 350 degrees; grease lightly. Ladle batter into skillet. Turn when bubbles appear; cook until lightly browned. Yield: 40 pancakes.

Phyllis McBee Gibbons, Laureate Alpha Nu
Wichita, Kansas

GERMAN PANCAKES

These are similar to French crêpes but have more substance. Children love these pancakes.

1 cup all-purpose flour	3 tablespoons sugar
1 cup milk	Vegetable oil for frying
3 eggs	
1/4 teaspoon salt	
(optional)	

Preheat 8-inch round skillet or omelet pan. Place first 5 ingredients in blender container; blend at Medium-High for 2 minutes. Pour enough batter into lightly oiled skillet to cover bottom. Brown on both sides, adding more oil if necessary. May serve with jam or sprinkled with sugar if desired. Yield: 4 servings.

Rosemarie Wilson, Preceptor Omicron
Germantown, Maryland

SWEDISH PANCAKES

2 cups milk	1 teaspoon sugar
4 eggs	1/2 teaspoon salt
1/4 cup oil	
1 2/3 cups all-purpose flour	

Preheat skillet on Medium-High. Place milk, eggs and oil in blender container; blend until mixed. Add remaining ingredients; blend well. Batter will be thin. Ladle 1/2 cup batter per pancake into lightly greased hot skillet, tipping and swirling until batter thinly covers bottom. Cook until light golden brown on each side. Yield: 9 pancakes.

Marjorie Espedal, Preceptor Gamma Theta
Arlington, Washington

MOM'S PANCAKES

This was our favorite thing for Mom to make. Even after I married, we went to Mom's for pancakes.

1 egg, slightly beaten	1 teaspoon (scant)
1 cup buttermilk	baking soda
3/4 cup all-purpose flour	1/4 teaspoon salt
1/2 teaspoon baking powder	

Preheat griddle. Combine egg and buttermilk in bowl, stirring until blended. Combine remaining ingredients in bowl. Add to egg mixture; mix well. Add small amount of milk if batter is too thick. Ladle batter onto hot griddle. Turn when bubbles form and cook until lightly browned. Yield: 6 to 8 servings.

Mary Sandholdt, Beta Omega
Oskaloosa, Iowa

DUTCH BABIES

1/4 cup margarine	Dash of salt
3 eggs	3/4 cup milk
3/4 cup all-purpose flour	

Preheat oven to 425 degrees. Place margarine in 9-by-13-inch baking pan; melt in oven. Set aside. Beat eggs in bowl. Stir in flour, salt and milk; mix well. Pour batter slowly into baking pan. Bake for 20 to 25 minutes or until puffy and browned. Cut into pieces. Yield: 6 servings.

Peggy Kemna, Xi Zeta Phi
Rolfe, Iowa

OVEN PANCAKES

3 eggs	3 tablespoons butter
1/2 cup all-purpose flour	or margarine
1/2 cup milk	Syrup or honey

Preheat oven to 400 degrees. Place all ingredients in blender container; blend until smooth. Pour into greased 8-inch baking pan. Bake for 10 minutes or until browned. Serve with syrup or honey. Yield: 2 servings.

Dorothy Lechman, Laureate Omicron
Merino, Colorado

WHOLE GRAIN PANCAKES

1 egg	1 tablespoon cooking oil
1 1/4 cups skim milk	1 1/2 cups Whole Grain
1 tablespoon honey	Mix

Preheat griddle. Combine egg, milk, honey and oil in bowl; mix well. Add Whole Grain Mix. Batter will be lumpy. Ladle batter onto greased hot griddle. Turn pancakes as soon as puffed and full of bubbles, but before bubbles break. Cook until lightly browned. Yield: 10 pancakes.

WHOLE GRAIN MIX

8 cups whole wheat flour	1 tablespoon salt
2 cups instant dry milk powder	2 teaspoons sugar
	3 cups oats
3 tablespoons baking powder	

Combine all ingredients in bowl; mix well. Store in tightly covered container. Yield: 13 cups.

Nancy F. Hydzik, Gamma Eta
Soda Springs, Idaho

WHOLE WHEAT PANCAKES

My neighbor gave me freshly ground whole wheat flour. I made up this recipe for a hearty breakfast, then we shared the pancakes.

2 egg whites	1/2 teaspoon salt
1 cup whole wheat flour	1 cup milk
1 tablespoon sugar	2 egg yolks
1 tablespoon baking powder	2 tablespoons vegetable oil

Preheat 8-inch griddle. Beat egg whites just until stiff peaks form. Set aside. Combine flour, sugar, baking powder and salt in bowl. Combine milk and egg yolks in bowl; mix well. Gradually stir into flour mixture, stirring until smooth. Gently fold in egg whites. Ladle batter onto lightly oiled hot griddle. Turn when bubbles appear; cook until lightly browned. Yield: 6 to 8 pancakes.

Rosalie Mirabelli, Theta
Salt Lake City, Utah

WHOLE WHEAT PANCAKES

This was my mother Helene Smeltekop's recipe for homemade pancakes. I still use this recipe for my family.

1 cup whole wheat flour	1¹/2 cups buttermilk or
¹/2 cup all-purpose flour	sour milk
1¹/2 teaspoons baking	3 to 4 tablespoons
soda	melted butter
¹/8 teaspoon salt	2 eggs, beaten

Preheat griddle. Combine all ingredients in bowl, mixing with spoon or whisk. Add additional milk if batter is too thick. Ladle batter onto lightly greased preheated griddle. Cook pancakes until bubbles form and break on top; turn. Cook until lightly browned. Yield: 4 servings.

Idamarie Roberts, Preceptor Mu
Las Vegas, Nevada

PINEAPPLE-COTTAGE CHEESE PANCAKES

2 eggs, separated	¹/4 teaspoon salt
8 ounces small curd	1 8-ounce can crushed
cottage cheese	pineapple, drained
¹/3 cup all-purpose flour	2 tablespoons sugar
¹/2 teaspoon baking	
powder	

Preheat griddle. Place egg yolks in mixer bowl; beat well. Stir in cottage cheese, flour, baking powder and salt; mix well. Stir in pineapple. Beat egg whites in mixer bowl until soft peaks form; add sugar gradually, beating until stiff. Fold into pineapple mixture. Spread ¹/4 cup batter to 3¹/2-inch circle on lightly greased preheated griddle. Cook for about 5 minutes on each side or until lightly browned.
Yield: 12 pancakes.

Ann Rascoe, Xi Delta Lambda
Niskayuna, New York

CORNMEAL PANCAKES

1 cup cornmeal	¹/3 cup sugar
1¹/2 cups cold water	1 teaspoon baking soda
1¹/2 cups sour milk or	1 egg, well beaten
buttermilk	2 tablespoons butter or
2 cups all-purpose flour	margarine

Preheat griddle. Combine cornmeal and cold water in saucepan; bring to a boil. Cook for 5 minutes. Pour into bowl. Add milk; mix well. Sift flour, sugar and baking soda into bowl. Stir into milk mixture. Add egg and butter; mix well. Ladle batter onto lightly greased hot griddle. Cook until bubbles form on top; turn and cook until lightly browned.
Yield: 24 pancakes.

Imogene Annette Mitcham, Xi Alpha Beta Omega
Jasper, Texas

CORN-FILLED PANCAKES

This is a simple version of an old family camping favorite. For the original, the cream-style corn was created by slitting each row of kernels of tender young corn. The creamy corn was pushed out with the back of a table knife.

1 16-ounce can	2 eggs
cream-style corn	1 cup pancake mix

Preheat griddle to 375 degrees or on Medium-High until water drops dance. Place corn in mixer bowl; beat in eggs with electric beater. Add pancake mix; mix well. Drop batter by ladlefuls onto lightly greased preheated griddle. Cook until bubbles form and edges begin to dry slightly; turn. Lower heat to 350 degrees; cook until done and underside is browned. Yield: 4 servings.

Ruth Parkison, Preceptor Beta Delta
Glenwood Springs, Colorado

GINGERBREAD WAFFLES

2 cups all-purpose flour	2 eggs, well beaten
1 teaspoon ginger	¹/4 cup sugar
¹/2 teaspoon salt	¹/2 cup molasses
1 teaspoon baking soda	1 cup buttermilk
1 teaspoon baking	¹/3 cup oil
powder	

Preheat waffle iron. Sift first 5 ingredients together into bowl. Cream eggs and sugar in large mixer bowl. Add molasses, buttermilk and oil; mix well. Add dry ingredients; stir until smooth. Pour batter into preheated waffle iron. Bake until lightly browned. May serve with butter and syrup or as dessert with whipped cream if desired.
Yield: 6 to 8 servings.

Cynthia L. Rahme, Delta Psi
Concord, North Carolina

WHOLE WHEAT PECAN WAFFLES

2 eggs, separated	¹/2 teaspoon salt
2 cups milk	¹/4 cup vegetable oil
2 cups whole wheat	Chopped pecans
flour	
4 teaspoons baking	
powder	

Preheat waffle iron. Beat egg whites in bowl until stiff peaks form. Combine egg yolks and next 5 ingredients; mix until smooth. Fold in egg whites. Sprinkle 1 tablespoon pecans on preheated waffle iron. Pour ¹/2 to ³/4 cup batter over pecans. Bake for about 3 minutes or until steaming stops. May serve with favorite syrup or fresh fruit and whipped cream if desired. Yield: 8 waffles.

Debra L. Stevens, Xi Chi
Farmington, New Mexico

WAFFLES

1 egg, beaten
1/3 cup salad oil

1 1/3 cups club soda
2 cups biscuit mix

Preheat waffle iron. Combine egg, oil and club soda in bowl; mix well. Stir in biscuit mix; mix well. Batter will be thin. Bake in preheated waffle iron. Leftover batter cannot be refrigerated for later use. Cooked waffles can be frozen if desired. Yield: 6 waffles.

Sandra K. Johnson, Alpha Xi
Chickasha, Oklahoma

LIGHT AND FLUFFY BELGIAN WAFFLES

2 eggs
1 tablespoon baking
  powder
1/3 cup sugar

1/2 teaspoon salt
2 cups club soda
2 cups all-purpose flour
1/4 cup melted margarine

Preheat Belgian waffle cooker. Combine eggs and baking powder in mixer bowl; beat well. Add sugar and salt; mix well. Add club soda and flour alternately, mixing well. Add margarine; mix well. Bake in preheated Belgian waffle cooker. Yield: 10 waffles.

Diana Jackson, Mu Kappa
Ellinwood, Kansas

WAFFLES

1 cup sifted self-rising
  flour
1 cup milk

1 egg
3 tablespoons vegetable
  oil

Preheat 7-inch waffle iron. Combine all ingredients in bowl; stir with wire whisk. Pour batter into preheated waffle iron. Bake for approximately 2 minutes or until lightly browned. Yield: 4 waffles.

Dot Deslattes, Xi Tau
Duncanville, Alabama

❖ EASY AMBROSIA

Assorted pieces of
  fruit such as oranges,
  apples, bananas and
  grapes
1 cup pecan halves
  (optional)
1 cup shredded coconut
  (optional)

1 6-ounce can frozen
  orange juice
  concentrate
10 (or more)
  maraschino cherries,
  cut into halves

Combine fruit in serving bowl; sprinkle with pecan halves and coconut. Spoon frozen orange juice over top; let stand until orange juice thaws. Stir fruit gently; top with cherries. Yield: variable.

Donna Lundy, Preceptor Gamma Gamma
Tulsa, Oklahoma

CHEESY PINEAPPLE CASSEROLE

1 cup self-rising flour
1 cup sugar
4 20-ounce cans sliced
  pineapple, drained,
  chopped
4 cups shredded
  Cheddar cheese

1/2 cup packed light
  brown sugar
8 ounces butter
  crackers, crushed
7/8 cup melted butter or
  margarine

Preheat oven to 350 degrees. Mix flour and sugar in large bowl. Add pineapple; mix well. Add cheese; mix well. Spread evenly in 9-by-13-inch baking dish. Sprinkle with brown sugar and cracker crumbs; drizzle with butter. Bake for 1 hour. Yield: 16 servings.

June Spence, Laureate Beta Iota
Ocala, Florida

CINNAMON APPLES

For a party, core the peeled apples and cook them whole. Stuff with mixture of cream cheese and pecans or walnuts.

8 to 10 medium Granny
  Smith apples
Lemon juice
1 8- to 10-ounce
  package red hot
  cinnamon candies

4 to 6 drops of red food
  coloring

Core apples and cut into quarters. Combine with lemon juice and enough water to cover in large bowl. Combine candies with water to cover in large saucepan. Cook over very low heat until candy dissolves, stirring with wooden spoon. Add food coloring as desired. Drain apples. Add to saucepan with water to cover. Simmer until tender but still firm; do not overcook. Store in covered container in refrigerator for up to 10 days. Yield: 8 to 10 servings.

Marian Daily, Preceptor Mu Sigma
Houston, Texas

CRANBERRY AND APPLE CASSEROLE

This recipe was a hit at the annual Christmas brunch for senior citizens. It is also great for a bridge luncheon.

2 to 3 tart cooking
  apples, chopped
2 cups cranberries
1 1/2 cups sugar
1/2 cup margarine

1 1/2 cups oats
1/2 cup packed light
  brown sugar
1/2 cup pecans

Preheat oven to 375 degrees. Combine apples, cranberries and sugar in bowl. Spoon into 11-by-13-inch baking dish sprayed with nonstick cooking spray. Mix remaining ingredients in bowl until crumbly. Spread over fruit. Bake for 35 to 45 minutes or until bubbly. May melt 1/4 cup margarine in baking dish before adding fruit if desired. Yield: 12 servings.

Kim Kafoglis, Delta Epsilon
Bowling Green, Kentucky

HOT CURRIED FRUIT

This recipe was served at a brunch honoring our Woman of the Year several years ago.

1 16-ounce can pears	1/2 cup packed light
1 16-ounce can peaches	brown sugar
1 16-ounce can	1/2 cup butter or
pineapple chunks	margarine
1 16-ounce can apricots	1 tablespoon curry
1 cup raisins	powder
1/2 cup pecans	

Preheat oven to 350 degrees. Drain canned fruits, reserving 1/2 cup juice. Layer or combine fruit as desired with raisins and pecans in 9-by-13-inch baking dish. Combine reserved juice and remaining ingredients in saucepan. Cook until mixture forms syrup of desired consistency. Pour over fruit. Bake for 1 hour. Yield: 12 servings.

Willie Sloan, Preceptor Omega
La Mesa, New Mexico

BAKED CURRIED FRUIT

1 small jar maraschino	2 teaspoons cornstarch
cherries	1/2 teaspoon curry
1 16-ounce can pears	powder
1 16-ounce can apricots	2 tablespoons butter
1 7-ounce can	or margarine
pineapple chunks	
1/4 cup packed light	
brown sugar	

Preheat oven to 325 degrees. Drain cherries and canned fruit. Combine in 1 1/2-quart baking dish. Combine brown sugar, cornstarch and curry powder in small bowl; sprinkle over casserole. Dot with butter. Bake for 1 hour. Yield: 8 servings.

Mary Fox, Laureate Omicron
Mt. Juliet, Tennessee

LAYERED FRUIT SALAD

2 medium red apples,	1 20-ounce can
chopped	pineapple chunks,
1 17-ounce can	drained
apricots, drained,	1/2 cup orange juice
sliced	1 teaspoon lemon juice
1 16-ounce can pears,	1 21-ounce can cherry
drained, sliced	pie filling
1 16-ounce can sliced	Coconut
peaches, drained	

Layer apples, apricots, pears, peaches and pineapple in large shallow bowl. Mix orange juice with lemon juice in small bowl; pour over fruit. Spread pie filling evenly over fruit. Chill for 2 hours. Top with coconut. Yield: 8 to 10 servings.

Betty Meck, Laureate Alpha Beta
Ft. Myers, Florida

SUNNY RAISIN BREAKFAST BARS

When I came home from the hospital with my newborn daughter, my mother would bring me hot coffee and these delicious bars during the early morning nursing.

1/2 cup crunchy peanut	2 1/2 cups Rice Krispies
butter	cereal
1/2 cup packed light	1 1/2 cup quick-cooking
brown sugar	oats
1/2 cup light corn syrup	1 cup raisins
1 teaspoon vanilla	
extract	

Combine peanut butter, brown sugar and corn syrup in large glass bowl. Microwave on High for 2 minutes. Stir in vanilla. Fold in cereal, oats and raisins. Press into buttered 9-by-13-inch dish. Let stand until cool. Cut into bars. Yield: 3 dozen.

Diane B. Lockman, Epsilon Delta
Crescent Springs, Kentucky

VEGETABLE BITES

4 eggs	1 1/2 cups cottage cheese
1 envelope vegetable	1 sheet frozen puff
soup mix	pastry, thawed
1 10-ounce package	Cooked sausage
frozen chopped broccoli,	
thawed, drained	

Beat eggs in large mixer bowl. Stir in soup mix, broccoli and cottage cheese. Chill for 20 minutes. Preheat oven to 400 degrees. Roll pastry to 11-inch-square on lightly floured surface. Place in 9-inch square baking pan; prick with fork. Spoon vegetable mixture into pastry-lined pan. Fold pastry edges over filling. Bake casserole for 40 minutes or until center is set. Cool for 10 minutes. Serve with sausage. Yield: 8 servings.

Beth Hildebrandt, Beta Mu
Rapid City, South Dakota

SURPRISE LAYERED SALAD

1 head lettuce, chopped	2 to 3 cups mayonnaise
1 green bell pepper,	2 tablespoons light
chopped	brown sugar
1 to 2 cups chopped	2 to 3 cups shredded
celery	Cheddar cheese
1 large onion, chopped	2 to 3 tablespoons
1 16-ounce can green	bacon bits
peas, drained	

Layer lettuce, green pepper, celery, onion and peas in large serving bowl. Spread evenly with mayonnaise. Sprinkle with brown sugar, cheese and bacon bits. Chill for 8 hours to overnight. Spoon through all layers to serve. May add hard-cooked eggs or grated carrots if desired. Yield: 10 to 12 servings.

Margaret A. Orlando, Xi Omicron
Phoenix, Arizona

RASPBERRY SURPRISE

My sorority sisters think this is all I know how to make because I always bring it to all "food" occasions.

1 6-ounce package
   raspberry gelatin
2 cups boiling water
1 cup applesauce

1 10-ounce package
   frozen sweetened
   raspberries

Dissolve gelatin in 2 cups boiling water in medium bowl. Stir in applesauce and frozen raspberries. Spoon into 4-cup serving bowl. Chill until set. Yield: 6 servings.

Ellen L. Kelley, Preceptor Omega
Waterford, Michigan

RED HOT APPLESAUCE SALAD

1 cup red hot cinnamon
   candies
3 cups boiling water
3 3-ounce packages
   red gelatin
4 cups applesauce,
   chilled
1/4 cup whipping cream

12 ounces cream cheese,
   softened
1/2 cup mayonnaise-
   type salad dressing
1/4 cup whipping cream
1/2 cup chopped nuts
Lettuce leaves

Dissolve candies in boiling water in large bowl. Stir in gelatin until dissolved. Cool to room temperature. Add chilled applesauce; mix well. Spoon into 9-by-13-inch dish. Chill until set. Combine remaining ingredients in medium bowl; mix well. Spread over congealed mixture. Chill for 3 hours or longer. Cut into squares. Serve on lettuce leaf. Yield: 15 servings.

Mary A. Connor, Preceptor Xi
Webster, North Dakota

VEGETABLE SANDWICH

This is great for sorority rushing.

1 can crescent rolls
4 ounces cream cheese,
   softened
1 1-serving packet
   spring garden
   or garden vegetable
   soup mix
2 to 3 tablespoons
   mayonnaise-type
   salad dressing

Assorted bite-sized
   vegetables such as
   broccoli, cauliflower,
   onion, bell peppers
   and tomatoes
Grated Parmesan
   cheese to taste

Preheat oven to temperature suggested on roll package. Unroll dough; do not separate. Place on cookie sheet. Bake according to package directions. Cool to room temperature. Combine cream cheese, soup mix and mayonnaise in small bowl; mix well. Spread over crust. Sprinkle with vegetables; top with cheese. Cut into squares. Yield: 12 to 14 servings.

Faye Janes, Preceptor Alpha Zeta
Brantford, Ontario, Canada

WAFFLE SAUCE

I serve this over waffles with a topping of fresh fruit.

2 cups milk
1/2 cup sugar
Salt to taste
1/2 cup milk
2 egg yolks, beaten
3 tablespoons
   cornstarch

1 tablespoon butter or
   margarine
1 teaspoon vanilla
   extract

Combine 2 cups milk, sugar and salt in heavy saucepan. Bring to a boil, stirring to mix well; remove from heat. Combine 1/2 cup milk, egg yolks and cornstarch in small bowl; mix well. Stir into hot mixture gradually. Cook for 1 minute or until thickened, stirring constantly. Stir in butter and vanilla. Yield: 3 cups.

Jan Landis, Theta Theta
Goshen, Indiana

RHUBARB AND BLUEBERRY JAM

5 cups finely
   chopped rhubarb
1 cup water
2 1/2 cups sugar

1 21-ounce can
   blueberry pie filling
1 6-ounce package
   raspberry gelatin

Simmer rhubarb in water in saucepan until tender. Stir in sugar. Add pie filling; mix well. Cook for 6 to 8 minutes, stirring constantly; remove from heat. Stir in gelatin until dissolved. Spoon into small jars or plastic freezer containers. Cool to room temperature; seal. Freeze; store opened jam in refrigerator. May substitute cherry pie filling for blueberry. Yield: 6 cups.

Merlyn Jenkins, Laureate Alpha Phi
Loveland, Colorado

MOCK APPLE BUTTER

4 cups chopped peeled
   zucchini
1/4 cup vinegar
2 cups sugar
1 teaspoon lemon juice

1 teaspoon cinnamon
Allspice to taste
2 or 3 drops of red
   food coloring

Place zucchini and vinegar in blender container; process until smooth. Combine with remaining ingredients in saucepan; mix well. Cook until of desired consistency, stirring constantly. Cool to room temperature. Spoon into jars; seal with 2-piece lids. Store in refrigerator or freezer. Yield: 4 small jars.

Marilyn Dierking, Xi Alpha Upsilon
Blue Springs, Missouri

Diana Kooima, Nu Alpha, Rock Valley, Iowa, makes Honey Butter by blending 1 1/2 cups butter at room temperature and 1 cup honey with electric mixer. Spoon into small containers and freeze.

CHOCOLATE GRAVY

Biscuits and chocolate gravy were served by my mother on special occasions. I have continued this tradition.

1/2 cup sugar	Salt to taste
2 tablespoons baking cocoa	1 cup milk
1 tablespoon all-purpose flour	1 tablespoon margarine
	1/2 teaspoon vanilla extract

Combine first 5 ingredients in medium saucepan; mix well. Cook until thickened, stirring constantly. Stir in margarine and vanilla. May serve over hot buttered biscuits if desired. Yield: 1 1/2 cups gravy.

Celia Mabry, Preceptor Kappa Lambda
Portland, Texas
*Allison Walters, Mu Omega
Watts, Oklahoma
*Maxine Mitchell, Preceptor Eta Beta
Boerne, Texas

HOT CHOCOLATE MIX

1 25-ounce package instant nonfat dry milk	2 cups confectioners' sugar
1 6-ounce jar nondairy creamer	1 16-ounce package instant chocolate drink mix

Combine milk powder with remaining ingredients in large bowl; mix well. Combine 1/4 cup mixture with 1 cup hot water. Store unused mixture in sealed container in cool dry place. Yield: 68 servings.

Denise Kozal
Ozark, Missouri

BAVARIAN MINT COFFEE

This mixture fills 4 small baby food jars. I decorate the jars with seasonal material and give as Christmas gifts.

2/3 cup nondairy creamer	1/4 cup baking cocoa
2/3 cup sugar	6 peppermint sticks, crushed
1/2 cup instant coffee	

Combine creamer powder with remaining ingredients in blender container. Process until smooth. Place 2 heaping teaspoons mixture in coffee cup. Fill with boiling water; stir. Yield: 40 servings.

Shirley Dorcy, Xi Beta Delta
Maple Grove, Minnesota

LEMON TEA

6 Earl Grey tea bags	Juice of 3 lemons
1 cup sugar	6 cups boiling water
1 cup water	

Combine tea bags, sugar and 1 cup water in large saucepan. Simmer for 10 minutes. Stir in lemon juice. Add 6 cups boiling water. Steep tea for 7 minutes.

Remove tea bags. Pour into pitcher. Chill completely before serving. Yield: 8 to 10 servings.

Mildred Johnstone, Xi Master
Lake Jackson, Texas

CRANBERRY TEA

4 cups cranberries	1/2 6-ounce can frozen orange juice concentrate
8 cups water	
1 cup red hot cinnamon candies	1/2 6-ounce can frozen lemonade concentrate
2 cups sugar	
12 whole cloves	

Combine cranberries with 4 cups water in saucepan. Bring to a boil. Cook until cranberries pop. Strain, discarding pulp. Combine remaining 4 cups water with next 3 ingredients in saucepan. Cook until candies and sugar dissolve. Combine with cranberry liquid in large container. Stir in orange and lemonade concentrates. Chill until serving time. Fill glass half full with mixture. Fill remainder of glass with water. Yield: 25 servings.

Mary M. Thompson, Preceptor Gamma
Hannibal, Missouri

CHAMPAGNE PUNCH

This is a favorite at sorority brunches, dinners and dessert parties. We vary the flavor of sherbet according to the holiday. We use raspberry for Valentine's day.

1 quart sherbet, softened	1 26-ounce bottle of sauterne
1 2-liter bottle of Champagne	Ginger ale or 7-Up

Place sherbet in punch bowl. Pour Champagne and sauterne over top; stir. Add ginger ale if desired. Spoon into punch cups. Yield: 18 servings.

Wendy Keserich, Preceptor Laureate Alpha Delta
Duncan, British Columbia, Canada

ORANGE JULIUS

1/2 6-ounce can frozen orange juice concentrate	1/4 cup sugar
	1/2 teaspoon vanilla extract
1/2 cup milk	5 or 6 ice cubes, crushed
1/2 cup water	

Combine all ingredients in blender container. Process until smooth. Yield: 4 servings.

Sharon L. Gulbrandson, Xi Gamma
Lakeville, Minnesota

Barbara M. Kruger, Preceptor Psi, Fremont, Nebraska, makes Marinated Fruit by preparing red apples, seedless grapes, temple oranges and pink grapefruit as for fruit cocktail and marinating the fruit in a light pink wine or non-alcoholic cider in refrigerator. Spoon into sherbet glasses; pour liquid over fruit. Sprinkle coconut on top.

The Great Outdoors

There's something about the outdoors that makes even the most simple foods taste great. A hot dog out of a microwave is ho-hum, but roast that same wiener over a campfire and you have a taste sensation. Maybe it's an instinct that goes back to the day our earliest ancestors first gathered around a cooking fire outside the cave. Or maybe it just takes us back to our own childhood camping expeditions. Whatever the explanation, there's no denying that "eating out" enhances most any meal. In the pages that follow, you'll find many of your old favorites for cookouts along with some exciting new dishes to help enhance the age-old appeal of eating in the great outdoors.

Home Sweet Home

Salmon Cookout

Sweet and Sour Barbecued Salmon
Baked Potatoes
Zucchini Salad
Ambrosia

See index for similar recipes.

This dinner is both easy and excellent. The salmon and potatoes are cooked on the grill. Just wrap the potatoes in foil and place them on the grill about 30 minutes before the salmon; turn frequently to prevent overbrowning.

Rozella Seale, Laureate Epsilon
Alhambra, California

SWEET AND SOUR BARBECUED SALMON

3 pounds salmon filets	1/2 cup mayonnaise
1/2 cup packed light brown sugar	1/4 cup catsup
1/4 teaspoon salt	2 tablespoons light vinegar
1/4 teaspoon pepper	1/2 teaspoon Worcestershire sauce
1/2 cup butter or margarine, chopped	

Arrange salmon filets skin side down on double layer of foil slightly larger than fish; pierce holes at 2-inch intervals around fish. Sprinkle with brown sugar, salt and pepper; dot with butter. Blend remaining ingredients in small bowl. Spread evenly over fish. Place foil and fish on grill over hot coals. Cover with additional foil or grill cover. Grill for 20 minutes or until fish flakes easily. Yield: 6 servings.

ZUCCHINI SALAD

8 small zucchini	1 teaspoon sugar
1 green bell pepper	1/2 teaspoon salt
4 tomatoes	1 avocado, chopped
4 green onions with tops	Bleu cheese

Chop first 4 vegetables into bite-sized pieces; combine with sugar and salt in covered container. Chill for 3 hours to overnight, stirring or turning container several times. Spoon into serving bowl; top with avocado. Crumble cheese over salad. Serve immediately. Yield: 6 servings.

AMBROSIA

1 16-ounce can fruit cocktail	2 cups miniature marshmallows
1 7-ounce can pineapple tidbits	1 cup coconut
2 11-ounce cans mandarin oranges	1/2 cup nuts
	1 cup whipped topping

Drain canned fruits and combine in serving bowl. Chill in refrigerator. Add marshmallows, coconut and nuts at serving time. Fold in whipped topping. May serve as salad or dessert. Yield: 6 to 8 servings.

Annual Goose Dinner

Currant and Jalapeño Jelly over
Cream Cheese
Crackers
Imperial Goose — Wild Rice
Broccoli Casserole
Tossed Salad — Bleu Cheese Dressing
Homemade White Bread
Fabulous Cheesecake — Banana Bread

See index for similar recipes.

My husband and three friends have hunted Canadian geese on the Eastern shore of Maryland for nearly 15 years. Through the years we have taken turns preparing the "goose dinner," and have shared new recipes we have discovered—many from Beta Sigma Phi cookbooks. Through the years of raising our children and changing careers, this annual event has produced some of our fondest memories of shared good times.

Jean Pessano, Preceptor Alpha Beta
Ocean City, New Jersey

CURRANT AND JALAPEÑO JELLY

1 12-ounce jar red currant jelly	2 1/2 tablespoons white vinegar
2 or 3 jalapeño peppers, seeded, chopped	

Melt jelly in saucepan over low heat. Stir in peppers and vinegar. Bring to a boil; reduce heat. Simmer for 5 minutes, skimming foam. Spoon into jar and seal. Store in refrigerator for up to 3 months. Serve over cream cheese with assorted crackers. Yield: 1 1/2 cups.

IMPERIAL GOOSE

1 goose	1/4 teaspoon dry
1/2 cup vinegar	mustard
2 cloves of garlic,	1/4 cup grated orange
minced	rind
2 tablespoons salt	1/4 teaspoon salt
1/4 cup minced onion	1/4 cup Port
1/2 teaspoon tarragon	1 16-ounce can
leaves	mandarin oranges
1/4 cup butter or	3 tablespoons
margarine	cornstarch
1/2 cup currant jelly	Wild rice
1 cup orange juice	

Cut goose into serving pieces; rinse and pat dry. Combine with vinegar, garlic, 2 tablespoons salt and cold water to cover in large bowl. Marinate in refrigerator overnight; drain. Place in slow cooker. Sauté onion and tarragon in butter in saucepan. Add jelly, orange juice, dry mustard, orange rind and 1/4 teaspoon salt; mix well. Cook over medium heat until jelly melts, stirring constantly; reduce heat. Stir in wine and oranges. Spoon into slow cooker. Cook on Low for 8 to 9 hours. Set slow cooker temperature to High. Stir in cornstarch. Cook for 30 minutes longer. May keep warm on Low to serve. Serve over rice. Yield: 8 servings.

BLEU CHEESE DRESSING

2 cups sour cream	1 clove of garlic, minced
1 tablespoon lemon juice	8 ounces bleu cheese,
1/2 teaspoon	crumbled
Worcestershire sauce	
1/8 teaspoon hot pepper	
sauce	

Combine all ingredients in small bowl; mix well. Chill until serving time. Yield: 8 servings.

FABULOUS CHEESECAKE

I usually serve strawberries in syrup over this cheesecake.

Graham cracker crumbs	Juice and grated rind of
4 pounds cream cheese,	1/4 lemon
softened	1 teaspoon vanilla
2 cups sugar	extract
7 eggs	Salt to taste

Preheat oven to 325 degrees. Spread layer of cracker crumbs in buttered springform pan. Beat cream cheese and sugar in mixer bowl until light. Beat in eggs. Add lemon juice, lemon rind, vanilla and salt; mix well. Spoon into prepared pan. Bake for 1 1/2 hours or until filling is firm around edges but still soft in center. Cool on wire rack. Chill overnight. Place on serving plate; remove side of pan. Yield: 12 servings.

BANANA BREAD

1/2 cup butter or	1 teaspoon baking soda
margarine, softened	3 tablespoons cold
1 cup sugar	water
1/2 teaspoon salt	2 cups all-purpose flour
1 teaspoon vanilla	3 bananas, mashed
extract	1/2 cup coarsely chopped
2 eggs, beaten	walnuts

Preheat oven to 325 degrees. Cream butter, sugar, salt and vanilla in mixer bowl. Stir in eggs. Dissolve baking soda in cold water in small bowl. Add flour alternately with baking soda mixture to creamed mixture, mixing well after each addition. Stir in bananas and walnuts. Spoon into greased and floured loaf pan. Bake for 1 hour. Remove to wire rack to cool. May bake in muffin cups if desired. Yield: 1 loaf.

Summer Gathering

Savory Lemon Chicken
Potato Salad — Baked Beans
Corn on the Cob
Fresh Fruit Salad

See index for similar recipes.

This is the meal we prepare for any large or small summer gathering, because it is delicious and easy.

Debbie Robinson, Xi Beta Nu
Moscow, Idaho

SAVORY LEMON CHICKEN

3 pounds chicken,	1 teaspoon prepared
cut up	mustard
1/3 cup vegetable oil	1/2 teaspoon tarragon
1/3 cup white cooking	leaves
wine	1/2 teaspoon onion
2 teaspoons lemon	powder
pepper	

Rinse chicken and pat dry. Combine with remaining ingredients in dish. Marinate in refrigerator for 1 hour. Drain, reserving marinade. Grill for 30 to 45 minutes or until cooked through, basting with reserved marinade. Yield: 6 servings.

Summer Picnic

Barbecued Chicken and Ribs
Potato Salad
Garden Salad
Assorted Salad Dressings
Rolls — Butter
Summer Potpourri

See index for similar recipes.

This is a typical menu for special summer afternoons with friends. The Summer Potpourri can be used as a party starter or dessert.

Sandra McCarthy, Laureate Gamma Delta
Windsor, Ontario, Canada

BARBECUED CHICKEN AND RIBS

1 cup packed light brown sugar	*1 cup catsup*
1 tablespoon dry mustard	*Salt and pepper to taste*
	Chicken pieces
	Ribs

Combine first 5 ingredients in large bowl; mix well. Rinse chicken and ribs; pat dry. Add to sauce. Marinate in refrigerator for 3 to 4 hours. Drain, reserving marinade. Grill chicken and ribs until cooked through, basting frequently with reserved sauce. Yield: variable.

POTATO SALAD

10 potatoes, peeled	*1 cup mayonnaise*
1 cup chopped celery	*1/8 teaspoon dry mustard*
4 hard-cooked eggs, chopped	*Paprika to taste*
Salt and pepper to taste	*Radishes*
	Hard-cooked eggs, sliced

Boil potatoes in water to cover until tender; drain and chop. Combine potatoes, celery, chopped eggs, salt and pepper, mayonnaise and mustard in large bowl; mix gently. Sprinkle with paprika. Chill until serving time. Garnish with radishes and sliced eggs. Yield: 12 servings.

SUMMER POTPOURRI

1 oval or oblong watermelon	*1 bunch seedless green grapes*
1 honeydew melon	*2 ounces light rum (optional)*
1 pint blueberries	
1 quart strawberries	

Cut 1 side from watermelon. Scoop out seedless pulp with melon baller; discard seeds and remaining pulp to form shell. Scoop honeydew melon into balls. Combine watermelon and honeydew balls with remaining fruit in large bowl. Add rum; mix gently. Chill shell and fruit until serving time. Spoon fruit into watermelon shell. Yield: 12 servings.

Cottage Drop-By Supper

Grilled Flank Steak
Chili Coleslaw
Creamy Horseradish Sauce
Marinated Mushrooms
Chocolate Brownies

This menu is easy to serve when company drops by at the cottage. Most of it can be made in advance. The steak can even be broiled inside if the weather or the mosquitoes don't cooperate.

Vera Wassill, Laureate Epsilon
Yorkton, Saskatchewan, Canada

GRILLED FLANK STEAK

1 1-pound flank steak	*1 tablespoon light brown sugar*
2 to 3 tablespoons soy sauce	*1 clove of garlic, crushed*
2 tablespoons lemon juice	*Freshly ground pepper to taste*
2 tablespoons olive oil	

Place steak in shallow dish just large enough to hold it. Whisk remaining ingredients together in medium bowl. Pour over steak. Marinate, covered, at room temperature for 1 to 2 hours or in refrigerator for up to 2 days. Drain steak and place on grill 4 inches from medium-hot coals. Grill for 3 to 4 minutes on each side for medium-rare. Yield: 4 servings.

CHILI COLESLAW

1 cup creamy cucumber salad dressing	*1 head cabbage, finely shredded*
1 tablespoon sugar	*4 carrots, grated*
1 teaspoon celery seed	*3 green onions*
1 1/2 teaspoons chili powder	

Combine salad dressing, sugar, celery seed and chili powder in large bowl; mix well. Add vegetables; mix well. Chill, covered, for up to 1 day. Yield: 8 servings.

CREAMY HORSERADISH SAUCE

1/2 cup mayonnaise *1/4 cup horseradish*

Combine mayonnaise and horseradish in small bowl; mix well. Store in refrigerator for up to 3 days. Serve with flank steak. Yield: 1/2 cup.

MARINATED MUSHROOMS

*1 pound small fresh
  mushrooms
1 small red bell pepper,
  chopped
2 green onions with
  tops, sliced
2 tablespoons red
  wine vinegar*

*1/3 cup olive oil
2 cloves of garlic,
  crushed
1/2 teaspoon each
  oregano and basil
Salt and cayenne pepper
  to taste*

Combine mushrooms, bell pepper and green onions in bowl. Whisk remaining ingredients together in small bowl. Add to mushroom mixture. Marinate at room temperature for 30 minutes or in refrigerator for up to 2 days. Yield: 4 servings.

CHOCOLATE BROWNIES

These are good served with ice cream or whipped cream and berries laced with Grand Marnier.

*1 3-ounce bittersweet
  or white chocolate
  bar
1 large package fudge
  brownie mix*

*1/3 cup water
2 tablespoons vegetable
  oil
1 egg*

Preheat oven to 350 degrees. Chop chocolate into 1/2-inch pieces. Combine brownie mix, water, oil and egg in medium mixer bowl; mix well. Stir in chocolate. Spoon into greased baking pan. Bake according to package directions. Cool on wire rack. Yield: 12 servings.

Patio Picnic

*Guacamole — Tortilla Chips
Beef and Chicken Fajitas
Homemade Tortillas
Vegetable Sauté*

This is a great outdoor menu that we like to share with friends on our patio overlooking the American River.

Lynn Hargrove, Xi Pi Epsilon
Auburn, California

GUACAMOLE

*2 large avocados, peeled
1 tablespoon lime juice
1/2 teaspoon each onion
  powder, coriander
  and garlic salt*

*1 tablespoon picante
  sauce
Tortilla chips*

Mash avocados with next 5 ingredients in serving bowl. Place 1 avocado pit in bowl until serving time. Serve with tortilla chips. Yield: 12 servings.

BEEF AND CHICKEN FAJITAS

*1 1/2 pounds chicken
  breast filets
1 1/2 pounds skirt steak
1 12-ounce can beer
2 tablespoons olive oil
2 teaspoons lime juice
2 teaspoons minced
  garlic
Worcestershire sauce
  and Tequila to taste
1/2 teaspoon oregano*

*1 tablespoon coarsely
  ground pepper
Homemade Tortillas
Vegetable Sauté
Toppings such as sour
  cream, shredded
  Cheddar and Monterey
  Jack cheeses, salsa,
  shredded lettuce and
  sliced black olives*

Rinse chicken and pat dry; trim fat from steak. Combine next 8 ingredients in large bowl; mix well. Pour half over chicken and half over beef in separate bowls. Marinate, covered, in refrigerator overnight. Drain, reserving marinades. Grill chicken and steak on covered grill until cooked through, brushing occasionally with marinade. Slice chicken and steak into strips. Sear in hot skillet. Serve with Homemade Tortillas, Vegetable Sauté, and remaining toppings. Yield: 12 servings.

HOMEMADE TORTILLAS

*2 1/2 cups all-purpose
  flour
1 1/2 tablespoons baking
  powder*

*1 1/2 teaspoons salt
1/2 cup shortening
1 cup (about) water*

Combine all ingredients in bowl; mix well, adjusting amount of flour and water as needed and kneading to form a smooth dough. Let rest, covered with warm towel, for 15 minutes. Shape into balls, working with a portion of the dough at a time and leaving remaining dough in bowl. Roll tortillas on lightly floured board. Bake on hot griddle until brown on both sides. Yield: 12 servings.

VEGETABLE SAUTÉ

*1 green bell pepper,
  sliced
2 or 3 tomatoes, chopped
1 red onion, sliced*

*Garlic salt and pepper
  to taste
1 or 2 teaspoons butter
  or margarine*

Sauté green pepper, tomatoes and onion with garlic salt and pepper in butter in large skillet until tender. Keep warm. Serve with fajitas. Yield: 12 servings.

❖ Wild West Birthday Party

Round-Up Wieners
On the Trail Mix
Billy the Kid Burgers
Barbecued Chicken — Buckaroo Beans
Pony Express Potatoes
Blue Jean Birthday Cake
Stage Coach Soda

See index for similar recipes.

This party is planned for my son's next birthday party. The invitation will show him, dressed in a cowboy outfit, on the front as a wanted poster. The invitation will read "'Wanted' Children to come celebrate a Wild West Birthday Party. Like Clint Eastwood would say, 'come have a good time and make my day.'" Decorations will include wanted posters of each child, and each guest will be given a cowboy hat and a sheriff's badge as a party favor. Songs of the wild west will be playing in the background. Tablecloths will be made of bandanna material and placemats will be of denim with bandanna napkins tucked in the pocket. A hitching post, a wooden horse and bales of hay will provide the western flavor. Entertainment will consist of pony rides, a horseshoe-pitching contest and panning for gold. The birthday cake, in the shape of a horseshoe, will be decorated like a pair of blue jeans.

Debbie Meegan, Xi Alpha
Lemont Furnace, Pennsylvania

ROUND-UP WIENERS

8 wieners	*Toppings such as heated*
8 hamburger buns	*chili, catsup, mustard,*
1/4 cup margarine or	*pickles or relish*
butter, softened	

Score wieners at 1/2-inch intervals, cutting to within 1/4 inch of opposite side. Shape each wiener into circle; secure ends with wooden picks. Grill 4 to 6 inches from medium coals for 6 to 8 minutes or until heated through. Spread buns with margarine. Toast on grill until light brown. Serve with desired toppings. Yield: 8 servings.

ON THE TRAIL MIX

4 cups crisp corn cereal	*1 cup peanuts*
squares	*1 cup raisins*
1 12-ounce package	*1/2 cup chopped dried*
candy-coated	*apple*
chocolate candies	

Combine all ingredients in large bowl; mix well. Yield: 7 1/2 cups.

BUCKAROO BEANS

1 small onion, chopped	*1/2 cup catsup*
2 tablespoons	*1/4 cup packed light*
margarine or bacon	*brown sugar*
drippings	
2 16-ounce cans pork	
and beans	

Sauté onion in margarine in saucepan until tender. Add remaining ingredients; mix well. Simmer until of desired consistency. Yield: 8 servings.

Company Cookout

Grilled Curried Chicken
Potatoes Fontecchio
Spinach Salad
Sourdough Bread
Chocolate Grand Marnier Cheesecake

See index for similar recipes.

This is the menu that I frequently use for dinner parties and it is always a big hit. I take the potatoes to potluck dinners and anyone who likes garlic likes it.

Candy Skaugrud, Delta
Seattle, Washington

GRILLED CURRIED CHICKEN

1 cup finely ground	*1/4 cup fresh tarragon*
salted peanuts	*leaves or*
1 pound bitter orange	*2 tablespoons dried*
marmalade	*tarragon*
1/2 cup olive oil	*1 teaspoon salt*
1/2 cup fresh orange juice	*8 chicken breasts*
1 6-ounce jar Dijon	*1 cup shredded coconut*
mustard	*1 cup dried currants*
2 teaspoons curry	
powder	

Combine first 8 ingredients in shallow baking dish; mix well. Rinse chicken and pat dry. Add to marinade, coating well. Marinate in refrigerator for 4 to 6 hours, turning occasionally. Preheat oven to 350 degrees. Bake chicken in marinade for 35 minutes. Drain, reserving marinade. Grill 4 inches from hot coals for 8 to 10 minutes on each side or until cooked through, brushing frequently with marinade. Place on serving platter; sprinkle with coconut and currants. Yield: 8 servings.

POTATOES FONTECCHIO

5¹/2 pounds tiny new potatoes	8 cloves of garlic, minced
1¹/2 cups extra-virgin olive oil	2 tablespoons coarse salt
1 large or 2 small bunches of fresh mint, chopped	Freshly ground pepper to taste

Preheat oven to 350 degrees. Scrub potatoes and pierce each 6 times with fork. Arrange in shallow baking pan. Bake for 2¹/2 hours. Cut each potato into halves. Toss with remaining ingredients in large bowl. Let stand for 30 minutes before serving. Yield: 8 servings.

CHOCOLATE GRAND MARNIER CHEESECAKE

¹/4 cup melted butter or margarine	4 eggs
1¹/2 cups Oreo cookie crumbs	¹/2 cup sour cream
32 ounces cream cheese, softened	6 ounces semisweet chocolate, melted
1 cup sugar	¹/3 cup Grand Marnier
	1¹/2 cups sour cream
	¹/4 cup sugar

Preheat oven to 300 degrees. Mix melted butter and cookie crumbs in medium bowl. Press over bottom and halfway up side of greased 10-inch springform pan. Beat cream cheese and 1 cup sugar in large mixer bowl until light and fluffy. Beat in eggs 1 at a time. Add ¹/2 cup sour cream; mix well. Beat in chocolate and liqueur. Spoon into prepared pan. Place in larger pan with ¹/4 inch water. Bake for 1 hour and 25 minutes or until set. Spread mixture of 1¹/2 cups sour cream and ¹/4 cup sugar over top. Bake for 5 to 10 minutes longer. Cool on wire rack. Chill overnight. Place on serving plate; remove side of pan. Yield: 12 to 16 servings.

Beverlee Harbin, Preceptor Omicron, Bethesda, Maryland, makes Pineapple Coleslaw by mixing a sauce made of one 15-ounce can crushed pineapple, drained, and 1 cup mayonnaise with ¹/2 head of cabbage, finely chopped. Chill before serving or overnight. This coleslaw will serve 6 to 10 people.

Pulling Together Barbecue

Pulled Brisket Barbecue
Whole Wheat Buns
Baked Beans — Corn on the Cob
Coleslaw — Pickles
Ice Cream
Iced Tea

See index for similar recipes.

My friends love my brisket barbecue, which has been the mainstay of many happy summer outings and picnics, but I love the fact that my wonderful husband and I sit down at the table and pull the brisket together. We talk and laugh and get kind of messy, but it is a special time for us.

Susan Hadley, Alpha Chi Iota
Orange, Texas

PULLED BRISKET BARBECUE

1 4-pound beef brisket or chuck roast	1 cup catsup
1 3¹/2-ounce bottle of liquid smoke	¹/2 cup chili sauce
2 cups chopped onions	3 tablespoons Worcestershire sauce
¹/4 cup vinegar	¹/4 teaspoon hot pepper sauce
¹/4 cup packed dark brown sugar	1 tablespoon salt
2 tablespoons spicy brown mustard	¹/4 teaspoon cayenne pepper
¹/2 lemon, sliced	¹/4 teaspoon black pepper
1 tablespoon dark molasses	10 to 12 whole wheat buns

Preheat oven to 325 degrees. Place brisket fat side up on rack in roasting pan. Pour liquid smoke over brisket; cover with foil. Roast for 3¹/2 hours; remove foil. Roast for 30 minutes longer. Remove and cool brisket, reserving pan drippings. Chill brisket and drippings overnight. Remove fat from brisket and surface of drippings, reserving 3 tablespoons of fat from drippings. Pull beef into shreds. Sauté onions in reserved fat in large saucepan over medium heat. Add 1 cup pan drippings and next 12 ingredients; mix well. Simmer for 20 minutes. Add beef. Simmer for 1 hour, adding additional pan drippings if needed for desired consistency. Serve on whole wheat buns. Yield: 10 to 12 servings.

Dinner on the Deck

Sesame and Ginger Chicken
Grilled Vegetable Kabobs with Rice
Grilled Peaches with Raspberry Purée
Toasted French Bread
Fruit Juice Cooler

See index for similar recipes.

My mother and I prepared this dinner as a surprise for my father's 50th birthday. His friends and neighbors gathered while he was working in the field. He returned home to this delicious meal and the company of friends to share it. We chose these recipes to suit his low-salt and low-fat diet.

Joan Lefsrud, Alpha Delta
Grande Prairie, Alberta, Canada

SESAME AND GINGER CHICKEN

4 4-ounce chicken breast filets	2 tablespoons honey
1 tablespoon toasted sesame seed	2 tablespoons reduced-sodium soy sauce
2 teaspoons grated ginger	Thin green onion strips

Rinse chicken; pat dry. Pound 1/4 inch thick between plastic wrap. Combine next 4 ingredients in bowl; mix well. Spray grill with nonstick cooking spray. Place chicken on grill. Grill for 4 minutes on each side, basting frequently with sauce. Place on serving platter; garnish with green onions. Yield: 4 servings.

GRILLED VEGETABLE KABOBS WITH RICE

1/2 cup oil-free Italian salad dressing	8 small onions
1 tablespoon minced parsley	8 cherry tomatoes
1 teaspoon basil	8 medium mushrooms
2 medium yellow squash, cut into 1-inch pieces	2 cups cooked long grain rice

Combine salad dressing, parsley and basil in small bowl. Chill, covered, in refrigerator. Alternate squash, onions, tomatoes and mushrooms on 8 skewers. Place on grill sprayed with nonstick cooking spray. Grill for 15 minutes or until vegetables are tender, basting frequently with salad dressing mix-

ture. Place 1/2 cup rice on each serving plate; top each with 2 vegetable kabobs. Yield: 4 servings.

GRILLED PEACHES WITH RASPBERRY PURÉE

1/2 10-ounce package frozen raspberries in light syrup, slightly thawed	1 1/2 tablespoons light brown sugar
1 1/2 teaspoons lemon juice	1/4 teaspoon cinnamon
	1 1/2 teaspoons rum extract
2 medium peaches, peeled, cut into halves	1 1/2 teaspoons margarine

Process raspberries and lemon juice in blender until smooth. Strain into small bowl. Chill, covered, in refrigerator. Place peach halves cut side up on 18-inch square piece of foil. Fill centers with mixture of brown sugar and cinnamon. Sprinkle with rum extract; dot with margarine. Seal foil; place packet on grill over medium coals. Grill for 15 minutes or until heated through. Place peaches on serving plates; spoon raspberry purée into centers. Yield: 4 servings.

FRUIT JUICE COOLER

2 6-ounce bottles of sparkling mineral water	1/4 cup unsweetened grapefruit juice
1 12-ounce can peach nectar	2 tablespoons lemon juice
1/2 cup unsweetened orange juice	

Chill all ingredients. Combine in large pitcher; mix well. Serve over ice. Yield: 4 servings.

Labor Day Picnic

Sliced Rare Roast Beef
Horseradish Sauce
Picnic Beans
Sliced Beefsteak Tomatoes
French Bread

See index for similar recipes.

This is an ideal dish for picnics and tailgate parties because it can be prepared in advance and served cold to a lot of people.

Frances Wilkerson, Preceptor Beta Sigma
Magalia, California

PICNIC BEANS

2 pounds dried small white navy beans	3 cups finely chopped celery
2 cups olive oil	1/2 cup finely chopped parsley
1¹/4 cups lemon juice	
1/2 cup light vinegar	2 tablespoons finely chopped onion
1/2 cup plus 1 tablespoon finely chopped green bell pepper	4¹/2 teaspoons salt
	1/4 teaspoon thyme

Soak and cook beans using package directions, taking care not to overcook, as beans should keep their shape. Combine remaining ingredients in large bowl. Drain and add beans. Marinate, tightly covered, in refrigerator for 8 hours or longer. Yield: 24 servings.

Poolside Party

Chicken Salad
Fruit Cup
Crackers
Old-Fashioned Lemonade

See index for similar recipes.

This menu is great by the pool on hot Florida days. The lemonade recipe was given to me by a best friend who moved from Florida to Seattle. I served it at her going-away party and I think of her every time I serve it. The Fruit Cup is a mixture of fresh fruits in season such as banana, green and red apple, orange, strawberries, red and green grapes, grapefruit, pineapple, peaches and blueberries. You can add coconut if you like.

Sharon Hogan, Xi Mu Eta
Jacksonville, Florida

CHICKEN SALAD

Chopped cooked chicken	*Sliced almonds*
Seedless green grapes	*Salt and pepper to taste*
Chopped celery or celery seed	*1 teaspoon vegetable oil*
	Mayonnaise

Combine chicken, grapes, celery and almonds in medium bowl. Add salt, pepper, oil and enough mayonnaise to moisten; mix gently. Yield: variable.

OLD-FASHIONED LEMONADE

2 lemons	1 tray of ice
3/4 cup sugar	2 cups cold water

Slice lemons very thin, discarding seed and ends. Combine with sugar in pitcher; mix with wooden spoon or potato masher until sugar dissolves. Add ice and water; mix well. Yield: 4 to 6 servings.

Tailgate Party

Steak Soup
Cob Salad
Crusty French Bread
Applesauce — Cookies

See index for similar recipes.

This is a good menu for a tailgate party during the football season or for a family gathering on a cold fall Sunday afternoon. It is also good for sorority potluck dinners because it makes a large amount. The soup recipe originally came from a restaurant in Portland, Oregon, which is no longer in existence, but the recipe goes on and on.

Norma Gilkey, Preceptor Kappa Tau
Glendora, California

STEAK SOUP

1 pound ground beef	2¹/2 quarts water
1¹/2 cups chopped onions	1 8-ounce can tomatoes, chopped
1¹/2 cups sliced carrots	
1 cup chopped celery	1/3 cup beef stock base
1 cup butter or margarine	Pepper to taste
	1 10-ounce package frozen mixed vegetables
1 cup all-purpose flour	

Preheat oven to 350 degrees. Pat ground beef into 1-inch layer in baking pan. Bake for 15 to 20 minutes or until done to taste; drain. Break into 1/2-inch pieces. Sauté onions, carrots and celery in butter in large saucepan over medium heat for 15 minutes or until tender. Stir in flour. Cook until bubbly. Stir in half the water. Bring to a boil and simmer for 10 minutes, stirring constantly. Add tomatoes, beef, stock base and pepper. Simmer for 10 minutes, stirring constantly. Add remaining water and frozen vegetables. Cook for 5 minutes or just until vegetables are tender; do not boil. Yield: 16 servings.

Front Porch Lunch

Beef Burgers Hawaiian
Baked Rice
Orange and Ginger Carrots
Combination Salad with
Bleu Cheese Dressing Deluxe
Piña Colada Cake
Iced Tea

See index for similar recipes.

I like to take an ordinary day and make memorable things happen. I invited a few friends and served this menu one day when my husband was coming home for lunch. We had laughter, conversation and good food while creating some good memories on our front porch.

Janet Newmyer, Beta Phi
Wilber, Nebraska

BEEF BURGERS HAWAIIAN

1¹/2 pounds lean ground beef	¹/4 cup soy sauce
1 teaspoon salt	1 tablespoon vinegar
¹/4 teaspoon pepper	¹/4 cup corn oil
1 13-ounce can pineapple tidbits, drained	2 tablespoons catsup
	¹/4 teaspoon pepper
2 cloves of garlic, minced	6 slices bacon

Combine ground beef with salt and ¹/4 teaspoon pepper in bowl; mix well. Shape into 6 patties. Press 5 or 6 pineapple tidbits into each patty; place in glass dish. Combine next 6 ingredients in small bowl; mix well. Pour over patties. Chill, covered, for 1 hour or longer. Drain patties and wrap each with slice of bacon; secure with wooden pick. Grill over hot coals for 8 to 10 minutes on each side. Yield: 6 servings.

BAKED RICE

1 cup uncooked rice	1 cup water
¹/2 cup margarine	1 4-ounce can mushrooms, undrained
1 10-ounce can onion soup	

Preheat oven to 350 degrees. Combine all ingredients in bowl; mix well. Spoon into 2-quart baking dish. Bake, covered, for 1 hour, stirring occasionally. Yield: 6 servings.

ORANGE AND GINGER CARROTS

8 medium carrots	¹/4 teaspoon each ginger and salt
¹/4 cup orange juice	1 tablespoon butter
1 teaspoon cornstarch	
1 tablespoon sugar	

Peel carrots and slice diagonally 1 inch thick. Cook in small amount of water in saucepan for 10 to 15 minutes or until tender; drain. Combine next 5 ingredients in small bowl; mix well. Pour over carrots. Cook over low heat for 3 minutes. Add butter; mix gently. Yield: 6 servings.

COMBINATION SALAD

1 tomato, cut into thin wedges	¹/2 cup chopped celery
4 or 5 mushrooms, sliced	¹/2 cucumber, sliced
¹/2 head lettuce, torn	Bleu Cheese Dressing Deluxe
1 carrot, shredded	

Reserve several tomato wedges and mushroom slices for top of salad. Combine remaining vegetables in salad bowl. Add salad dressing; toss to mix well. Top with reserved vegetables. Yield: 6 servings.

BLEU CHEESE DRESSING DELUXE

1 cup mayonnaise	1 tablespoon lemon juice
¹/2 cup sour cream	1 clove of garlic, minced
¹/4 cup wine vinegar	2 ounces bleu cheese
1 tablespoon anchovy paste	

Combine first 6 ingredients in medium bowl; mix well. Crumble in bleu cheese; mix lightly. Chill, covered, for 1 hour or longer. Yield: 6 servings.

PIÑA COLADA CAKE

1 2-layer package yellow cake mix	1 cup coconut
1 20-ounce can crushed pineapple, drained	8 ounces whipped topping
1 cup sugar	Nuts
1 small package French vanilla instant pudding mix	

Prepare and bake cake mix using package directions. Pierce holes in cake with fork. Heat pineapple and sugar in saucepan just until sugar melts. Pour over cake. Chill in refrigerator. Prepare pudding mix using package directions. Spread over cake; sprinkle with coconut. Top with layer of whipped topping; sprinkle with nuts. Chill until serving time. Yield: 12 servings.

Thank You Cookout

Grilled Chicken with Mustard Sauce
Grilled Corn on the Cob
Grilled Peppers
Oven-Roasted New Potatoes
Snickerdoodles

See index for similar recipes.

We prepared this meal to thank good friends who helped us move. We still remember that happy time with good friends in our first home. The grilled corn was basted with a mixture of ½ cup melted butter, the juice of 1 lime and cayenne pepper. Green, red and yellow bell peppers were grilled with a drizzle of olive oil.

Susan Senser, Mu Eta
San Antonio, Texas

GRILLED CHICKEN WITH MUSTARD SAUCE

1 chicken, cut up	*¼ cup honey*
¼ cup olive oil	*3 tablespoons*
½ cup vegetable oil	*Champagne*
½ cup Dijon mustard	
¼ cup whole grain mustard	

Rinse chicken and pat dry. Combine with remaining ingredients in bowl; mix well. Marinate in refrigerator for 8 hours. Drain, reserving marinade. Grill chicken until cooked through, basting with reserved marinade. Yield: 4 servings.

SNICKERDOODLES

1 cup shortening	*2 teaspoons cream of tartar*
1½ cups sugar	*2 eggs*
2¾ cups all-purpose flour	*2 tablespoons sugar*
1 teaspoon baking soda	*2 teaspoons cinnamon*

Preheat oven to 400 degrees. Cream shortening and 1½ cups sugar in mixer bowl until light and fluffy. Add dry ingredients and eggs; mix well. Shape into balls. Coat with mixture of 2 tablespoons sugar and cinnamon; place on cookie sheet. Bake for 8 minutes. Cool on cookie sheet for several minutes. Remove to wire rack to cool completely. Yield: 4 dozen.

Clean Kitchen Favor

Barbecued Spareribs
Corn on the Cob — Potato Salad
Strawberry Shortcake
Tea — Coffee

See index for similar recipes.

When we were stationed at Schofield Barracks in Hawaii, we were in the process of clearing quarters in government housing. We had cleaned all day getting ready for the dreaded inspection and my stove was spotless and my refrigerator bare. Military families take care of each other, so a dear friend asked us over to share this meal. We have served the combination many times in the years since then.

Marilyn Dixon, Xi Alpha Lambda
Warner Robins, Georgia

BARBECUED SPARERIBS

1½ cups catsup	*1 tablespoon sugar*
¼ cup minced instant onion	*3 tablespoons water*
3 tablespoons Worcestershire sauce	*2 pounds spareribs*

Combine first 5 ingredients in medium bowl; mix well. Let stand for 30 minutes. Cut ribs into serving portions. Grill until nearly done. Brush with sauce. Cook until done to taste. Yield: 4 servings.

POTATO SALAD

6 medium potatoes	*1 cup chopped dill pickles*
3 tablespoons celery seed	*2 cups mayonnaise*
3 tablespoons dillweed	*1½ tablespoons mustard*
1 teaspoon salt	*1 tablespoon sugar*
¼ cup minced instant onion	

Cook potatoes in jackets in water to cover in saucepan until tender; drain. Peel and chop potatoes. Combine with celery seed, dillweed, salt, onion and pickles in medium bowl; mix well. Add mixture of mayonnaise, mustard and sugar; mix gently. Yield: 4 to 8 servings.

Saturday Barbecue

Shish Kabob
Tossed Salad
To-Die-For Cheesecake
Fruit Fizz

See index for similar recipes.

We host barbecue suppers for the young men in my husband's office to celebrate a successful fishing trip or just to relax on a Saturday afternoon. Our patio is comfortable and this is a relaxed way to serve a do-it-yourself meal where all that is needed are trays of prepared fixings and hot coals. We marinate the meat for the kabobs overnight and skewer them with onion, green peppers, mushroom caps, cherry tomatoes, zucchini cubes and hard cheeses and grill them. The Fruit Fizz is a blended mixture of fresh fruit such as strawberries, lemon juice and seltzer.

Marsha Korkowski, Xi Alpha Epsilon
Easton, Pennsylvania

TO-DIE-FOR CHEESECAKE

24 ounces cream cheese, softened	*5 eggs*
1 cup sugar	*1 tablespoon lemon juice*
1 tablespoon vanilla extract	*1 square German's sweet chocolate, melted*

Preheat oven to 350 degrees. Beat cream cheese with sugar and vanilla in medium bowl until light. Beat in eggs 1 at a time. Reserve 1/3 cup mixture. Add lemon juice to remaining mixture; spoon into buttered 10-inch springform pan. Stir chocolate into reserved mixture. Drizzle chocolate mixture over top; swirl with knife. Bake for 40 to 45 minutes or until center begins to crack. Cool on wire rack. Chill until serving time. Place on serving plate; remove side of pan. Yield: 12 servings.

Sue Nelson, Xi Zeta Omicron, Fresno, California, makes Chicken Kabobs by combining 2 cups vegetable oil, 1 cup lemon juice, 1/2 cup chopped parsley, 1 thinly sliced onion and garlic salt and pepper to taste in a large bowl. Add 2 pounds boneless chicken cut into 1-inch cubes; mix well. Refrigerate overnight. Thread chicken on skewers. Grill over medium hot coals for 15 minutes or until done.

Suburban Pig-Picking

Barbecued Pork Loin
Collard Greens with Ham Hocks
Potato Salad — Coleslaw
Corn Bread — Iced Tea

See index for similar recipes.

We call this meal a suburban pig-picking because it is country cooking done on a dual-burner gas grill in town. Preheat 1 burner to 400 degrees and leave the remaining burner unlit to cook pork and greens together.

Sandra W. Parrish, Xi Beta Xi
Dublin, Georgia

BARBECUED PORK LOIN

1 4- to 5-pound pork loin or Boston butt	*2 tablespoons mustard*
1 cup vinegar	*1/2 tablespoon crushed red pepper, or to taste*
1/4 cup catsup	

Preheat 1 gas burner to 400 degrees; leave remaining burner unlit. Place pork over unlit burner. Grill for 1 hour per pound or until done to taste. Slice or chop pork as desired, discarding fat. Combine remaining ingredients in medium bowl; mix well. Serve with or over pork. Yield: 6 to 8 servings.

COLLARD GREENS WITH HAM HOCKS

Collard greens	*Ham hocks*

Wash greens well, discarding stems. Place large saucepan half full of water on gas grill preheated to 400 degrees. Bring to a boil; add greens and ham hocks. Cook for 1 hour to 1 1/2 hours or until done to taste, stirring frequently. Drain and chop greens. Yield: variable.

SUMMERTIME RUM SNO-BALLS

1 large can pineapple juice	*1 cup lemon juice*
1 quart orange juice	*1 cup grenadine*
	1 fifth of rum

Combine all ingredients in large plastic container; mix well. Cover; place in freezer overnight. Remove from freezer. Chop and stir mixture with large spoon until broken up. Cover; return to freezer. This will remain in a slushy state. Yield: 20 to 30 servings.

Page D. Meyer, Xi Alpha Delta
River Ridge, Louisiana

BOURBON SLUSH

This has been enjoyed at several sorority functions.

2 tea bags
1 cup boiling water
1 cup sugar
6 ounces frozen
  orange juice

12 ounces frozen
  lemonade
1 to 2 cups Southern
  Comfort bourbon
7 cups water

Steep tea bags in boiling water; discard bags. Dissolve sugar in tea. Combine with remaining ingredients in large container; mix well. Freeze to soft slush. Yield: 10 to 12 servings.

*Gwendolyn S. Crouse, Beta Sigma
Mt. Home AFB, Idaho*

MISSISSIPPI CAVIAR

This is a great Southwest recipe. It is different.

3 jalapeño peppers
3 cans black-eyed peas,
  drained, rinsed
1 onion, chopped

1 large jar pimentos
1 15-ounce jar Italian
  salad dressing
Chili and Lime Doritos

Chop jalapeño peppers using seeds from one. Combine peppers and next 4 ingredients in bowl; toss to mix. Refrigerate for 12 hours; serve with Doritos. Yield: 12 servings.

*Kelly R. Krause, Alpha Beta Rho
Windsor, Missouri*

TEXAS CAVIAR

2 14-ounce cans
  black-eyed peas,
  drained
1 can Shoe Peg corn,
  drained
2 medium tomatoes,
  chopped
4 green onions,
  chopped
1/2 cup parsley, chopped

2 cloves of garlic,
  minced
1 medium-sized green
  pepper, chopped
1 jalapeño pepper,
  chopped
1/2 cup onion, chopped
1 8-ounce bottle of
  Italian salad dressing
Tortilla chips

Combine first 9 ingredients in large bowl; mix well. Pour salad dressing over mixture; toss to mix. Refrigerate, covered, for at least 2 hours; drain. Serve with tortilla chips. Yield: 12 servings.

*Beverly Musil, Alpha Chi Psi
China Spring, Texas*

LOW-CALORIE GOOD TASTIN' DIP

4 ripe tomatoes, finely
  chopped
4 green onions with
  stems, chopped
1 small can chopped
  ripe olives
1 small can chopped
  green chilies

1 tablespoon olive oil
1 tablespoon vinegar
2 teaspoons garlic salt
2 teaspoons seasoned
  salt

Combine all ingredients; toss to mix. Refrigerate, covered, for at least 4 hours or overnight. May serve with tortilla chips, potato chips, green peppers, carrots or celery sticks if desired.

*Jeanice Holland, Alpha Phi
Roswell, New Mexico*

CLARABELLE'S PÂTÉ

I gave a friend some "Texas Pâté" from Nieman Marcus for Christmas. I wanted the flavor, not the price.

2 15-ounce cans black
  beans, drained
2 cups canned peeled
  tomatoes
1 teaspoon cumin
1 teaspoon chili powder

1 teaspoon garlic
  powder
1 teaspoon onion
  powder
1/2 teaspoon salt
8 ounces green chilies

Combine all ingredients in bowl. Place half the mixture in blender container; purée until smooth. Repeat process. Combine mixtures in bowl, stirring well. May serve with tortilla chips or saltines if desired. Yield: 7 cups.

*Clare Gaia, Epsilon Chi
Kingman, Arizona*

MICHELLE'S SALSA AND HOMEMADE CHIPS

This was a staple at our house while growing up and has been refined over the years. It makes me feel like I'm at home again whenever I eat this!

1 large can stewed
  tomatoes
1 small can tomato
  sauce
2 or 3 fresh tomatoes,
  diced
2 large onions, diced
1 large green pepper,
  diced
1 large red pepper, diced

2 stalks celery, chopped
4 or 5 green chili
  peppers, diced
Jalapeño peppers
  to taste
Hot red peppers to taste
1 package flour tortillas
Butter (optional)
Salt (optional)

Preheat oven to 275 degrees. Combine first 10 ingredients in large bowl; mix well. Place in airtight containers or covered glass jars. The longer it stands the more potent and better it becomes. Cut tortillas into quarters. Place on baking stone or cookie sheet. Brush with butter and salt. Bake for 15 minutes or until golden brown and crisp. Store in airtight container or serve hot with salsa.

*Michelle Jensen, Tau Pi
Sterling, Illinois*

Billie Brown, Preceptor Alpha Chi, Kendallville, Indiana, makes Beef Jerkie by sprinkling thin slices of roast beef with liquid smoke and marinating in refrigerator overnight. Thread on toothpicks and hang on rack. Bake in preheated 200-degree oven overnight with cookie sheet underneath.

ZESTY BRUSSELS SPROUTS

I serve this as an appetizer but a sorority sister serves it as snacks, salad or quick side dish.

2 10-ounce bags frozen Brussels sprouts	5 tablespoons hot horseradish
1¹/2 cups sugar	Salt to taste
1 cup cider vinegar	2 teaspoons dry mustard

Cook Brussels sprouts according to package directions; drain. Combine remaining ingredients in large bowl; mix well. Add Brussels sprouts; toss lightly until well mixed. Refrigerate at least 6 hours or overnight. Yield: 6 servings.

Phyllis Carver, Laureate Beta Eta
Lakeland, Florida

MAKEOVER PINWHEELS

This is my favorite treat to take to work at the hospital. A patient and 3 nurses called for the recipe in one day.

16 ounces cream cheese, softened	1 large can diced olives
8 ounces shredded Cheddar cheese	1 small jar diced pimentos
2 envelopes ranch dressing mix	1 small bunch green onions, diced
1 small can diced jalapeño peppers	1 green bell pepper, diced
	12 large tortillas

Combine first 8 ingredients in bowl; mix well. Spread mixture on each tortilla. Roll up tightly to enclose filling. Slice into ¹/2-inch rolls. Yield: 10 to 12 dozen.

JoDee Huck, Beta Omega
Gering, Nebraska

MEXICAN PINWHEELS

8 ounces cream cheese, softened	3 green onions, finely chopped
1 4-ounce can deviled ham	1 4-ounce can diced green chilies
1 2-ounce can chopped black olives	6 8-inch flour tortillas

Combine first 5 ingredients; mix well. Spread evenly on each tortilla. Roll up securely to enclose filling; wrap in plastic wrap. Refrigerate overnight. Slice into ³/4-inch rolls. May be frozen and thawed when ready to slice and serve if desired. Yield: 48 pieces.

Elaine Martin, Preceptor Alpha
Missoula, Montana

HOT TEXAS BITES

4 large boneless chicken breasts, skinned	12 slices bacon Pepper to taste Fajita seasoning to taste
1 small jar jalapeño peppers, sliced	

Cut each chicken breast into approximately six 1-inch strips. Place 1 or 2 jalapeño slices on end of each strip. Roll up. Wrap ¹/2 slice bacon around chicken; secure with toothpick. Season moderately with pepper and fajita seasoning. Cook over medium coals for approximately 10 to 15 minutes or until done, turning once. Can be frozen and reheated. Yield: 24 appetizers.

Beth Clements, Alpha Chi Psi
China Spring, Texas

STROMBOLI

This is a great dish for tailgate parties or picnics!

1 loaf frozen bread dough, thawed	¹/2 pound mozzarella cheese, shredded
2 eggs, separated	2 to 3 thin slices boiled ham
1 tablespoon Parmesan cheese	¹/2 cup hot pepper rings
1 teaspoon parsley	1 can mushrooms, drained, chopped
¹/2 teaspoon garlic powder	Green bell pepper (optional)
1 teaspoon oregano	Black olive slices (optional)
¹/4 teaspoon pepper	1 jar pizza sauce
2 tablespoons olive oil	
¹/2 pound pepperoni, sliced	

Preheat oven to 350 degrees. Roll out dough on cookie sheet. Combine egg yolks and next 6 ingredients in bowl; mix well. Spread over dough. Layer next 7 ingredients on dough. Roll up jelly-roll fashion to enclose filling. Place seam down on cookie sheet. Brush with egg white. Bake for 30 to 40 minutes or until browned. Slice; serve with heated pizza sauce for dipping. Yield: 4 servings.

Carol Shuck, Xi Lambda Lambda
Canton, Ohio

CRAB CROSTINI

8 ounces lump crab meat	1 tablespoon Dijon-style mustard
¹/2 cup diced red bell pepper	2 teaspoons grated Parmesan cheese
2 tablespoons plus 2 teaspoons mayonnaise	4 to 5 drops of hot pepper sauce
2 tablespoons chopped parsley	4 ounces Italian bread, cut into 16 slices
1 tablespoon chopped chives	
1 tablespoon fresh lime juice	

Preheat broiler. Line broiler pan with foil. Combine first 9 ingredients in bowl; blend well. Spread 1 tablespoon crab mixture on each bread slice. Place on broiler pan; broil 4 inches from heat for 5 to 6 minutes or until lightly browned. Yield: 8 servings.

Marjorie Wentz, Laureate Gamma
Great Falls, Montana

CHICK 'N' DIP

3/4 cup Dijon-style mustard	4 chicken breasts, skinned, boned, cut into 1-inch chunks
2 tablespoons honey	
1/2 teaspoon cayenne pepper	
1/4 teaspoon garlic salt	3/4 cup crushed salted pretzels

Preheat oven to 400 degrees. Combine first 4 ingredients in bowl. Reserve half the mixture. Dip chicken into remaining mustard mixture; roll in pretzels to coat well. Place on large cookie sheet. Bake for 10 minutes or until tender. Serve with reserved mustard mixture for dipping. Yield: 4 servings.

Tracy Adams, Mu Omega
Tahlequah, Oklahoma

BUFFALO WINGS

2 1/2 pounds chicken wings	1/2 cup butter or margarine, melted
1/4 cup cayenne pepper sauce	

Preheat oven to 400 degrees. Split wings at joints; place on 9-by-13-inch baking pan. Bake for 1 hour or until brown and crispy, turning once. Combine pepper sauce and butter in bowl. Place several wings in bowl at a time; coat completely. May serve with celery and bleu cheese dip if desired. Yield: 24 wings.

Bonnie Fralick, Alpha Epsilon
Minnetonka, Minnesota

SWEET AND SOUR WINGS

2 1/2 to 3 pounds chicken wings	3/4 cup soy sauce
	1 teaspoon dry mustard
3/4 cup packed light brown sugar	4 to 5 teaspoons crushed garlic cloves

Rinse wings; pat dry. Place in large bowl. Combine remaining ingredients; pour over wings. Refrigerate, covered, for 24 hours. Preheat oven to 325 degrees. Place wings in 9-by-13-inch baking pan. Bake for 1 1/2 hours or until done, turning once. May be cooked on barbecue grill if desired. Yield: 6 servings.

Christine Olah, Iota
Shelburne, Vermont

BLESSED DEVILED EGGS

Our family members tell me these are a must at our reunion each year, and my sorority knows these are the only things I can cook.

8 eggs, 1 week old	7 tablespoons mayonnaise-type salad dressing
3 dashes of salt	
3 dashes of pepper	
3 drops of mustard	Paprika

Place eggs in saucepan; cover with water. Let stand for 3 hours. Sprinkle salt in water, 3 shakes (Father, Son and Holy Spirit). Bring to a boil; boil for 10 minutes on High. Remove from heat. Place eggs in cold water, changing water until cool. Let stand at room temperature for 1 1/2 hours. Peel eggs; cut in half. Remove yolks; place in mixing bowl. Set whites aside. Mash yolks with fork; sprinkle with salt and pepper in 3 shakes, repeating phrase. Add mustard, repeating phrase. Add mayonnaise-type dressing (Father, Son and Holy Spirit Praise the Lord Amen); blend well. Fill whites with yolk mixture. Sprinkle lightly with paprika. Yield: 16 servings.

Patty Anton, Laureate Alpha Rho
St. Petersburg, Florida

PENNSYLVANIA DUTCH PICKLED EGGS AND RED BEETS

No family picnic in this area would be complete without these beautiful red pickled eggs.

1 pound fresh red beets	3 or 4 whole cloves
1/2 cup vinegar	1/2 cup water
1/2 teaspoon salt	Small piece of stick cinnamon
1/4 cup packed light brown sugar	6 hard-cooked eggs

Wash beets; remove leaves and stems, leaving about 1 inch root end. Place in saucepan; cover with water. Cook until tender; drain. Remove skin. Combine next 6 ingredients in saucepan; boil for 10 minutes. Place beets in vinegar mixture; refrigerate for several days. Add eggs; let stand for 2 more days. Yield: 6 servings.

Dottie Flinchbaugh, Laureate Kappa
York, Pennsylvania

GREEN CHILI WON TONS WITH GUACAMOLE DIP

This is a family favorite for get-togethers. The women make won tons in the kitchen while the men barbecue outside.

Vegetable oil for deep-frying	1 package won ton wrappers
1 pound shredded Monterey Jack cheese	All-purpose flour
	Guacamole Dip
1 3-ounce can chopped green chilies	

Preheat oil in deep-fryer. Combine cheese and green chilies in bowl; mix well. Place 1 teaspoonful mixture in center of each wrapper. Fold opposite corners over filling to middle. Wet finger with water; dab corners to seal. Repeat for remaining corners. Roll each won ton in flour. Drop into hot oil; cook for 30 seconds or until golden brown. Remove with slotted spoon; drain on paper towels. Serve with guacamole dip. Yield: 4 to 6 servings.

Jayme Kreitman, Psi Upsilon
Apopka, Florida

MARINATED HOT DOGS

This is a favorite hors d'oeuvres at Beta Sigma Phi socials.

1 cup catsup
1 cup bourbon
1/2 cup packed light
  brown sugar
1 tablespoon chopped
  onion
2 teaspoons
  Worcestershire
  sauce

1/8 teaspoon Tabasco
  sauce
2 packages mini hot
  dogs or 2 pounds
  hot dogs, cut up

Combine all ingredients in Crock•Pot. Set temperature on High until mixture is hot; reduce temperature to Medium. The longer they cook, the better they are. May cook overnight with temperature on Low if desired. Yield: 10 to 20 servings.

Beth Marconi, Xi Eta Nu
Norristown, Pennsylvania

❖ BREAKFAST TAKEALONGS

2/3 cup butter
  or margarine
2/3 cup sugar
1 egg
1 teaspoon vanilla
  extract
3/4 cup all-purpose
  flour
1/2 teaspoon salt

1/2 teaspoon baking
  soda
1 1/2 cups oatmeal
1 cup shredded Cheddar
  cheese
1/2 cup nuts or wheat
  germ
6 crisp-fried bacon
  slices, crumbled

Preheat oven to 350 degrees. Cream butter and sugar in mixer bowl. Add egg and vanilla; beat until well blended. Add flour, baking soda and salt; mix well. Stir in remaining ingredients. Drop by rounded tablespoonfuls onto greased cookie sheet. Bake for 12 to 14 minutes or until done. Cool on cookie sheet 1 minute before placing on wire rack. Store loosely in airtight container. Yield: 3 dozen.

Gloria Martin, Xi Alpha Zeta
Madison Heights, Michigan

CHEERIO BARS

1/2 cup honey
1/3 cup plus 2
  tablespoons sugar
1/2 cup margarine

1/3 cup plus 2
  tablespoons butter
1 cup marshmallows
8 cups Cheerios

Combine honey and sugar in saucepan; heat, stirring, until sugar is dissolved. Reduce heat; add next 3 ingredients, stirring until marshmallows melt. Remove from heat; stir in Cheerios. Press into buttered 9-by-13-inch pan. Let cool; cut into squares. Yield: 18 servings.

Norma Bullerman, Beta Delta
Calmar, Iowa

GOOBER-BACON SANDWICH

Peanut butter
2 slices bread, plain or
  toasted
2 slices crisp-fried
  bacon, crumbled

6 sweet pickle slices or
  sweet relish
Mayonnaise

Spread peanut butter generously on 1 slice bread. Sprinkle with bacon. Place pickles evenly over bacon. Spread mayonnaise on remaining bread slice. Place on top. Serve hot or cold. Yield: 1 sandwich.

Laura Hulburd, Alpha Theta
Corvallis, Oregon

CHEESE STICKS

My kids love these for sack lunch snacks.

1 cup butter or
  margarine
2 cups all-purpose flour
2 cups Rice Krispies

2 cups sharp Cheddar
  cheese
Tabasco sauce to taste

Preheat oven to 375 degrees. Spray cookie sheet with nonstick cooking spray. Combine butter and flour in bowl; mix well with fork. Add Rice Krispies, cheese and Tabasco; mix well. Shape into sticks; place on cookie sheet. Bake for 15 to 18 minutes or until lightly browned. Cool on cookie sheet a few minutes to avoid breaking. Freezes well for up to 3 months. Yield: 6 to 7 dozen.

Claudia M. Long, Kappa Kappa
Meriden, Kansas

ORIENTAL CASHEW CRUNCH

This is a great recipe for Superbowl Sunday in January.

1 16-ounce package
  Original Quaker Oat
  Squares cereal
1 3-ounce can chow
  mein noodles
1 cup cashews

1/3 cup vegetable oil
3 tablespoons soy sauce
1 teaspoon garlic
  powder
1 teaspoon onion
  powder

Preheat oven to 250 degrees. Combine cereal, noodles and cashews in 9-by-13-inch baking pan; set aside. Combine remaining ingredients in small bowl; pour quickly over cereal mixture. Stir to coat evenly. Bake for 1 hour, stirring every 20 minutes. Let cool. Store in airtight container. Yield: 10 cups.

Roxanna Privratsky, Alpha Sigma
Devils Lake, North Dakota

CAPE MAY CRACKERS

1/2 cup vegetable oil
1 package ranch-style
  dressing mix
1/2 teaspoon lemon-
  pepper

Parmesan cheese
1 box oyster crackers
Old Bay seasoning
  and red pepper

Pour oil in bowl. Add next 3 ingredients; mix well. Add crackers; stir occasionally for 5 to 6 hours. Add seasoning to taste. Store in tightly sealed container. May use wheat thins for variety if desired. Yield: 12 servings.

Elizabeth Bennett, Laureate Alpha Epsilon
Newport News, Virginia

CRISPIX MIX

This snack takes about 15 minutes to make. It is really delicious.

1 cup packed light
  brown sugar
1/2 cup light corn
  syrup
1/2 cup margarine
1 teaspoon baking
  soda

1 teaspoon vanilla
  extract
1 12-ounce box Crispix
  cereal
1 12-ounce jar dry
  roasted peanuts

Combine sugar, corn syrup and margarine in large glass bowl. Microwave for 6 to 8 minutes or until bubbly, stirring once. Add baking soda and vanilla; mix well. Place cereal and peanuts in large glass bowl. Pour syrup mixture over cereal and peanuts. Microwave for 1 1/2 minutes. Pour onto large cookie sheet. Let cool; break apart. Yield: 12 servings.

Jeanette A. Tims, Xi Gamma Alpha
Norfolk, Nebraska
*Betty Faggard, Laureate Delta Xi
High Island, Texas

NO-BAKE PARTY MIX

1 package ranch-style
  dressing mix
1 tablespoon
  lemon-pepper
1 tablespoon dillweed

5 packages small
  crackers
Pecans to taste
Peanuts to taste
1 cup vegetable oil

Combine first 6 ingredients in paper sack. Add oil. Shake vigorously. Pour into airtight containers; cover tightly. Let stand for 1 hour before serving. May substitute pretzels, Cheez-ets, oyster crackers and Chex cereals for crackers if desired. Yield: 1 gallon.

Michele Levo, Kappa Mu
Miami, Oklahoma

CRISPIX CEREAL CANDY

4 1/2 cups Crispix cereal
1 cup peanuts (optional)
6 squares almond bark

1 tablespoon (heaping)
  peanut butter

Combine cereal and peanuts in large bowl; mix well. Combine almond bark and peanut butter in double boiler. Cook over low heat until melted, stirring until smooth. Pour over cereal; toss together. Drop by spoonfuls onto waxed paper. Yield: 5 cups candy.

Brenda Keys, Beta Omicron
Winslow, Indiana

PARTY SNACK

This is good year-round for lunches but mostly at Christmas time for snacks.

2 cups Corn Chex
2 cups Rice Chex
2 cups Wheat Chex
1 cup Cheerios
1 cup croutons
1/4 cup margarine,
  melted
1 1/4 teaspoons
  seasoned salt

4 1/2 teaspoons
  Worcestershire sauce
1 cup round or stick
  pretzels
1 cup dry roasted
  peanuts

Preheat oven to 250 degrees. Combine cereals and croutons in large bowl; mix well. Combine margarine and seasonings in small bowl. Pour over cereal and croutons. Add pretzels and peanuts; coat evenly. Spread onto cookie sheet. Bake for 1 hour, stirring every 15 minutes. Let cool; store in airtight container. Yield: 10 cups snack mix.

Carol Knuth, Xi Alpha Rho
Grand Island, Nebraska

GRANOLA BARS

This is a wonderful munchie for kids and grown-ups.

1 1/4 cups packed light
  brown sugar
3/4 cup margarine or
  butter
4 cups quick oats
3/4 cup snipped pitted
  prunes

1/2 cup sliced
  unblanched almonds
1/2 cup coarsely chopped
  pecans
1 tablespoon ground
  cinnamon

Preheat oven to 350 degrees. Combine sugar and margarine in 9-by-13-inch baking pan. Bake for 5 minutes or until melted, stirring occasionally; mix well. Add remaining ingredients, stirring until well blended. Press firmly with fingertips into an even layer. Bake for 30 to 35 minutes or until golden brown. Cool in pan on rack for 15 minutes. Cut into 3-by-5-inch bars. Let cool completely. Remove from pan. Yield: 36 bars.

Marie L. Eschels, Preceptor Tau
Cocoa Beach, Florida

QUICK ENERGY GORP

1/2 cup raisins
1/2 cup cashews
1/2 cup "M & M's"
  Plain Chocolate
  Candy
1 cup granola

1/2 cup cut-up dried
  apricots
1/2 cup sunflower seeds
1/2 cup cut-up dried
  apples

Combine all ingredients in large bowl; mix well. Pour into several plastic bags. Seal with twisters. Yield: 4 cups.

Joan Bowers, Preceptor Mu
Las Vegas, Nevada

GORP

We used this recipe for a trail mix at church camp where I served as a staff and board member. It makes a great topping for ice cream.

10 tablespoons plus 2 teaspoons butter or margarine	6 cups oats
1 cup packed light brown sugar	1 package "M & M's" Plain Chocolate Candy
1/3 cup honey	3/4 cup raisins
1 egg	3/4 cup peanuts
1 teaspoon vanilla extract	

Preheat oven to 350 degrees. Combine butter, brown sugar and honey in mixer bowl; beat until light and fluffy. Blend in egg and vanilla. Add oats; mix well. Pour into 9-by-13-inch baking pan; spread evenly. Bake for 30 minutes, stirring every 10 minutes. Let cool for 1 hour; break into small chunks. Combine chunks, "M&M's," raisins and peanuts in large bowl; mix well. Store, covered, in refrigerator. May use colored "M&M's" Plain Chocolate Candy to correlate with seasons if desired. Yield: 10 cups.

Norma Borgmann, Preceptor Delta
Patoka, Illinois

QUICK ENERGY BALLS

1 cup confectioners' sugar	1 cup mini chocolate chips
1 cup peanut butter	4 tablespoons water
1/2 cup dry nonfat milk	Graham cracker crumbs, crushed

Combine first 5 ingredients in bowl; mix well. Shape into balls. Roll in crushed crumbs.
Yield: 2 to 3 dozen balls.

Kathleen Radcliffe, Laureate Beta
Lancaster, Pennsylvania

CHINESE FRIED PECANS

6 cups water	Vegetable oil for frying
4 cups pecans	Salt
1/2 cup sugar	

Pour 6 cups water in 3-quart saucepan; bring to a boil. Add pecans; bring to a boil. Cook for 1 minute. Rinse pecans under hot water; drain. Place sugar in large bowl. Add warm pecans; toss until evenly coated. Pour 1 to 2 inches oil into skillet. Add half pecans using slotted spoon. Fry for 5 minutes or until golden, stirring constantly. Drain in sieve over bowl. Let cool on waxed paper in single layer. Sprinkle with salt. Repeat for remaining pecans. Store in airtight container. Yield: 4 cups pecans.

Isabel O'Connell, Xi Beta Xi
Ocala, Florida

SNACK NUTS

4 1/2 cups shelled raw peanuts	1/2 teaspoon salt
2 cups sugar	1 cup water
	1 tablespoon coarse salt

Preheat oven to 300 degrees. Place peanuts, sugar, 1/2 teaspoon salt and water in large heavy saucepan. Bring to a boil; boil for 30 to 35 minutes or until all liquid is absorbed. Spread peanuts on greased 10-by-15-inch baking pan. Sprinkle with 1/2 tablespoon coarse salt; bake for 20 minutes. Stir; sprinkle with remaining 1/2 tablespoon coarse salt. Bake for 20 minutes longer. Let cool completely. Store in airtight container. Yield: 18 servings.

Vickie Thomas, Preceptor Tau
Weiser, Idaho

SUGARED PEANUTS

I like to triple this recipe and put it in holiday tins for teacher gifts, bake sales and last minute gifts.

12 ounces raw peanuts	1 cup sugar
1/2 cup water	

Preheat oven to 300 degrees. Place peanuts in large skillet. Add water and sugar; mix well. Cook on medium-high heat, stirring constantly, until all liquid is absorbed. Spread onto greased 9-by-13-inch baking pan. Bake for 15 minutes; stir. Bake for 15 minutes longer. Let cool completely; store in airtight container. Yield: 2 cups peanuts.

Becky J. Antes, Xi Beta Lambda
Syracuse, Nebraska

WHITE TRASH

I made this for a Florida State Seminoles vs. Florida Gators football game tailgate party. We won the game and the "White Trash" was great.

1 18-ounce box Golden Graham cereal	2 cups creamy peanut butter
1 15-ounce box golden raisins	1 teaspoon vanilla extract
3 cups roasted peanuts, mixed nuts or pecans	1 1-pound box confectioners' sugar
1/2 cup margarine	
12 ounces chocolate morsels	

Combine cereal, raisins and peanuts in large container; mix well. Combine margarine, chocolate morsels and peanut butter in saucepan. Heat until melted, stirring constantly. Do not boil. Add vanilla; let cool. Pour over cereal mix; mix until well coated. Pour into large brown paper bag. Add confectioners' sugar; shake. Store in tightly covered containers. Yield: 12 cups candy.

Betty Futch, Preceptor Chi
Tallahassee, Florida

ENERGY BARS

I like to take these on long walks as they are easy to carry and an excellent source of energy. Calories yes, but very little fat.

2 cups quick-cooking oats	1/4 cup honey
3 tablespoons margarine	1 cup raisins
3 cups miniature marshmallows	1 cup nuts or sunflower seeds (optional)
1/2 cup chunky peanut butter	1/2 cup chocolate chips (optional)

Preheat oven to 350 degrees. Place oats on 9-by-13-inch baking pan. Bake for 15 minutes or until golden. Combine margarine, marshmallows, peanut butter and honey in saucepan; cook over low heat until melted, stirring constantly. Remove from heat; stir in oats, raisins and nuts. Pour into 9-inch square pan lined with aluminum foil and greased; spread evenly. Place chocolate chips on top; press down. Chill until firm. Return to room temperature; remove foil and cut into squares. Yield: 16 servings.

*Phoebe Harrison, Theta Master
Albany, Oregon*

POPCORN BALL PERFECTION

I made up this recipe 35 years ago. My son says they are still the best popcorn balls he has tasted.

1 pound light brown sugar	2 teaspoons vanilla extract
1/4 cup butter or margarine	4 gallons popped popcorn
1/2 teaspoon salt	1/2 cup walnut halves
3/4 cup cream or milk	

Combine sugar, butter, salt and cream in saucepan; bring to a boil. Cook to hard-crack stage. Remove from heat; stir in vanilla. Pour over popcorn. Add walnuts; mix well. Shape into balls.
Yield: 5 dozen balls.

*Patricia R. Convath, Alpha Lambda
Cheney, Washington*

POPPYCOCK

2/3 cup sugar	2/3 cup pecans
1/2 cup butter or margarine	1/3 cup almonds
1/4 cup light corn syrup	4 cups popcorn, popped
1/2 teaspoon vanilla extract	

Preheat oven to 300 degrees. Combine first 3 ingredients in 1 1/2-quart heavy saucepan. Cook over medium heat, stirring constantly, until sugar is dissolved and mixture comes to a boil. Continue cooking, stirring occasionally, to soft-crack stage or 290 degrees on candy thermometer. Mixture will have light caramel color. Remove from heat; stir in vanilla. Toast pecans and almonds in oven until almonds are lightly browned. Spread popcorn, pecans and almonds on lightly greased 9-by-13-inch baking pan. Pour hot syrup over top. Toss to coat completely. Let cool; break into chunks. Store in tightly covered container. Yield: 1 pound.

*Velda Kloke, Preceptor Alpha Chi
Harvard, Nebraska*

MOLASSES BALLS

1 1/2 cups light molasses	1 cup toasted unsalted sunflower seeds
1/4 cup salted butter	
2 cups raisins	6 cups popped popcorn

Heat molasses in saucepan over medium heat. Add butter; mix well. Add raisins and sunflower seeds; stir until evenly distributed. Place popcorn in 9-by-13-inch dish. Drizzle mixture over popcorn, mixing until thoroughly coated. Lightly grease hands; shape into balls. Wrap in waxed paper; store in refrigerator. Yield: 6 to 8 servings.

*Daisy Burkhardt, Laureate Sigma
Mountain Home, Idaho*

SOFT CARAMEL CORN

2 1/2 cups packed light brown sugar	1 can sweetened condensed milk
1 cup light corn syrup	2 large bowls popped popcorn
2 cups butter or margarine	

Combine brown sugar, corn syrup and butter in saucepan; bring to a boil. Cook to firm-ball stage. Add condensed milk; mix well. Pour over popcorn; mix until coated. Yield: 36 servings.

*Helen Cutler
Challis, Idaho*

PAGODA FRUIT SALAD

1 8-ounce can pear halves	1 5-ounce jar bleu cheese spread
1 8-ounce can peach slices	1 head lettuce
1 8-ounce can figs	1/2 cup mayonnaise
1 8-ounce can cherries	1/4 cup honey

Drain fruits, reserving 2 teaspoons syrup; chill. Shape cheese spread into small balls; chill. Line serving plate with lettuce leaves, building up center slightly. Place 4 pear halves around center. Fill pears with cheese balls. Thread kabob stick with 2 peach slices, fig and cherry. Stick kabob into pear half. Repeat for 3 more kabobs. Place remaining fruit around edge. Combine mayonnaise, honey and reserved syrup in small serving bowl; blend well. Serve separately. Yield: 8 servings.

*Colleen Romano, Xi Gamma Delta
Delta, British Columbia, Canada*

BEAUTIFUL FRUIT SALAD

2 cans fruit cocktail	Pineapple chunks
1 1/2 cups sugar	Fresh strawberries or
1/4 cup cornstarch	frozen whole
Banana slices	strawberries

Drain fruit cocktail, reserving juice. Combine sugar, cornstarch and reserved juice in saucepan; mix well. Cook until thickened; let cool. Glaze will be clear. Add remaining ingredients; mix gently.
Yield: 6 to 8 servings.

Kim Erwin, Xi Lambda Tau
Urich, Missouri

WALKING SALAD

I ate these on hikes while a camp counselor. They were great! I've made them for my own family.

1 large red delicious apple	1/2 tablespoon raisins
2 tablespoons (heaping) peanut butter	1/2 tablespoon chopped celery
	1 teaspoon chopped nuts

Core apple, keeping bottom intact. Combine remaining ingredients in small bowl. Fill apple with mixture. Wrap in foil or plastic wrap. Refrigerate until ready to pack or eat. Yield: 1 serving.

Valerie Jones, Preceptor Xi
Aurora, Nebraska

BANANA-NUT SALAD

4 medium bananas, sliced	3/4 to 1 cup coarsely crushed lightly salted peanuts
4 to 5 ounces coleslaw salad dressing	

Place 1/4 banana slices into 2-quart salad bowl. Drizzle 1/4 salad dressing over bananas. Sprinkle with 1/4 peanuts. Repeat layers, ending with peanuts. Chill for 2 to 2 1/2 hours before serving.
Yield: 4 to 6 servings.

Barbara Beeson, Laureate Epsilon Epsilon
Amarillo, Texas

TURNIP-HORSERADISH SALAD

1 gallon ice water	1 1/2 cups white vinegar
1 gallon turnips, washed, peeled, shredded	1 1/2 cups water
	2 tablespoons salt
3 cups sugar	2 tablespoons freshly ground horseradish

Pour ice water over turnips in large pan. Let stand for 30 minutes; drain excess liquid. Combine sugar, vinegar and water in saucepan; heat through. Pour hot sugar mixture over turnips. Add salt and horseradish; mix well. Chill overnight. Yield: 16 servings.

Gertrude Gladish, Beta Omicron
Petersburg, Indiana

ROSE'S TACO SALAD

1 head lettuce, torn into pieces	1 16-ounce can red beans, rinsed, drained
8 ounces shredded mozzarella cheese	3 pounds ground chuck
8 ounces shredded Cheddar cheese	3 packages taco seasoning
8 medium-large tomatoes, diced	2 cups sour cream
1 large red onion, diced	1 16-ounce jar picante sauce
	1 large bag corn chips

Combine lettuce, cheeses, tomatoes, onion and beans in large bowl. Brown ground chuck in skillet; drain. Add seasoning according to package directions. Combine sour cream and picante sauce in medium mixer bowl; blend well. Combine lettuce mixture, ground beef and sauce in 8- to 9-quart bowl when ready to serve. Add chips. Yield: 12 servings.

Rose M. Bloss
St. Catherine, Missouri

COLORED PASTA SALAD

This is perfect for end-of-the-year sorority picnics.

2 pounds colored pasta spirals, uncooked	1/2 can sliced black olives
1/4 pound salami, cubed	1 small bottle of stuffed olives
1/4 pound Colby cheese, cubed	1 small bottle of pepperoncini
1/4 pound provolone cheese, cubed	1 large bottle of Italian salad dressing
1/4 pound cooked ham, cubed	
1/2 pound pepperoni, sliced	

Cook pasta according to package directions; drain and rinse. Combine pasta and next 8 ingredients in large bowl. Add salad dressing; toss to mix. Chill. Yield: 8 to 10 servings.

Carolyn M. Cline, Xi Sigma
Jamestown, New York

MOZZARELLA AND PASTA SALAD

1 8-ounce package macaroni	8 ounces cooked ham, chopped
Parmesan Dressing	1 4-ounce can diced green chilies, drained
10 ounces fresh spinach, torn into pieces	1 cup grated Parmesan cheese
8 ounces mozzarella cheese, cubed	

Cook macaroni according to package directions; drain. Combine macaroni and Parmesan Dressing in large bowl; toss lightly. Add next 4 ingredients; mix well. Cover; chill. Sprinkle 2 tablespoons Parmesan cheese over each serving. Yield: 6 to 8 servings.

PARMESAN DRESSING

1 egg
1 cup salad oil
$^{1}/_{2}$ cup grated
  Parmesan cheese
$^{1}/_{4}$ cup white wine
  vinegar
$^{1}/_{2}$ to 1 teaspoon pepper
1 or 2 cloves of garlic,
  minced

Place egg in blender container; cover and blend for 5 seconds. Blend in salad oil gradually until thickened. Add $^{1}/_{2}$ cup Parmesan cheese, vinegar, pepper and garlic. Blend until smooth.

Susan Potter, Delta Zeta
Traverse City, Michigan

FIESTA TORTELLINI

1 10-ounce package
  spinach tortellini
  with cheese
1 cup chopped raw
  carrots
$^{1}/_{2}$ cup chopped celery
$^{1}/_{4}$ cup chopped black
  olives
$^{3}/_{4}$ cup chopped red
  sweet peppers
3 tablespoons chopped
  onion
1 tablespoon Louisiana-
  style hot sauce
1 medium tomato,
  chopped
$^{1}/_{2}$ teaspoon garlic
  powder
$^{3}/_{4}$ cup Italian salad
  dressing

Cook tortellini according to package directions. Rinse with cold water. Add remaining ingredients; toss gently. Chill. Toss again before serving. Yield: 6 to 8 servings.

Christine Greenleaf, Xi Alpha Theta
Limestone, Maine

SEASIDE MACARONI SALAD

This is an especially colorful and attractive salad that makes any cookout more festive.

1 16-ounce package
  shell macaroni
1 cup sour cream
1 cup mayonnaise
2 tablespoons sugar
2 tablespoons vinegar
1 tablespoon parsley
  flakes
1 teaspoon salt
$^{1}/_{2}$ teaspoon pepper
$1^{1}/_{2}$ pounds crab meat
  or imitation, chopped
1 bunch green onions,
  chopped
1 cup chopped celery
1 cup frozen peas

Cook macaroni according to package directions. Rinse under cold water; drain well. Mix next 7 ingredients in small bowl. Combine macaroni, crab meat, onions, celery and peas in large bowl; toss lightly. Add dressing; mix to coat. Chill; serve. Yield: 12 servings.

Dianne L. Waldo, Lambda Lambda
Emporia, Kansas

SHRIMP RING

I made this for an end-of-the-year sorority salad dinner party. It travels well in a covered container.

2 cans shrimp or
  8 ounces fresh
  shrimp, cooked
1 10-ounce can cream
  of mushroom soup
1 tablespoon
  unflavored gelatin
3 tablespoons water
6 ounces cream cheese
3 green onions, chopped
1 cup mayonnaise
1 cup finely chopped
  celery
Crackers

Drain shrimp, reserving liquid from 1 can; mince shrimp. Heat soup in saucepan. Dissolve gelatin in water; add to soup. Stir in cream cheese; heat until melted. Remove from heat. Add shrimp, reserved liquid, green onions, mayonnaise and celery; mix well. Pour into greased 1-quart ring mold. Chill overnight. Serve with crackers. Yield: 4 cups.

Sharon Weaver, Preceptor
Carson City, Nevada

CRUNCHY PEANUT SALAD

2 cups frozen peas,
  thawed, drained
1 cup unsalted peanuts
6 slices crisp-fried
  bacon, crumbled
$^{1}/_{4}$ cup chopped red
  onion
$^{1}/_{2}$ cup salad dressing or
  mayonnaise
$^{1}/_{4}$ cup zesty Italian
  dressing

Combine peas, peanuts, bacon and onion in bowl; toss to mix. Chill. Combine salad dressing and Italian dressing; mix well. Chill. Pour dressing over salad when ready to serve; toss to mix. Yield: 6 servings.

Janet Annison, Lambda Delta
Amherstburg, Ontario, Canada

CHICKEN SALAD

$1^{1}/_{2}$ cups cooked
  cubed chicken
$^{1}/_{3}$ cup seedless green
  grapes
$1^{1}/_{2}$ ounces shredded
  Swiss cheese
$^{1}/_{3}$ cup chopped celery
$^{1}/_{8}$ cup chopped
  onion
$^{1}/_{4}$ cup sour cream
$^{3}/_{4}$ cup mayonnaise
$^{1}/_{2}$ teaspoon lemon juice
Pepper and salt to taste
Lettuce leaves
Tomato slices
4 to 6 croissants, split
  into halves
Green grapes

Combine first 9 ingredients in large bowl; mix well. Refrigerate, covered, until ready to serve. Place lettuce leaf and tomato slice on each croissant half. Spoon chicken salad on top. Garnish with green grapes. Yield: 4 to 6 servings.

Barbara S. Clark, Preceptor Alpha Omicron
Asheville, North Carolina

HOMEMADE CHICKEN SALAD

This is an excellent dish for a salad luncheon served on a lettuce leaf with a roll or crackers.

8 ounces shell macaroni, cooked, cooled	1 cup chopped celery
	1/2 cup chopped onion
1 chicken, cooked, shredded	1/2 cup chopped sweet pickle
6 hard-cooked eggs, chopped	1 small jar green olives, chopped
1 package frozen mixed carrots and peas, cooked, cooled	Mayonnaise Dressing
	Lettuce leaves

Combine first 8 ingredients in large bowl. Cover with Mayonnaise Dressing. Chill for 4 hours. Serve on lettuce leaves. Yield: 12 servings.

MAYONNAISE DRESSING

1/2 cup all-purpose flour	3/4 cup white vinegar
3/4 cup sugar	4 eggs, beaten
2 teaspoons salt	1 tablespoon butter
2 teaspoons dry mustard	2 cups mayonnaise-type salad dressing
1/8 teaspoon paprika	
1 cup water	

Combine first 5 ingredients in bowl. Add water and vinegar; mix well. Add eggs, butter and salad dressing; stir with whisk until well blended. Yield: 12 servings.

Barb Bova, Alpha Gamma
Marshalltown, Iowa

CHICKEN-RICE SALAD

I prepared this salad for our salad dinner we held to celebrate the revealing of our sorority secret sisters. It was a big hit!

1 6-ounce package wild rice mix	3/4 cup chopped celery
	Salt and pepper to taste
2 tablespoons diced onion	1/3 cup salad oil
	1/2 cup cider vinegar
2 cups cooked diced chicken	1/2 cup sugar
	1 teaspoon salt
2 cups raw broccoli flowerets	8 cherry tomatoes, halved

Prepare wild rice according to package directions, using seasoning packet. Combine rice and next 5 ingredients in 3-quart serving bowl. Combine oil, vinegar, sugar and 1 teaspoon salt in saucepan; bring to a full boil. Pour boiling mixture over salad. Stir to mix well; refrigerate overnight. Garnish with tomato halves. Recipe doubles well. Yield: 6 to 8 servings.

Leslyn M. Rose, Kappa Beta
Dowagiac, Michigan

ROQUEFORT POTATO SALAD

1 tablespoon tarragon vinegar	2 pounds red potatoes
	1 head leafy lettuce
2 tablespoons cider vinegar	1/2 bunch parsley or watercress
4 tablespoons minced onion	1/2 cup Roquefort or bleu cheese
1 teaspoon Dijon-style mustard	1/4 cup cream
	6 slices crisp-fried bacon, crumbled
1 tablespoon minced parsley	2 tablespoons chopped chives
Salt and pepper to taste	

Combine first 6 ingredients in small bowl; mix well. Boil potatoes in jackets for 20 to 30 minutes or until tender. Slice warm potatoes into bowl. Pour 1/4 cup dressing over potatoes; mix gently. Line large platter with lettuce leaves. Arrange potatoes on leaves with parsley. Add cheese and cream to remainder of dressing; spoon over potatoes. Sprinkle with bacon and chives. Yield: 8 servings.

Nancy Hutton, Xi Epsilon Beta
Woodstock, Virginia

MICROWAVE POTATO SALAD

3 or 4 eggs	1 tablespoon mustard
1/2 cup sugar	Salt and pepper to taste
2 tablespoons vinegar	1 cup mayonnaise
1 medium onion, chopped	10 to 12 medium potatoes, cooked

Combine eggs, sugar and vinegar in microwave-safe bowl; mix with whisk. Microwave for 3 to 4 minutes, whisking every 15 to 20 seconds, until texture of pudding. Do not overcook. Add onion, mustard, salt and pepper; mix well. Add mayonnaise; mix well. Chop potatoes. Combine dressing and potatoes in large bowl; mix gently. Yield: 8 servings.

Anne G. Smith, Preceptor Mu
Mitchell, South Dakota

RISING SUN POTATO SALAD

4 cups cooked peeled potatoes, cut into 1/2-inch cubes	3/4 cup chopped celery including leaves
	2 tablespoons chopped green onions
3 tablespoons vinegar	1/4 cup mayonnaise
1 teaspoon salt	3/4 teaspoon ginger
2 tablespoons salad oil	4 slices crisp-fried bacon, crumbled
1 cup pineapple tidbits, drained	
1 cup water chestnuts	

Combine first 8 ingredients in large bowl; mix well. Refrigerate overnight. Combine mayonnaise, ginger and bacon; mix well. Add to salad 1 hour before serving. Yield: 4 to 6 servings.

Lila Jean Stewart, Laureate Alpha Epsilon
Longmont, Colorado

SUMMERTIME POTATO SALAD

4 cups cooked potatoes,
  cut into 1/2-inch pieces
1/2 cup each chopped
  red, green and yellow
  bell peppers
1/4 cup chopped celery
1/4 cup chopped red
  onion
1/4 cup chopped fresh
  chives
1 tablespoon chopped
  parsley
1/4 cup salad oil
2 tablespoons red wine
  vinegar
1 teaspoon dried thyme
Salt and pepper
  to taste

Combine potatoes, peppers, celery, onion, chives and parsley in large bowl; toss gently to mix. Combine remaining ingredients in small bowl. Pour over potato mixture; toss gently. Serve at room temperature or chilled. Yield: 12 servings.

Deborah Beakey, Xi Beta Alpha
Great Bend, Kansas

ARTICHOKE AND RICE SALAD

1 package chicken
  Rice-A-Roni
2 6-ounce jars
  marinated artichokes
2 green onions, chopped
1/2 green pepper, chopped
1/2 cup chopped celery
1 cup diced shrimp, ham
  or chicken
1/2 cup black olives
1/4 cup mayonnaise
1/2 to 3/4 teaspoon curry
  powder
Lettuce leaves

Cook Rice-A-Roni according to package directions; let cool. Drain and chop artichokes, reserving marinade. Combine rice, artichokes and next 5 ingredients in large bowl. Combine reserved marinade, mayonnaise and curry powder in bowl; mix well. Pour over rice mixture; toss to mix. Chill; serve on lettuce leaves. Yield: 6 to 8 servings.

Kathy Boyer, Xi Epsilon Phi
Shawnee, Kansas

MARINATED BLACK-EYED PEA SALAD

3 16-ounce cans
  black-eyed peas,
  drained well
1 16-ounce jar salsa
1 8-ounce bottle of
  Italian salad dressing
1 green bell pepper,
  chopped
1 onion, chopped
3 small tomatoes,
  chopped

Combine all ingredients in large bowl; toss to mix. Refrigerate overnight. Yield: 10 to 12 servings.

Mary Morgan, Preceptor Epsilon Lambda
Friendswood, Texas

EGG AND KIDNEY BEAN SALAD

3 hard-cooked eggs,
  chopped
1 16-ounce can kidney
  beans, drained, rinsed
1 small onion, chopped
1/2 cup mayonnaise
Salt
Pepper

Combine first 4 ingredients in large bowl; toss to mix. Add salt and pepper to taste; chill. Yield: 4 to 6 servings.

Deborah Blessman, Theta Psi
Crossville, Tennessee

FRENCH GREEN BEAN SALAD

My mother liked to fix cold vegetable salads to have with barbecue meat. This is one of my favorites.

2 pounds (about) fresh
  whole green beans
  or cut French
  green beans
2 cups water
Salt to taste
1 red onion
1/4 cup vinegar
1 cup olive oil
1 clove of garlic, crushed
Salt and pepper to taste
1 tablespoon paprika

Rinse beans; cut off ends and push through French bean cutter. Combine beans, water and salt in saucepan; boil for 10 minutes. Drain; rinse in cold water. Cut onion into quarters; slice one way to create strings of onion. Add to green beans. Combine remaining ingredients; mix well. Add to salad. Refrigerate overnight or serve warm.
Yield: 4 servings.

Melanie Worsham, Xi Gamma Chi
Santee, California

BROCCOLI SALAD

4 cups broccoli flowerets
1 cup chopped celery
1 cup red grapes
1 cup white grapes
1/4 cup chopped green
  onions
1/4 cup slivered almonds
1/2 pound bacon,
  crisp-fried, crumbled
1 cup mayonnaise-type
  salad dressing
1/3 cup sugar
1 tablespoon vinegar

Combine first 7 ingredients in large bowl; toss lightly. Combine remaining ingredients in small bowl; mix well. Pour over salad; toss lightly.
Yield: 8 servings.

Jean Riley, Delta Sigma
Waverly, Missouri

BROCCOLI SALAD

4 cups broccoli flowerets
1 pound bacon, diced,
  crisp-fried, drained
1 cup raisins, plumped
  in warm water
1/2 cup sunflower seeds
1/2 cup slivered almonds
2 tablespoons minced
  onion
1 cup salad dressing or
  mayonnaise
1/2 cup sugar
2 tablespoons vinegar

Combine first 6 ingredients in large bowl; mix gently. Combine remaining ingredients in bowl; mix well. Pour over salad; stir. Serve. Yield: 12 servings.

Tammy Dolezal, Gamma Beta
Columbus, Nebraska
*Dorothea Campion, Xi Gamma Xi
Fairfield Bay, Arkansas

COUNTRY COLESLAW

1 large head cabbage,
   finely cut
1 cup diced celery
1 green bell pepper,
   chopped
1/2 medium onion,
   chopped

2 cups sugar
1/2 cup cider vinegar
2 teaspoons salt
1 teaspoon celery seed
1/2 teaspoon powdered
   mustard

Combine first 4 ingredients in large bowl; mix gently.
Combine remaining ingredients in bowl; mix well.
Pour over cabbage mixture. Refrigerate for at least 6
hours or up to 1 week. Yield: 20 servings.

Helen Vallely, Preceptor Chi
Terre Haute, Indiana

FIESTA SLAW

This recipe is great with your sparerib barbecue.

3 cups mayonnaise
1/2 cup vinegar
1 package taco
   seasoning
1/2 teaspoon chili
   powder
1/2 teaspoon garlic salt
Salt and pepper to taste
1 small head purple
   cabbage, shredded

1 small head cabbage,
   shredded
3 carrots, peeled, sliced
   julienne-style
2 large yellow bell
   peppers
2 large red bell peppers,
   seeded, sliced
   julienne-style

Combine mayonnaise and vinegar in large bowl.
Add taco seasoning, chili powder, garlic salt, salt and
pepper; mix well. Stir in cabbage, carrots and peppers; mix gently. Yield: 10 to 15 servings.

Candace Vassallo, Xi Delta Rho
Williamsport, Pennsylvania

NUTTY NOODLE SALAD

I hunted down this recipe at a large pig roast by asking
everyone, "Who brought this tasty dish?" I wrote it on
a napkin and still have it in my recipe file.

1 head cabbage
2 ounces slivered
   almonds, toasted
3 scallions, chopped
2 1/2 tablespoons
   vegetable oil
3 tablespoons red wine
   vinegar

2 tablespoons sugar
1 3-ounce package
   oriental noodle soup
   with beef flavor
   packet

Slice cabbage into 1/4-by-2-inch strips. Combine cabbage, almonds and scallions in large bowl. Combine
oil, vinegar, sugar and beef flavor packet from noo-
les in bowl; mix well. Crumble uncooked noodles
over cabbage just before serving. Pour vinaigrette
over mixture; toss to mix. Yield: 15 to 20 servings.

Valerie Burke, Xi Delta Gamma
Manassas, Virginia

RUFFLE TRIO AND EGG SALAD

12 ounces ruffle trio
   macaroni
12 hard-cooked eggs,
   chopped
1 green bell pepper,
   chopped

4 stalks celery, chopped
1 cup nonfat
   mayonnaise
Shredded carrots
   (optional)

Cook macaroni according to package directions.
Combine macaroni, eggs, green pepper, celery and
mayonnaise in large bowl; mix well. Garnish with
carrots. Refrigerate. Yield: 20 servings.

Virginia Lamore, Preceptor Epsilon Iota
Lady Lake, Florida

POLISH SLAW

This is a great slaw for picnics because it contains no
mayonnaise.

1 head cabbage,
   shredded
1 medium white onion,
   chopped
1 medium green bell
   pepper, chopped
1 small carrot,
   shredded

1/2 cup sugar
1 cup white vinegar
3/4 cup salad oil
2 teaspoons sugar
1 teaspoon dry mustard
1/2 teaspoon garlic salt
1 teaspoon celery seed

Layer first 4 ingredients in large salad bowl, sprinkling 2 tablespoons sugar over each layer. Combine
next 6 ingredients in 2-quart saucepan; bring to a
boil. Pour over layered mixture. Let stand for 1 hour;
stir. Let stand for 2 hours; stir. Refrigerate. Can be
stored at room temperature for 3 days.
Yield: 10 servings.

Sue Jolly, Epsilon Pi
Houston, Texas

CORN SALAD

This is quick and easy and goes great with barbecue.

2 11-ounce cans white
   Shoe Peg corn,
   drained
4 medium tomatoes,
   chopped
1 small onion, chopped

1/2 medium green bell
   pepper, chopped
2 tablespoons
   mayonnaise
Salt and pepper
   to taste

Combine all ingredients in large bowl; mix gently.
Chill. Yield: 12 to 15 servings.

Jane Lee Davis, Alpha Alpha
Decatur, Alabama

CUCUMBER SALAD

This recipe was handed down by my grandfather from
Canada.

6 medium cucumbers
2 quarts buttermilk
3/4 cup sour cream

1/3 cup vinegar
1 tablespoon salt
1 teaspoon pepper

Chill cucumbers; grate and drain. Combine remaining ingredients in large bowl; blend well. Add cucumbers; stir. Yield: 12 servings.

Karen M. Sedillo, Alpha Nu
Farmington, New Mexico

AUNT BARB'S CALICO SALAD

1 large can sauerkraut, drained
1 cup chopped celery
1 cup chopped onion
1 cup chopped green bell pepper
1 4-ounce can pimento, chopped
1 1-pound can garbanzo beans, drained
1/3 cup vinegar
1/2 cup salad oil
1/2 cup sugar
1/4 cup water

Combine first 6 ingredients in large bowl. Combine remaining ingredients in small bowl; blend well. Pour over vegetables. Refrigerate for 24 hours. May add small can whole kernel yellow corn, drained, for color if desired. Yield: 8 servings.

Margaret Turner, Laureate Xi
Fairmont, West Virginia

MANDARIN ORANGE SALAD

1/3 cup sliced almonds
2 tablespoons sugar
1/2 small head iceberg lettuce
1/2 small bunch romaine lettuce
1 11-ounce can mandarin oranges
2 stalks celery, chopped
2 green onions, chopped
1/3 cup bottled Caesar dressing
2 tablespoons sugar
Dash of red pepper sauce

Combine almonds and sugar in sauté pan. Cook over low heat, stirring constantly, until sugar is melted and almonds are coated. Let cool; break apart. Tear lettuce into bite-sized pieces. Drain oranges, reserving 2 tablespoons juice. Place lettuce, celery, green onions and oranges in large plastic bag. Combine reserved liquid, dressing, sugar and pepper sauce in small bowl. Pour into bag; toss well. Yield: 6 to 8 servings.

Karen L. Smith, Delta Psi
Leonardo, New Jersey

ONION SALAD

I don't really like raw onion, but I love this salad.

1/2 cup sugar
1/3 cup water
1/3 cup cider vinegar
1 1/2 teaspoons salt
4 Spanish onions
1 cup mayonnaise
1 teaspoon celery seed

Combine sugar, water, vinegar and salt in large glass bowl; stir until sugar is dissolved. Cut onions in half; slice into thin slices. Add to vinegar mixture. Refrigerate, covered, for at least 4 hours or overnight. Drain onions well in colander; do not rinse.

Combine mayonnaise and celery seed in bowl; stir into onions. Refrigerate, covered, for 1 to 2 hours or several days. Yield: 10 to 20 servings.

Diane Monk, Xi Epsilon Iota
Port McNeill, British Columbia, Canada

B.L.T. SALAD

1 pound bacon
1 head lettuce, cut into small pieces
3 or 4 ripe tomatoes, chopped
1 small onion, thinly sliced
2/3 cup salad dressing
2 tablespoons vinegar
2 tablespoons sugar

Fry bacon until almost crisp; let cool. Chop into small pieces. Combine lettuce, tomatoes and onion in salad bowl. Add bacon. Combine salad dressing, vinegar and sugar in small bowl. Add to lettuce mixture; mix well. Chill until serving time. Yield: 4 to 6 servings.

Nadeen Steffey, Preceptor Tau
Erie, Pennsylvania

SOUTHWESTERN SALAD

This recipe is wonderful for a picnic or barbecue because it does not need refrigeration.

1 15-ounce can black beans, drained
1 15-ounce can low-sodium whole kernel corn, drained
2 cloves of garlic, finely minced
1 bunch green onions, finely sliced
6 cherry tomatoes, quartered, seeded
1 small bunch fresh cilantro, finely chopped
1/2 cup chopped red and green bell pepper (optional)
1/3 cup vinegar
Cilantro

Combine beans and corn in large bowl. Add next 5 ingredients; mix well. Pour vinegar over salad; blend well. Refrigerate at least 1 hour. Garnish with cilantro. Yield: 6 to 8 servings.

Diane Higgins, Psi Sigma
Palm Beach Gardens, Florida

RANCH CRUNCHY PEA SALAD

1 10-ounce package frozen baby peas, thawed
1 cup diced celery
1 cup chopped cauliflower
1/4 cup diced green onions
1 cup chopped cashews
1/2 cup sour cream
1 cup prepared ranch salad dressing
Bacon, crisp-fried, crumbled

Combine first 7 ingredients in large bowl; toss to mix. Chill. Garnish with bacon just before serving. Yield: 6 to 8 servings.

Marjorie R. Murray, Zeta Master
Colorado Springs, Colorado

SPINACH SALAD

1 bag fresh spinach,
   washed, torn into
   bite-sized pieces
1 can water chestnuts,
   sliced
1 cup fresh mushrooms,
   sliced
2 hard-cooked eggs,
   sliced
5 strips crisp-fried
   bacon, crumbled

1/2 cup catsup
1/4 cup sugar
1/4 cup vinegar
1 small onion, grated
3 tablespoons salad oil
2 tablespoons
   Worcestershire sauce
Salt and pepper to taste

Combine first 5 ingredients in large salad bowl; toss to mix. Combine remaining ingredients in blender container; blend well. Pour over salad just before serving; toss to mix. Yield: 6 to 8 servings.

Kathleen F. Toepperwein, Preceptor Mu Sigma
Houston, Texas

SWEET POTATO SALAD

4 medium sweet
   potatoes, cooked
1/2 cup mayonnaise
1/2 cup plain yogurt
1 teaspoon curry powder
Salt to taste
2 medium Granny
   Smith apples,
   chopped

2 medium oranges,
   peeled, chopped
1/2 cup raisins
1/2 cup chopped dates
1 20-ounce can
   pineapple chunks,
   drained

Peel sweet potatoes; cut into chunks about the size of pineapple. Combine mayonnaise, yogurt, curry powder and salt in large bowl; mix well. Add sweet potatoes and remaining ingredients; toss well. Refrigerate for at least 3 hours. Yield: 6 servings.

Saundra Nobbe, Theta Nu
Batesville, Indiana

ZUCCHINI SALAD

Everyone loves this recipe. It has been given out many times to sorority girls and many others. It is published in the San Fernando Valley Council Cookbook called "Spirit of 76."

2/3 cup cider vinegar
2 tablespoons wine
   vinegar
1/3 cup salad oil
1/2 cup sugar
1 teaspoon salt
1/2 cup chopped onion

1/2 cup chopped green
   bell pepper
1/2 cup sliced celery
5 to 7 zucchini, sliced
1 2-oz. jar pimento,
   drained

Combine first 5 ingredients in small bowl; mix well. Combine remaining ingredients in large bowl. Add vinegar mixture; toss to mix. Refrigerate at least 6 hours or overnight. Yield: 15 to 20 servings.

Irene M. Forsyth, Laureate Gamma Upsilon
Auburn, California

MARINATED SUMMER SALAD

3 avocados, chopped
3 tomatoes, chopped
2 red or green bell
   peppers, chopped
2 cucumbers, sliced
1 bunch green onions,
   chopped

2 small jars marinated
   artichokes, drained,
   chopped
1 bottle of cheese and
   garlic salad dressing

Combine first 6 ingredients in large bowl; mix well. Add salad dressing; toss to mix. Marinate in refrigerator for at least 1 hour or overnight. Yield: 6 servings.

René Castellino, Xi Xi Lambda
San Jose, California

TOMATOES PIQUANTE

6 tomatoes, peeled,
   sliced
2/3 cup salad oil
1/4 cup tarragon wine
   vinegar
1/2 cup snipped parsley
1/4 cup sliced green
   onions

1/2 teaspoon basil
1/2 teaspoon thyme
1/2 teaspoon marjoram
1 teaspoon salt
1/4 teaspoon pepper
1 clove of garlic,
   minced

Place tomatoes in deep bowl. Combine remaining ingredients in bowl; mix well. Pour over tomatoes. Refrigerate, covered, for several hours or overnight. Serve with slotted spoon. Yield: 8 to 10 servings.

Fran McMullen, Preceptor Kappa Rho
Hilltop Lakes, Texas

PATIO POT ROAST

1 3- to 4-pound
   blade-bone pot
   roast, 1 1/2 to
   2 inches thick
Salt and pepper
   to taste
3 tablespoons all-
   purpose flour
1 tablespoon light
   brown sugar

1/2 teaspoon dry
   mustard
1/2 cup catsup
1 tablespoon
   Worcestershire sauce
1 tablespoon vinegar
Vegetables, sliced, such
   as carrots, celery
   and onions

Brown roast on grill over medium-hot coals for 30 minutes. Season with salt and pepper. Combine next 7 ingredients in bowl; mix well. Place half the sauce in center of large piece of heavy-duty aluminum foil. Place roast on top of sauce. Top with vegetables; add remaining sauce. Fold foil over and seal tightly. Place on another piece of foil on grill. Cook over medium-hot coals for 1 1/2 to 2 hours or to desired doneness. Yield: 8 servings.

Linda Hollingsworth, Tau Pi
Sterling, Illinois

BARBECUED ROAST AND VEGETABLES

Friends of ours from Toledo served this at a dinner party. It was delicious.

2 tablespoons butter or margarine	2 tablespoons light brown sugar
1 onion, chopped	1 teaspoon dry mustard
1/2 cup chopped celery	1 teaspoon salt
3/4 cup water	1/4 teaspoon pepper
1 cup catsup	1 eye of round roast
2 tablespoons vinegar	Vegetables such as potatoes, green bell peppers, mushrooms, carrots
2 tablespoons lemon juice	
2 tablespoons Worcestershire sauce	

Preheat grill. Melt butter in saucepan. Add onion and celery; cook until tender. Add next 9 ingredients; simmer for 15 minutes. Place roast on grill over medium-hot coals. Grill for 20 minutes or until brown, turning occasionally. Place roast in large pan. Add sauce and vegetables. Cover; cook on grill for 1 1/2 to 2 hours or until desired doneness.
Yield: 8 servings.

Beverly J. Beaver, Xi Beta Xi
Huntingdon, Pennsylvania

MARINATED CHUCK ROAST BARBECUE

1/2 cup cooking oil	1/2 clove of garlic, crushed
1/4 cup soy sauce	2 tablespoons lemon juice
4 teaspoons Worcestershire sauce	1 beef chuck roast, cut into 2-inch squares
2 tablespoons wine vinegar	Vegetables such as tomatoes, corn, green bell pepper, potatoes
2 teaspoons dry mustard	
3/4 teaspoon salt	
1 teaspoon black pepper	Pineapple chunks
1/2 teaspoon dried parsley flakes	

Combine first 10 ingredients in bowl; mix well. Place beef cubes in bowl; pour marinade over beef cubes. Refrigerate, covered, overnight. Thread beef cubes on skewers alternately with vegetables and pineapple chunks. Grill over medium-hot coals to desired doneness. Yield: 8 servings.

Kathy Gasper, Nu Mu
Salina, Kansas

DELICIOUS BARBECUED BRISKET

1 8-to 10-pound brisket, trimmed or untrimmed	2 tablespoons sugar
	1/2 teaspoon garlic powder
2 tablespoons salt	2 tablespoons meat tenderizer
1/2 teaspoon cayenne pepper	Barbecue Sauce
1 tablespoon paprika	

Preheat oven to 400 degrees. Let brisket stand at room temperature for 1 hour. Combine next 6 ingredients in bowl; stir until well mixed. Rub into both sides of brisket until most is absorbed. Wrap brisket loosely in heavy-duty foil. Place on rack in roaster. Bake for 45 minutes; reduce heat to 325 degrees and continue cooking 5 to 6 hours (about 40 minutes per pound) or until fork tender. Remove from oven; drain. Trim excess fat. Brush with Barbecue Sauce; bake, uncovered, for 30 to 45 minutes or grill over medium-hot coals to desired doneness. Chill for 30 minutes before slicing. Serve with warm Barbecue Sauce. Yield: 12 to 15 servings.

BARBECUE SAUCE

1 20-ounce bottle of catsup	Dash of black pepper
	1/4 teaspoon cayenne or red pepper
1 10-ounce bottle of Worcestershire sauce	Juice of 2 fresh lemons
	4 tablespoons sugar
4 tablespoons dry mustard	1/4 cup molasses
	2 tablespoons steak sauce
1/2 teaspoon garlic powder	1/2 cup margarine, melted
1 teaspoon salt	
1/2 cup cooking oil	

Combine first 12 ingredients in bowl. Mix with wire whisk until well blended. Add margarine when ready to use; mix well. May thin by gradually adding small amounts of vinegar or Worcestershire sauce if de-sired. Yield: 8 cups.

Myrt Mortimore, Preceptor Epsilon Nu
San Angelo, Texas

TEXAS BRISKET

This recipe was used at one of many inaugural balls for President George Bush.

Garlic powder to taste	1 1/2 teaspoons salt
Salt to taste	1 teaspoon garlic powder
Pepper to taste	1 teaspoon chili powder
Paprika to taste	1 1/2 teaspoons pepper sauce
Chili powder to taste	
1 large beef brisket	1/3 cup Worcestershire sauce
1 cup vinegar	
1/2 cup vegetable oil	3 bay leaves
1/4 cup water	1 1/2 teaspoons paprika
1/4 cup lemon juice	

Combine first 5 ingredients in bowl; mix well. Dry rub brisket with mixture. Cover; let stand at room temperature for 1 hour. Combine remaining ingredients in saucepan; simmer for 15 minutes. Grill brisket over medium-hot coals for 2 to 4 hours or to desired doneness, basting often with sauce.
Yield: 8 servings.

Janet Gutowsky, Xi Omega Nu
Rosenberg, Texas

ZESTY BEEF BRISKET

1 3- to 5-pound beef brisket	2 tablespoons light brown sugar
Water	1 tablespoon Worcestershire sauce
2 teaspoons salt	
1/4 teaspoon pepper	1 teaspoon instant coffee
1 medium onion, sliced	
1/2 cup catsup	

Place brisket in large heavy saucepan; add enough water to cover. Add salt, pepper and onion. Cover; simmer for 3 hours or until tender. Combine remaining ingredients in bowl. Remove brisket from liquid. Baste with sauce. Grill over medium-hot coals for 15 to 20 minutes or until browned, turning and basting with sauce. Yield: 8 servings.

Tami Zimmerschied, Mu Omega
Sweet Springs, Missouri

CALIFORNIA BARBECUED STEAK

1 2 1/2-pound top sirloin steak, 2 inches thick	3 tablespoons hoisin sauce (optional)
3/4 cup catsup	3 tablespoons minced green onions
3/4 cup chili sauce	3 cloves of garlic, crushed
1 1/2 tablespoons soy sauce	1/2 teaspoon salt
3 tablespoons honey	1/8 teaspoon pepper

Place steak in plastic food bag. Combine remaining ingredients in bowl; mix well. Pour over steak. Fasten bag; place in shallow pan. Let marinate in refrigerator for 24 hours, turning occasionally. Remove steak; pat dry. Broil 4 inches from heat, basting with marinade several times, to desired doneness. Yield: 10 servings.

Glena Jackson
Barstow, California

KOREAN STEAK

1 flank steak, tenderized twice, cut into fourths	1/4 cup sherry
	Vegetable oil for frying
1/2 cup sugar	1 egg, beaten
1/2 cup soy sauce	2 stalks green onions, minced
1 clove of garlic, minced	1 cup all-purpose flour

Place steak pieces in shallow pan. Combine sugar, soy sauce, garlic and sherry in saucepan; mix well. Heat until sugar is melted. Pour over steak; marinate for 30 minutes. Preheat oil in skillet. Combine egg and onions in bowl; mix well. Dredge steak pieces in flour; dip in egg mixture. Fry in hot oil until coating is browned. Cut into small finger-sized pieces. Serve hot or cold. Leftovers can be frozen. Yield: 4 servings.

Joy Fujii-Donaldson, Xi Sigma Alpha
Dinuba, California

CHUCKWAGON PEPPER STEAK

1 3-pound 2-inch thick round roast	1 cup wine vinegar
	1/2 cup salad or olive oil
2 teaspoons unseasoned meat tenderizer	3 tablespoons lemon juice
2 tablespoons instant minced onion	1/4 cup peppercorns, coarsely crushed, or 2 tablespoons cracked pepper
2 teaspoons thyme	
1 teaspoon marjoram	
1 bay leaf	

Preheat grill. Sprinkle roast evenly on both sides with tenderizer. Pierce deeply with fork; place in shallow pan. Combine next 7 ingredients in bowl; mix well. Pour over and around roast. Let stand at room temperature for 1 to 2 hours, turning every 30 minutes. Remove meat from marinade. Pound half the peppercorns into each side with wooden mallet. Grill 6 inches above hot coals for 15 minutes on each side or until roast is done. Yield: 8 servings.

Joan Haase, Laureate Theta
Aiken, South Carolina

CARNE ASADA

This is a family favorite that is great for camping trips.

2 to 3 pounds London broil or beef filets	1/2 green bell pepper, chopped (optional)
1 cup salsa	1 1/2 teaspoons crushed oregano leaves
2 cloves of garlic, crushed	2 tablespoons liquid smoke
1 medium onion, chopped	

Slice beef into 1/4-inch slices. Place in shallow bowl. Combine remaining ingredients in bowl; mix well. Pour over beef. Let marinate in refrigerator for at least 2 days or up to 4 days. Grill over medium-hot coals until done. Yield: 4 to 6 servings.

Joyce Steele, Xi Nu
Los Alamos, New Mexico

❖ SESAME SEED STEAK TERIYAKI

I always serve this recipe for special occasions such as birthdays and anniversaries.

1 2/3 cup soy sauce	3 teaspoons sesame seed, toasted
1/3 cup water	
2 tablespoons sugar	1 3-pound boneless rump or round roast, 1/4 to 1/3 inch thick
1 piece gingerroot, crushed	
1 clove of garlic, crushed	

Combine first 6 ingredients in bowl; mix well. Place roast in shallow dish. Pour sauce over roast; marinate for 2 1/2 hours. Grill over hot coals for a few minutes or until done to taste. Yield: 8 to 10 servings.

O. Nadine Litle, Laureate Alpha Phi
Loveland, Colorado

BARBECUED SKIRT STEAK

1/2 cup barbecue sauce   *1/4 cup honey*
1/4 cup Italian dressing   *5 pounds skirt steak*

Combine first 3 ingredients in large bowl; mix well. Place steak in marinade; let marinate in refrigerator for at least 8 hours or overnight. Grill over medium-hot coals to desired doneness. Yield: 6 to 8 servings.

Bonnie L. Munson, Lambda Delta
Long Grove, Illinois

SHISH KABOBS

I won a recipe round-up with this recipe in 1979. My friends and family still enjoy making their own.

8 ounces French   *1 onion*
  dressing   *1 large green bell pepper*
8 ounces barbecue   *1 1/2 pounds sirloin*
  sauce   *steak, cut into*
8 new potatoes   *chunks*
8 ounces fresh   *Cherry tomatoes*
  mushrooms

Combine dressing and barbecue sauce in large container; mix well. Parboil potatoes for 15 to 20 minutes. Place cleaned mushrooms on top of potatoes; cover and let steam. Cut onion and green pepper into quarters; separate into bite-sized pieces. Drain potatoes and mushrooms. Place steak and vegetables in sauce. Marinate for at least 2 hours. Preheat grill. Thread steak on skewers alternating with vegetables. Grill over medium-hot coals for 6 minutes on each side. Yield: 6 servings.

Cyndy Meyer, Xi Epsilon Nu
Enid, Oklahoma

GRILLED LAMB CHOPS

1/3 cup honey   *2 cloves of garlic,*
1 cup dry white wine   *crushed*
2 tablespoons white   *1/2 teaspoon salt*
  wine vinegar   *2 to 4 lamb chops,*
2 tablespoons melted   *trimmed*
  margarine
1 tablespoon chopped
  fresh or dry mint

Combine first 7 ingredients in bowl; mix well. Place lamb chops in shallow pan; pour marinade over chops. Refrigerate, covered, for 12 hours or overnight. Preheat and grease grill. Drain chops; grill over medium-hot coals for 5 minutes on each side or until browned on outside and juicy pink in center. Yield: 2 to 4 servings.

Lucille V. Lindgren, Laureate Epsilon
Glasgow, Montana

PORK AND VEGETABLE SHISH KABOBS

Our chapter held a husband-wife barbecue social and served this as the main dish. They were delicious, fast, easy and a big hit with the men.

1 6-ounce can frozen   *Salt and pepper to taste*
  orange juice   *5 pounds pork loin, cut*
1 1/2 6-ounce orange   *into 1 1/2-inch cubes*
  juice cans water   *Cherry tomatoes*
1/2 cup soy sauce   *Onion wedges*
4 tablespoons light   *Green bell pepper*
  brown sugar   *wedges*
2 tablespoons   *Red bell pepper wedges*
  Worcestershire sauce   *Fresh mushrooms*
1 clove of garlic,   *(optional)*
  crushed

Combine orange juice, water and next 5 ingredients in bowl; mix well. Place pork cubes in airtight container. Pour marinade over pork cubes; refrigerate, covered, overnight, stirring once or twice. Preheat grill. Thread pork cubes on skewers alternating with vegetables. Grill over medium-hot coals for 10 to 15 minutes or until done, turning often and basting with marinade. Yield: 10 to 12 servings.

Dena Reger, Pi Delta
Princeton, Missouri

ONE POUND PORK CHOPS IN RED SAUCE

This is a good recipe to start the day before and barbecue when you want, especially if all you have to do is hand your husband a fork and a pan of chops!

2 cups soy sauce   *1/3 cup water*
1 cup water   *1 14-ounce bottle of*
1 tablespoon dark   *catsup*
  molasses   *1 12-ounce bottle of*
1/2 cup packed light   *chili sauce*
  brown sugar   *1/2 cup packed light*
1 teaspoon salt   *brown sugar*
6 1-pound pork   *1 teaspoon dry*
  chops   *mustard*

Combine first 5 ingredients in saucepan; mix well. Bring to a boil; let cool. Place pork chops in 9-by-13-inch dish; pour mixture over chops. Refrigerate, covered, overnight. Preheat oven to 375 degrees. Remove chops from marinade; place in 9-by-13-inch baking pan. Cover with foil; bake for 2 hours. Combine remaining ingredients in saucepan; bring to a boil. Dip chops in sauce; return to baking pan. Reduce oven temperature to 350 degrees; bake for 30 minutes. Grill over medium-hot coals until brown on both sides. May refrigerate, covered, overnight before grilling if desired. Yield: 6 servings.

Beryl Jean Thompson, Preceptor Iota
Devils Lake, North Dakota

BARBECUED PORK

1 large pork loin or Boston butt	10 tablespoons Worcestershire sauce
1 cup margarine	5 teaspoons hickory salt
1 cup catsup	5 teaspoons paprika
1 cup packed light brown sugar	5 teaspoons dry mustard
5 tablespoons lemon juice	5 teaspoons chili powder
10 tablespoons vinegar	1 1/4 cups water or broth
	Buns

Preheat oven to 325 degrees. Bake pork loin in covered roaster until done; shred. Combine next 11 ingredients in saucepan; simmer for 1 hour. Add meat; simmer, covered, for 1 to 2 hours. Serve on buns. Yield: 12 to 15 servings.

Rachel O'Neill
Lighthouse Point, Florida

PORK BARBECUE

This recipe has been used as our money maker at our Oktoberfest in September for the last 15 years and is a big seller.

25 pounds pork	6 dashes of Tabasco sauce
Water	
1 1/2 cups lemon juice	1/2 cup plus 1 tablespoon vinegar
1 1/2 cups minced onion	
3 teaspoons salt	1 1/2 cups packed light brown sugar
2 tablespoons dry mustard	
1 52-ounce bottle of catsup	1 cup plus 3 tablespoons A-1 sauce
	94 buns

Preheat oven to 325 degrees. Bake pork in covered roaster until done and fork tender. Reserve pan juices. Shred pork; add small amount of water to keep moist. Remove fat from pan juices; add enough water to make 6 1/4 cups stock. Combine stock and next 9 ingredients in large saucepan; mix well. Simmer for 1 hour. Add meat. Let simmer, covered, for about 2 hours. Serve on buns. May substitute beef for pork if desired. Yield: 94 servings.

Stella Stinauer, Xi Xi Alpha
Havana, Illinois

TEX-MEX RIBS

3 pounds ribs	1 clove of garlic, crushed
1 5-ounce can tomato paste	1 teaspoon oregano
1 cup water	1/4 teaspoon cayenne pepper
2 tablespoons red wine vinegar	3 tablespoons vegetable oil
1/4 cup packed light brown sugar	

Cut ribs into serving-size pieces; place in large saucepan. Cover with boiling water; boil for 30 to 45 minutes. Combine next 7 ingredients in small saucepan. Simmer, uncovered, for 10 minutes, stirring often. Stir in oil. Brush ribs with sauce. Grill on well-greased grill about 5 inches above medium-hot coals for 20 minutes, turning and basting frequently. May broil if desired. Yield: 4 to 6 servings.

Glenda West, Xi Epsilon Epsilon
Owen Sound, Ontario, Canada

CAMPER'S STEW

If camping with a group, let each family contribute 1 of the stew items, crackers and/or cornbread.

1 large can Dinty Moore stew	1 16-ounce can tomatoes
1 16-ounce can corn	1 16-ounce can chili
1 16-ounce can green beans	1 package onion soup mix
1 16-ounce can pinto beans	

Combine all ingredients in large stew pan; mix well. Simmer, covered, for 1 to 2 hours. May serve with crackers or cornbread if desired.
Yield: 8 to 10 servings.

Anita Hess, Laureate Nu
Conway, Arkansas

LOW COUNTRY BOIL

Each year in the fall, we have a dock party at a member's home. We always make the Low Country Boil. It's great.

6 medium Irish potatoes	6 ears corn on the cob
1 quart water	3 pounds shrimp, deheaded
3 pounds sausage, cut into 1-inch pieces	

Place potatoes in large heavy saucepan; add water. Cook for about 5 minutes. Add sausage and corn; resume cooking until potatoes are tender. Add shrimp; cook until shrimp are pink. Drain; spread in large baking pans on picnic table. May serve with saltines, catsup and cold beer if desired.
Yield: 6 servings.

Dora B. Sauls, Xi Gamma Psi
St. Marys, Georgia

GARBAGE CAN DINNER

This is a real topic of conversation and a great way to have fun at an outside barbecue. It is great for a crowd!

1 clean new galvanized garbage can	Fresh whole vegetables such as potatoes, corn on the cob, cabbage, carrots, cauliflower, onions, broccoli, mushrooms and green bell peppers
Clean pop cans, filled 1/2 full with water	
Sausage, precooked	

Fill bottom of garbage can with pop cans. Place screen over pop cans. Place sausage on screen. Layer vegetables on top of sausage. Small vegetables can be placed in cheesecloth. Place garbage can directly on hot coals in fire pit. Cook, covered with lid, for 45 minutes; remove from fire. May serve with cheese sauce if desired. Yield: 24 servings.

Kara Johnson, Iota
Devils Lake, North Dakota

SAUSAGE BURGERS

1 pound ground beef
1 pound sausage
1/4 cup finely chopped
  onions
6 tablespoons
  Worcestershire
  sauce
3 tablespoons liquid
  smoke
1/2 teaspoon garlic
  powder

Preheat grill. Combine all ingredients in large bowl; mix well. Shape into patties. Grill over medium-hot coals for 3 to 5 minutes or until desired doneness. Yield: 6 to 8 servings.

Jo Evelyn Hanna, Delta Lambda
Graham, Texas

MEAL-IN-A-BUNDLE

2 pounds lean chuck,
  cut into 1-inch cubes
6 medium potatoes,
  peeled, diced
6 tablespoons chopped
  onions
6 carrots, cut into
  1/4-inch slices
1/2 cup chopped parsley
2 10-ounce cans
  condensed cream of
  mushroom soup
Tabasco sauce to taste
6 tablespoons water
Salt and pepper
  to taste

Preheat grill. Divide first 6 ingredients into 6 equal portions. Place each portion on 18-inch square of heavy-duty aluminum foil. Add Tabasco sauce and 1 tablespoon water to each portion. Season each with salt and pepper. Bring up corners of foil; twist at top to close. Store in cool place. Line grill with heavy-duty aluminum foil. Grill bundles 2 inches above hot coals for 1 hour. Yield: 6 servings.

Irene A. Fritz, Xi Zeta Omicron
Trenton, Ontario, Canada

CINDY'S BARBECUED RABBIT

Our family began raising rabbits to eat and show. We have enjoyed the hobby immensely, and it saves money on our food bill.

1 fryer rabbit, cut up
1 green bell pepper,
  chopped
1 onion, chopped
1 small can sliced
  mushrooms
Barbecue sauce

Preheat grill. Make a square dish out of heavy-duty aluminum foil; spray with nonstick cooking spray.

Arrange rabbit on foil; place on grill. Add pepper, onion and mushrooms around rabbit. Add barbecue sauce to cover; cook slowly for 1 to 2 hours or until done. Yield: 8 servings.

Cindy Freiberg, Xi Eta Omega
Janesville, Iowa

CHICKEN TERIYAKI

3/4 cup soy sauce
1/4 cup vinegar
1 teaspoon garlic
  powder
2 teaspoons sugar
1 teaspoon rosemary
1 teaspoon ginger
1 to 2 pounds chicken
  pieces

Combine first 6 ingredients in shallow glass dish; mix well. Add chicken. Refrigerate, covered, overnight. Preheat grill. Grill over medium-hot coals for 45 to 55 minutes or until done, brushing with marinade. Yield: 8 servings.

Carla Hefley, Alpha Epsilon
Tulsa, Oklahoma

GRILLED CHICKEN BUNDLES

1/4 pound process
  American cheese
4 chicken breasts,
  skinned, boned,
  cut in half
16 slices bacon
1/4 cup barbecue sauce

Cut cheese into 1/2-by-1-by-1-inch chunks. Make vertical slit in each chicken breast half to form pocket. Place cheese in pocket. Roll into a bundle; wrap crisscross with 2 slices bacon, securing with wooden toothpicks. Grill, using indirect heat, about 6 inches above medium-hot coals for 30 to 40 minutes or until tender, turning every 15 minutes. Grill bundles over direct heat during last 10 minutes to crisp bacon, turning 2 or 3 times and brushing with barbecue sauce. Bundles can be made ahead, wrapped and refrigerated. Yield: 4 to 6 servings.

Amy Ogborn, Gamma Theta
Cedar Rapids, Iowa

GRAPEFRUIT CHICKEN BREASTS

4 8-ounce chicken
  breasts
Juice of 2 lemons
1/4 teaspoon thyme
1/4 teaspoon salt
4 ounces salad oil
Juice of 1 grapefruit
1/4 teaspoon rosemary
1/4 teaspoon pepper

Place chicken in shallow dish. Combine remaining ingredients in bowl; mix well. Pour over chicken; refrigerate, covered, for 24 hours. Preheat grill. Grill over medium-hot coals until done, turning and basting with marinade. May decorate with citrus slices if desired. Yield: 4 servings.

Joan Hayn, Beta Master
San Diego, California

BACON-WRAPPED CHICKEN-MUSHROOM KABOBS

This is a yummy barbecue recipe we enjoy each summer. It is a quick and great make-ahead recipe so you can visit with friends and relatives.

2 large chickens	2 small green onions,
10 large mushrooms,	minced
cut in half	1 8-ounce can sliced
1/4 cup soy sauce	pineapple, drained
1/4 cup cider vinegar	1 8-ounce package
2 tablespoons honey	sliced bacon
2 tablespoons salad oil	

Preheat grill. Debone chicken; cut into chunks. Combine chicken and next 6 ingredients in large bowl. Cut each pineapple slice into 3 pieces. Cut each bacon slice into pieces; wrap bacon around chicken chunk and mushroom half. Thread on skewers, alternating with pineapple pieces, leaving space between each so bacon can cook completely. Grill over medium-hot coals for about 20 minutes, turning once, basting with sauce mixture. Yield: 4 servings.

Carol Kelly, Xi Lambda
Richland, Washington

PRESIDENT'S BARBECUED CHICKEN

This dish is great for Sunday afternoon barbecues. Everyone will ask for the recipe.

1 cup butter or	2 teaspoons dried leaf
margarine	oregano
3/4 cup lemon juice	4 fryers, cut into halves
2 teaspoons garlic salt	3 teaspoons salt
2 tablespoons paprika	1/2 teaspoon pepper

Melt butter in small saucepan; stir in next 4 ingredients. Place chicken in shallow dish; sprinkle with salt and pepper. Pour marinade over chicken; cover. Marinate for 3 to 4 hours at room temperature, turning occasionally. Drain, reserving marinade. Preheat grill; cover rack with foil. Place chicken, skin side up, on foil; brush generously with reserved marinade. Grill for 45 minutes to 1 hour and 15 minutes or until done, turning and brushing with marinade occasionally. Yield: 8 servings.

Kathy Samol, Xi Eta Xi
Edinboro, Pennsylvania

LIME CHICKEN

6 chicken breast halves,	1 teaspoon salt
skinned, boned	1/4 teaspoon pepper
1 clove of garlic	6 tablespoons butter or
2 tablespoons fresh lime	margarine
juice	1/2 cup white wine
2 green onions, minced	
1 teaspoon dried	
tarragon	

Preheat oven to 400 degrees. Rub chicken with clove of garlic. Place chicken in 9-by-13-inch baking dish. Sprinkle chicken with lime juice, green onions, tarragon, salt and pepper. Dot with butter; pour wine over chicken. Bake, uncovered, for 40 minutes, basting every 10 minutes and turning after 20 minutes. Let cool. Refrigerate, covered, for 3 hours or overnight. Yield: 6 servings.

Patricia Ann Sherrill, Laureate Delta
Shelbyville, Tennessee

GARLIC GRILLED CHICKEN

4 skinless boneless	2 cloves of garlic,
chicken breast halves	minced
1 cup picante sauce	1/2 teaspoon ground
2 tablespoons vegetable	cumin
oil	1/2 teaspoon dried
1 tablespoon lime	whole oregano
juice	1/4 teaspoon salt

Place chicken between plastic wrap; flatten to 1/4-inch thickness. Cut chicken into 1-inch wide strips; place in 9-by-12-inch shallow dish. Combine remaining ingredients in bowl; mix well. Pour over chicken. Refrigerate, covered, for 1 to 2 hours. Preheat grill. Thread 8 to 10 pieces chicken on each skewer. Grill over medium-hot coals for 6 to 8 minutes or until done, basting with remaining marinade. May serve with additional picante sauce if desired.
Yield: 4 to 6 servings.

Lisa Smith, Xi Xi Iota
Texarkana, Texas

GRILLED TURKEY BREAST

My family and I have raised and been associated with turkeys for 41 years. I have cooked turkey just about every way possible.

1/4 cup soy sauce	1/4 teaspoon dry
1/4 cup vegetable oil	mustard
1/4 cup wine or sherry	Pepper to taste
2 tablespoons lemon	Garlic salt to taste
juice	1 pound turkey breast
2 tablespoons	steaks, 3/4 to 1 inch
dehydrated onion	thick

Combine first 8 ingredients in shallow dish; blend well. Add turkey, turning to coat both sides. Refrigerate, covered, for at least 5 hours, turning occasionally. Grill over medium-hot coals for 6 to 8 minutes per side or until done, basting with marinade. Steaks are done when there is no pink in center; do not overcook. Yield: 4 servings.

Marnell Comer, Omega Mu
Ridgeway, Missouri
*Evann J. Clayton, Mu Epsilon
Jefferson City, Missouri

GRILLED WHOLE TURKEY WITH LIME

1 12-pound turkey
1/2 cup butter or
   margarine
Juice of 6 limes
2 tablespoons
   Tequila

2 tablespoons finely
   chopped fresh oregano
   or 1 teaspoon dried
   oregano
Salt to taste
Freshly ground pepper

Preheat grill. Have butcher butterfly turkey. Cut off excess skin and fat. Rinse and pat dry. Insert meat thermometer in thickest part, not touching bone. Melt butter in saucepan; add remaining ingredients, mixing well. Place turkey, skin side down, on oiled grill about 6 inches above heat. Mop turkey with lime mixture. Grill for 1 1/2 to 2 hours or until meat thermometer reads 170 degrees, turning and basting with lime mixture every 15 minutes. Yield: 6 servings.

Jean Wawiorka, Epsilon Beta
Waukesha, Wisconsin

BROILED COMPANY TURKEY FILETS

1/4 cup mayonnaise
1/4 cup soy sauce
3 tablespoons olive oil
1 tablespoon water
1 tablespoon lemon juice
2 teaspoons oregano

2 cloves of garlic,
   pressed
3/4 teaspoon pepper
4 turkey breast
   tenderloins

Whisk mayonnaise slowly into soy sauce in bowl. Stir in next 6 ingredients; mix well. Pour marinade into plastic bag; add turkey. Press air out of bag; seal. Refrigerate for 24 hours or longer, moving turkey around inside bag once or twice. Preheat grill. Grill turkey over medium-hot coals for 12 minutes on each side or until done, basting with marinade. Yield: 4 servings.

Cathy Royce, Epsilon Beta
Elm Grove, Wisconsin

GRILLED HALIBUT STEAKS

1/2 cup white wine
2 or 3 cracked
   peppercorns
1/2 teaspoon salt

2 halibut steaks, 1 1/2
   inches thick, 6 inches
   in diameter

Combine wine, peppercorns and salt in shallow dish; mix well. Add steaks; marinate, at room temperature, for 30 to 45 minutes, turning frequently. Preheat grill. Place steaks in basket grill; cook over medium-hot coals for 6 to 8 minutes on each side or until done, basting with marinade. Surface of fish will show each layer of flesh in a white outlined pattern when done. Yield: 4 servings.

Mary Swartout, Preceptor Beta Sigma
Magalia, California

BARBECUED HALIBUT

1/2 cup butter or
   margarine, softened
1 tablespoon snipped
   fresh basil or
   1 teaspoon dried basil
1 tablespoon snipped
   parsley

2 teaspoons lemon juice
Cooking oil
4 1/2-pound halibut,
   salmon or shark steaks,
   cut 1 inch thick

Combine first 4 ingredients in bowl; blend well. Preheat grill; brush grill rack with cooking oil. Place fish on grill; lightly brush with butter mixture. Grill, uncovered, over medium-hot coals for 5 minutes. Turn; brush with butter mixture. Grill for 3 to 7 minutes or until done. Dollop remaining butter mixture on top of fish. Yield: 4 servings.

Jill Knoechel, Xi Delta
St. John's, Newfoundland, Canada

BARBECUED BASS

Nonstick cooking spray
2 pounds bass filets, cut
   into serving pieces
3 tablespoons lemon
   juice
2 tablespoons dried
   minced onion

1 tablespoon Cavenders
   seasoning
1/4 cup barbecue sauce
1/4 cup picante sauce

Spray filets on both sides with nonstick cooking spray. Sprinkle with lemon juice, onion and seasoning. Let stand for 5 minutes. Combine barbecue and picante sauces in bowl; mix well. Preheat grill. Grill filets, covered, over medium-hot coals for 4 minutes, basting with sauce. Turn; cook, covered, for 4 minutes or until fish flakes. Yield: 4 servings.

Mary Masterson, Xi Epsilon Rho
Center, Texas

CALGARY STAMPEDE SALMON BARBECUE

Because I'm from the coast, I like to serve the "cowboys" something different!

1 cup soya sauce
2 tablespoons light
   brown sugar
1 tablespoon dry
   mustard

Juice of 1 lemon
4 to 6 salmon steaks
Salt to taste
Fresh ground pepper to
   taste

Combine first 4 ingredients in shallow dish; mix well. Add steaks; marinate for 2 to 3 hours. Preheat grill. Drain steaks; reserve marinade. Grill steaks over medium-hot coals for 4 to 5 minutes on each side or until done, basting with marinade. Sprinkle with salt and pepper. May serve with crab fettucini and fresh vegetables if desired. Yield: 4 to 6 servings.

Lysle Barmby, Xi Omicron
Bragg Creek, Alberta, Canada

INDIAN-STYLE BARBECUED SALMON

1/4 cup lemon juice	1/4 cup butter or
1/4 cup packed light	margarine
brown sugar	Salmon filets
1/4 cup honey	

Preheat grill; spray with nonstick cooking spray. Combine first 4 ingredients in bowl; mix well. Grill salmon, skin side down, over medium-hot coals for 10 to 12 minutes on each side or until done, basting with sauce. Yield: 4 servings.

Carol L. Anderson, Xi Epsilon Alpha
Spokane, Washington

GRILLED SHRIMP

2 pounds fresh shrimp	Juice of 1 lemon
1 cup olive oil or	1 tablespoon
vegetable oil	Worcestershire sauce
1 cup dry sherry	1 tablespoon soy sauce
1 cup soy sauce	Tabasco sauce to taste
1 clove of garlic	(optional)
1 cup butter or	
margarine	

Peel, devein and rinse shrimp. Combine next 4 ingredients in shallow dish; mix well. Add shrimp; marinate for 20 to 25 minutes. Combine remaining ingredients in bowl; mix well. Preheat grill. Drain shrimp; reserve marinade. Thread shrimp on skewers. Grill over medium-hot coals for 2 minutes on each side or until shrimp turn pink, basting with marinade. Serve with butter sauce. Yield: 6 servings.

Betty Snavely, Laureate Sigma
Lilburn, Georgia

FAVORITE SHRIMP

1 pound large shrimp	1 tablespoon Tabasco
1 16-ounce bottle of	sauce
Italian dressing	1 tablespoon lemon juice
1/3 cup soy sauce	1/4 teaspoon celery seed

Peel, devein and rinse shrimp. Combine remaining ingredients in shallow dish; mix well. Add shrimp; refrigerate for 6 hours, turning shrimp often. Preheat grill. Drain shrimp; reserve marinade. Thread shrimp on skewers. Grill over medium-hot coals for 3 minutes on each side or until shrimp turn pink, basting with marinade. Yield: 6 servings.

Elizabeth Taubert, Theta Psi
Cookeville, Tennessee

TRI-TIP ROAST MARINADE

1/2 cup wine	1 teaspoon ground
1/2 cup soy sauce	ginger
1/2 teaspoon garlic	
powder	

Combine all ingredients in bowl; mix well. Marinate roast overnight in refrigerator, turning once or twice. Grill for 20 to 30 minutes on each side, basting frequently with marinade. Heat remaining marinade to a boil; pour over sliced roast to serve. Yield: 1 cup.

Charlotte Carter, Laureate Alpha
Roseburg, Oregon

BEEF AND CHICKEN MARINADE

1 8-ounce bottle of	2 teaspoons
Italian salad dressing	Worcestershire sauce
1/4 cup soy sauce	1 clove of garlic, crushed
2 tablespoons brown	1 green bell pepper,
sugar	sliced
2 tablespoons lemon	1 medium onion, sliced
juice	

Combine first 5 ingredients in bowl; mix well. Rub garlic over desired meat. Pour marinade over meat. Place green pepper and onion on top. Refrigerate, covered, for 24 hours, turning meat once. Barbecue as desired. May use top round steak, London broil, tenderloin or chicken breasts and wings if desired. Yield: enough marinade for 4 pounds meat.

Shelly Bailey, Beta Delta
Havre, Montana

NEVER-A-TOUGH-STEAK MARINADE

This is a great marinade and makes an average steak great.

3 tablespoons	1 1/2 teaspoons cider
vegetable oil	vinegar
1 teaspoon fresh lemon	1/2 teaspoon salt
juice	Pepper to taste
Pinch of sugar	

Combine all ingredients in bowl; mix well. Marinate steak in marinade for at least 2 hours. Grill as desired. Yield: marinade for 1 steak.

Linda McMillan, Gamma Tau
Pearl, Mississippi

ORIENTAL MARINADE

After my third child, I wanted to cut calories and still eat something mouth-watering! This is it!

1/2 cup soy sauce	1/4 teaspoon ground
1/4 cup water	ginger
2 tablespoons vinegar	1/2 teaspoon garlic
1 tablespoon cooking oil	powder
1 teaspoon sugar	

Combine all ingredients in 1-gallon zip lock plastic bag. Place meat in bag; seal bag. Refrigerate for 4 to 6 hours. Grill as desired. Yield: 1 cup.

Denise R. Wheaton, Xi Zeta Omega
Lewis, Kansas

TERIYAKI STEAK MARINADE FOR BARBECUE

This is an old recipe I have used for over 25 years. My family loves steak fixed this way!

1 clove of garlic, minced
2 tablespoons light brown sugar
1/2 teaspoon ground ginger
1/2 teaspoon coarsely ground black pepper
2 tablespoons water
1 tablespoon cooking oil
1/4 cup soy sauce

Combine garlic and brown sugar in bowl. Add remaining ingredients; mix well. Place steak in marinade, turning to coat well. Let stand at room temperature for 1 hour or refrigerate overnight, turning once or twice. Drain well; grill as desired. Yield: 1/2 cup.

*Mary Jane Happy, Xi Delta Chi
Camden, Missouri*

SWEET-SOUR MARINADE FOR MEAT

I use this recipe all summer long. It is fast, easy, delicious and can be made ahead of time.

1 cup soy sauce
1 cup catsup
1/2 cup sugar
2 tablespoons hoisin sauce
1 tablespoon sherry
1 tablespoon wine vinegar
6 cloves of garlic, minced
2 tablespoons fresh ginger, peeled, minced

Combine all ingredients in bowl; mix well. Pour over meat. Marinate at least 2 hours or overnight in refrigerator. Good on spareribs, leg of lamb, chicken or fish. May be stored in refrigerator, covered, for up to 1 month. Yield: 2 1/2 cups.

*Patricia Anderson, Rho
Spearfish, South Dakota*

BARBECUE SAUCE

2 tablespoons chopped onion
2 tablespoons butter or margarine
1 clove of garlic, crushed
1 cup catsup
4 tablespoons white vinegar
1/2 teaspoon chili powder
1/2 teaspoon paprika
4 teaspoons sugar
2 tablespoons prepared mustard
2 teaspoons Worcestershire sauce
1/2 teaspoon salt
1 cup water

Sauté onion in butter in medium saucepan until transparent. Add garlic. Combine remaining ingredients in bowl; mix well. Add to onion-garlic mixture; simmer over low heat for 15 to 20 minutes. Refrigerate until ready to use. Marinate steak at least 20 minutes or longer. Yield: 2 1/2 cups.

*Beth Couillard, Pi Kappa
Petitcodiac, New Brunswick, Canada*

BARBECUED SPARERIB SAUCE

This tastes like a famous rib restaurant's sauce in Montreal, Canada, that has the best tasting ribs anywhere.

1 1/2 cups catsup
4 tablespoons dark corn syrup
1 1/2 teaspoons chili powder
2 teaspoons oregano
1 cup packed light brown sugar
6 tablespoons wine vinegar
6 to 10 tablespoons sweet-sour barbecue sauce
4 teaspoons salt
2 teaspoons pepper
4 teaspoons garlic powder
1 bottle of V.H. garlic sauce

Combine all ingredients in saucepan; boil for 2 minutes. Use to marinate spareribs for at least 1 hour and as a basting sauce during grilling. Yield: Approximately 3 cups.

*Marian Lyne, Nu
Hampton, New Brunswick, Canada*

PORK RIB MARINADE BARBECUE SAUCE

1 cup packed light brown sugar
1 teaspoon pepper
1 tablespoon salt
1 tablespoon paprika
1 cup tomato sauce
1 tablespoon Worcestershire sauce
2 tablespoons soy sauce
1 tablespoon garlic sauce

Combine all ingredients in saucepan; bring to a boil. Cool; marinate ribs in refrigerator overnight. Grill as desired, basting with sauce. Yield: enough for 2 pounds ribs.

*Debbie Geer, Zeta Pi
Corning, California*

RAY'S MARINADE AND BARBECUE SAUCE

Pat's husband, Ray, is the originator of this recipe. He is the Number 1 Chef at all sorority barbecues.

32 ounces catsup or tomato sauce
1/4 cup soy sauce
1 cup honey
3 tablespoons vinegar or 1 tablespoon lemon juice
2 tablespoons cooking sherry (optional)
1 tablespoon dry oregano leaves
2 teaspoons black pepper
1 bay leaf
1 teaspoon curry powder
1 teaspoon garlic salt

Combine all ingredients in bowl; mix well. Marinate meat for 2 to 3 hours before cooking. Baste with sauce during cooking. Great on steak or chicken. Yield: approximately 5 cups.

*Pat Lopez, Preceptor Beta Epsilon
Mohave Valley, Arizona*

CAJUN BARBECUE SAUCE

1 large can tomato juice
1 large bottle of catsup
1 box light brown sugar
1 cup chopped onion
5 tablespoons
Worcestershire sauce
Salt and pepper to taste
2 lemons

Combine first 6 ingredients in large saucepan. Cut lemons into quarters; remove seeds. Add to mixture. Simmer over low heat for 4 hours or all day. Yield: Approximately 2 quarts.

Mary Florene Stafford
Brackettville, Texas

CHICKEN BARBECUE SAUCE

1/2 cup margarine
1 tablespoon garlic
   powder
2 tablespoons lemon
   juice
1/4 teaspoon thyme
Salt and pepper to taste
1/4 cup dry white wine

Combine first 5 ingredients in saucepan; heat until margarine is melted. Add wine; heat but do not boil. Yield: sauce for 1 chicken.

Shirley Fitch, Preceptor Rho
Flagstaff, Arizona

AUNT RUBY'S BARBECUE BASTING SAUCE

My aunt said this was the same basting sauce used at her 4-H chicken barbecue.

1 cup butter or
   margarine
2 cups vinegar
2 cups water
Salt to taste
2 tablespoons
   Worcestershire sauce

Melt butter in saucepan. Add remaining ingredients; mix well. Use to baste beef, pork or chicken. Yield: 5 cups.

Elizabeth McKnight, Theta Theta
Goshen, Indiana

CHICKEN BARBECUE SAUCE

The chicken does not burn! Everyone raves about the flavor of the chicken.

1 egg, beaten
1/2 cup vegetable oil
1 cup vinegar
1 tablespoon salt
1 teaspoon poultry
   seasoning
1 teaspoon white
   pepper

Combine egg and oil in saucepan; beat until well mixed. Add remaining ingredients; mix well. Heat over low heat, stirring frequently, but do not boil. Baste chicken while grilling, turning often. Can be stored, covered, in refrigerator for several days. Yield: approximately 2 cups.

Judy Lance, Xi Gamma
Toccoa, Georgia

TANNIS' BARBECUE SAUCE

This recipe was created throughout an entire summer cooking over a campfire while building a house to live in! It has a full-bodied zesty taste.

1 cup catsup
1/4 cup fresh lemon juice
1/4 cup honey
2 teaspoons
   Worcestershire sauce
2 small dry red chili
   peppers, crushed
1 teaspoon onion salt
1/2 teaspoon cloves

Combine all ingredients in small saucepan; heat over medium heat, stirring frequently, until all ingredients are well blended. Baste chicken or pork while barbecuing. May add slightly more honey for pork if desired. Yield: 1 1/2 cups.

Tannis Chequis, Beta Nu
Kitimat, British Columbia, Canada

DELICIOUS BARBECUE SAUCE

10 cups catsup
2 tablespoons dry
   mustard
2 cups packed dark
   brown sugar
2 tablespoons liquid
   smoke
Hickory seasoning
1 cup finely chopped
   onion
1/2 cup Heinz 57 steak
   sauce
1 tablespoon
   Worcestershire sauce
2 tablespoons hot red
   pepper sauce
1 tablespoon A-1 sauce

Combine all ingredients in large saucepan; simmer over low heat for 40 minutes, stirring frequently. Brush over meat while grilling. Yield: approximately 3 quarts.

Marjorie C. Burkdoll, Delta Master
Ogden, Utah

CHILI SAUCE

This sauce is great on barbecued hamburgers. We also enjoy it with roast beef, pork and chicken.

30 ripe tomatoes,
   peeled, chopped
4 onions, diced
1 celery heart, diced
2 red bell peppers,
   chopped
1 green bell pepper,
   chopped
4 cups sugar
2 cups vinegar
2 tablespoons pickling
   spice
2 tablespoons pickling
   salt

Combine all ingredients in saucepan; bring to a boil. Reduce heat; cook, stirring frequently, until thickened or for at least 3 hours. Pour into sterilized jars; seal. Yield: 6 pints.

Louise Lawson, Preceptor Gamma
Souris, Manitoba, Canada

MUSTARD SAUCE

This sauce is very good served over Polish sausages.

1/4 cup dry mustard	*1/3 cup sugar*
1/2 cup white vinegar	*1 egg yolk, beaten*

Combine mustard and vinegar in saucepan; whisk until well blended. Let stand at room temperature for 6 hours or overnight. Add remaining ingredients; mix well. Cook over low heat for 10 to 15 minutes or until thickened, stirring frequently.
Yield: 1 cup.

Carole J. Payne, Omega Nu
Jamesport, Missouri

TERIYAKI SAUCE

1/2 cup soy sauce	*Dash of dry mustard*
1/4 cup bourbon or sherry	*1 clove of garlic, crushed*
2 tablespoons dark brown sugar	*1/2 teaspoon ginger*

Combine all ingredients in bowl; mix well. Use as a marinade for beef or chicken. Yield: 1 cup.

Pat Jordan, Preceptor Alpha
Missoula, Montana

JOHN'S KRAUT FOR SAUSAGE

1 pound bacon, cut into small pieces	*1 large jar sauerkraut, drained*
2 large green bell peppers, chopped	*1 medium can tomato sauce*
2 large onions, chopped	

Fry bacon in large skillet until browned; remove from drippings. Sauté peppers and onions in drippings until tender. Add bacon, sauerkraut and tomato sauce. Simmer for approximately 30 minutes. Keep warm in Crock•Pot. Use less tomato sauce for a thicker sauce. May serve over hot dogs, Polish sausage or bratwurst if desired.
Yield: approximately 1 quart.

Betty Nix, Xi Lambda Sigma
Royalton, Illinois

ONION BURGERS

2 pounds ground beef	*1 envelope onion soup mix*
2 tablespoons sour cream	*1/2 cup cornflake crumbs*
2 tablespoons catsup	*Buns*
1/2 teaspoon parsley flakes	

Combine all ingredients in bowl; mix well. Shape into patties of desired size. Grill to desired doneness. Serve hot on buns. May broil if desired; do not fry.
Yield: 6 to 10 servings.

Linda Hrabik, Omega Tau
Jackson, Missouri

BURGUNDY BEEFBURGERS

2 pounds ground chuck	*2 tablespoons sliced green onions*
1 cup soft bread crumbs	*1/2 cup butter or margarine*
1 egg	*1/4 cup dry red wine*
1 teaspoon salt	
Dash of pepper	

Combine first 5 ingredients in large bowl; toss with fork until well mixed. Shape into 8 patties, about 1/2 inch thick. Cook onions in butter in saucepan until just tender; add wine. Cook patties over hot coals for 13 to 15 minutes or until desired doneness, turning once; brush frequently with sauce. Heat remaining sauce to serve with beefburgers. May serve with hamburger buns if desired. Yield: 8 servings.

Charlotte J. Zeiller, Xi Mu Nu
Dunnellon, Florida

CORNED BEEF BARBECUES

2 pounds ground beef	*1 teaspoon chili powder*
1 onion, chopped	*2 tablespoons all-purpose flour*
1 can corned beef, mashed	*Dash of garlic powder*
1 medium-sized bottle barbecue sauce	*12 buns*
2 tablespoons dark brown sugar	*1 small cabbage, shredded*

Cook ground beef and onion in skillet until browned; drain well. Add next 6 ingredients; mix well. Bring to a boil. Serve on buns with shredded cabbage.
Yield: 12 servings.

Doris Grachek, Xi Eta
Omaha, Nebraska

OLD-TIME HOT DOGS

1/2 pound ground beef	*1/2 teaspoon Worcestershire sauce*
1 medium onion, chopped	*10 hot dogs, cooked*
1 8-ounce can tomato sauce	*10 hot dog buns*
1 tablespoon chili powder	

Sauté ground beef and onion in large skillet over medium heat, stirring often, until beef is browned; drain well. Add tomato sauce, chili powder and Worcestershire sauce. Bring to a boil; reduce heat and simmer for 10 minutes. Serve hot dogs in buns topped with beef mixture. May add your favorite regular toppings if desired. May add a little cinnamon to beef mixture and it will taste like it came from a New York pushcart, a little oregano will give a Greek or Italian flavor and a teaspoon of cumin will make it an authentic chili dog, if desired.
Yield: 10 servings.

Mary Elizabeth Beitel, Beta Nu
Encampment, Wyoming

WISCONSIN BRATWURST

8 bratwurst sausages
2 or 3 onions, thinly
  sliced
1/2 cup butter
  or margarine
1 can beer

Bratwurst buns or
  potato buns
Dill pickles
German mustard to
  taste

Grill bratwurst over medium-hot charcoal until browned. Sauté onions in butter in saucepan for 10 to 15 minutes. Add beer and grilled bratwurst; cover and steam over low heat until ready to serve. Serve on buns with pickles and mustard. May serve with German potato salad and sliced tomatoes if desired. Yield: 8 servings.

Mary Croarkin, Laureate Chi
Macon, Missouri
*Marge Wolf, Xi Beta Epsilon
Rogers, Arkansas

HOT TURKEY SANDWICHES

1 16- to 18-pound
  turkey, baked
1 pound ground beef
1 pound pork sausage
3 loaves dry bread,
  cubed

1 onion, diced
1/2 tablespoon ground
  sage
Buns

Bake turkey according to package directions; reserve broth. Preheat electric roaster to 350 degrees. Debone and dice turkey. Combine turkey and next 5 ingredients in large bowl; mix well. Pour into roaster; cook for 1 hour. Reduce temperature to 325 degrees; cook for 2 to 3 hours or until broth is absorbed. Serve on buns. Yield: 12 dozen sandwiches.

Michele Elsbernd, Preceptor Beta Delta
Fort Atkinson, Iowa

SWISSY SPREAD

This recipe is a favorite picnic standard after hikes in the Rocky Mountains.

1 cup grated Swiss
  cheese
1 cup cottage cheese
1/2 cup chopped green
  pepper
1/2 teaspoon dillweed
Salt and pepper to
  taste

2 tablespoons
  mayonnaise
2 tablespoons chopped
  green onion tops
1 package pita bread,
  halved
Alfalfa sprouts
  (optional)

Combine first 7 ingredients in bowl; mix well. Spoon filling into pita bread; top with sprouts. Yield: 6 to 8 servings.

Marcia Bohnenblust, Zeta Delta
Greeley, Colorado

HOT BACKYARD SUPPER BUNS

3/4 cup chopped chicken
  or tuna
1/4 cup mayonnaise
1/3 cup diced celery
1 tablespoon minced
  onion

1 tablespoon lemon juice
1/4 teaspoon salt
1/2 cup grated American
  cheese
4 sandwich buns

Preheat oven to 350 degrees. Combine first 7 ingredients in bowl; mix well. Spread between buns. Wrap in aluminum foil. Bake for 15 minutes. May be frozen and heated when ready to use if desired. Yield: 4 sandwiches.

Lenette F. Pettigrew
Fort Wayne, Indiana

CALICO BEANS

1/2 pound ground beef
1/2 pound bacon, diced
1/4 cup chopped onion
1/2 cup catsup
1 teaspoon mustard
3/4 cup packed dark
  brown sugar

2 tablespoons vinegar
1 teaspoon salt
1 large can pork and
  beans
1 large can lima beans
1 large can kidney beans

Preheat oven to 350 degrees. Cook first 3 ingredients in skillet until beef is browned; drain. Combine remaining ingredients in bean pot or casserole; add beef mixture, mixing well. Bake for 40 minutes. May be cooked in Crock•Pot if desired. Yield: 8 servings.

Linda Endorf
Mitchell, South Dakota

THREE-BEAN CASSEROLE

This is a wonderful outdoor entreé. The aroma brings out neighbors to check on activities.

1 pound ground beef
1 cup chopped onion
3/4 cup 1-inch pieces
  bacon
2 31-ounce cans pork
  and beans
1 30-ounce can kidney
  beans, drained
1 30-ounce can butter
  beans, drained

1 cup catsup
1 tablespoon liquid
  smoke
3 tablespoons cider
  vinegar
1 tablespoon (scant) salt
1 tablespoon chopped
  green bell pepper
  (optional)

Preheat oven to 350 degrees. Brown ground beef and onion in skillet; drain. Sauté bacon in skillet; drain. Combine beef, onions, bacon and remaining ingredients in large crock; mix well. Bake for 2 hours. May simmer outdoors in electrical crock or slow cooking pot. Yield: 10 to 12 servings.

Ruth F. Blayden, Laureate Lambda
Salmon, Idaho

BEANS FOR A CROWD

10 slices bacon, cut into pieces	2 teaspoons dried oregano
1¹/₂ cups chopped onions	2 teaspoons dry mustard
1 15-ounce can lima beans	Freshly ground pepper to taste
1 15-ounce can kidney beans	Salt to taste
	1 red bell pepper, chopped
1 15-ounce can Great Northern beans	1 yellow bell pepper, chopped
1 15-ounce can pinto beans	1 green bell pepper, chopped
¹/₄ cup honey	2 10-ounce packages frozen corn
3 tablespoons cider vinegar	2 stalks celery, diced
2 teaspoons ground cumin	1 28-ounce can plum tomatoes, drained, chopped

Preheat oven to 350 degrees. Crisp-fry bacon in large skillet; remove and crumble bacon, reserving drippings in skillet. Add onions to drippings; cook over low heat until soft, but not brown. Drain beans, reserving liquid; combine liquids. Stir 1 cup bean liquid, honey, vinegar and seasonings into onions. Add bacon and remaining ingredients; mix well. Pour into 11-by-15-inch baking dish. Bake for 1¹/₂ hours or until thickened and bubbly.
Yield: 12 servings.

Betty J. Erickson, Xi Epsilon Gamma
Walnut, California

NEW ORLEANS BAKED BEANS

5 slices bacon	2 tablespoons dark brown sugar
3 large onions, chopped	
1 green bell pepper, chopped	1 tablespoon Worcestershire sauce
1 cup chopped cooked ham	Salt and pepper to taste
2 10-ounce cans tomato soup	

Preheat oven to 350 degrees. Crisp-fry bacon in skillet; reserve 4 tablespoons drippings in skillet. Sauté onions and peppers in drippings until almost tender. Add bacon and remaining ingredients; mix well. Pour into greased baking dish. Bake for 40 minutes.
Yield: 4 servings.

Shirley Siler, Theta Omega
San Angelo, Texas

SALE BARN BEANS

6 slices bacon	¹/₄ cup dry red wine
1 envelope onion soup mix	1 cup cubed sharp Cheddar cheese
4 cups cooked red beans	¹/₄ teaspoon salt
¹/₂ cup barbecue sauce	
¹/₄ cup chili sauce	

Preheat oven to 350 degrees. Sauté bacon in large skillet until crisp; drain and crumble. Combine bacon and remaining ingredients in 2-quart casserole or saucepan; mix well. Bake or cook for 10 to 15 minutes or until cheese is melted and mixture is bubbly. Yield: 6 servings.

Ginny Cooper, Xi Omicron
Harlingen, Texas

PATIO BEANS

I like to fix this over a Coleman stove when we get together with Boy Scout leaders. The aroma drives the hunger thermometer sky high! It is excellent to serve with hamburgers.

3 slices bacon	1 16-ounce can pork and beans
¹/₃ cup chopped green bell pepper	¹/₄ to ¹/₃ cup barbecue sauce
¹/₃ cup chopped onion	
1 cup drained whole kernel corn	

Crisp-fry bacon in large skillet, reserving 1 tablespoon drippings; crumble. Sauté green pepper and onion in reserved drippings until softened. Add corn, pork and beans and barbecue sauce; mix well. Cook over medium-low heat until heated through; do not boil. Stir in crumbled bacon; serve hot.
Yield: 4 servings.

Diane Trembly, Xi Alpha Epsilon
Durango, Colorado

SATISFACTION SIX-BEAN CASSEROLE

Men go out of their way to tell me how much they like this casserole. It is hearty and substitutions can be made easily. It is a great covered dish and no leftovers.

¹/₂ pound spicy bulk sausage	1 16-ounce can white kidney beans, drained
¹/₄ pound pepperoni, thinly sliced	1 16-ounce can butter beans, drained
¹/₄ pound smoked kielbasa, sliced	1 16-ounce can lima beans, drained
¹/₄ cup barbecue sauce	1 10-ounce can tomato soup, undiluted
1 16-ounce can pork and beans, undrained	3 ounces tomato paste
1 16-ounce can red kidney beans, undrained	¹/₂ cup packed dark brown sugar
	6 slices bacon, partially cooked
1 16-ounce can chili beans, undrained	

Preheat oven to 325 degrees. Shape sausage into 1-inch balls. Brown in skillet and drain. Combine sausage and next 12 ingredients in 5-quart casserole or small roasting pan. Arrange bacon over top. Baked, uncovered, for 1¹/₂ hours. Serve hot or cold.
Yield: 16 servings.

Linda D. Swim, Preceptor Zeta
Marysville, Kansas

FIVE-BEAN CASSEROLE

The Peters family has an annual Putt and Pork. We go golfing, then barbecue. This recipe is perfect for it.

1 16-ounce can cut green beans, drained	1 6-ounce can tomato paste
1 16-ounce can wax beans, drained	1 cup packed dark brown sugar
1 16-ounce can lima beans, drained	1 small onion, chopped
1 31-ounce can pork and beans	1 green bell pepper, chopped
1 24-ounce can chili beans	1 pound mild Italian sausage, browned, drained
1 6-ounce can tomato sauce	

Preheat oven to 250 degrees. Combine all ingredients in 4-quart casserole or bean pot; mix well. Bake, covered, for 4 hours. Yield: 24 servings.

Maggie Peters, Xi Alpha Beta
Fremont, Nebraska

BAKED CORN CASSEROLE

A good friend shared this recipe with me. I've never found a child who did not like it.

1/2 cup margarine, melted	1 16-ounce can whole kernel corn, drained
1 16-ounce can cream-style corn	1 8 1/2-ounce box Jiffy corn muffin mix
8 ounces sour cream	

Preheat oven to 375 degrees. Combine all ingredients in casserole; mix well. Bake for 45 minutes to 1 hour or until golden brown and crusty on top. Yield: 8 servings.

Jenny Fuller, Xi Zeta Omega
Kinsley, Kansas

JALAPEÑO CORN

4 or 5 jalapeño peppers	1 cup yellow cornmeal
1 1/2 cups water	1 tablespoon baking powder
2 eggs, beaten	1 1/2 teaspoons salt
2 16-ounce cans cream-style corn	2 cups shredded Velveeta cheese
2/3 cup corn oil	
2 cups sour cream	

Preheat oven to 350 degrees. Boil jalapeño peppers in water in saucepan until tender. Combine eggs, corn, oil and sour cream in large bowl; mix well. Combine cornmeal, baking powder and salt in bowl; mix well. Add to egg mixture. Drain jalapeño peppers; remove seeds and chop. Add jalapeño peppers and cheese to batter; mix well. Pour into greased 9-inch square baking pan. Bake for 1 hour. Yield: 12 servings.

Kathy M. Parker, Xi Phi Alpha Omega
Wichita Falls, Texas

GRILLED MUSHROOMS WITH BACON

24 large whole mushrooms	1/4 cup packed dark brown sugar
24 slices bacon	1/4 teaspoon onion powder
1 cup margarine, melted	1/4 teaspoon garlic powder
1 cup teriyaki sauce	
1/4 cup liquid smoke	

Preheat grill. Wrap each mushroom with bacon slice, securing end with toothpick. Combine remaining ingredients in bowl; mix well. Place mushrooms in 9-by-13-inch baking pan. Pour marinade over mushrooms. Grill over medium-hot coals for 30 minutes or until bacon is done, basting occasionally with marinade. Yield: 8 to 10 servings.

Sandra Cox, Alpha Zeta
Brownwood, Texas

EGGPLANT PARMESAN

1 large eggplant	6 ounces sliced mozzarella cheese
1/2 cup vegetable oil	1 cup grated Parmesan cheese
1/2 teaspoon dried oregano, crushed	1 15-ounce jar Marinara sauce, heated
1/2 teaspoon dried rosemary, crushed	
1/4 teaspoon garlic powder	

Preheat grill. Rinse eggplant well; do not peel. Slice eggplant crosswise into 1/2-inch slices. Combine next 4 ingredients in bowl. Brush sides of eggplant slices with oil mixture. Cut mozzarella cheese slices to fit eggplant slices; set aside. Grill eggplant on covered grill over medium-hot coals for 5 minutes on each side, turning often and basting with oil. Arrange mozzarella cheese slices on eggplant slices; spoon Parmesan cheese over each. Grill until cheeses melt. Place eggplant on serving dish; spoon Marinara sauce over eggplant before serving. Yield: 6 to 8 servings.

Evie Russel
Gering, Nebraska

BAKED POTATO STRIPS

3 large baking potatoes	Garlic salt to taste
1/2 cup butter or margarine, melted	1 cup shredded cheese (optional)

Preheat oven to 400 degrees. Slice unpeeled potatoes lengthwise into large slices. Place on 9-by-13-inch baking pan. Coat with butter; sprinkle with garlic salt. Bake for 1 hour. Sprinkle with cheese; bake until cheese is melted. Can also be cooked on grill in foil. Yield: 6 servings.

Aleta O'Neal
Windsor, Missouri

POTATOES ON THE GRILL

This is an easy recipe with a "throw-away" foil pan. I receive many compliments on it.

6 potatoes, peeled,
    sliced lengthwise
    as for French fries
1 small onion, sliced
1 small green bell
    pepper, diced

4 tablespoons butter or
    margarine
Paprika to taste
Salt and pepper to taste
Garlic salt to taste

Preheat grill. Spray large piece of heavy-duty foil generously with nonstick cooking spray. Arrange potatoes, onion and green pepper on foil. Cut butter into small pieces; place evenly over potatoes. Add remaining ingredients. Fold foil into packet to seal. Grill over medium-hot coals for 30 minutes on each side. Yield: 6 servings.

Denise Nielsen, Xi Lambda Lambda
North Canton, Ohio

BRONSON DILLY TATERS

4 red potatoes
1 green bell pepper
1/2 large onion, chopped
1 tablespoon margarine,
    melted

2 teaspoons dill
    seasoning
1 tablespoon water

Preheat grill. Cut potatoes into quarters. Slice green pepper into 1-inch pieces. Layer potatoes, green pepper and onion on large piece of aluminum foil. Drizzle with margarine; sprinkle with dill. Add water; wrap foil to seal edges. Grill over medium-hot coals for 10 minutes on each side or until potatoes are done. Yield: 4 servings.

Marilyn Waltz, Preceptor Lambda Phi
Salton Sea Beach, California

LIPTON ONION POTATOES

I have cooked this many times for barbecue parties and camping. It is easy, great eating and goes with any meat.

5 or 6 medium potatoes
1/4 cup margarine,
    melted
2 packages onion
    soup mix

Salt and pepper to taste
Sour cream

Preheat oven to 350 degrees. Wash and scrub potatoes; do not peel. Cut into 1/4-inch thin slices; place in 9-by-13-inch baking pan. Drizzle with margarine; sprinkle with soup mix. Add salt and pepper; cover with foil. Bake for 1 hour or until tender, stirring twice. Serve plain or with sour cream. Can be baked on grill in pan or foil, turning several times. Yield: 6 servings.

Linda Elliott, Alpha Mu
Rapid City, South Dakota

❖ CASHEW RICE

We serve this at every barbecue. It is such a favorite! Great with barbecue chicken, steak and ribs.

4 fresh mushrooms,
    sliced or 1 4-ounce
    can sliced mushrooms,
    drained
1 green bell pepper, diced
1 onion, diced

6 tablespoons butter or
    margarine
1 1/4 cups long grain rice
2 cans consommé
1 cup salted cashews

Preheat oven to 350 degrees. Sauté mushrooms, green pepper and onion in butter in skillet. Combine mushrooms, green pepper, onion, rice and consommé in lightly greased 2-quart casserole. Bake, covered, for 45 minutes or until moisture is absorbed. Add cashews during last 10 minutes of cooking. Yield: 6 servings.

Mary Roberson, Xi Epsilon Pi
Sacramento, California

REFRIGERATOR PICKLES

2 cups sugar
1 cup vinegar
1 green bell pepper,
    chopped

1 large onion, chopped
1 tablespoon salt
1 teaspoon celery salt
7 cups sliced cucumbers

Combine first 6 ingredients in saucepan; cook over medium heat until pepper is tender. Cool to room temperature. Place cucumbers in large canning jars; pour vinegar mixture over cucumbers. Refrigerate for at least 24 hours. Use no salt or celery salt if on salt-free diet. Yield: 2 pints.

Barbara Osterman, Preceptor Mu
Las Vegas, Nevada

CHOP SUEY PICKLE RELISH

This was my mother's recipe. At a recent family gathering, relatives fondly remembered it as one of her favorite recipes.

6 large cucumbers,
    peeled
11 small onions
3 large sweet green bell
    peppers
3 large sweet red bell
    peppers
1/2 cup salt

2 cups vinegar
1 cup water
2 tablespoons celery
    salt
3 tablespoons mixed
    pickling spices
4 cups sugar
1 teaspoon curry powder

Slice cucumbers, onions and peppers very thin; combine in large bowl. Sprinkle with salt; add water to cover. Let stand overnight. Drain; rinse in clear water twice. Drain well; place in large kettle. Add next 5 ingredients; boil for 10 minutes. Add curry powder just before removing from heat. Pack into hot sterilized jars; seal at once. Yield: 4 to 6 pints.

Roxanne Petersen, Lambda Epsilon
Ankeny, Iowa

SWEET DILL PICKLES

1/2 gallon dill pickles, drained
2 tablespoons pickling spices
3/4 cup tarragon vinegar
3 cups sugar

Cut pickles into chunks; place in jar. Tie pickling spices in cheesecloth bag. Combine remaining ingredients in bowl, stirring until sugar dissolves. Pour over pickles; seal jar tightly. Invert jar every day for several days. Refrigerate. Yield: 1/2 gallon.

Barbara Perini, Mu
Santa Monica, California

HOT SWEET PICKLES

This pickle recipe was given to a friend by a friend in Arkansas.

1 gallon sliced dill pickles
8 cups sugar
1 small bottle of Tabasco sauce
2 6-ounce bottles of Louisiana hot sauce
1 head garlic, separated into cloves
10 jalapeño peppers

Drain pickles in colander; discard pickle juice, saving jar. Place remaining ingredients in gallon jar; add pickles. Place lid on jar, sealing well. Turn upside down; invert every 12 hours for 5 days. Store in refrigerator. Yield: 1 gallon.

Eileen Holash
Whittier, California

MOM'S BREAD AND BUTTER PICKLES

This was my mom's recipe. I remember helping slice the vegetables. I do most of it with my food processor. It is a great condiment and wonderful on hamburgers.

6 pounds unpeeled cucumbers
8 onions, thinly sliced
2 green bell peppers, thinly sliced
2 red bell peppers, thinly sliced
1/2 cup salt
1 quart cracked ice
5 cups sugar
1 1/2 teaspoons turmeric
1 1/2 teaspoons mustard seed
1 teaspoon celery seed
1/2 teaspoon ground cloves
1 quart white vinegar

Slice cucumbers thinly to make 1 gallon. Place cucumbers, onions and peppers into 2-gallon stone crock. Combine salt and ice; pack on top. Cover with weighted lid; let stand for 3 hours. Combine remaining ingredients in bowl; mix well. Remove cucumber mixture from crock; drain. Place in large kettle. Pour vinegar mixture over cucumber mixture. Bring to a boil over low heat; remove from heat. Ladle immediately into hot sterilized jars; seal. Yield: 8 pints.

Gay Meyer, Preceptor Mu Beta
Santa Rosa, California

BREAD AND BUTTER PICKLES

2 cups sliced cucumber
3/4 cup thinly sliced onion
1 cup sugar
1/2 cup distilled white vinegar
1 teaspoon salt
1/2 teaspoon mustard seed
1/4 teaspoon celery seed
1/4 teaspoon turmeric

Combine all ingredients in 2-quart microwave-safe bowl. Microwave on High for 10 to 15 minutes or until cucumbers are crisp-tender and onion translucent, stirring every 2 minutes. Ladle into glass jars prewashed in hot water to prevent cracking. Cover; cool slightly. Refrigerate for up to 1 month. Yield: 2 1/2 cups.

Lisa Hiett, Delta Gamma Iota
Moreno Valley, California

BRAZILIAN BREAD

1 yeast cake
4 cups all-purpose flour
3/4 cup vegetable oil
Pinch of salt
1 cup milk
Salt and pepper to taste
Tomato slices
Green bell pepper slices
Chopped onion
Thinly sliced cooked meat of your choice
Jalapeño peppers, sliced (optional)
1 egg yolk, beaten

Preheat oven to 350 degrees. Dissolve yeast cake according to package directions. Combine first 5 ingredients in large bowl; mix well. Divide dough into 2 balls; roll out to 1/4-inch thickness. Sprinkle with salt and pepper. Layer next 5 ingredients on dough; roll up jelly-roll fashion. Place in 9-by-13-inch baking pan; brush with egg yolk. Let rise for 10 minutes. Bake for 35 minutes. Yield: 8 servings.

Stella Beck, Preceptor Kappa Lambda
Portland, Texas

CHEESE BREAD

My granddaughter gave me this recipe. It is a nice alternative to garlic bread and very popular at potluck dinners.

8 ounces Monterey Jack cheese, shredded
8 ounces Cheddar cheese, shredded
8 ounces mozzarella cheese, shredded
Mayonnaise
3 loaves French bread
Johnny's Salad Elegance

Preheat oven to 350 degrees. Combine cheeses in bowl; add enough mayonnaise to mix well. Split loaves lengthwise; spread cheese mixture on each side of bread. Sprinkle salad elegance over cheese. Place bread on cookie sheets. Bake for 15 minutes or until lightly browned and cheese is melted. Cut in desired pieces; serve hot. Yield: 24 servings.

Eleanor Tafil, Preceptor Laureate Alpha Upsilon
Seattle, Washington

GREEK BREAD

1 large loaf French bread	Tops of 1 bunch green
1/2 cup margarine,	onions, chopped
melted	1 small jar chopped ripe
8 ounces shredded	olives
mozzarella cheese	1/2 cup mayonnaise
1 small jar chopped	
mushrooms	

Preheat oven to 350 degrees. Cut bread in half lengthwise. Combine remaining ingredients in bowl; mix well. Spread on bread; place on large cookie sheet. Bake for 30 minutes or until browned. Cut into serving pieces; serve hot. Yield: 6 servings.

Jean Spiller, Laureate Psi
Pasadena, Texas

PIZZA STICKS

I took these to a sorority fun night. Everyone loved them.

1 11-ounce can soft	1/4 teaspoon garlic
breadsticks	powder
24 thin pepperoni slices	1/2 cup pizza sauce,
2 tablespoons grated	heated
Parmesan cheese	
1/2 teaspoon Italian	
seasoning	

Preheat oven to 350 degrees. Separate and unroll breadsticks. Place 3 pepperoni slices in single layer over half of each breadstick. Fold remaining half over top; seal end and twist. Place on ungreased cookie sheet. Combine next 3 ingredients in bowl; sprinkle evenly over each breadstick. Bake for 15 to 20 minutes. Serve with pizza sauce. Yield: 8 sticks.

Justine Peace, Epsilon Eta
Muncy, Pennsylvania

CINNAMON ICE CREAM

This ice cream is unique and gets rave reviews.

3 1/2 cups sugar	2 egg yolks, beaten
3/4 cup water	4 cups half and half
3 tablespoons cinnamon	2 teaspoons vanilla
6 cups milk	extract

Combine 2 cups sugar, water and cinnamon in saucepan. Cook over low heat, stirring constantly, until smooth and sugar is dissolved. Set syrup aside. Scald milk in top of double boiler over hot water; add 1 1/2 cups sugar, stirring until dissolved. Pour milk mixture slowly over egg yolks, stirring constantly. Return to top of double boiler; cook over hot water until thickened, stirring constantly. Remove from hot water; chill. Add syrup, half and half and vanilla; mix well. Freeze in ice cream freezer. Yield: 4 quarts.

Karen Ashley, Rho Lambda
Levelland, Texas

MINTED PINEAPPLE SORBET

1 2 1/2-pound ripe	1 teaspoon dried mint
pineapple	2 tablespoons fresh
1 cup water	lemon juice
1/2 cup sugar	

Peel and core pineapple; cut into 1-inch chunks. Combine water, sugar and mint in microwave-safe dish. Microwave, uncovered, on High for 2 minutes. Cover tightly with microwave-safe wrap; microwave on High for 3 minutes. Strain mint syrup through a fine sieve; set aside to cool at room temperature. Refrigerate until chilled. Place pineapple chunks in food processor or blender container; blend until smooth. Add chilled syrup and lemon juice; blend for several seconds to combine. Freeze sorbet in ice cream maker according to manufacturer's directions. Yield: 4 to 6 servings.

Donna Weeks, Omicron Epsilon
Cawker City, Kansas

SHERBET ICE CREAM

Juice of 3 oranges	1 small can condensed
Juice of 3 lemons	milk, whipped
1 small can crushed	1/2 pint whipping cream,
pineapple	whipped
3 cups sugar	Milk
Dash of salt	

Combine first 5 ingredients in large bowl; let stand until sugar is dissolved. Add condensed milk and whipped cream; mix well. Fold in enough milk to fill 1-gallon ice cream freezer container. Freeze according to manufacturer's directions. Yield: 1 gallon.

Jerri Franks, Xi Gamma Nu
Richardson, Texas

GRANDMA'S FROZEN CUSTARD

2 1/2 cups sugar	1 teaspoon vanilla
1/2 cup all-purpose flour	extract
2 quarts milk	Half and half
3 eggs, beaten	

Combine sugar and flour in bowl; mix well. Heat milk just to a boil in heavy 4-quart saucepan; reduce heat. Remove 2 cups milk from saucepan; stir into beaten eggs. Return mixture to milk in saucepan, stirring constantly. Add flour and sugar mixture to milk mixture very slowly, beating constantly with wire whisk to keep lumps from forming. Cook, stirring constantly, over medium-low heat until thickened. Refrigerate overnight. Just before freezing, add vanilla and enough half and half to fill freezer container; mix well. Freeze according to manufacturer's directions. Yield: 8 to 12 servings.

Jody Prokupek, Xi Epsilon Rho
Sturgis, Michigan

BANANA SPLIT SQUARES

This is a popular dessert at family reunions. It disappears very quickly. There are no leftovers to take home.

1/3 cup butter or margarine, softened	1 teaspoon baking powder
1 cup sugar	1/2 cup chopped walnuts or pecans
1 egg	
2 small bananas, mashed	2 cups miniature marshmallows
1 teaspoon vanilla extract	1 cup semisweet chocolate chips
11/4 cups all-purpose flour	1 cup maraschino cherries, chopped
1/4 teaspoon salt	1/2 cup chopped nuts

Preheat oven to 350 degrees. Combine butter and sugar in mixer bowl; beat until creamy. Add egg, bananas and vanilla; mix well. Combine flour, salt and baking powder; mix well. Stir into banana mixture; mix well. Stir in walnuts. Pour into greased 9-by-13-inch baking pan. Bake for 20 minutes. Sprinkle with remaining ingredients; bake for 8 to 10 minutes or until tests done. Yield: 12 servings.

Yvonne Sorge, Xi Kappa Theta
Lebanon, Ohio

LOTS OF BROWNIES

1 cup butter or margarine, melted	1 cup pecans
1/2 cup cocoa	2 squares chocolate
5 eggs, lightly beaten	1/3 cup margarine
23/4 cups sugar	1/3 cup milk
1 teaspoon vanilla extract	1 box confectioners' sugar
21/4 cups all-purpose flour	

Preheat oven to 325 degrees. Combine butter and cocoa in bowl; cool. Add eggs, sugar and vanilla; mix well. Combine flour and pecans; fold into egg mixture. Do not beat. Pour into greased 10-by-16-inch baking pan. Bake for 20 to 25 minutes or until tests done. Let cool. Combine chocolate, margarine and milk in saucepan; mix well. Heat just to a boil; remove from heat. Stir in confectioners' sugar; beat well. Pour over cooled brownies. Yield: 48 brownies.

Janice A. Duggins, Xi Theta Tau
Harrisburg, Illinois

BROWN SUGAR STICKY BARS

This is such an easy recipe with such good results. My children loved these brown sugar brownies!

2 eggs, beaten	1/2 teaspoon salt
2 cups packed light brown sugar	1/2 teaspoon baking soda
14 tablespoons all-purpose flour	2 teaspoons vanilla extract
	2 cups walnut pieces

Preheat oven to 350 degrees. Combine eggs and brown sugar in bowl. Add flour, salt and baking soda; mix well. Stir in vanilla. Fold in walnuts. Spread in greased 9-by-13-inch baking pan. Bake for 20 minutes; cut while hot. Yield: 21/2 dozen bars.

Marjorie S. Klar, Laureate Zeta Kappa
Colusa, California

CHOCOLATE CHIP COOKIES

21/4 cups sifted all-purpose flour	1 teaspoon vanilla extract
1 teaspoon baking powder	1 package instant chocolate or vanilla pudding
1 cup softened margarine	2 eggs, beaten
1/4 cup sugar	1 12-ounce package chocolate chips
3/4 cup packed light brown sugar	1 cup nuts

Preheat oven to 375 degrees. Combine flour and baking powder in bowl; mix well. Combine next 5 ingredients in mixer bowl; beat until smooth and creamy. Beat in eggs. Gradually add flour mixture; mix well. Stir in chocolate chips and nuts. Drop by rounded teaspoonfuls onto ungreased cookie sheet. Bake for 8 minutes or until golden brown. Yield: 3 to 4 dozen cookies.

Marilyn Borras, Xi Epsilon Xi
Stafford, Virginia

HONEY DATE BARS

This was found in my mother's recipes. It is truly delicious. She is now 94 years old. This is very good for those on restricted sugar and fat diets.

3 eggs, beaten	1/2 teaspoon salt
1 cup honey	1 cup chopped dates
11/2 cups all-purpose flour	1 cup chopped nuts
1 teaspoon baking powder	

Preheat oven to 325 degrees. Combine eggs and honey in mixer bowl; blend well. Sift flour, baking powder and salt together in bowl; stir into egg mixture. Fold in dates and nuts. Spread mixture 1/4 inch thick in 9-by-13-inch baking pan. Bake for 30 minutes or until lightly browned. Cut into bars. Yield: 24 to 36 bars.

Ila Jeane Lepp, Preceptor Nu Chi
Orland, California

SUNFLOWER SEED MUNCH COOKIES

This is a great snack to curb both the sweet and salty cravings!

1/2 cup margarine	15 to 20 whole club crackers
1/2 cup butter	1/4 cup sunflower seeds
10 tablespoons sugar	

Preheat oven to 350 degrees. Combine margarine, butter and sugar in saucepan; bring to a boil. Place crackers, side by side, in 9-by-13-inch jelly roll pan. Pour butter mixture over crackers. Sprinkle with sunflower seeds. Bake for 10 minutes; immediately remove cookies from pan to foil.
Yield: 8 to 10 servings.

Susan K. McDonald, Xi Alpha Omega
Powell, Wyoming

PINEAPPLE BARS

2 cups all-purpose flour	8 ounces cream cheese,
2 cups sugar	softened
2 eggs, beaten	1 tablespoon margarine
1 20-ounce can crushed	1³/4 cups confectioners'
pineapple and juice	sugar
1 teaspoon baking	Slivered almonds
powder	
1 teaspoon vanilla	
extract	

Preheat oven to 350 degrees. Combine first 6 ingredients in large bowl; mix well. Pour into greased 9-by-13-inch baking pan. Bake for 35 minutes; let cool in pan. Combine next 3 ingredients in mixer bowl; mix well. Spread on cooled cake. Garnish with almonds. Yield: 24 bars.

Lynn Charles, Beta Omega
Scottsbluff, Nebraska

BANANA BUTTERMILK CAKE

This is an especially nice cake because it is not too sweet. It packs well in school lunch bags.

¹/2 cup butter or	¹/2 teaspoon salt
margarine	¹/3 cup buttermilk
1¹/2 cups sugar	1 cup ripe bananas,
2 eggs, beaten	mashed
2 cups all-purpose flour	1 teaspoon vanilla
³/4 teaspoon baking soda	extract
¹/2 teaspoon baking	Confectioners' sugar
powder	

Preheat oven to 350 degrees. Cream butter and sugar in mixer bowl. Add eggs; mix well. Sift flour, soda, baking powder and salt in bowl. Combine buttermilk, bananas and vanilla; mix well. Blend flour mixture into batter alternately with banana mixture; mix well. Pour into greased and floured 9-by-12 glass baking dish. Bake for 45 minutes or until lightly browned and toothpick comes out clean. Sprinkle with confectioners' sugar. May also frost with creamy chocolate frosting if desired.
Yield: 12 servings.

Barbara Nees, Tau Eta
Hemet, California
*Bonnie Kingston, Xi Eta Xi
Edinboro, Pennsylvania

BEAN CAKE

This is a fun cake to take on picnics. Everyone thinks it is a spice cake and would never guess the recipe includes pears and pork and beans!

1¹/4 cups vegetable oil	1 teaspoon nutmeg
2¹/4 cups sugar	3 cups all-purpose flour
3 eggs	1 teaspoon vanilla
1¹/2 cups chopped	extract
canned pears, drained	¹/2 cup butter, softened
1 cup pork and beans,	1 teaspoon vanilla
drained, rinsed	extract
1 teaspoon salt	3 ounces cream cheese
1 teaspoon baking	1 1-pound package
powder	confectioners' sugar
2 teaspoons cinnamon	Milk or cream

Preheat oven to 350 degrees. Combine oil, sugar and eggs in mixer bowl; mix well. Place pears and beans in blender container; blend. Sift next 5 ingredients in bowl. Add pear-bean mixture to batter alternately with dry ingredients; mix well. Add 1 teaspoon vanilla; mix well. Pour into greased tube pan. Bake for 1 hour or until tests done. Cool in pan for 20 minutes. Combine butter, 1 teaspoon vanilla, cream cheese and confectioners' sugar in mixer bowl; beat until smooth. Add small amount of milk if frosting is too thick. Spread on cooled cake. Yield: 15 servings.

Teresa Groff, Zeta Kappa
Emerson, Iowa

PICNIC CAKE

This cake does not need frosting. It transports well and is delicious.

1³/4 cups boiling water	1³/4 cups all-purpose
1 cup uncooked oatmeal	flour
1 cup packed light	1 teaspoon baking soda
brown sugar	1 teaspoon salt
1 cup sugar	1 tablespoon cocoa
¹/2 cup margarine	12 ounces semisweet
2 extra large eggs,	chocolate chips
beaten	³/4 cup chopped pecans

Preheat oven to 350 degrees. Pour water over oatmeal in large bowl. Let stand for 10 minutes. Add brown sugar, sugar and margarine, stirring until margarine melts. Add eggs; mix well. Sift flour, baking soda, salt and cocoa into bowl. Add to batter, mixing well. Add half the chocolate chips. Pour batter into greased and floured 9-by-13-inch pan; sprinkle pecans and remaining chocolate chips over top. Bake for 40 minutes or until cake tests done. Yield: 16 to 20 servings.

Mary Hill, Nu
Montrose, Colorado
*Dorothy Stevens, Preceptor Delta
Montgomery, Alabama

COCOA BANANA CUPCAKES

This is a great recipe for very ripe bananas and needs no frosting. Kids love them.

2 ripe bananas	1 cup sugar
1/2 cup butter or margarine, chilled	1/4 cup cocoa
2 teaspoons lemon juice	1/2 teaspoon cinnamon
1/4 cup milk	2 eggs
1 1/2 cups all-purpose flour	1/2 cup walnuts or pecans (optional)
1 1/4 teaspoons baking soda	

Preheat oven to 350 degrees. Place bananas and butter in food processor bowl; process for 20 seconds or until blended. Combine lemon juice and milk; set aside. Add next 5 ingredients to banana mixture; process for 10 seconds or until well mixed. Add eggs; process for 10 seconds. Add milk mixture; process for 10 seconds or until well mixed. Add walnuts. Spoon mixture into greased muffin cups. Bake for 20 minutes. Yield: 18 to 20 muffins.

Ruth Ann Fleming, Gamma Eta
Lighthouse Point, Florida

PINEAPPLE CAKE

I always take this camping, to barbecues and potlucks. It is very filling.

1 1/2 cups raisins	1 1/2 cups sugar
3 cups all-purpose flour	1/2 cup shortening
2 teaspoons baking soda	1 cup raisin water
1 teaspoon cinnamon	1 medium can crushed pineapple
1 teaspoon nutmeg	1/2 cup nuts
2 eggs, well beaten	

Preheat oven to 350 degrees. Dredge raisins in small amount of flour. Combine remaining flour and next 3 ingredients in bowl; mix well. Combine eggs, sugar, shortening, raisin water and pineapple in large bowl; mix well. Stir in flour mixture; mix well. Add raisins and nuts. Pour into 9-by-13-inch baking pan. Bake for 35 to 40 minutes or until tests done. May top with confectioners' sugar frosting if desired. Yield: 24 servings.

Jane Thiel, Preceptor Zeta
Nampa, Idaho

CHIPS OF PEANUT BUTTER CAKE

1/2 cup butter or margarine, softened	1 cup milk
1 cup peanut butter	1 teaspoon baking powder
2 cups packed light brown sugar	1/2 teaspoon baking soda
2 1/4 cups all-purpose flour	1 teaspoon vanilla extract
3 eggs	6 ounces chocolate chips

Preheat oven to 350 degrees. Combine butter and peanut butter in bowl; blend well. Stir in brown sugar and flour until crumbly. Reserve 1 cup crumb mixture. Add eggs to remaining mixture; beat well. Add next 4 ingredients; beat until well blended. Pour into greased 9-by-13-inch baking pan; sprinkle reserved crumb mixture on top. Sprinkle chocolate chips over crumb mixture. Bake for 35 to 40 minutes or until tests done. Yield: 12 to 16 servings.

Sandra Kellough, Preceptor Alpha Beta
Marrero, Louisiana

FRUIT PLATTER PIZZA

This recipe is great for annual picnics and family reunions.

1 2-layer package yellow cake mix	1 teaspoon vanilla extract
4 tablespoons water	1 pint fresh strawberries, rinsed, sliced
2 eggs	
4 tablespoons margarine or butter	2 dozen seedless grapes, halved
4 tablespoons light brown sugar	3 bananas, sliced
12 ounces cream cheese	1/2 cup apricot preserves
1/2 cup sugar	2 tablespoons water

Preheat oven to 375 degrees. Combine first 5 ingredients in mixer bowl; mix well. Pour into heavily greased 11-by-15-inch baking pan. Bake for 15 minutes; cool. Combine next 3 ingredients in mixer bowl; mix well. Spread on cooled crust. Arrange fruit in desired pattern over cream cheese mixture. Combine preserves and 2 tablespoons water in saucepan; heat until preserves are melted. Let cool; brush over fruit. Refrigerate until serving time. Yield: 15 servings.

Eunice Warren, Beta Lambda
Fremont, Nebraska

SNOWBALLS

My grandmother always made these when we were small. My daughter went to District 4-H competition with this recipe.

1 12-ounce box vanilla wafers, crushed	1 cup chopped pecans
1/2 cup melted butter or margarine	1 6-ounce can frozen orange juice, thawed, undiluted
1 cup confectioners' sugar	Confectioners' sugar

Combine first 4 ingredients in bowl; mix well. Add juice; blend well. Chill; shape into bite-sized balls. Roll in confectioners' sugar; refrigerate for 24 hours before serving. Yield: 40 balls.

Donna Wheeler
Seminole, Texas

Around the Dinner Table

No one needs to be reminded that times have changed when it comes to the traditional family dinner hour. Dad's taking a night class, Mom's working late, Bobby has a rehearsal, Sally has a soccer game. It seems like there is always something that is pulling us apart at dinner time. Well, maybe we can't have Ozzie and Harriet style family dinners every night, but most of us can find one day a week to set aside for a night of togetherness. In this chapter we've included traditional as well as contemporary versions of family favorites. From hearty beef roasts with all the trimmings to lighter fare such as seafood, pasta, and salad, there's sure to be something here that will call your family home to the dinner table.

Home Sweet Home

Saturday Supper

Burgundy Rump Roast
Golden Parmesan Potatoes
Marshmallow-Limeade Freeze

When my children were growing up, they always liked to bring their friends over for Saturday supper. This was a meal that they usually asked me to serve.

Pat Ellsworth, Preceptor Epsilon Lambda
Spring Valley, Illinois

BURGUNDY RUMP ROAST

1 4-ounce can mushrooms, drained	1 3-pound boneless rump roast
2 tablespoons margarine	1 envelope onion soup mix
2 cups Burgundy	

Preheat oven to 375 degrees. Sauté mushrooms in margarine in skillet until light brown. Add 1/2 cup wine and roast. Cook until most of the wine evaporates and roast is light brown, turning to brown evenly on all sides. Line roasting pan with double thickness of foil. Place roast and mushrooms in prepared pan; sprinkle with soup mix. Add remaining 1 1/2 cups wine. Seal foil in tent over roast. Roast for 2 1/2 hours. Yield: 6 servings.

GOLDEN PARMESAN POTATOES

6 large potatoes	3/4 teaspoon salt
1/4 cup sifted all-purpose flour	1/8 teaspoon pepper
1/4 cup grated Parmesan cheese	1/3 cup melted margarine
	Chopped fresh parsley

Preheat oven to 375 degrees. Peel potatoes and cut into quarters. Toss with mixture of flour, cheese, salt and pepper in bag. Arrange in melted margarine in 9-by-13-inch baking dish. Bake for 1 hour, turning once. Sprinkle with parsley. Yield: 6 servings.

MARSHMALLOW-LIMEADE FREEZE

2 eggs, slightly beaten	1 14-ounce can pineapple tidbits, drained
1/3 cup confectioners' sugar	
1/4 cup lime juice	1 16-ounce can peaches, drained
1 tablespoon margarine	
2 cups miniature marshmallows	1 cup whipped cream
	Green food coloring
1/8 teaspoon salt	

Combine eggs, confectioners' sugar, lime juice, margarine, marshmallows and salt in saucepan. Cook over low heat until thickened and smooth, stirring constantly. Cool to room temperature. Fold in fruit, whipped cream and food coloring. Spoon into mold. Freeze until firm. Let stand at room temperature for 30 minutes before serving. Yield: 6 to 8 servings.

Stress-Reliever Supper

Baked Chicken Sandwiches
French Green Beans
Fabulous Fruit Salad
Devil's Food Cake with Fluff Icing

After I moved to a small country town, a group of close friends from the city came for an afternoon of exploring rural attractions and small-town life. This menu was chosen because I could prepare it in advance, leaving only a few simple things to do at serving time, and I had time to visit with my friends. They thought that the meal was great and the day in the country was a good stress-reliever.

Sandra Coblentz, Alpha Beta Rho
Windsor, Missouri

BAKED CHICKEN SANDWICHES

16 slices white bread	3 hard-cooked eggs, chopped
1/2 cup butter or margarine, softened	2 tablespoons finely chopped onion
4 ounces fresh mushrooms	3/4 cup mayonnaise
2 tablespoons butter or margarine	1 10-ounce can cream of chicken soup
2 cups chopped cooked chicken	1 cup sour cream
1/3 cup sliced black olives	1/4 cup sherry
	Paprika to taste

Trim crusts from bread. Spread both sides with softened butter; arrange 8 slices in greased 9-by-13-inch baking dish. Sauté mushrooms in 2 tablespoons margarine in skillet. Combine with chicken, olives, eggs, onion and mayonnaise in large bowl; mix gently. Spoon into prepared dish; arrange remaining bread over top. Mix next 3 ingredients in small bowl. Spoon over casserole; sprinkle with paprika. Chill overnight. Preheat oven to 325 degrees. Bake casserole for 30 to 35 minutes or until set and golden brown. Yield: 8 servings.

FRENCH GREEN BEANS

2 16-ounce cans French-style green beans	1/4 cup lemon juice
2 teaspoons sugar	2 tablespoons butter or margarine
2 teaspoons chervil	1 ounce sliced almonds
8 ounces sliced fresh mushrooms	1 tablespoon butter or margarine
2 tablespoons butter or margarine	

Preheat oven to 350 degrees. Combine undrained beans with sugar and chervil in saucepan. Bring to a boil over medium heat. Cook for 5 minutes; drain. Sauté mushrooms in 1 tablespoon butter in skillet until tender. Add to beans with lemon juice and 2 tablespoons butter; toss gently. Spoon into 2-quart baking dish. Bake for 10 minutes or until heated through. Sauté almonds in 1 tablespoon butter in skillet. Sprinkle over casserole. Yield: 8 servings.

FABULOUS FRUIT SALAD

1 21-ounce can apricot pie filling	2 11-ounce cans mandarin oranges
2 tablespoons fresh lemon juice	1 16-ounce can fruit cocktail
1 20-ounce can pineapple chunks	7 or 8 small bananas, sliced

Mix pie filling and lemon juice in large serving bowl. Drain canned fruit. Add to pie filling mixture; mix well. Chill overnight to several days. Add sliced bananas at serving time. Yield: 15 servings.

DEVIL'S FOOD CAKE

1 cup shortening	2 eggs
6 tablespoons baking cocoa	3/4 cup buttermilk
1 cup water	1 1/2 teaspoons baking soda
2 cups all-purpose flour	1 teaspoon vanilla extract
2 cups sugar	Fluff Icing
1/2 teaspoon salt	

Preheat oven to 350 degrees. Combine shortening, baking cocoa and water in 3-quart saucepan. Bring to a boil, stirring to mix well; remove from heat. Stir in sifted mixture of flour, sugar and salt. Stir in next 4 ingredients, mixing well. Spoon into 2 greased and floured 8- or 9-inch cake pans. Bake for 35 minutes. Cool in pans for several minutes; remove to wire rack to cool completely. Spread Fluff Icing between layers and over top and side of cake. Yield: 16 servings.

FLUFF ICING

2 tablespoons all-purpose flour	1/4 cup vegetable shortening
1/2 cup milk	1/2 cup sugar
1/4 cup margarine, softened	1 teaspoon vanilla extract

Blend flour and milk in saucepan. Cook until thickened, stirring constantly. Cool to room temperature. Cream margarine and shortening in medium mixer bowl for 4 minutes. Add sugar; beat for 4 minutes. Add cooled mixture and vanilla; beat until smooth. Yield: enough for 2-layer cake.

Comfort Dinner

Sweet and Sour Spareribs
Mashed Potatoes
Corn
Hot Rolls
Apple Pie or Butter Tarts

See index for similar recipes.

This is a simple menu that my husband loves. My mom used to cook these spareribs and the smells in the house when I cook them bring back wonderful memories of my mom's kitchen in the winter after school. They remind me of more simple and secure times.

Sharon A. Wilson, Xi Beta Zeta
Belleville, Ontario, Canada

SWEET AND SOUR SPARERIBS

2 1/2 pounds spareribs	2 tablespoons cornstarch
2 cups water	
1/4 cup soy sauce	1/2 cup water
1 teaspoon salt	1/2 16-ounce can drained pineapple tidbits
3 tablespoons light brown sugar	
3 tablespoons vinegar	

Cut spareribs into 1-inch lengths, then cut between ribs. Combine with 2 cups water, soy sauce and salt in electric skillet. Bring to a boil. Simmer, covered, for 1 hour or until spareribs are tender. Cook, uncovered, until water evaporates. Combine remaining ingredients in medium bowl; mix well. Add to electric skillet. Cook until thickened, stirring constantly. Yield: 4 servings.

Gigi Horn, Preceptor Kappa Lambda, Corpus Christi, Texas, makes Pineapple-Carrot Salad by combining 1 chilled 20-ounce can crushed pineapple with juice and 2 or 3 grated carrots in salad bowl. Stir in 1/4 cup mayonnaise-type salad dressing. Serve very cold.

Fish Fry

Southern Fried Catfish
Coleslaw
Hush Puppies

I grew up in Louisiana where fresh fish was always available. Since I have been married, we have lived in Georgia, Germany, Guam and several other places where fish was sometimes hard to find. When we go home, the first thing we always want is a big family fish fry in the backyard. The winter-time substitute is a big pot of my father's special chili.

W. Mae Jones, Laureate Psi
Altus, Oklahoma

SOUTHERN FRIED CATFISH

5 pounds catfish	1/2 teaspoon sugar
1 cup buttermilk	1 teaspoon salt
1 cup cornmeal	1 teaspoon red pepper
1/2 cup all-purpose flour	Vegetable oil for frying
1 tablespoon baking	Parsley sprigs and
powder	lemon wedges

Combine fish with buttermilk in large dish; let stand for 30 minutes or longer. Mix cornmeal, flour, baking powder, sugar, salt and red pepper in large bag. Add fish 1 piece at time; shake to coat well. Heat 2 to 3 inches oil to 375 degrees in heavy saucepan. Fry fish in hot oil for 4 to 5 minutes on each side or until golden brown. Garnish with parsley and lemon. Yield: 8 to 10 servings.

COLESLAW

1 medium head cabbage,	1/2 cup water
shredded	1/2 cup sugar
1 cup shredded carrots	1 teaspoon celery seed
1/2 cup finely chopped	1 1/2 teaspoons salt
onion	1/2 cup vegetable oil
1 cup white vinegar	

Combine cabbage, carrots and onion in large serving bowl. Mix vinegar, water, sugar, celery seed and salt in medium saucepan. Bring to a boil and cook until sugar dissolves; remove from heat. Stir in oil. Add to vegetables; mix well. Chill, covered, for 4 hours or longer. Yield: 8 to 10 servings.

HUSH PUPPIES

2 cups cornmeal	1 cup finely chopped
1/2 cup all-purpose flour	onion
2 teaspoons baking	3/4 cup buttermilk
powder	1/2 cup water
1/2 teaspoon baking soda	1/2 cup vegetable oil
1 teaspoon salt	Vegetable oil for frying

Mix dry ingredients in medium bowl. Add onion, buttermilk, water and 1/2 cup oil; mix well. Drop by spoonfuls into 375-degree oil in heavy saucepan. May fry in same oil in which fish are cooked. Yield: 25 to 30 hush puppies.

❖ Winter Sunday Dinner

Prime Rib Roast
Steamed Broccoli and Carrots
Mashed Potatoes
Yorkshire Pudding
Brown Gravy
Apple Pie
Ice Cream
Coffee — Tea
White Wine

See index for similar recipes.

During the winter we usually have 8 to 10 family members for Sunday dinner and this is their favorite dinner. I microwave the broccoli and carrots separately in 1/2 cup water until tender and mash the potatoes with a small amount of milk and butter.

Gwen Goodridge, Laureate Alpha
Winnipeg, Manitoba, Canada

PRIME RIB ROAST

1 5- to 6-pound prime	Garlic salt and pepper
rib roast	to taste

Preheat oven to 350 degrees. Sprinkle roast lightly with garlic salt and pepper; place in roasting pan. Roast, uncovered, for 1 1/2 hours. Roast, covered, for 1 hour longer or until done to taste. Reserve 3 to 4 tablespoons drippings for Yorkshire Pudding. Slice roast very thin with sharp knife. Yield: 8 to 10 servings.

YORKSHIRE PUDDING

1 cup all-purpose flour	*3 to 4 tablespoons beef*
1 cup milk	*drippings*
2 eggs	

Preheat oven to 375 degrees. Combine flour, milk and eggs in medium bowl; mix well with spoon. Heat beef drippings in 9-by-13-inch baking pan. Spoon batter into pan. Bake for 35 minutes or until puffed and brown. Yield: 8 to 10 servings.

APPLE PIE

1 cup shortening	*1¹/2 cups sugar*
2 cups all-purpose flour	*2 tablespoons*
1 teaspoon salt	*all-purpose flour*
¹/2 cup (or less) cold	*1 teaspoon cinnamon*
water	*Butter or margarine*
6 Granny Smith apples,	*Vanilla ice cream*
peeled, sliced	

Preheat oven to 350 degrees. Cut shortening into mixture of 2 cups flour and salt with pastry blender in bowl. Add water gradually, mixing with fork until mixture forms ball. Divide into 2 portions. Roll on floured surface. Fit 1 portion into pie plate. Toss apples with sugar and 2 tablespoons flour in bowl. Spoon into prepared pie plate. Sprinkle with cinnamon; dot with butter. Top with remaining pastry. Trim and seal edge; cut vents. Bake for 1 hour. Cool for 1¹/2 hours. Serve with ice cream. Yield: 8 servings.

Famous Meal

Filet Mignon
Twice-Baked Potatoes
Breaded Tomatoes
Wilted Spinach Salad — Bread Pudding
Strawberry Cheesecake

See index for similar recipes.

This is the "famous meal" I serve to guests, and everyone seems to love it, including my husband. We wrap the filets with bacon, spread them with Worcestershire sauce and cook them on the grill. I mash the cooked potatoes with sour cream, green onions, celery seed, garlic salt and salt; stuff the mixture into the potato shells; top with cheese and bake for 45 minutes.

Ruthann Gray, Lambda Mu
Easton, Missouri

BREADED TOMATOES

8 cups tomatoes	*8 slices bread, torn*
¹/4 cup melted butter or	*1¹/4 cups sugar*
margarine	

Combine all ingredients in medium saucepan; mix well. Simmer for 15 to 20 minutes or until of desired consistency. Yield: 8 servings.

WILTED SPINACH SALAD

Spinach, torn	*Lemon juice*
Cherry tomatoes	*Catsup*
Green onions, chopped	*Worcestershire sauce*
Cucumbers, chopped	*Salt*
Sugar	*Bacon*
Mustard	

Combine spinach, cherry tomatoes, green onions and cucumbers in salad bowl. Combine desired amounts of next 6 ingredients in bowl. Cook bacon in skillet for 6 to 8 minutes or until crisp; drain, reserving 3 tablespoons drippings. Stir in catsup mixture. Bring to a boil, stirring constantly. Spoon over salad; crumble bacon over top. Yield: variable.

BREAD PUDDING

4 eggs	*¹/2 teaspoon cinnamon*
1 cup sugar	*2 teaspoons vanilla*
4 cups milk	*extract*
8 to 10 slices bread, torn	*¹/4 cup sugar*
¹/2 cup melted margarine	*¹/4 teaspoon cinnamon*

Preheat oven to 350 degrees. Beat eggs and 1 cup sugar in large bowl. Let stand for several minutes. Stir in milk, bread, margarine, ¹/2 teaspoon cinnamon and 2 teaspoons vanilla. Spoon into baking dish; sprinkle with mixture of ¹/4 cup sugar and ¹/4 teaspoon cinnamon. Place in larger pan with a small amount of water. Bake for 45 minutes. Yield: 8 servings.

STRAWBERRY CHEESECAKE

Graham cracker crumbs	*Juice of ¹/2 lemon*
48 ounces cream cheese,	*1 teaspoon vanilla*
softened	*extract*
2 cups sugar	*Fresh strawberries*
6 eggs, at room	
temperature	

Spread layer of cracker crumbs in greased 8- or 9-inch springform pan. Preheat oven to 325 degrees. Combine cream cheese, sugar, eggs, lemon juice and vanilla in large mixer bowl; beat for 6 to 8 minutes. Spoon evenly into prepared pan. Place in larger pan; add enough hot water to come halfway up side of springform pan. Bake for 2 hours; turn off oven. Let cheesecake stand in closed oven for 1 hour. Cool on rack for 2 hours. Place on serving plate; remove side of pan. Top with strawberries. Yield: 12 servings.

Pig-Out Supper

Lasagna
Green Salad
French Bread
Mound Bars
Iced Tea with Fresh Mint

This is the menu that I like to serve when I ask friends for dinner. It is fun for a group of people to make and "pig out" together.

Kathay E. Beam, Eta Beta
Robbinsville, North Carolina

LASAGNA

1 pound ground chuck	1 small onion, finely
2 15-ounce cans	chopped
tomato sauce	24 ounces cottage cheese
1 6-ounce can tomato	12 ounces mozzarella
paste	cheese, shredded
1 tablespoon minced	12 ounces mild or
garlic	medium Cheddar
1/2 tablespoon Italian	cheese, shredded
seasoning	Shredded Parmesan
1 tablespoon pepper	cheese
1 package lasagna	
noodles	

Preheat oven to 350 degrees. Brown ground chuck in skillet, stirring until crumbly; drain. Add tomato sauce and tomato paste; mix well. Stir in garlic, Italian seasoning and pepper. Simmer for several minutes. Cook noodles using package directions; drain. Mix onion and cottage cheese in small bowl. Layer noodles, cottage cheese mixture, mozzarella cheese and beef mixture 1/2 at a time in 10-by-13-inch baking dish sprayed with nonstick cooking spray. Top with Cheddar cheese and Parmesan cheese. Bake for 30 minutes or until bubbly. Yield: 8 servings.

GREEN SALAD

1 medium head red leaf	8 radishes, sliced
lettuce, torn	1/2 cup shredded
1 each red and green bell	mozzarella cheese
pepper, coarsely	1/2 cup toasted croutons
chopped	Salad dressing
1 pound small carrots,	
sliced	

Combine salad ingredients with salad dressing; toss to mix well. Serve immediately. Yield: 8 servings.

MOUND BARS

2 cups graham cracker	1/2 cup sugar
crumbs	2 cups coconut
1/2 cup melted butter or	3 tablespoons peanut
margarine	butter
1 14-ounce can	1 cup semisweet
sweetened condensed	chocolate chips
milk	

Preheat oven to 375 degrees. Mix first 5 ingredients in large bowl; mix well. Spoon into greased 10-by-13-inch baking pan. Bake for 15 minutes. Cool on wire rack. Spread with peanut butter. Melt chocolate chips in saucepan over low heat. Spread over top. Chill for 45 minutes. Cut into bars. Yield: 3 dozen.

ICED TEA WITH FRESH MINT

Fresh mint	3 cups water
1 family-size tea bag	1/4 cup sugar
1/2 cup (about) water	Mint sprigs

Wash and crush mint. Remove paper tag from tea bag. Combine with mint in glass 1-cup measure. Fill with water. Microwave on High for 6 minutes. Let stand for 10 minutes. Strain into pitcher. Add 3 cups water, sugar and 1 sprig of mint; mix well. Serve over ice. Yield: 8 servings.

Branding Crew Dinner

Meat Loaf — Spaghetti Corn
Celery and Carrot Sticks
Whole Wheat Bread
Quick Cherry Dessert

See index for similar recipes.

When I couldn't get back in time to serve dinner, I set the table up and prepared this hearty menu for a branding crew to serve to themselves.

Alma J. Baldwin, Laureate Alpha Iota
Steamboat Springs, Colorado

MEAT LOAF

1 cup tomato juice	1/4 teaspoon pepper
3/4 cup quick-cooking	11/2 pounds lean ground
oats	beef
1 egg or egg white	1/2 cup catsup
1/4 cup chopped onion	2 tablespoons light
1/2 teaspoon salt	brown sugar
(optional)	1/8 teaspoon nutmeg

Preheat oven to 350 degrees. Combine first 6 ingredients in large bowl; mix well. Add ground beef; mix lightly. Press into 4-by-8-inch loaf pan. Combine catsup, brown sugar and nutmeg in small bowl. Spread over meat loaf. Bake for 1 hour; drain. Let stand for 5 minutes. Yield: 8 servings.

SPAGHETTI CORN

1 16-ounce can whole kernel corn	2 teaspoons chopped onion
1 16-ounce can cream-style corn	1 cup chopped Monterey Jack cheese
1 cup broken uncooked spaghetti	1/2 cup melted butter or margarine

Preheat oven to 350 degrees. Combine undrained whole kernel corn with remaining ingredients in large bowl; mix well. Spoon into buttered baking dish. Bake, covered, for 30 minutes. Bake, uncovered, for 30 minutes longer. Yield: 8 servings.

WHOLE WHEAT BREAD

2 envelopes dry yeast	2 teaspoons baking powder
3/4 cup 105- to 115-degree water	2 teaspoons salt
1 1/4 cups buttermilk	3 1/2 cups all-purpose flour
1 cup whole wheat flour	
1/4 cup shortening	Butter or margarine, softened
2 tablespoons sugar	

Dissolve yeast in warm water in large bowl. Add buttermilk, whole wheat flour, shortening, sugar, baking powder, salt and 1 1/2 cups all-purpose flour; mix at low speed for 30 seconds, scraping bowl constantly. Beat at medium speed for 2 minutes, scraping bowl occasionally. Stir in enough remaining all-purpose flour to form a soft and slightly sticky dough. Knead on floured surface 200 times or for 5 minutes. Roll into 9-by-18-inch rectangle. Roll from narrow side; press ends and fold under to seal. Place seam side down in greased 5-by-9-inch loaf pan. Brush lightly with butter. Let rise in warm place for 1 hour or until doubled in bulk; center should be 2 inches above top of pan. Preheat oven to 425 degrees. Place loaf pan on lowest oven rack. Bake for 30 to 35 minutes or until bread tests done. Brush again with butter. Remove to wire rack to cool. Yield: 1 loaf.

QUICK CHERRY DESSERT

1 3-ounce package cherry gelatin	1 21-ounce can cherry pie filling
1 cup boiling water	1 cup grated apple

Dissolve gelatin in boiling water in medium bowl. Stir in remaining ingredients. Spoon into 8-inch square dish. Chill until firm. May add chopped nuts, whipped cream or a cream cheese topping if desired. May serve as salad or dessert. Yield: 9 servings.

Sweetheart Dinner

Lasagna
Spinach Salad
Garlic Toast
Pistachio Ice Cream — Sugar Cookies

See index for similar recipes.

This was the first meal that I cooked for my husband before we were married and, after 27 years, it is still his favorite. The salad is made of spinach, broccoli, red onions, cucumbers, carrots, celery and Italian dressing.

Lynn McNew, Beta Epsilon Omicron
Brackettville, Texas

LASAGNA

2 tablespoons olive oil	1 10-ounce package lasagna noodles
3 cloves of garlic, minced	1 pound ground beef
1 6-ounce can tomato paste	1 pound bulk sausage
2 large onions, chopped	1 medium onion, chopped
2 8-ounce cans tomato sauce	2 cloves of garlic, minced
2 teaspoons chili powder	4 to 5 mushrooms, sliced
1 teaspoon sugar	1 pound mozzarella cheese, shredded
1 teaspoon salt	2 cups cottage cheese
Pepper to taste	

Preheat oven to 375 degrees. Combine first 9 ingredients in pressure cooker. Cook at 15 pounds pressure using manufacturer's instructions for 10 minutes. Reduce pressure quickly while running cold water over cooker. Cook noodles using package directions for 7 minutes or until *al dente*. Brown ground beef and sausage with 1 onion, 2 cloves of garlic and mushrooms in skillet, stirring frequently; drain. Layer noodles, meat mixture, spaghetti sauce and mixture of cheeses 1/2 at a time in 9-by-13-inch baking dish. Bake for 30 to 40 minutes or until heated through. Yield: 6 to 9 servings.

Beth Biedenfeld, Beta Delta, Ossian, Iowa, makes Shrimp and Pea Salad by combining 1 pound cooked shrimp, 10 ounces frozen peas, thawed, 1 chopped tomato, 3 cups cooked minute rice, 1 cup mayonnaise, 1/4 cup chopped onion and Italian salad dressing to taste in large bowl; toss together to mix. Chill and serve.

Indian Dinner

Tandoori Chicken (Murghi)
Cucumbers in Yogurt (Raita)
Broccoli in Garlic Oil
(Hare Gobhi Ki Sabzi)
Golden Rice (Kismis Pilau)
Naan Bread
Caramel Apples

This menu was served by Indian friends after we shared a yoga class. I have continued to serve and enjoy it on other occasions.

Adrienne C. McAlevey, Xi Beta Xi
Ocala, Florida

TANDOORI CHICKEN

6 to 8 chicken quarters	2 teaspoons paprika
2 cloves of garlic	1/2 teaspoon each cumin
1 tablespoon chopped	and cayenne pepper
ginger	1 teaspoon each garam
1 to 1 1/2 cups yogurt	marsala, turmeric,
Juice of 1 lemon	chili powder and salt
1 tablespoon tomato	Vegetable oil
paste	

Rinse chicken and pat dry, discarding wing tips and skin. Prick all over with fork and make diagonal 1/2-inch deep cuts 1 inch apart. Place in glass dish. Process garlic and ginger in food processor until smooth. Add next 10 ingredients; process until smooth. Pour over chicken. Marinate in refrigerator for 4 hours to overnight, turning several times. Let stand at room temperature for 1 hour. Preheat oven to 500 degrees. Remove chickens to rack in very large shallow roasting pan; brush with oil. Roast for 25 to 30 minutes or until cooked through. May broil for 3 to 4 minutes longer if desired to brown.
Yield: 6 to 8 servings.

CUCUMBERS IN YOGURT

1 medium cucumber	1/4 teaspoon cumin
2 tablespoons chopped	2 tablespoons chopped
green bell pepper	parsley
1/2 teaspoon salt	Pepper to taste
1 tablespoon chopped	1 cup plain yogurt
fresh mint or 1	Mint leaves or paprika
teaspoon dried mint	

Peel cucumber and cut into halves lengthwise. Scoop out seed and slice crosswise. Combine with green pepper and salt in colander; let stand for 15 minutes. Rinse and drain well; pat dry. Combine with next 4 ingredients in medium bowl; mix well. Chill, covered, for 1 hour or longer. Stir in yogurt at serving time; garnish with mint leaves or paprika.
Yield: 6 to 8 servings.

BROCCOLI IN GARLIC OIL

1 bunch broccoli	1/2 teaspoon salt
3 tablespoons canola oil	1 to 2 tablespoons
8 to 10 cloves of garlic	chopped parsley
1/3 teaspoon turmeric	

Cut broccoli into spears; peel stems. Rinse in cold water and drain for 5 minutes. Heat oil in skillet large enough to hold broccoli in single layer over medium-high heat. Sauté garlic in oil in skillet for 1 to 2 minutes or until golden brown. Add turmeric and broccoli. Cook for 1 minute without stirring; sprinkle with salt. Turn broccoli carefully with spatula or tongs. Cook for 1 minute; reduce heat. Simmer, covered, for 8 to 10 minutes or until broccoli is tender but still green. Cook, uncovered, until moisture evaporates and broccoli is glazed. Sprinkle with parsley; serve immediately. Yield: 6 to 8 servings.

GOLDEN RICE

1/2 cup thinly sliced	1 tablespoon light
green onions	brown sugar
1/2 cup shredded carrot	1/4 teaspoon each
2 tablespoons margarine	cinnamon and ginger
1 cup orange juice or	1/2 teaspoon each curry
apple juice	powder and salt
1 cup water	1/2 cup chopped peanuts,
1 cup long grain rice	almonds or cashews
1/2 cup golden raisins	

Sauté green onions and carrot in margarine in medium saucepan until tender-crisp. Stir in orange juice, water and next 7 ingredients. Bring to a boil; reduce heat. Simmer, covered, for 20 to 30 minutes or until rice is tender and liquid is absorbed. Stir in peanuts at serving time. Yield: 6 to 8 servings.

NAAN BREAD

4 cups all-purpose flour	1 teaspoon salt
1 tablespoon sugar	2 eggs
1 tablespoon baking	1/4 cup yogurt
powder	3/4 cup milk
1 teaspoon (scant)	2 tablespoons vegetable
baking soda	oil

Mix dry ingredients in deep bowl; make well in center. Add eggs, yogurt, milk and oil to well; mix to form sticky dough, adding warm water if necessary. Knead on floured surface until smooth and elastic. Shape into golf ball-sized balls; place on buttered baking sheet. Let rest, covered with damp cloth, for

1 hour. Preheat oven to 450 degrees. Pat dough balls into 6-inch circles. Place on baking sheet. Bake for 3 minutes or until puffed and light brown. Serve immediately. Yield: 6 to 8 servings.

CARAMEL APPLES

This can also be made with bananas, pears or plums.

6 apples	1/2 cup sugar
6 tablespoons all-purpose flour	2 tablespoons water
2 tablespoons cornstarch	1 tablespoon vegetable oil
2 egg whites	1 tablespoon sesame seed
Vegetable oil for deep frying	

Peel and core apples and cut into quarters. Toss with a small amount of flour. Sift remaining flour and cornstarch into medium bowl. Add egg whites; mix well. Add apple; stir to coat well. Deep fry in hot oil until golden brown; drain well. Heat sugar and water in small saucepan until sugar dissolves. Add 1 tablespoon oil. Cook until sugar is light golden brown. Stir in apples and sesame seed. Serve immediately in lightly oiled individual dishes. May place bowl of cold water on table for guests to dip apples to firm caramel. Yield: 6 to 8 servings.

Cheer-Up Dinner

Glazed Walnuts
Cream of Pumpkin Soup
Spinach Salad
Pita Crisps
Kahlua Brownies
Wine or Sparkling Cider

See index for similar recipes.

This is my favorite meal to take to sorority sisters that have just had a baby, just come home from the hospital or need some cheering up. I always take it in zip-lock bags, plastic tubs and foil tins so there are no dishes to return and no clean up. The brownies can be made from scratch or if I am in a hurry, I use a mix, add nuts and substitute coffee liqueur for part of the water.

Anne Fugit, Xi Pi Rho
Napa, California

GLAZED WALNUTS

3/4 cup walnut halves	1/4 teaspoon each cumin and salt
2 teaspoons vegetable oil	Dried red pepper flakes to taste
2 teaspoons sugar	

Preheat oven to 425 degrees. Toss walnuts with oil in small bowl. Add remaining ingredients; mix well. Spread in single layer on baking sheet. Bake for 7 to 8 minutes or until golden brown, stirring several times. Yield: 2 to 4 servings.

CREAM OF PUMPKIN SOUP

1/2 cup chopped onion	1/2 teaspoon curry powder
2 tablespoons butter or margarine	1/2 cup half and half
1 16-ounce can pumpkin	Salt and pepper to taste
1 14-ounce can chicken broth	Sour cream or plain yogurt

Sauté onion in butter in saucepan. Add pumpkin, chicken broth and curry powder. Bring to a boil; reduce heat. Simmer, covered, for 15 minutes. Process in food processor until smooth. Combine with half and half, salt and pepper in saucepan. Heat just to serving temperature; do not boil. Top with sour cream or yogurt. Yield: 4 servings.

SPINACH SALAD

1/2 cup corn oil	8 slices bacon
1 tablespoon sugar	2 bunches spinach, torn
2 tablespoons grated onion	1 cup fresh bean sprouts
1/3 cup catsup	2 hard-cooked eggs, chopped
1/4 cup rice vinegar	1 7-ounce can sliced water chestnuts, drained
1 tablespoon soy sauce	
1 teaspoon paprika	

Combine first 7 ingredients in jar; mix well. Chill until serving time. Fry bacon until crisp; drain and crumble. Combine spinach, bean sprouts, bacon, eggs and water chestnuts in salad bowl. Add dressing; toss lightly to coat well. Yield: 2 to 4 servings.

PITA CRISPS

6 pita bread rounds	1 teaspoon garlic salt
3 tablespoons butter or margarine, softened	1 tablespoon grated Parmesan cheese

Preheat oven to 350 degrees. Split pita rounds and cut each piece into quarters. Mix remaining ingredients in small bowl. Spread on pitas; place on baking sheet. Bake for 5 minutes or just until crisp. Yield: 2 to 4 servings.

Healthy Dinner

Smoked Lean Pork Kabobs
Chicken Kabobs
Wheat Thins
Peel-A-Pound Soup
Beef Elegant — Rice
Cucumbers Marinated in Soy Sauce
Italian Salad
Hobo Bread
Slimma Banana Bars
Dairy-Rich Rice Pudding
Tea — Coffee

See index for similar recipes.

Two of our chapter members made this low-fat, low-cholesterol meal to demonstrate their program on nutrition. Everyone was given recipes and were glad to discover how good everything tasted.

Gloria Nelson, Preceptor Delta Phi
Barrie, Ontario, Canada

PEEL-A-POUND SOUP

It will take more calories to digest this no-fat soup than it provides.

1 large onion, chopped	1 bunch celery, chopped
1 head cabbage, shredded	1 16-ounce can tomatoes
6 fresh tomatoes, chopped	1 clove of garlic, crushed
1 large green bell pepper, chopped	Salt and pepper to taste
	Grated Parmesan cheese

Combine fresh vegetables, canned tomatoes, garlic, salt and pepper with water to cover in large saucepan. Simmer for 2½ to 3 hours. Sprinkle servings with cheese. Yield: 8 servings.

ITALIAN SALAD

½ cup corn oil	1 bunch celery, chopped
1 cup vinegar	2 green bell peppers, chopped
1 teaspoon salad seasoning	1 head cauliflower, chopped
1 teaspoon crushed garlic	2 purple onions, sliced
1 bunch broccoli, chopped	6 carrots, julienned

Combine oil, vinegar, salad seasoning and garlic in small bowl; mix well. Combine remaining ingredients in salad bowl. Add dressing; toss to coat well. May use diet zesty Italian salad dressing if preferred. Yield: 8 servings.

BEEF ELEGANT

1½ pounds thinly sliced round steak	1 cup chopped onion
⅓ cup all-purpose flour	¼ cup red wine
Salt and pepper to taste	1¾ cups beef broth
3 tablespoons vegetable oil	1 4-ounce can sliced mushrooms
	3 cups cooked rice

Pound steak to tenderize and cut into 1-inch strips. Coat with mixture of flour, salt and pepper. Brown in oil in skillet. Add onion. Cook for 2 to 3 minutes, stirring frequently. Stir in wine, beef broth and undrained mushrooms. Simmer, covered, for 20 to 30 minutes or until beef is tender. Serve over rice. Yield: 6 servings.

HOBO BREAD

2 cups raisins	¼ cup corn oil
2 cups water	½ teaspoon salt
4 teaspoons baking soda	4 cups all-purpose flour
Sugar to taste	

Bring raisins and water to a boil in saucepan. Stir in baking soda. Let stand, covered, overnight. Add sugar, oil and salt; mix well. Stir in flour 1 cup at a time. Fill 3 oiled coffee cans ½ full. Preheat oven to 350 degrees. Bake bread for 1 hour. Remove to wire racks to cool. Yield: 3 small loaves.

SLIMMA BANANA BARS

½ cup margarine, softened	1 teaspoon each baking powder and baking soda
¾ cup sugar	½ teaspoon salt
1 teaspoon vanilla extract	1 cup mashed banana
1½ cups all-purpose flour	

Preheat oven to 350 degrees. Cream margarine, sugar and vanilla in large mixer bowl until light and fluffy. Mix dry ingredients together. Add to creamed mixture alternately with banana, mixing well after each addition. Spoon into lightly greased 9-by-13-inch baking pan. Bake for 20 to 25 minutes or until golden brown. Cool on wire rack. Cut into bars. Yield: 4 dozen.

Doris Ebner, Preceptor Eta Beta, Boerne, Texas, cooks a Working Woman's Roast by placing roast on foil. Cover with 1 package dry onion soup mix; seal tightly. Place in baking pan. Bake in preheated 250-degree oven for 5 hours.

Home-Style Oven Dinner

Oven Swiss Steak
Scalloped Corn
Baked Potatoes — Cheese Sauce
Crescent Rolls
Chilled Peach Halves — Taffy Bars
Coffee — Tea

See index for similar recipes.

Enjoy your time with the family while this easy dinner is cooking in the oven.

Sharon Kennedy Lyster, Preceptor Gamma Epsilon
DeLand, Florida

OVEN SWISS STEAK

3 pounds boneless round steak, 3/4 inch thick	1/2 cup each chopped celery and carrot
6 tablespoons all-purpose flour	3 tablespoons chopped onion
1 teaspoon salt	1/2 teaspoon Worcestershire sauce
Shortening	6 tablespoons shredded sharp process American cheese
1 8-ounce can stewed tomatoes	

Preheat oven to 350 degrees. Cut steak into serving pieces. Pound mixture of flour and salt into steak; reserve remaining flour mixture. Brown steak in a small amount of shortening in skillet; remove to shallow baking dish. Stir reserved flour mixture into drippings in skillet. Add next 5 ingredients; mix well. Bring to a boil, stirring constantly. Spoon over steak. Bake, covered, for 2 hours or until steak is tender. Sprinkle with cheese. Bake until cheese melts. Yield: 6 servings.

SCALLOPED CORN

1 small onion, chopped	1/4 teaspoon pepper
1/2 small green bell pepper, chopped	3/4 cup milk
2 tablespoons margarine or butter	4 ears of fresh corn, cooked
2 tablespoons all-purpose flour	1 egg, slightly beaten
1 1/2 teaspoons dry mustard	1/3 cup cracker crumbs
1/2 teaspoon each paprika and salt	1 tablespoon melted margarine or butter

Preheat oven to 350 degrees. Sauté onion and green pepper in 2 tablespoons margarine in saucepan over medium heat for 2 minutes or until tender, stirring occasionally; remove from heat. Stir in flour, dry mustard, paprika, salt and pepper. Cook until bubbly, stirring constantly; remove from heat. Stir in milk gradually. Bring to a boil, stirring constantly. Cook for 1 minute, stirring constantly. Cut enough kernels from corn to measure 2 cups. Stir corn and egg into onion mixture. Spoon into ungreased 1-quart baking dish. Top with mixture of cracker crumbs and 1 tablespoon margarine. Bake for 30 to 35 minutes or until bubbly. May substitute frozen or canned corn for fresh. May add 1/2 cup shredded Cheddar cheese to sauce for scalloped corn. Yield: 6 servings.

CHEESE SAUCE

6 tablespoons butter or margarine	1 cup sour cream
1 cup shredded sharp process American cheese	2 tablespoons chopped green onions

Beat butter and cheese in mixer bowl until well mixed. Add sour cream and green onions; mix well. Serve with baked potatoes. Yield: 6 servings.

TAFFY BARS

1/3 cup light molasses	1 1/4 cups sifted all-purpose flour
1/2 cup shortening	1/2 teaspoon baking soda
3/4 cup packed light brown sugar	1/2 teaspoon salt
1 egg	3/4 cup chopped walnuts

Preheat oven to 350 degrees. Heat molasses and shortening in saucepan until bubbly; remove from heat. Stir in brown sugar. Beat egg in mixer bowl. Add molasses mixture gradually, beating until fluffy. Sift in dry ingredients; mix well. Stir in walnuts. Spoon into greased 9-inch square baking dish. Bake for 20 to 30 minutes or until tests done. Cool on wire rack. Cut into bars. Yield: 6 to 8 servings.

DAIRY-RICH RICE PUDDING

1 quart skim milk	1/2 cup raisins
1 egg	1 teaspoon rum or vanilla extract
1 package low-calorie vanilla pudding mix	1/4 teaspoon each nutmeg and cinnamon (optional)
1/2 cup instant rice	Salt to taste
3 tablespoons sugar or equivalent sugar substitute	

Preheat oven to 350 degrees. Combine milk, egg and pudding mix in mixer bowl; mix well. Stir in remaining ingredients. Spoon into baking dish. Bake for 1 hour, stirring occasionally during first 40 minutes. Chill until serving time. May sprinkle servings with additional nutmeg or cinnamon. Yield: 10 servings.

Sunday Evening Family Dinner

Glazed Ham — Barbecued Chicken
Potato Salad — Baked Beans
Chicken Caesar Salad — Garlic Bread
Pineapple Upside-Down Cake

This menu includes all my family's favorite dishes. I began cooking it at noon and cooked until everyone arrived. After dinner, they asked if they could have doggie bags for leftovers. As I cleaned up, I could smile in the knowledge that it was a successful evening once again.

Karen M. Ing, Epsilon Alpha
Garland, Texas

GLAZED HAM

1 small fully cooked
  ham, drained
1/4 cup melted butter or
  margarine
1/4 cup packed light
  brown sugar

1 small jar maraschino
  cherries (optional)
1 8-ounce can sliced
  pineapple (optional)
12 walnuts or pecans

Preheat oven to 350 degrees. Place ham in foil-lined baking pan. Blend butter and brown sugar in bowl. Spread over ham. Top with remaining ingredients. Bake, covered with foil, for 1 hour. Yield: 8 servings.

BARBECUED CHICKEN

1 chicken
1/4 cup white wine
  Worcestershire sauce

Salt and pepper to taste
Barbecue sauce

Rinse chicken well. Cook in water to cover in large saucepan over medium-high heat for 1 hour. Cool for 30 minutes or longer. Cut into serving pieces. Marinate in mixture of Worcestershire sauce, salt and pepper in bowl. Grill over medium-low heat for 15 to 25 minutes or until done to taste. Turn off grill. Brush chicken with barbecue sauce. Leave chicken on hot grill for 5 minutes longer. Yield: 8 servings.

POTATO SALAD

5 large baking potatoes
1 large white onion,
  finely chopped
3 hard-cooked eggs,
  chopped
1 8-ounce jar sweet
  pickle relish

5 tablespoons light
  mayonnaise-type
  salad dressing
Mustard to taste
1/4 cup sugar
Salt and pepper
  to taste

Cook potatoes in water to cover in large saucepan until fork-tender. Peel and chop potatoes. Combine with remaining ingredients in large bowl; mix gently. Chill for 1 hour. Yield: 10 servings.

BAKED BEANS

1 29-ounce can baked
  beans
1 medium white onion,
  finely chopped
1/2 cup packed light
  brown sugar

1 tablespoon syrup
1 tablespoon catsup
1/2 teaspoon
  Worcestershire sauce
1/4 teaspoon mustard

Preheat oven to 350 degrees. Combine all ingredients in large bowl; mix well. Spoon into 1-quart baking dish. Bake for 1 hour. Yield: 6 servings.

CHICKEN CAESAR SALAD

1 head romaine lettuce,
  torn
Juice of 1 lemon
Chopped grilled chicken
2 hard-cooked eggs,
  chopped

1/2 teaspoon freshly
  ground pepper
1/4 cup Caesar salad
  dressing
Croutons

Toss lettuce with lemon juice in large wooden bowl. Add chicken, eggs, pepper and salad dressing; toss lightly. Top with croutons. Yield: 6 servings.

GARLIC BREAD

1 loaf French bread
1/2 cup melted butter or
  margarine

1/2 teaspoon crushed
  garlic
1/4 teaspoon salt

Preheat oven to 350 degrees. Slice bread 1/4 of the way through. Spoon mixture of remaining ingredients between slices; wrap in foil. Bake for 20 minutes or until heated through.
Yield: 6 to 10 servings.

PINEAPPLE UPSIDE-DOWN CAKE

1 1/2 cups butter
  or margarine
1 cup packed light
  brown sugar
24 pecan or walnut
  halves
1 16-ounce can
  pineapple chunks,
  drained

1 12-ounce jar
  maraschino cherries,
  drained
1 2-layer package
  white cake mix
1/2 teaspoon cinnamon

Preheat oven to 350 degrees. Melt butter in 9-by-13-inch cake pan. Stir in brown sugar, pecans, pineapple and cherries. Prepare cake mix using package directions and adding cinnamon. Spoon into prepared pan. Bake for 35 to 40 minutes or until cake tests done. Cool on wire rack. Invert servings onto serving plates. Yield: 15 servings.

Greek Dinner

*Stuffed Mushrooms with Pesto
Agrastada — Lemon Rice Pilaf
Greek Salad*

I fell in love with Greek food on a visit to the Greek Isles. I brought these favorite recipes back with me, but I had to do a lot of experimenting to get them right. This meal was special not only because I relived memories of Greece, but also because I shared it with a friend who was born and reared in Greece. There's nothing like a well qualified critic, and my dinner passed with flying colors!

Sharon L. See
Albuquerque, New Mexico

STUFFED MUSHROOMS WITH PESTO

1/2 cup mayonnaise	20 medium-large
1/2 cup chopped parsley	mushroom caps
1 tablespoon grated	2 tablespoons chopped
Parmesan cheese	parsley
2 tablespoons chopped	2 tablespoons finely
almonds	chopped onion
1/4 teaspoon chopped	2 tablespoons butter
garlic	1/4 teaspoon each salt
1/2 teaspoon chopped	and pepper
basil	

Combine first 6 ingredients in small bowl; mix well and set aside. Rinse and drain mushroom caps. Combine 2 tablespoons parsley, onion, butter, salt and pepper in small bowl; mix well. Spoon into mushroom caps; arrange on glass plate. Microwave on High for 3 to 4 minutes. Top with mayonnaise mixture. Yield: 20 mushroom caps.

AGRASTADA

21/2 pounds chicken	Juice of 1 lemon
breasts	1/4 cup melted margarine
Salt to taste	Pepper to taste
5 eggs	

Rinse chicken well. Bring to a boil in salted water in saucepan; reduce heat. Simmer, covered, for 30 minutes or until tender. Drain, reserving 2/3 cup broth. Chop chicken, discarding skin and bones. Place in baking dish. Preheat oven to 350 degrees. Combine reserved broth with remaining ingredients and additional salt to taste in medium bowl; mix well. Spoon over chicken. Bake for 25 to 30 minutes. Yield: 2 to 4 servings.

LEMON PILAF

1 cup each chopped	1/4 teaspoon pepper
celery and green onions	3 cups cooked brown
2 tablespoons butter or	rice
margarine	1 tablespoon grated
1 teaspoon salt	lemon rind

Sauté celery and green onions in butter in skillet until tender. Add remaining ingredients; mix well. Spoon into glass dish. Microwave on High until heated through. Yield: 2 to 4 servings.

GREEK SALAD

2 to 3 tomatoes, chopped	1/4 cup white vinegar
1 red onion, chopped	1/2 cup olive oil
Feta cheese, crumbled	2 teaspoons sugar
Black or green olives	Salt to taste

Combine tomatoes, onion, cheese and olives in salad bowl. Combine remaining ingredients in small bowl; mix well. Add to salad; toss to coat well. Serve chilled or at room temperature. Yield: 2 to 4 servings.

Family Barbecue Supper

*Barbecued Brisket — Scalloped Potatoes
Green Bean Casserole — Light Rolls
Cherry Fluff Dessert — Iced Tea*

See index for similar recipes.

My family considers this meal a special treat. I often take the barbecued brisket to dinners and someone always asks for the recipe.

Patricia Hanavan, Omicron Beta
Bosworth, Missouri

BARBECUED BRISKET

1 4- to 5-pound brisket	1 teaspoon each onion
2 tablespoons liquid	powder, garlic powder,
smoke	celery salt, salt and
2 tablespoons	pepper
Worcestershire sauce	11/2 cups barbecue sauce

Line roasting pan with foil, shiny side up. Place brisket on foil. Combine next 7 ingredients in small bowl; mix well. Spread over brisket; seal foil. Marinate in refrigerator for 10 to 12 hours. Preheat oven to 300 degrees. Bake brisket for 4 to 5 hours. Pour barbecue sauce over brisket. Bake for 11/2 hours longer. Yield: 12 servings.

Winter Warmer

Black Bean Soup
Old-Fashioned Corn Bread
No-Crust Apple Pie

This was my favorite supper when my sister and I were growing up in Buffalo, New York. There was a lot of snow in the winter and I remember coming in from playing in the snow, sleigh riding or ice skating to a warm house and a supper of big bowls of hot bean soup and corn bread finished off with warm apple pie.

Evelyn Oberlander, Laureate Nu
Allison Park, Pennsylvania

BLACK BEAN SOUP

3 cups dried black beans	4 cloves of garlic,
1 teaspoon salt	minced
10 cups water	1 bay leaf
1 cup each chopped	2 15-ounce cans whole
celery, onion, carrot	tomatoes, chopped
and green bell pepper	1 8-ounce can
2 teaspoons each basil	no-salt-added
and oregano	tomato sauce
1 teaspoon black pepper	1 11-ounce can white
1/2 teaspoon cumin	corn
1/4 to 1/2 teaspoon	
ground red pepper	

Bring beans to a boil in salted water in large saucepan. Cook for 1 minute. Let stand, covered, for 1 hour; do not drain. Add next 11 ingredients; mix well. Simmer, covered, for 1 1/2 hours or until beans are tender. Add tomatoes, tomato sauce and corn. Simmer, uncovered, for 30 minutes longer. Discard bay leaf. Yield: 10 to 12 servings.

OLD-FASHIONED CORN BREAD

1 cup yellow cornmeal	1/4 teaspoon salt
3/4 cup sifted all-	1/2 tablespoon melted
purpose flour	margarine
2 1/2 teaspoons baking	1 cup skim milk
powder	1 egg
1/2 teaspoon sugar	

Preheat oven to 400 degrees. Mix dry ingredients in medium bowl. Whisk melted margarine into milk and egg in small bowl. Stir in dry ingredients just until moistened. Spoon into 8-inch square baking pan sprayed with nonstick cooking spray. Bake for 20 minutes or until golden brown. Yield: 9 servings.

NO-CRUST APPLE PIE

6 apples, peeled, sliced	1/4 cup all-purpose flour
1/2 cup sugar	1/2 teaspoon baking
1/2 cup water	powder
1 teaspoon cinnamon	1/2 teaspoon salt
3 tablespoons butter or	Ice cream
margarine, softened	
1/4 cup packed light	
brown sugar	

Preheat oven to 350 degrees. Combine apples, sugar, water and cinnamon in medium saucepan. Cook for 10 minutes; apples will be partially cooked. Spoon into buttered 9-inch pie plate. Cream butter and brown sugar in mixer bowl until light. Sift in remaining dry ingredients; mix well. Sprinkle over apples. Bake for 45 minutes. Serve with ice cream if desired. May double recipe to bake in 9-by-13-inch baking pan. Yield: 6 to 8 servings.

Week-Night Family Supper

Stuffed Pork Chops
Baked Sweet Potatoes
Spinach and Mushroom Salad
Strawberries with Amaretto Cream

See index for similar recipes.

This is a quick but good week-night family dinner at home. We "bake" the sweet potatoes in the microwave and serve them with a pat of butter. The salad is made with torn fresh spinach, thinly sliced mushrooms, sliced onion rings and bottled salad dressing. The fresh strawberries are served with a mixture of 6 tablespoons of sour cream and 2 tablespoons of Amaretto.

Mardi Nesmith, Laureate Alpha Rho
St. Petersburg, Florida

STUFFED PORK CHOPS

4 to 8 3/4-inch thick	Thinly sliced celery
pork chops	Sliced almonds
1 package stove-top	Pepper to taste
stuffing mix	2 tablespoons corn oil

Cut a pocket in each pork chop. Prepare stuffing mix using package directions and adding celery and almonds; cool slightly. Stuff into pockets in chops; secure with wooden picks. Sprinkle with pepper.

Cook in oil in heavy medium skillet until brown on both sides and cooked through. Yield: 4 servings.

Southern Sunday Supper

Cajun Pork Roast — Tomato Fritters
Squash Casserole
Baked Sweet Potatoes
Baking Powder Biscuits
Coconut Cake

See index for similar recipes.

For people born and raised in the South, any get-together is an excuse to eat. You name it and we Southerners will eat right through it. This menu is my favorite Sunday supper: I just put it on the table and everyone eats like there ain't no tomorrow.

Linda Necrason, Xi Nu Alpha
Winter Park, Florida

CAJUN PORK ROAST

2 teaspoons each thyme, paprika and oregano	1/2 teaspoon each red pepper and white pepper
1 teaspoon garlic powder	1 2-pound boneless pork roast
1/2 teaspoon each cumin, nutmeg and salt	Vegetable oil

Preheat oven to 350 degrees. Combine first 9 seasonings in small bowl. Rub roast lightly with oil and seasoning mixture. Place in shallow roasting pan. Roast for 1 hour or to 155 degrees on meat thermometer. Let stand for 5 to 10 minutes before slicing. Yield: 4 to 6 servings.

TOMATO FRITTERS

2 tomatoes, sliced	Vegetable oil
1 cup cornmeal	1/2 teaspoon salt

Coat tomatoes with cornmeal. Cook in oil in skillet until golden brown on both sides; drain. Season with salt. Yield: 4 to 6 servings.

SQUASH CASSEROLE

6 slices bacon	Salt and pepper to taste
2 cups mashed cooked squash	1/2 cup bread crumbs
1 tablespoon chopped onion	1 cup shredded Cheddar cheese

Preheat oven to 350 degrees. Cook bacon in skillet until crisp; drain. Crumble bacon, reserving 2 tablespoons drippings. Mix bacon, reserved drippings, squash, onion, salt and pepper in bowl. Spoon into greased 2-quart baking dish. Top with bread crumbs and cheese. Bake until brown. Yield: 4 to 6 servings.

BAKING POWDER BISCUITS

2 cups all-purpose flour	1/2 teaspoon salt
1 teaspoon baking powder	1/3 cup shortening
	1/2 to 3/4 cup milk

Preheat oven to 400 degrees. Sift flour, baking powder and salt into bowl. Work in shortening with fork or fingers. Add enough milk gradually to form dough, mixing until moistened. Roll on floured cloth; cut out as desired. Place on baking sheet. Bake for 10 minutes. Yield: 16 biscuits.

COCONUT CAKE

1 cup butter or margarine, softened	1 cup milk
2 cups sugar	1 teaspoon vanilla extract
4 eggs	1/2 teaspoon almond extract
3 cups sifted cake flour	
1 tablespoon baking powder	1 recipe seven-minute frosting
1/2 teaspoon salt	Grated fresh coconut

Preheat oven to 350 degrees. Grease three 9-inch cake pans and line bottoms with waxed paper. Cream butter in mixer bowl until light. Add sugar gradually, beating for 10 minutes. Beat in eggs 1 at a time. Add sifted dry ingredients to batter alternately with milk and flavorings, mixing well after each addition. Spoon into prepared cake pans. Bake for 25 to 30 minutes or until layers test done. Cool in pans for 10 minutes; remove to wire racks to cool completely. Spread frosting between layers and over top and side of cake; sprinkle with coconut. Yield: 16 servings.

CHEESE SOUP

3 stalks celery, chopped	1 cup sour cream
2 carrots, grated	1 cup cubed Velveeta cheese
3 green onions, chopped	
1/4 cup margarine	1 tablespoon green pepper flakes
3 10-ounce cans cream of potato soup	
2 10-ounce cans chicken broth	

Sauté celery, carrots and green onions in margarine in saucepan until tender. Stir in soup and broth; simmer for 20 minutes. Add sour cream and cheese; heat until cheese is melted. Sprinkle pepper flakes over top. Yield: 8 servings.

Ginger McGraw, Preceptor Beta
Marshall, Missouri

BROCCOLI-BEER-CHEESE SOUP

This is a great make-ahead recipe to come home to on a cold night.

2 cups water
1 tablespoon margarine
1/4 cup chopped onion
2 chicken bouillon cubes
6 8-ounce packages egg
  noodles
1/8 teaspoon garlic salt
1 10-ounce package
  frozen chopped
  broccoli

1 10-ounce can cream
  of mushroom soup
1 1/2 cups milk
6 ounces beer
1 cup shredded Cheddar
  cheese or cubed
  Velveeta cheese
Salt and pepper to taste

Combine water, margarine, onion and bouillon cubes in large saucepan; bring to a boil. Add noodles and garlic salt. Boil for about 5 minutes or until noodles are partially cooked. Add broccoli, soup, milk, beer and cheese. Cook, stirring, over medium heat until smooth and thoroughly heated. Add salt and pepper. Yield: 6 servings.

Sue Trowbridge, Preceptor Beta Omega
Emporia, Kansas

VEGETARIAN CHILI

Charlie and Barbara Ward, world-class chili cooks, served this chili at the First Invitational James Beard House Chili Cookoff sanctioned by the International Chili Society on September 20, 1992, in Manhattan, New York.

1 tablespoon vegetable
  oil
1 tablespoon margarine
1 tablespoon minced
  garlic
2 tablespoons chili
  powder
1 teaspoon ground
  cumin
1/2 teaspoon crushed
  oregano
1/4 teaspoon black
  pepper
2 1/2 cups fresh green
  beans, cut into
  1/4-inch pieces
1 1/2 cups shredded
  carrots

1 cup diced celery
1 16-ounce can peeled
  and diced tomatoes
  with juice
1/2 cup water
1 cup diced onions
1 large red bell pepper,
  diced
1 large green bell
  pepper, diced
1 long green Anaheim
  chili pepper, diced
1 16-ounce can red
  kidney beans with
  liquid
Salt to taste

Heat oil and margarine in large Dutch oven. Add garlic, chili powder, cumin, oregano and black pepper; sauté over low heat for 1 to 2 minutes, stirring constantly. Add beans, carrots, celery, juice from tomatoes and water; mix well. Cover; cook for 10 minutes. Add onions and peppers. Cook, covered, for 10 minutes longer. Add tomatoes and kidney beans. Cook, covered, for 10 minutes longer. Add

salt. May substitute one 8-ounce can hot Mexican sauce for 1/2 cup water for spicier chili if desired. Yield: 4 to 6 servings.

Barbara Ward, Laureate Alpha Theta
Lake Havasu City, Arizona

WHITE CHILI AND CHICKEN SOUP

This is an easy reduced-calorie and hearty dinner. I serve it with a tossed salad and corn bread.

1 16-ounce package
  navy beans
1 small onion, chopped
2 tablespoons margarine
3 cooked chicken breast
  halves, cut into small
  cubes
1 4-ounce can green
  chilies, chopped

8 cups chicken bouillon
Pepper to taste
1 small can white corn,
  drained
Green chili salsa
Sour cream
Grated Cheddar cheese

Soak beans in cold water in bowl overnight. Sauté onion in margarine in saucepan until tender. Place beans, sautéed onion, chicken, green chilies, bouillon and pepper into Crock•Pot; mix well. Cook on Low for 8 to 10 hours or until beans are soft. Add corn just before serving. Garnish with salsa, sour cream and/or cheese. Yield: 8 servings.

Ginny Weeber, Xi Beta Sigma
Redmond, Oregon

MOM'S CLAM CHOWDER

My mother made this many times to take to friends or family who were ill or "just because." It is great served with dark bread, a tray of cheese and a bowl of fruit.

4 to 6 slices bacon, diced
3 green onions with
  tops, chopped
5 medium potatoes, cut
  into 1/2-inch cubes
1 stalk celery, sliced
1 carrot, finely sliced
1 clove of garlic, minced
2 cups water

1 teaspoon salt
1/2 teaspoon pepper
1 teaspoon
  Worcestershire sauce
4 drops of Tabasco sauce
2 cups chopped clams
  with juice
1 pint half and half

Sauté bacon in large heavy kettle until crisp. Add onions, potatoes, celery, carrot and garlic; mix well. Add water and next 4 ingredients; mix well. Simmer, covered, for 15 minutes or until potatoes are tender. Mash potatoes lightly with potato masher. Heat clams and juice in saucepan for 3 minutes or until tender; add to vegetable mixture. Add half and half, stirring well. Heat until very hot but do not boil. Yield: 6 servings.

Sue Wise, Omicron Epsilon
Cawker City, Kansas

CORN-SHRIMP SOUP CAJUN STYLE

1 large onion, chopped
1/2 cup chopped green
  onions
1/2 medium green bell
  pepper, chopped
1/2 cup tomato paste
2 16-ounce cans whole
  kernel corn
2 16-ounce cans cream-
  style corn

1 10-ounce bottle of
  catsup
2 cups shrimp
8 ounces smoked
  sausage, diced
Salt and pepper to taste
Hot sauce to taste

Simmer onion, green onions and green pepper in tomato paste in large heavy kettle for 10 minutes. Add corn and catsup; cook for 1 hour over medium heat, stirring frequently. Add shrimp and sausage; cook for 30 minutes longer. Add salt, pepper and hot sauce; mix well. Water may be added as needed. Yield: 6 servings.

Earline Hall, Preceptor Alpha Beta
Marrero, Louisiana

CHICKEN JAMBALAYA

9 chicken thighs
1 pound smoked sausage
3 medium onions,
  chopped
4 ribs celery, chopped
5 cloves of garlic,
  crushed
2 green bell peppers,
  chopped
3 tablespoons light
  olive oil
1 large can tomatoes

1 small can tomato
  paste
Cayenne pepper to taste
Chili powder to taste
1 teaspoon parsley
  flakes
1 tablespoon
  Worcestershire sauce
Tabasco sauce to taste
3 bay leaves
Salt and pepper to taste
1 cup rice

Boil chicken and sausage in water in large saucepan until tender; drain, reserving liquid. Bone chicken; cut chicken and sausage into bite-sized pieces. Sauté onions, celery, garlic and green peppers in olive oil in large heavy kettle until tender. Add chicken, sausage, tomatoes, tomato paste and seasonings; cook for 30 to 45 minutes over low heat. Add 2 1/2 cups reserved liquid and rice. Cook, covered, until rice is tender, stirring frequently. Yield: 8 servings.

Karen Patterson, Tau Pi
Sterling, Illinois

NANCY'S SPECIAL POTATO SOUP

2 bunches green onions,
  chopped
2 stalks celery, chopped
2 tablespoons margarine
8 medium potatoes,
  peeled, cubed
2 carrots, sliced
4 cups chicken broth

1 teaspoon Nature's
  Seasons
1/4 teaspoon garlic salt
Pinch of thyme
1 cup half and half
2 cups whipping cream
2 cups shredded mild
  Cheddar cheese

Sauté onion and celery in margarine in large heavy kettle until tender. Stir in next 6 ingredients; simmer, covered, for about 20 minutes or until vegetables are tender. Mash vegetables with potato masher. Add half and half, cream and cheese. Cook until cheese is melted. Yield: 6 to 8 servings.

Nancy J. Chaffee, Xi Beta Epsilon
Rogers, Arkansas

TURKEY TACO SOUP

2 teaspoons vegetable
  oil
1 pound ground turkey
1 cup chopped onion
1/2 cup chopped green
  bell pepper
1 15-ounce package
  taco seasoning mix
1 15-ounce can pinto
  beans

1 cup thick and chunky
  salsa
1 8-ounce can tomato
  sauce
2 cups water
6 taco shells
1/2 cup shredded
  Cheddar cheese

Heat oil in large saucepan over medium-high heat. Add turkey, onion and green pepper; cook, stirring, until turkey is browned. Add taco seasoning, beans, salsa, tomato sauce and water. Bring to a boil, stirring well. Reduce heat; simmer, uncovered, for 30 to 40 minutes. Heat taco shells; crush. Ladle soup into bowls; top with crushed taco shells. Sprinkle with cheese. Yield: 6 servings.

Florene Brouillette, Preceptor Alpha Xi
Natchitoches, Louisiana

WILD TOMATO SOUP

3 tablespoons butter or
  margarine
3 tablespoons vegetable
  oil
1 cup chopped onion
1/2 cup diced carrot
1/2 cup chopped celery
6 large ripe tomatoes or
  2 16-ounce cans
  tomatoes, chopped

3 cups chicken or beef
  stock
1/2 cup wild rice
Salt and pepper to taste
1/2 teaspoon minced
  fresh basil or oregano
1/2 cup whipping cream
  (optional)
Chopped fresh parsley
  or dill

Heat butter and oil in saucepan over medium-high heat. Add onion, carrot and celery; cook for about 10 minutes or until vegetables are transparent, stirring frequently. Add tomatoes, stock and rice, stirring well. Bring to a boil; reduce heat. Simmer, covered, for 1 hour. Stir in salt, pepper and basil. Add cream for creamy soup. Ladle soup into bowls. Garnish with parsley or dill. Yield: 4 servings.

Val Goodwin, Alpha Epsilon
Carman, Manitoba, Canada

❖ MARINATED ASPARAGUS

2 pounds fresh
  asparagus
1/3 cup chopped parsley
1/3 cup sliced black
  olives
1/3 cup sliced green
  olives
2 ounces pimento
2 tablespoons chopped
  green onion
1 1/2 cups vegetable oil
1/2 cup red wine vinegar

2 teaspoons lemon juice
1 teaspoon
  Worcestershire sauce
1 tablespoon dried basil
2 teaspoons ground
  pepper
1 teaspoon dried
  oregano
1/2 teaspoon garlic
  powder
1/2 teaspoon salt
1/4 teaspoon sugar

Cook asparagus in small amount of water in covered saucepan for 6 to 8 minutes or until tender; drain. Place in 9-by-13-inch shallow dish. Arrange parsley, olives, pimento and green onion over asparagus. Combine remaining ingredients in container; cover and shake well. Pour over asparagus. Chill, covered, for 8 hours. Yield: 8 servings.

Ellen René Stanley, Mu Xi
Whitestown, Indiana

BROCCOLI SALAD

3/4 cup buttermilk
4 tablespoons
  mayonnaise
1 tablespoon lemon juice
1/2 teaspoon garlic salt

4 cups chopped fresh
  broccoli
2 medium tomatoes,
  diced

Combine buttermilk, mayonnaise, lemon juice and garlic salt in bowl. Add broccoli and tomatoes, stirring lightly; chill. Yield: 4 to 6 servings.

Tonua Mock, Xi Gamma Psi
St. Marys, Georgia

CHINESE LETTUCE SALAD

5 slices bacon
1 head lettuce, torn into
  pieces
4 green onions, chopped
1/4 cup chopped celery
1/4 cup sliced radishes
1 3-ounce can chow
  mein noodles
4 tablespoons sesame
  seeds

1/2 cup sliced almonds,
  toasted
4 tablespoons sugar
6 tablespoons vinegar
2 teaspoons
  monosodium
  glutamate
1/2 teaspoon pepper
1/2 cup oil

Fry bacon in skillet until crisp; drain and crumble. Toss bacon, lettuce, onions, celery and radishes together in salad bowl. Add noodles, sesame seeds and almonds just before serving. Combine remaining ingredients in bowl; mix until sugar is dissolved. Pour over salad; toss lightly. Yield: 6 to 8 servings.

Diane Kelly, Zeta Eta
Derby, Kansas

CUCUMBER SALAD

1 3-ounce package
  lime gelatin
1 cup boiling water
1 cup cottage cheese

1 cup grated cucumber
1/4 cup grated onion
1/2 cup mayonnaise

Dissolve gelatin in boiling water in bowl; cool. Add remaining ingredients; chill until set.
Yield: 4 to 6 servings.

Frances W. Farrar, Laureate Delta
Shelbyville, Tennessee

MANDARIN SALAD

1/4 head iceberg lettuce,
  torn into pieces
1/4 head romaine
  lettuce, torn into pieces
2 medium stalks celery,
  chopped
2 green onions with
  tops, thinly sliced

1/4 cup vegetable oil
2 tablespoons sugar
1/4 teaspoon salt
2 tablespoons vinegar
Dash of pepper
1 small can mandarin
  oranges, drained
1/4 cup sliced almonds

Place lettuce, celery and onions in plastic storage bag; refrigerate. Combine next 5 ingredients in glass jar; shake well. Refrigerate. Pour dressing over lettuce mixture in bag just before serving. Add oranges and almonds to mixture; shake until well coated. Yield: 4 servings.

Rita Owens, Rho
Waynesboro, Virginia
*Carol Kay Marbert, Laureate Theta
Columbia, South Carolina

COTTAGE CHEESE-SPINACH SALAD

1 3-ounce package
  lemon gelatin
1 cup boiling water
1/2 cup cold water
1 1/2 tablespoons vinegar
1/2 cup mayonnaise
Salt and pepper to taste

1 cup chopped fresh
  spinach
3/4 cup small curd
  cottage cheese
1/3 cup diced celery
1 tablespoon chopped
  green onions

Dissolve gelatin in boiling water in mixer bowl. Add next 5 ingredients; blend well. Chill for 30 minutes or until firm. Whip until fluffy. Fold in spinach and remaining ingredients. Pour into salad mold; chill until firm. Yield: 4 to 6 servings.

Charlene Little, Preceptor Gamma Mu
Twenty-Nine Palms, California

CARNE GUISADA

1 pound beef sirloin, cut
  into strips or cubes
1/4 cup vegetable oil
1 white onion, chopped
2 tomatoes, chopped
2 tablespoons
  all-purpose flour

1 cup water
1 jalapeño pepper,
  chopped
2 tablespoons cumin
1/4 to 1/2 teaspoon salt
8 flour tortillas

Brown beef in oil in heavy skillet. Add onion; sauté until onion is tender. Add tomatoes. Mix flour with water in bowl; stir into beef mixture. Add jalapeño pepper, cumin and salt. Cook until beef is tender and sauce begins to thicken. Heat tortillas; spoon beef mixture onto each tortilla. Roll and serve.
Yield: 4 servings.

Sarah Moore, Beta Pi
Baker, Montana

AMERICAN STIR-FRY

1 pound round or sirloin steak, sliced into thin strips	2 tablespoons cornstarch
1/4 cup soy sauce	2 cups broccoli flowerets
1/8 cup water	2 medium carrots, sliced diagonally
1 tablespoon lemon juice	2 cups sliced fresh mushrooms
1 tablespoon honey	1 8-ounce package baby corn, thawed
2 green onions with tops, chopped	2 tablespoons beef broth or water
1/8 teaspoon garlic powder	4 cups hot cooked rice

Combine first 7 ingredients in bowl; marinate for 2 hours. Drain steak, reserving marinade. Add enough water to marinade to make 1 cup. Add cornstarch; mix well. Spray wok or skillet with nonstick cooking spray. Stir-fry broccoli and carrots for 3 minutes. Add mushrooms; stir-fry for 2 minutes. Add corn; stir-fry for 2 minutes. Remove vegetables from wok. Pour beef broth into wok. Add steak; stir-fry for 2 to 3 minutes. Push steak from center of wok. Stir cornstarch mixture; add to center of wok, stirring until thickened. Return vegetables to wok; stir and heat through. Serve over rice. Yield: 6 servings.

Carol Nelson, Xi Alpha Psi
Brandon, South Dakota

ROUND STEAK SAUERBRATEN

This "Old World" recipe is a family favorite and constantly requested by friends.

1 1/2 pounds round steak, 1/2 inch thick	1 teaspoon Worcestershire sauce
1 tablespoon shortening	1/4 teaspoon ground ginger
1 envelope brown gravy mix	1 bay leaf
2 cups water	1/2 teaspoon salt
1 tablespoon instant minced onion	1/4 teaspoon pepper
1 tablespoon light brown sugar	Hot buttered egg noodles
2 tablespoons wine vinegar	

Preheat oven to 350 degrees. Cut steak into 1-inch squares. Brown steak in shortening in skillet; remove steak. Add gravy mix and water to skillet. Bring to a boil, stirring constantly. Stir in next 8 ingredients; add steak. Pour into 1 1/2-quart casserole; bake, covered, for 1 1/2 hours. Remove bay leaf. Serve over noodles. Yield: 6 servings.

Lynn Demi, Xi Gamma Nu
Hendersonville, Tennessee

BRAISED SIRLOIN TIPS

1 2-pound beef sirloin tip, cut into 1-inch cubes	2 tablespoons soy sauce
	1 clove of garlic, minced
2 tablespoons vegetable oil	1/4 teaspoon onion powder
1 10-ounce can beef consommé	2 tablespoons cornstarch
1/3 cup red Burgundy wine or cranberry cocktail	1/4 cup water
	4 cups hot cooked rice

Brown beef on all sides in oil in large heavy skillet. Add next 5 ingredients. Heat to boiling. Reduce heat; simmer, covered, for 1 hour or until beef is tender. Blend cornstarch and water in cup; stir slowly into beef mixture. Cook until gravy thickens and boils for 1 minute, stirring constantly. Serve over rice.
Yield: 8 servings.

Ann Lassmann, Psi Master
Victoria, Texas
*Sue Sheeley
Marion, Iowa

JAPANESE SUKIYAKI

This is a wonderfully nutritious meal.

1 pound round steak, thinly sliced	1 1/2 cups sliced mushrooms
2 tablespoons vegetable oil	1/2 cup sliced green onions
1 10-ounce can beef broth	1 tablespoon soy sauce
1 1/2 cups celery, chopped into 1-inch pieces	1 cup broccoli flowerets
1 green bell pepper, sliced	2 tablespoons cornstarch
1 medium onion, thinly sliced	1/4 cup water
	8 cups steamed rice

Brown steak in oil in large skillet. Add next 7 ingredients; stir well. Simmer for 5 minutes. Add broccoli; simmer for additional 5 minutes, stirring often. Mix cornstarch and water together in small bowl. Pour into beef mixture, stirring until thickened. Serve over rice. Yield: 8 servings.

Jerri Gazaille, Xi Pi Alpha
Abilene, Texas

VEAL DIANNE

1 pound veal, cut into 1/2-inch strips	2 stalks celery, diced
2 tablespoons vegetable oil	1 16-ounce can stewed tomatoes
1 medium onion, chopped	1 10-ounce package frozen mixed vegetables
1 small green bell pepper, chopped	Salt and pepper to taste

Sauté veal in oil in 10-inch skillet until browned. Add remaining ingredients. Simmer, uncovered, for 20 minutes. Serve over rice. Yield: 4 servings.

Dianne Lauer, Xi Alpha Epsilon
Easton, Pennsylvania

CRAZY MEATBALLS

2 pounds ground beef	1 16-ounce can cranberries
1 pound ground sausage	
1 cup bread crumbs	1 12-ounce bottle of chili sauce
3 eggs	
1 4-ounce package onion soup mix	1 1/2 cups water
1 16-ounce can sauerkraut with juice	1 cup packed dark brown sugar

Preheat oven to 350 degrees. Combine ground beef, sausage, crumbs, eggs and soup mix in large bowl; mix well. Shape into meatballs; place in 9-by-13-inch baking pan. Combine remaining ingredients in large bowl; mix well. Pour over meatballs. Bake for 2 hours. May substitute ground turkey for ground beef and sausage if desired. Yield: 25 to 30 large meatballs.

Kaye Schramm, Laureate Beta Epsilon
Sequim, Washington

TAMALE PIE

I love this recipe because it takes only 35 minutes from frozen ground beef to serving on table.

1 pound ground beef	1 16-ounce can whole kernel corn, drained
2 teaspoons chili powder	
1 10-ounce can condensed tomato soup	1/2 cup salsa or taco sauce
1 cup chopped green bell pepper	1/2 cup water
	1 package Jiffy corn muffin mix

Preheat oven to 400 degrees. Combine ground beef and chili powder in large skillet; cook over medium heat until browned. Stir in next 5 ingredients; cook, covered, for 5 minutes. Pour into greased 2-quart casserole. Prepare muffin mix according to package directions. Spoon evenly over beef mixture. Bake for 20 to 25 minutes or until corn bread is browned. Yield: 6 servings.

Brenda Carr, Xi Kappa Mu
Keystone Heights, Florida

EASY LASAGNA

12 ounces cottage cheese	6 ounces uncooked lasagna noodles
1 egg	
1 teaspoon crushed dried basil	1 30-ounce jar spaghetti sauce
1/4 teaspoon crushed oregano	4 ounces mozzarella cheese slices
1 pound lean ground beef	1/2 cup Parmesan cheese

Preheat oven to 350 degrees. Combine first 4 ingredients in bowl; mix well. Cook ground beef in skillet, stirring until crumbly; drain well. Layer 1/3 noodles in greased 9-by-12-inch baking dish. Spoon enough spaghetti sauce over noodles to cover. Add ground beef. Layer another 1/3 noodles over ground beef. Add cottage cheese mixture; top with mozzarella cheese. Spoon enough spaghetti sauce over cheese to cover. Layer remaining noodles; cover with remaining spaghetti sauce. Sprinkle with Parmesan cheese. Cover with foil. Bake for 1 hour; let stand for 15 minutes before serving. Yield: 6 to 8 servings.

Nancy Hentzell, Xi Omicron
San Benito, Texas

SPAGHETTI PIE

7 ounces uncooked spaghetti	1 teaspoon oregano
	1 tablespoon garlic salt
2 tablespoons butter or margarine	1 16-ounce can whole tomatoes, drained, diced
2 eggs, beaten	
1/3 cup Parmesan cheese	1 6-ounce can tomato sauce
1 pound ground beef	
1 small onion, chopped	1 cup cottage cheese
1 small green bell pepper, chopped	8 ounces shredded mozzarella cheese
1 tablespoon sugar	

Preheat oven to 350 degrees. Cook spaghetti according to package directions; drain. Combine spaghetti, butter, eggs and Parmesan cheese in large bowl; mix well. Pour mixture into 2 greased 9-inch pie plates. Press mixture to cover as pie crusts. Brown ground beef lightly in skillet, stirring until crumbly. Add onion, green pepper and sugar; cook for 6 minutes. Add oregano, garlic salt, tomatoes and tomato sauce. Cook for additional 10 to 15 minutes over medium heat. Spoon cottage cheese over spaghetti crusts in pie plates. Spoon ground beef mixture over cottage cheese. Bake for 20 minutes. Spread mozzarella cheese over top; bake for 5 to 10 minutes longer or until cheese is melted. Let cool for 5 to 6 minutes before serving. May freeze 1 pie if desired. Yield: 8 servings.

Annie Cavalli, Xi Alpha Psi
Leadville, Colorado

BEEF CHOW MEIN

1 1/2 pounds round steak,
  cut into thin strips
1 cup chopped onions
1 green bell pepper,
  chopped
1/4 cup vegetable oil
1 cup diced celery
3/4 cup water
1/2 tablespoon salt
1/8 teaspoon pepper

1 20-ounce can bean
  sprouts, drained
1/3 cup cold water
2 tablespoons
  cornstarch
2 tablespoons soy sauce
1 tablespoon sugar
Chow mein noodles or
  rice

Sauté steak, onions and green pepper in oil in skillet. Add celery, 3/4 cup water, salt and pepper; cook, covered, for 5 minutes. Add bean sprouts; heat to boiling. Blend 1/3 cup water, cornstarch, soy sauce and sugar in small bowl; stir into meat mixture. Simmer for 5 minutes. Serve over chow mein noodles or over rice with noodles on top. Yield: 6 servings.

Ruby Chambers, Gamma Eta
Sherman, Texas

ZESTY GREEK CHILI

This dish is not only very tasty but low in calories.

2 pounds lean ground
  beef or ground turkey
Salt and pepper to taste
1 12-ounce can tomato
  paste
2 1/2 cups beef stock
1 medium eggplant,
  peeled, diced
2 cloves of garlic,
  minced

1 teaspoon oregano
1/2 teaspoon ground
  nutmeg
1/8 teaspoon ground red
  pepper
1 large onion, chopped
3 to 4 cups cooked rice
1/4 cup grated Parmesan
  cheese

Shape ground beef into large flat patty. Brown in nonstick 10-inch skillet over medium heat. Turn; brown other side. Break into chunks; season with salt and pepper. Combine tomato paste and beef stock in bowl; add to ground beef. Stir in next 6 ingredients; simmer, covered, for 15 minutes. Uncover; simmer for 10 minutes. Serve over rice; sprinkle with cheese. Yield: 6 servings.

Lucille Foley, Xi Upsilon
Pensacola, Florida

CHEESY HAM CASSEROLE

Great-grandma made this casserole when the grandchildren stayed overnight. We all loved it!

1/2 cup mayonnaise-
  type salad dressing
2 cups broccoli flowerets
1 1/2 cups diced cooked
  ham
1 1/2 cups corkscrew
  noodles, cooked,
  drained

1/2 cup chopped green
  bell pepper
1/4 cup milk
1 1/2 cups shredded sharp
  Cheddar cheese
3/4 cup herb-seasoned
  croutons

Preheat oven to 350 degrees. Combine first 6 ingredients and 1 cup cheese in large bowl; mix well. Spoon into greased 1 1/2-quart casserole. Sprinkle with remaining cheese and croutons. Bake for 30 minutes. Yield: 4 to 6 servings.

Kimberly Tjugum, Xi Beta
Madison, Wisconsin

RAVIOLI ROULADE

This spinach dish is my children's favorite. They love to make it, too.

1 package crescent rolls
1 egg, beaten
1 tablespoon water
1 8-ounce can spinach,
  well drained

1 4-ounce can deviled
  ham
1/3 cup Parmesan cheese
1 jar spaghetti sauce

Preheat oven to 375 degrees. Separate rolls into triangles. Beat egg and water in small bowl. Combine spinach, ham and cheese in bowl; mix well. Spoon spinach mixture on each triangle. Roll up starting at wide end; arrange, points down, on greased cookie sheet. Brush each roll with egg mixture. Bake for 15 minutes or until golden brown. Heat spaghetti sauce in saucepan; spoon over rolls. Yield: 4 servings.

Linda King, Beta Beta Chi
Cedar Hill, Texas

APPLE STUFFED PORK CHOPS WITH CIDER PAN GRAVY

1 medium onion,
  chopped
6 tablespoons butter or
  margarine
4 slices raisin bread,
  crumbled
1 large apple, peeled,
  cored, chopped
1/4 cup chopped parsley
1 teaspoon salt

1/2 teaspoon thyme
1/2 teaspoon pepper
1 egg, slightly beaten
4 double pork loin
  chops, 1 1/2 inches thick
1/2 cup water
2 tablespoons all-
  purpose flour
1 cup apple cider

Sauté onion in 3 tablespoons butter in large skillet until tender. Remove from heat. Stir in next 7 ingredients; mix well. Cut deep pocket in each chop; fill with bread mixture. Fasten opening with wooden toothpick. Brown chops on both sides in 3 tablespoons butter in large skillet, turning once. Add water; bring to a boil. Reduce heat; simmer, covered, for 40 minutes. Remove chops to serving plate. Sprinkle flour over pan drippings, stirring until smooth. Stir in cider; cook, stirring, until gravy is thickened. Serve with chops. Yield: 4 servings.

Karen L. Young, Xi Epsilon
Smithsburg, Maryland

BAKED PORK CHOPS WITH CRANBERRIES

6 loin pork chops, 3/4 inch thick	1 1/2 teaspoons salt
2 cups fresh cranberries	1/8 teaspoon pepper
3/4 cup sugar	1/3 cup water

Pat pork chops with damp paper towels. Trim fat from chops; heat small amount of fat in large skillet. Add chops; cook for about 15 minutes or until browned on both sides. Remove chops; pour fat from skillet. Return chops to skillet with remaining ingredients. Bring to a boil; reduce heat and simmer for 1 hour or until done. Use cranberry sauce as gravy. May serve with whipped potatoes if desired. Yield: 4 servings.

Jan Manning, Xi Gamma Theta
Largo, Florida

EASY COUNTRY SPARERIBS

8 pork country-style spareribs	1 medium jar spaghetti sauce
Seasoned salt to taste	

Preheat oven to 325 degrees. Sprinkle ribs on both sides with seasoned salt. Place ribs in 9-by-13-inch baking dish; pour sauce over ribs. Cover with foil; bake for 1 1/2 hours. Yield: 4 servings.

Kimberly Tulloch, Epsilon Alpha
Garland, Texas

MONTREAL SPARERIB SAUCE

1 cup applesauce	1/2 teaspoon pepper
1/2 cup catsup	1/2 teaspoon paprika
2 cups packed dark brown sugar	1/2 teaspoon garlic powder or 2 cloves of garlic, minced
6 tablespoons lemon juice	1/2 teaspoon cinnamon
1/2 teaspoon salt	

Combine all ingredients in large saucepan; mix well. Heat to boiling. Use as basting sauce for baked spareribs. Yield: enough for 12 spareribs.

Nancy Noon-Ward, Xi Gamma Tau
Mission, British Columbia, Canada

COUNTRY SPARERIBS AND SAUERKRAUT

This homely country supper goes together in minutes.

1 32-ounce jar sauerkraut	2 pounds country-style spareribs, cut into serving pieces
1/4 cup dry white wine	Freshly ground black pepper to taste
2 tablespoons all-purpose flour	
2 whole bay leaves, broken in half	

Preheat oven to 350 degrees. Drain sauerkraut in colander; rinse with cold water. Place in roasting pan sprayed with nonstick cooking spray. Sprinkle wine and flour over sauerkraut; toss lightly with fork. Add bay leaves evenly, submerging in sauerkraut. Place spareribs on top. Add pepper. Bake, covered, for 1 1/2 hours or until tender. Yield: 4 servings.

Rosemarie Peterson, Preceptor Alpha Eta
Merrill, Wisconsin

UPSIDE-DOWN PIZZA

This is a wonderful dish for company on a cold night.

4 pounds Italian sausage, cut into 1-inch pieces	2 tablespoons oregano
	2 tablespoons basil
	2 eggs
5 cups tomato sauce	Pepper to taste
2 cups cottage cheese	4 cups shredded mozzarella cheese
1/2 cup Parmesan cheese	
3/4 cup chopped parsley	Pizza Dough

Preheat oven to 350 degrees. Brown sausage in skillet; drain. Stir in tomato sauce. Combine next 7 ingredients in bowl; mix well. Spoon tomato mixture into two 12-inch pie plates. Spoon cottage cheese mixture over tomato mixture. Sprinkle with cheese. Cover with Pizza Dough, tucking in edges. Bake for 35 to 45 minutes or until crust is browned. Yield: 10 servings.

PIZZA DOUGH

1 tablespoon quick yeast	1 teaspoon salt
2 1/3 cups all-purpose flour	1 1/4 cups lukewarm water
1/3 teaspoon pepper	2 tablespoons olive oil

Combine first 4 ingredients in bowl; mix well. Stir in water and oil; mix well. Knead dough on lightly floured surface for 8 to 10 minutes or until smooth. Place in greased bowl; let rise, covered, for 1 hour. Punch down; roll out on lightly floured surface. Yield: enough to cover two 12-inch pie plates.

Leslie White, Kappa Pi
Carleton Place, Ontario, Canada

SHEPHERD'S PIE

1 package instant beef broth	1/4 cup frozen peas
	2 tablespoons chopped fresh mint
1 cup hot water	4 ounces boned cooked lamb, cubed
1/2 cup diced carrot	
1/2 cup chopped leeks	1 cup hot water
1/4 cup diced celery	2/3 cup instant potato flakes
1 small clove of garlic, minced	
2 teaspoons margarine	
2 tablespoons all-purpose flour	

Dissolve beef broth in hot water. Sauté carrot, leeks, celery and garlic in margarine in 2-quart saucepan over medium heat for several minutes or until leeks and celery are softened. Sprinkle flour over mixture; stir quickly to combine. Cook, stirring constantly, for 1 minute; stir in beef broth gradually. Add peas and mint; mix well. Reduce heat to low; cook, stirring occasionally, for about 10 minutes or until carrot is tender and mixture thickens. Add lamb; cook for 2 to 3 minutes or until mixture is heated through. Combine water and potato flakes in small bowl; beat with fork until light and fluffy. Divide lamb mixture into 2 greased 1½-cup casseroles; top with potato mixture. Spread over center of each casserole. Broil for 2 to 3 minutes or until potato mixture is lightly browned. Yield: 2 servings.

Virginia P. Cook, Laureate Gamma Alpha
Sarasota, Florida

LIVER AND ONIONS

1 medium onion, sliced	2 teaspoons water
2 tablespoons margarine	2 teaspoons lemon juice
1 pound sliced beef liver	1 teaspoon
Salt and pepper to taste	Worcestershire sauce

Separate onion slices into rings. Sauté onion in margarine in skillet until tender; remove from skillet. Add liver; sprinkle with salt and pepper. Cook over medium heat for 3 minutes; turn. Add onion; cook for 2 to 3 minutes or until liver is slightly pink in center. Remove liver and onion to serving plate. Stir remaining ingredients into pan drippings; heat through. Pour over liver and onion. Yield: 4 servings.

Herminia V. Martinez, Alpha Pi Gamma
Edinburg, Texas

PEPPER STEAK

I've used this recipe for 14 years. It tastes wonderful.

1 pound moose, venison	¼ cup water
or beef steak	¼ cup soya sauce
Salt to taste	2 tomatoes, cut into
Paprika to taste	eighths
2 tablespoons margarine	2 green bell peppers, cut
2 cloves of garlic,	into strips
minced	1 cup sliced green onions
1½ cups beef consommé	6 cups cooked rice
2 tablespoons cornstarch	

Cut steak into strips. Sprinkle with salt and paprika. Brown steak in margarine in large skillet. Add garlic and consommé; simmer for 30 minutes. Combine cornstarch, water and soya sauce; stir into steak mixture, stirring until gravy thickens. Add tomatoes, green peppers and onions; simmer, covered, for 2 minutes. Serve over rice. Yield: 4 servings.

Maria Hedderson, Xi Gamma Tau
Mission, British Columbia, Canada

HIGH DESERT VENISON STEAK

¼ cup chopped onion	½ cup crushed croutons
3 tablespoons butter or	2 pounds venison
margarine	tenderloin steaks
1 cup all-purpose flour	Lemon pepper to taste
2 teaspoons basil	½ cup chopped celery
1 teaspoon paprika	½ cup chopped bacon

Sauté onion in 2 tablespoons margarine in large skillet for 2 minutes. Combine flour, basil, paprika and croutons in bowl; mix well. Coat steaks with flour mixture; place in skillet over onion. Simmer, uncovered, for 15 minutes; add 1 tablespoon butter and water as needed. Turn steaks; sprinkle each with lemon pepper. Add celery and bacon; cook for 15 minutes over low heat. Yield: 4 servings.

Keri Satterlee, Zeta Beta
Madras, Oregon

NASSAU OVEN-BARBECUED CHICKEN

4 skinned chicken	2 tablespoons tarragon
breasts	wine vinegar
1 cup tomato juice	1 teaspoon chili powder
1 cup chili sauce	½ teaspoon garlic salt
2 teaspoons	
Worcestershire sauce	

Preheat oven to 350 degrees. Place chicken in 9-by-15-inch baking pan; bake for 30 minutes. Combine remaining ingredients in bowl; mix well. Pour over chicken, reserving small amount for basting. Bake for 30 minutes or until chicken is tender, basting frequently with reserved sauce. Yield: 4 servings.

Ellen Connelly, Laureate
Goderich, Ontario, Canada

CHINESE CHICKEN WITH ALMONDS

4 chicken breasts, cut	1 8-ounce can bamboo
into strips	shoots
4 tablespoons vegetable	1 large green bell
oil	pepper, chopped
½ teaspoon ginger	Water
1 cup soy sauce	½ cup slivered almonds
2 stalks celery, chopped	1 tablespoon cornstarch
1 4-ounce can	Cooked rice
mushrooms	

Place chicken in oil in skillet; sprinkle with ginger. Pour ½ cup soy sauce over chicken. Cook over medium heat for about 2 minutes. Add next 4 ingredients; cook for 35 to 40 minutes or until chicken tests done. Add remaining ½ cup soy sauce, ½ cup water and almonds. Mix cornstarch with ⅓ cup water; add to chicken mixture, stirring until thickened. Serve over rice. Yield: 4 servings.

Fern Caraway, Preceptor Beta Mu
San Manuel, Arizona

CRANBERRY CHICKEN

I made this dish for a sick sorority sister and her family before I found out they did not care for cranberries. They ate the entire recipe in one sitting!

1/3 cup all-purpose flour	3/4 cup sugar
1 teaspoon salt	1/4 cup chopped onion
2 1/2 pounds boneless skinned chicken breasts	1 teaspoon grated orange peel
4 tablespoons margarine	3/4 cup orange juice
1 1/2 cups fresh or frozen cranberries	1/4 teaspoon cinnamon
	1/4 teaspoon ginger

Mix flour and salt in shallow bowl; coat chicken in mixture. Brown chicken on both sides in margarine in skillet. Combine remaining ingredients in saucepan; bring to a boil. Remove from heat when cranberries pop open. Drain excess fat from skillet; pour cranberry mixture over chicken. Simmer, covered, for 35 to 40 minutes or until chicken tests done. May serve sauce over mashed potatoes if desired. Yield: 4 to 6 servings.

Roberta Foreman, Laureate Sigma
Dunwoody, Georgia

CHICKEN AND SAUSAGE STEW

It is nice to come home to the smell of cooked stew after a busy day at work, especially on a cold winter evening.

1 cup cooked sliced carrots	2 bay leaves
1/2 cup chopped onion	2 15-ounce cans navy beans, drained
1 6-ounce can tomato paste	4 boneless chicken breasts, frozen individually
1/2 cup red wine	8 ounces Polish sausage, sliced 1/4 inch thick
1 teaspoon garlic powder	
1/2 teaspoon dry thyme	
1/8 teaspoon ground cloves	

Preheat 4-quart Crock•Pot on Low. Combine first 8 ingredients in Crock•Pot; mix well. Add beans. Arrange chicken on top of bean mixture. Place sausage over chicken. Cover; cook on Low for 9 to 10 hours or on High for 5 1/2 to 6 hours. Remove bay leaves before serving. Yield: 4 servings.

Arlene Haldeman, Omicron Master
Granite City, Illinois

CHICKEN CORDON BLEU

4 skinned boneless chicken breasts	1/2 cup crushed cornflakes or 1/2 cup herb-seasoned bread crumbs
1/4 teaspoon pepper	
4 slices 98% fat free ham	
3/4 cup shredded mozzarella cheese	1/4 teaspoon garlic powder
1/2 teaspoon paprika	1/3 cup skim milk

Preheat oven to 350 degrees. Place each chicken breast between 2 pieces heavy-duty plastic wrap; flatten to 1/4-inch thickness, using mallet or rolling pin. Sprinkle with pepper. Place 1 slice ham and 3 tablespoons mozzarella cheese on each breast. Roll up jelly-roll fashion, tucking in sides; secure with wooden toothpicks. Mix paprika, cereal and garlic powder in shallow bowl. Dip each chicken roll in milk; roll in cereal mixture. Place in 7-by-11-inch baking dish sprayed with nonstick cooking spray. Bake for 30 minutes or until lightly browned and tests done. Yield: 4 servings.

Janet Cox, Epsilon
Wichita, Kansas

❖ PECAN STUFFED CHICKEN BREASTS

1 large celery stalk, chopped	2 teaspoons parsley flakes
1 small onion, minced	1/4 cup water
2 tablespoons butter or margarine	4 whole boneless chicken breasts
1/2 teaspoon salt	2 tablespoons lemon juice
1/4 teaspoon pepper	Salt and pepper to taste
2 cups crumbled toast	
1 cup coarsely chopped pecans	

Preheat oven to 400 degrees. Sauté celery and onion in butter in skillet over medium heat until soft. Add 1/2 teaspoon salt and 1/4 teaspoon pepper. Stir in toast, pecans, parsley and water; remove from heat. Place each chicken breast on double foil square; brush both sides with lemon juice. Sprinkle with salt and pepper to taste. Spoon 1/4 of stuffing on center of each breast; close foil tightly. Place on cookie sheet. Bake for 20 minutes. Open bundles; brush with drippings. Bake, uncovered, for 20 additional minutes. Yield: 4 servings.

Diana H. Jones, Xi Delta Phi
Fairfield Glade, Tennessee

MA-MA PIERINI'S CHICKEN AND RIGATONI

This is an original Italian recipe given to me by my Ma-Ma Pierini. No exact ingredients have ever been written down, but it is an excellent dish.

Vegetable oil	1 large frying chicken, cut up
1 large onion, chopped	Salt and pepper to taste
8 stalks celery, chopped	3 cans tomato paste
1 cup chopped celery leaves	2 packages rigatoni

Add enough oil to cover bottom of large saucepan. Add onion, celery and celery leaves; sauté until tender. Add chicken; mix well. Add salt and pepper. Cook, covered, over low heat for about 1 hour or until chicken loses pink color, stirring occasionally.

Add tomato paste and enough water to cover chicken. Cook over medium heat until mixture comes to a boil. Reduce heat to low; simmer for about 1 hour or until sauce is thickened and chicken is done, stirring occasionally. Cook rigatoni according to package directions. Do not overcook. Drain well. Remove chicken from saucepan onto serving plate. Pour about half the sauce over rigatoni; toss until mixed. Pour remaining sauce over chicken. Yield: 6 to 8 servings.

Judy Long, Xi Omicron
Greenville, Mississippi

COLA-SAUCED CHICKEN LEGS

1 10-ounce can cola	*1 teaspoon mustard*
1/2 cup catsup	*5 or 6 chicken legs and*
1 large onion, chopped	*thighs, skinned*

Combine cola, catsup, onion and mustard in electric skillet; bring to a boil. Add chicken; reduce heat to low. Simmer, covered, for 30 to 40 minutes or until chicken is tender. Yield: 6 servings.

Irene Schafer, Laureate Gamma Alpha
Sarasota, Florida

CHICKEN IN YOGURT

Everybody loves this recipe but they don't know how the chicken is cooked.

6 chicken thighs	*1 teaspoon mustard*
2 tablespoons margarine	*1 cup plain yogurt*

Fry chicken in margarine in skillet until lightly browned. Combine mustard and yogurt in small bowl; mix well. Dip chicken in yogurt mixture and return to skillet. Cook over low heat for 30 minutes or until chicken is tender. May serve with rice or mashed potatoes if desired. Yield: 6 servings.

Pia Valdes, Theta Phi
Terrell, Texas

EASY POT PIE

2 9-inch prepared pie crusts	*1 16-ounce can cream of chicken soup*
1 16-ounce can mixed vegetables, drained	*1 onion, minced*
1 cup sour cream	*3 cups diced chicken or turkey*

Preheat oven to 350 degrees. Place 1 crust in 9-inch pie plate. Combine next 5 ingredients in bowl; mix well. Pour into prepared crust. Top with remaining crust. Bake for 1 hour. Let stand for 5 minutes before cutting. Yield: 6 to 8 servings.

Suzanne Blickenstaff, Mu Chi
DuBois, Pennsylvania

CHICKEN POT PIE WITH CELERY SEED CRUST

1/3 cup butter	*1 10-ounce package*
2 1/3 cups all-purpose flour	*frozen mixed vegetables, thawed*
1/3 cup chopped onion	*1 teaspoon celery seed*
1 1/2 teaspoons salt	*2/3 cup plus 2*
1/4 teaspoon pepper	*tablespoons*
1 3/4 cups chicken broth	*shortening*
2/3 cup milk	*5 tablespoons water*
2 cups cooked diced chicken	

Preheat oven to 425 degrees. Melt butter in saucepan; blend in 1/3 cup flour, onion, 1/2 teaspoon salt and pepper. Cook, stirring, until bubbly. Remove from heat; stir in broth and milk. Heat to boiling, stirring constantly, for 1 minute. Stir in chicken and vegetables. Combine 2 cups flour, celery seed and 1 teaspoon salt in bowl; cut in shortening. Sprinkle with water, 1 tablespoon at a time, mixing until all flour is moistened and dough cleans side of bowl. Shape dough into ball. Roll out 2/3 dough on lightly floured board into 13-inch square. Place pastry into 9-inch square baking pan. Pour chicken mixture into crust. Roll out remaining dough; place over filling. Cut slits in center. Bake for 30 to 35 minutes or until lightly browned. Yield: 6 servings.

Joannie Thomas, Delta Epsilon
Bowling Green, Kentucky

TACO TURKEY MEAT LOAF

1 pound ground turkey	*1/4 cup chopped onion*
1 small can tomato sauce	*2 tablespoons pepper*
1/3 cup crushed corn chips	*1 package taco seasoning*
	Taco sauce

Preheat oven to 350 degrees. Combine first 6 ingredients in bowl; mix well. Place in 4-by-8-inch loaf pan. Bake for 45 to 50 minutes or until done. Spoon taco sauce over top. Bake for 5 minutes longer or until sauce is heated. Yield: 4 to 6 servings.

Karen Dobbins, Xi Lambda Mu
Laurie, Missouri

TUNA LASAGNA

1 7-ounce can tuna	*1 small onion, chopped*
8 ounces cooked noodles	*8 ounces shredded*
1 10-ounce can cream of mushroom soup	*Cheddar cheese*

Preheat oven to 350 degrees. Pour mixture of first 4 ingredients into greased 8-inch square baking pan. Sprinkle cheese over top. Bake for 30 minutes. Let stand for 10 minutes. Yield: 4 servings.

Sally Jansen, Xi Delta Iota
Marshalltown, Iowa

OVERNIGHT TUNA CASSEROLE

This delicious recipe was a blessing while I was losing 70 pounds last year.

1   10-ounce can cream
   of mushroom soup
1 cup milk
1   6-ounce can water-
   pack tuna, drained,
   flaked

1 cup uncooked elbow
   macaroni
1 cup frozen peas
1/2 cup chopped onion
1 cup shredded Cheddar
   cheese

Combine soup and milk in 2-quart microwave-safe bowl; whisk until well blended. Stir in tuna, macaroni, peas, onion and 3/4 cup cheese; mix well. Refrigerate, covered, for at least 12 hours or overnight. Cover with lid or vented plastic wrap. Microwave on High for 15 to 17 minutes or until bubbly. Sprinkle with 1/4 cup cheese. Let stand, uncovered, for 5 to 7 minutes or until cheese is melted. Yield: 4 servings.

Judy Cooperrider, Xi Chi Gamma
Livermore, California

STUFFED FISH FILETS

Old recipes were left in a kitchen drawer of the house we recently purchased. This one was dated 1935.

11/2 pounds fish filets
3/4 teaspoon salt
1/8 teaspoon pepper
3 slices bacon, diced
1 cup corn bread crumbs

1 cup soft white bread
   crumbs
3/4 teaspoon salt
1/8 teaspoon pepper
1 cup evaporated milk

Preheat oven to 350 degrees. Cut fish into 9-by-11/2-by-1/2-inch thick strips. Sprinkle with 3/4 teaspoon salt and 1/8 teaspoon pepper. Arrange strips around inside of greased custard cups or ramekins. Cook bacon in skillet until lightly browned. Stir in remaining ingredients. Spoon into center of fish rings. Set cups in shallow baking pan. Bake for 45 minutes or until stuffing is firm in center. Yield: 6 servings.

Nancy Scheirer, Preceptor Beta Nu
Manitou Beach, Michigan

SALMON CROQUETTES

Vegetable oil for frying
1   15-ounce can pink
   salmon
1/4 onion, grated
1 cup cracker crumbs

1 teaspoon salt
1/4 teaspoon pepper
1 egg
1 tablespoon pickle juice

Preheat oil in deep skillet to 375 degrees. Place salmon in large bowl; remove bones. Add remaining ingredients; mix well. Shape into patties; drop into hot oil. Cook until browned. Yield: 12 croquettes.

Tracey Smith, Tau Omega
Carthage, Texas

MANHATTAN CLAM-SAUCED LINGUINE

1/2 cup chopped onion
2 teaspoons minced
   garlic
1 tablespoon olive oil
1   28-ounce can crushed
   tomatoes
1 teaspoon thyme
1 teaspoon basil

1/2 teaspoon salt
1/8 teaspoon pepper
1   6-ounce can chopped
   clams, drained
1   8-ounce package
   linguine, cooked
Grated Parmesan cheese

Sauté onion and garlic in olive oil in skillet until tender. Stir in next 5 ingredients; simmer, uncovered, for 30 minutes. Add clams; heat through. Serve over linguine. Sprinkle with cheese. Yield: 6 servings.

Beverly Frayne
Humble, Texas

CRAB SUPPER PIE

1 cup shredded Swiss
   cheese
1 unbaked 9-inch pie
   shell
1   7-ounce can crab,
   drained, flaked
2 green onions with
   tops, sliced
3 eggs, beaten
1 cup light cream

1/2 teaspoon salt
2 tablespoons finely
   chopped parsley
1/2 teaspoon grated
   lemon peel
1/4 teaspoon dry
   mustard
Dash of mace
1/4 cup sliced almonds

Preheat oven to 400 degrees. Sprinkle cheese evenly in pie shell. Place crab over cheese; sprinkle with green onions. Combine next 7 ingredients; pour over crab. Top with almonds. Bake for 15 minutes. Reduce oven temperature to 325 degrees; bake for 45 minutes. Let stand for 10 minutes before serving. Yield: 4 to 6 servings.

Susan Curry, Xi Delta Zeta
Mississauga, Ontario, Canada

SCALLOPS PROVENÇAL

12 ounces fresh scallops
   or 1   12-ounce package
   frozen scallops,
   thawed
1/4 cup all-purpose flour
1/4 teaspoon salt
Dash of pepper

1/4 cup vegetable oil
1 small clove of garlic,
   finely chopped
2 tablespoons margarine
Snipped parsley
Lemon wedges

Cut large scallops into 11/2-inch pieces. Pat scallops with paper towels. Mix flour, salt and pepper in bowl; coat scallops with flour mixture. Heat oil in 10-inch skillet. Cook scallops for 4 to 5 minutes or until light brown, turning carefully. Sauté garlic in margarine in 1-quart saucepan over low heat for about 2 minutes. Pour over scallops. Sprinkle with parsley. Serve with lemon wedges. Yield: 4 servings.

Sue Penny, Alpha Theta
Oromocto, New Brunswick, Canada

QUICK SHRIMP ÉTOUFFÉ

1 small onion, diced
1/2 cup butter or
  margarine
2 10-ounce cans cream
  of mushroom soup
2 cups water

1 16-ounce can diced
  Ro-Tel tomatoes
1 pound peeled small or
  medium shrimp
Cooked rice

Sauté onion in butter in large saucepan. Add soup, water and tomatoes; bring to a boil. Stir in shrimp; reduce heat to low. Cook for 1 hour. Serve over rice. Yield: 8 servings.

Martha Connell, Chi
Shreveport, Louisiana

SHRIMP SCAMPI

This recipe brings back wonderful memories of my growing up along the bayous of southern Louisiana.

2 pounds medium
  fresh shrimp, peeled,
  deveined
1/2 cup olive oil
1/2 cup butter
1/2 cup white wine
1/4 cup lemon juice
1 teaspoon oregano

3 cloves of garlic, finely
  chopped
3 tablespoons parsley,
  chopped
Salt and pepper to taste
French bread or cooked
  rice

Preheat oven to 375 degrees. Arrange shrimp in 9-by-13-inch baking dish. Mix next 9 ingredients in saucepan; heat through. Pour over shrimp. Bake for 20 minutes or until shrimp turn pink. Serve with French bread or over rice. Yield: 2 to 4 servings.

Mary R. Simmons, Alpha Beta Rho
Windsor, Missouri

SHRIMP STUFFED PEPPERS

6 green bell peppers
1 large onion, chopped
2 tablespoons butter or
  margarine
1 pound shrimp, peeled,
  deveined
1 cup plus 2
  tablespoons Italian-
  style bread crumbs
1 egg, beaten

2 or 3 cloves of garlic,
  finely chopped
1 to 2 tablespoons
  chopped parsley
10 to 12 green olives,
  chopped
1 cup grated Parmesan
  cheese
Salt and pepper to taste
Butter or margarine

Preheat oven to 350 degrees. Cut green peppers in half lengthwise; remove seeds and membrane. Sauté onion in 2 tablespoons butter in skillet. Add shrimp; cook until shrimp turn pink. Place in bowl. Stir in 1 cup bread crumbs and next 7 ingredients. Spoon into green pepper halves; sprinkle with 2 tablespoons bread crumbs. Top with small amount of butter. Place in 9-by-13-inch baking pan. Add 1/2 inch water to pan. Bake for 1 hour. Yield: 4 to 6 servings.

Mary Greco Hill, Preceptor Alpha Eta
Kirkland, Washington

ASPARAGUS CASSEROLE

This is a wonderful addition to any meal, especially if guests are invited!

4 15-ounce cans
  asparagus
2 10-ounce cans cream
  of celery soup
1 small jar Cheez Whiz

1/2 teaspoon white
  pepper
10 hard-cooked eggs,
  sliced
3 stacks buttery crackers

Preheat oven to 350 degrees. Drain asparagus, reserving half the liquid. Combine soup, Cheez Whiz and reserved liquid in large skillet; mix well. Simmer until cheese is melted. Add pepper. Layer 2 cans asparagus, 1/2 the egg slices, 1/2 the crackers and 1/2 the sauce in greased deep 3-quart casserole. Repeat layers. Bake for 50 minutes. Yield: 6 to 8 servings.

Kim Tucker, Zeta Alpha
Sheridan, Arkansas

BROCCOLI-CORN CASSEROLE

1 egg, beaten
1 10-ounce package
  frozen broccoli
1 16-ounce can cream-
  style corn
1/4 teaspoon salt

1 tablespoon grated
  onion
1 cup herb-seasoned
  stuffing mix
3 tablespoons
  margarine, melted

Preheat oven to 350 degrees. Combine first 5 ingredients in large bowl. Toss stuffing mix with margarine in small bowl until coated. Stir 3/4 cup stuffing mixture into broccoli mixture. Spoon into ungreased 2-quart baking dish. Sprinkle with remaining stuffing mixture. Bake for 45 minutes. Yield: 6 to 8 servings.

Helen Dix, Laureate Alpha Theta
Rifle, Colorado

DUTCH MESS

I grew up in Pella, Iowa, a Dutch community. My grandmother served this twice a week in the spring.

3 bunches leaf lettuce
3 bunches green onions
  with tops, chopped
8 medium potatoes,
  peeled
1 pound bacon, cut into
  1-inch pieces

1/2 cup vinegar
1/4 cup sugar
6 to 8 hard-cooked eggs,
  sliced

Preheat large ovenproof serving dish in 325-degree oven. Wash lettuce; cut into pieces. Combine lettuce and green onions in bowl. Boil potatoes in enough water to cover in saucepan until done; drain. Place in preheated dish; mash. Fry bacon in skillet. Add vinegar and sugar; simmer for 1 minute. Layer eggs and lettuce over potatoes. Pour bacon mixture over lettuce; stir. Serve immediately. Yield: 6 servings.

Beverly Gingery
Roseburg, Oregon

SOUTHERN STUFFED PEPPERS

6 large green bell peppers	1 clove of garlic, crushed
6 slices bacon, diced	1/2 cup canned sliced mushrooms
8 ounces chicken livers, chopped	2 cups cooked rice
1 cup chopped onion	1 teaspoon salt
1 cup sliced celery	1/2 teaspoon pepper
	Dash of cayenne pepper

Preheat oven to 375 degrees. Slice stem end from peppers; remove seeds. Cook peppers in small amount of boiling water in saucepan for about 5 minutes. Remove from water; drain. Sauté bacon, livers, onion, celery and garlic until onion and celery are tender. Add remaining ingredients; mix well. Stuff peppers with mixture. Place in 9-by-13-inch baking dish; add 1/2 inch of water. Bake, covered, for 20 to 25 minutes or until done. May freeze stuffed peppers and cook later if desired. Yield: 6 servings.

Virginia K. Baker, Xi Omicron
Harlingen, Texas

SPINACH CASSEROLE

2 10-ounce packages chopped frozen spinach	1 can artichoke hearts, cut into small pieces
1 10-ounce can cream of chicken soup	1/2 cup Parmesan cheese

Preheat oven to 350 degrees. Cook spinach according to package directions in saucepan; drain. Add soup, artichoke hearts and 1/4 cup cheese; mix well. Pour into greased 9-inch square baking dish. Top with remaining cheese. Bake for 20 to 30 minutes or until heated through. Yield: 4 to 6 servings.

Jennifer Petty, Chi
Shreveport, Louisiana

SQUASH DRESSING

8 to 10 yellow squash, sliced	1 10-ounce can cream of mushroom soup
1 large onion, chopped	1 10-ounce can cream of chicken soup
1/4 cup butter or margarine	Salt and pepper to taste
3 6-ounce packages corn bread mix	1/2 cup Cheddar cheese, shredded
1 10-ounce can cream of celery soup	

Preheat oven to 350 degrees. Cook squash with onion in boiling water in large covered saucepan for 30 minutes; drain well. Stir in butter. Cook corn bread using package directions; cool. Break corn bread into small pieces in large bowl. Add squash and soups; mix well. Add salt and pepper. Spoon into greased 9-by-13-inch baking dish. Sprinkle cheese over top. Bake, covered, for 30 minutes. Yield: 8 servings.

Sherron Boswell, Xi Alpha Gamma Gamma
Huntsville, Texas

HOG JOWL AND TURNIP GREENS

6 ounces cured hog jowl	1 bunch turnip greens
3 quarts water	Salt and pepper to taste

Boil hog jowl in 3 quarts water in large covered saucepan for 45 minutes. Rinse turnip greens. Add to saucepan; cook, covered, for 1 hour longer or until turnips are tender. Add salt and pepper. Place jowl in center of platter surrounded by turnip greens. Serve pot likken or juice in bowl to be used for dunking corn bread. Yield: 6 servings.

Patricia L. White, Preceptor Kappa Lambda
Portland, Texas

MIXED VEGETABLE CASSEROLE

8 ounces frozen California blend vegetables	1 cup shredded Cheddar cheese
1 16-ounce can whole kernel corn, drained	1/2 cup milk
	Salt and pepper to taste
1 16-ounce can cream of broccoli soup	1 cup bread or cracker crumbs
1/4 cup chopped onion	1/4 cup margarine

Preheat oven to 350 degrees. Combine first 7 ingredients in 2-quart casserole; mix well. Bake for 30 minutes. Mix bread crumbs and margarine together in small bowl; sprinkle on top. Bake for 30 minutes longer. Serve hot. Yield: 6 to 8 servings.

Susan Moore, Zeta Nu
Princeton, Missouri

SPAGHETTI AND BROCCOLI

My grandmother made this dish and called it green spaghetti.

8 slices bacon, cut in half	4 tablespoons Italian-style bread crumbs
2 tablespoons olive oil	
4 cloves of garlic, crushed	Salt and pepper to taste
1 bunch broccoli, cut up	1 1-pound package spaghetti
2 tablespoons butter or margarine	Grated Parmesan cheese

Brown bacon in olive oil with garlic in large skillet. Boil broccoli in salted water in large saucepan until tender. Remove broccoli with slotted spoon, reserving liquid in saucepan. Add broccoli, 4 cups reserved liquid, butter, bread crumbs, salt and pepper to bacon mixture, mixing well. Simmer, covered, for 10 minutes. Cook spaghetti in reserved liquid in large saucepan; drain. Pour broccoli mixture over spaghetti. Sprinkle with Parmesan cheese. Yield: 6 servings.

Diane Anton, Epsilon Alpha
Lake Havasu City, Arizona

ITALIAN-STYLE VEGETABLE STIR-FRY

1 clove of garlic, minced
1/2 green bell pepper, diced
1/3 cup chopped green onions
1 tomato, diced
2 tablespoons olive oil
1/2 cup chicken stock
1 teaspoon dried basil
1/2 teaspoon dried oregano
1/2 teaspoon salt
1 14-ounce can red kidney beans, drained, rinsed
3 cups cooked rigatoni pasta

Stir-fry first 4 ingredients in olive oil in skillet over medium heat for 3 to 5 minutes or until soft. Add chicken stock, seasonings and kidney beans; heat through. Add pasta; toss gently. Yield: 6 servings.

I. Krauss, Alpha Mu
Preeceville, Saskatchewan, Canada

VEGETABLE STUFFED SHELLS

1/2 cup chopped leeks, white part only
2 teaspoons margarine
1/2 cup coarsely shredded carrot
1/2 cup coarsely shredded yellow squash
1/2 cup coarsely shredded zucchini
1/4 teaspoon dried basil
1 1/2 ounces jumbo pasta shells, cooked, drained
1 ounce coarsely shredded Monterey Jack cheese

Preheat oven to 350 degrees. Sauté leeks in margarine in large nonstick skillet over medium-high heat for about 5 minutes or until soft. Add carrot, squash and zucchini; mix well. Cook for about 3 minutes or until vegetables are soft. Stir in basil. Fill shells with vegetable mixture; sprinkle with cheese. Place in 8-inch square baking pan sprayed with nonstick cooking spray. Bake, covered, for 15 minutes. Yield: 2 servings.

Karina Nelson, Xi
Victoria, British Columbia, Canada

MEATLESS SAUCE AND PASTA DINNER

1 9-ounce can tomatoes
1 10-ounce can Ro-Tel tomatoes
1 clove of garlic, chopped
1 tablespoon Worcestershire sauce
1 tablespoon basil
1 teaspoon oregano
1 tablespoon wine vinegar
1 16-ounce jar mushroom pieces or 1 can white beans
Salt and pepper to taste
1 onion, sliced
4 cups cooked pasta

Combine first 9 ingredients in large skillet; mix well. Place onion slices on top. Cook on medium-high for 15 minutes. Reduce heat; simmer, covered, for 1 hour. Serve over favorite pasta. Yield: 4 servings.

Lynn C. Campbell, Rho
Deadwood, South Dakota

HOMEMADE EGG NOODLES

3 egg yolks
1 whole egg
3 tablespoons cold water
1 teaspoon salt
2 cups sifted all-purpose flour

Beat egg yolks and whole egg in mixer bowl until very light. Beat in cold water and salt. Stir and work flour in with hands. Divide dough into 3 portions. Roll out each portion on lightly floured cloth-covered board until very thin. Dust both sides lightly with flour. Roll up jelly-roll fashion. Cut into 1/4-inch wide strips. Unroll strips; let dry before using. Can be stored in freezer. Yield: 10 ounces.

Cathi Lynn Iacovetto, Theta
Gillette, Wyoming

GROSMAMA'S DUMPLINGS

This was one of my German Grandmother's favorite recipes. It is a great way to use leftover mashed potatoes.

2 slices bread
1/2 cup milk
1 cup cooked mashed potatoes
2 tablespoons beef or chicken broth
1 cup all-purpose flour
2 eggs, slightly beaten
2 quarts (or more) beef or chicken broth

Soak bread in milk in small bowl. Combine bread, potatoes, 2 tablespoons broth, flour and eggs in bowl; mix well. Heat 2 quarts broth in large saucepan to a boil. Drop mixture by tablespoonfuls into boiling broth. Cook for 15 to 20 minutes or until dumplings float on top of broth. Remove with slotted spoon. Yield: 4 servings.

Betty Hoback, Epsilon Master
Kansas City, Missouri

ARMENIAN RICE PILAF

This recipe is one of the first Armenian dishes an Armenian girl learns to cook. It is easy and delicious.

1/2 cup vermicelli, broken into small pieces
1/2 cup butter or margarine
2 cups long grain rice
4 cups chicken broth
1/2 tablespoon salt

Sauté vermicelli in butter in heavy saucepan until golden brown, stirring constantly. Add rice, stirring constantly, for 2 to 3 minutes or until rice is well coated. Combine broth and salt in saucepan; bring to a boil. Add boiling broth to rice mixture. Cook, covered, on low heat for 25 minutes or until liquid is absorbed. Stir lightly with fork; let set for 10 minutes before serving. Yield: 8 servings.

Dorothy Taminosian, Laureate Alpha Beta
Fort Myers, Florida

SPANISH CHEESE RICE

1 7-ounce can diced
chilies
1 cup uncooked rice
2 cups grated Monterey
Jack cheese
1 chicken bouillon cube

1¹/₂ cups boiling water
1 8-ounce can tomato
sauce
1 8-ounce sauce can
water

Preheat oven to 350 degrees. Arrange chilies over bottom of baking dish. Add rice. Sprinkle with 1 cup cheese. Dissolve bouillon cube in 1¹/₂ cups boiling water; pour over mixture. Sprinkle with remaining cheese. Pour remaining ingredients over mixture. Bake, covered, for 1 hour. Yield: 6 to 8 servings.

Patricia Nutting, Preceptor Tau
Elko, Nevada

MA'S HOMEMADE BISCUIT MIX

6 cups all-purpose flour
3 tablespoons baking
powder

1 tablespoon salt
1 cup shortening

Mix dry ingredients in large bowl; cut in shortening until particles are fine. Store in large glass or plastic container with tightfitting lid at room temperature. Yield: 7 cups.

BISCUITS

2¹/₂ cups Ma's
Homemade Biscuit
Mix

³/₄ cup milk

Preheat oven to 450 degrees. Place mix in bowl. Stir in milk; mix slowly. Knead lightly until well blended. Roll or pat out on lightly floured surface to ¹/₂-inch thickness. Cut with 2-inch biscuit cutter. Place in ungreased 9-by-13-inch baking pan. Bake for 12 to 15 minutes or until browned. Yield: 12 biscuits.

Fay Bullock, Laureate Alpha Epsilon
Langley, British Columbia, Canada

MIRACLE BISCUITS

2 cups self-rising flour
1 cup milk

¹/₂ cup mayonnaise

Preheat oven to 350 degrees. Mix all ingredients together in bowl. Dough will be sticky. Add additional flour as needed to work and knead dough with hands. Roll dough out on lightly floured surface to ¹/₂-inch thickness; cut into biscuits. Place on greased cookie sheet. Bake for 15 to 20 minutes or until lightly browned. Sticky dough may be dropped by tablespoonfuls into greased muffin cups and baked in preheated 400-degree oven for 15 minutes. Yield: 8 to 10 biscuits.

Tammie Raye Parino, Theta Rho
Royalton, Illinois
*Ruth Smith, Preceptor Gamma Rho
Bourbonnais, Illinois

BROCCOLI CORN BREAD

1 10-ounce package
frozen chopped
broccoli, thawed
1 8-ounce package corn
bread mix
¹/₃ cup finely diced
chicken
1 cup shredded Cheddar
cheese

3 eggs, beaten
¹/₂ cup butter or
margarine, melted
¹/₂ teaspoon salt
¹/₄ to ¹/₂ teaspoon garlic
powder
¹/₄ teaspoon ground red
pepper

Preheat oven to 375 degrees. Press broccoli between paper towels. Combine remaining ingredients in large bowl; mix well. Stir in broccoli. Pour into greased 8-inch square baking pan. Bake for 30 minutes or until golden brown. Cool slightly; cut into squares. Yield: 8 servings.

Sandra McDonald
Wintersville, Ohio
*Susan J. F. Bourne, Xi Epsilon Eta
Centreville, Virginia
*Denice Nall, Zeta Alpha
Sheridan, Arkansas

❖ MEXICAN RICE CORN BREAD

1 cup cornmeal
1 teaspoon salt
¹/₂ teaspoon baking soda
1 cup milk
2 eggs, beaten
¹/₄ cup vegetable oil
1 16-ounce can
cream-style corn

2 cups cooked rice
¹/₂ cup finely chopped
onions
2 tablespoons chopped
jalapeño peppers
8 ounces grated
Cheddar cheese

Preheat oven to 350 degrees. Sift dry ingredients together in large bowl. Add remaining ingredients; stir until well blended. Pour into greased 12-inch ovenproof skillet sprinkled with cornmeal. Bake for 40 to 45 minutes or until browned.
Yield: 8 to 10 servings.

Pauline Dennis, Laureate Pi
Dallas, Texas

PUMPKIN AND PECAN CORN BREAD

1 cup whole wheat flour
1 cup yellow cornmeal
1 tablespoon baking
powder
1 tablespoon sugar
¹/₂ teaspoon baking soda

¹/₂ cup pumpkin purée
¹/₃ cup butter or
margarine, melted
1 egg
1 cup milk
³/₄ cup pecan pieces

Preheat oven to 400 degrees. Mix first 5 ingredients in bowl. Beat pumpkin, butter, egg and milk together in large mixer bowl. Add flour mixture all at once. Add pecans; stir with fork until mixture is moist. Do not overmix. Spoon into greased and floured 4-by-8-inch loaf pan. Yield: 10 servings.

Vicki Elworthy, Delta Lambda
Delta, British Columbia, Canada

APPLE-CINNAMON BREAD

I make this bread on Sunday and eat it for breakfast during the week. It is excellent warmed in the microwave and is sugar-free.

1 16-ounce can frozen apple juice	5 cups unbleached flour
1/2 juice can water	2 teaspoons baking powder
3 eggs	2 teaspoons baking soda
1 cup butter or margarine, melted	4 teaspoons cinnamon

Preheat oven to 350 degrees. Beat apple juice, water, eggs and butter in large mixer bowl until frothy. Add remaining ingredients; mix just until blended. Pour into 2 well-greased 4-by-8-inch loaf pans. Sprinkle additional cinnamon on top. Bake for approximately 50 minutes or until knife inserted in center comes out clean. Yield: 2 loaves.

Denise Smith, Alpha Chi
Albuquerque, New Mexico

GRAPE NUT BREAD

My guests love this bread. It is delicious when toasted and freezes well.

1 cup Grape Nuts	4 cups sifted all-purpose flour
2 cups buttermilk	1 teaspoon baking powder
2 cups sugar	1/2 teaspoon salt
2 eggs, beaten	
2 teaspoons baking soda	
Small amount of warm water	

Preheat oven to 350 degrees. Soak Grape Nuts in buttermilk for 45 minutes in large bowl. Add sugar, eggs and baking soda which has been dissolved in small amount of warm water. Sift remaining ingredients together in bowl; add to mixture. Stir until well blended. Pour into greased 4-by-8-inch loaf pan. Bake for 1 hour. Yield: 1 loaf.

Maxine T. Olson, Laureate Phi
Sun City, Arizona

GREEN TOMATO BREAD

This is a great way to use remaining green tomatoes before frost. Freeze bread and have something special for any occasion.

2/3 cup raisins	3 1/3 cups all-purpose flour
2/3 cup boiling water	1/2 teaspoon baking powder
2/3 cup shortening	
2 2/3 cups sugar	1 teaspoon cloves
4 eggs	1 teaspoon cinnamon
2 cups ground green tomatoes	2/3 cup chopped nuts
2 teaspoons baking soda	

Preheat oven to 350 degrees. Soak raisins in boiling water. Cream shortening and sugar in large mixer

bowl. Add eggs, tomatoes, plump raisins and water; beat well. Mix remaining ingredients together in bowl; add to mixture. Pour into well-greased 5-by-9-inch loaf pan. Bake for 1 hour and 10 minutes or until toothpick inserted in center comes out clean. Yield: 1 loaf.

Sophia H. Holmes, Laureate Alpha Epsilon
Williamsburg, Virginia
*Lois Cassel, Xi Chi
Greenville, Ohio

PORK AND BEAN LOAF

I served this loaf at one of our sorority meetings.

1 cup raisins	3 cups all-purpose flour
1 cup boiling water	1 teaspoon baking soda
3 eggs	1 teaspoon cinnamon
1 cup vegetable oil	1/2 teaspoon baking powder
2 cups sugar	
1 teaspoon vanilla extract	1/2 teaspoon salt
1 14-ounce can deep brown beans, pork removed	1 cup chopped walnuts (optional)

Preheat oven to 325 degrees. Soak raisins in boiling water. Beat eggs, oil, sugar, vanilla and beans in mixer bowl until beans are well broken. Add plump raisins, water and remaining ingredients; mix well. Pour into 2 well-greased 4-by-8-inch loaf pans. Bake for 50 minutes to 1 hour or until toothpick inserted in center comes out clean. Yield: 2 loaves.

Dorothy W. Darnley, Xi Eta
Scarborough, Ontario, Canada

WHOLE WHEAT FRENCH BREAD

This is a quick and easy recipe because the second rising occurs during baking. It is also healthy!

2 tablespoons yeast	4 1/2 to 5 cups unbleached flour
3 1/2 cups warm water	
1/8 cup honey	Cornmeal
1 tablespoon salt	Sesame or poppy seed (optional)
3 cups whole wheat flour	

Preheat oven to 400 degrees. Dissolve yeast in warm water in large bowl. Stir in honey, salt and flour. Dough will be slightly stiff. Let rise, covered, in warm place for 1 hour or until doubled in bulk. Punch down; knead for 1 to 2 minutes or until elastic. Divide into 2 portions; shape each into long loaf. Place loaves on greased 9-by-13-inch baking sheet sprinkled with cornmeal. Slash tops; brush with water. Sprinkle with sesame seed. Bake for 30 minutes. Yield: 2 loaves.

Bonnie Jo Nay, Xi Alpha Delta
Pleasant Hill, Oregon

TRADITIONAL SODA BREAD

2 pounds all-purpose flour
2 teaspoons cream of tartar
1 teaspoon bread soda
1 teaspoon salt
2 cups milk

Preheat oven to 400 degrees. Sift dry ingredients together into bowl. Make well in center; pour milk into well. Mix with knife until soft dough is formed. Knead with floured hands, adding additional milk if necessary. Dough should be soft. Shape and place in greased and floured 9-inch round baking pan. Cut cross on top to allow for rising. Bake for 30 minutes. Cover with foil; bake for 30 minutes longer. Yield: 1 round loaf.

Susan O'Brien, Kappa Chi
Manhattan, Kansas

COTTAGE CHEESE DILL BREAD

This recipe originally came from Peggy Fleming, world champion figure skater.

2 packages active dry yeast
1/2 cup warm water
2 teaspoons sugar
2 cups creamed cottage cheese
2 tablespoons minced onion
2 tablespoons dillweed
1 teaspoon baking powder
2 teaspoons salt
2 tablespoons sugar
2 eggs
4 1/2 cups all-purpose flour

Sprinkle yeast on warm water; stir until blended. Stir in sugar. Combine next 7 ingredients; mix well. Add yeast mixture; mix well. Add flour to make stiff dough. Knead on lightly floured surface until smooth and elastic. Place dough in greased bowl; turn to bring greased side up. Let rise, covered, in warm place for 1 to 1 1/2 hours or until doubled in bulk. Preheat oven to 350 degrees. Punch down; turn out onto lightly floured surface. Knead few times; divide into 2 equal portions. Shape each portion into loaf in well-greased 5-by-8-inch loaf pan. Bake for 30 minutes. Remove from pans; cool on rack. May brush tops with melted butter if desired. Yield: 2 loaves.

Sandra Freeman, Xi Gamma
Manchester, Connecticut
*Alma Hopkins, Theta Xi
Guthrie, Oklahoma

DILLY CASSEROLE BREAD

1 package yeast
1/4 cup warm water
1 cup cottage cheese
1 tablespoon butter or margarine
1 egg
2 tablespoons sugar
1 teaspoon salt
1 tablespoon onion flakes
2 teaspoons dillseed
1/4 teaspoon baking soda
2 1/4 to 2 1/2 cups all-purpose flour
Melted butter or margarine

Preheat oven to 350 degrees. Dissolve yeast in warm water in large bowl. Add cottage cheese and butter. Stir in egg. Add sugar, salt, onion flakes and dillseed. Mix baking soda and flour together in bowl; add to batter. Turn out onto floured surface; knead 3 to 5 times. Let rise, covered, for about 40 minutes or until doubled in bulk. Shape into round loaf; place in greased 8-inch iron skillet. Bake for 40 to 45 minutes or until browned. Brush top with melted butter. May sprinkle with salt if desired. Yield: 1 round loaf.

Sharon Carlile
Zillah, Washington
*Joan Buck, Xi Kappa
Keene, New Hampshire
*Karen Wright, Pi Zeta
Floral City, Florida

HOT ROLLS

Our Senior Center cooked these for our Founder's Day Dinner. Sixty rolls were gone in a jiffy.

1 box Jiffy white cake mix
1 package dry yeast
1/4 teaspoon salt
1 1/2 cups warm water
3 cups all-purpose flour

Preheat oven to 350 degrees. Mix cake mix, yeast and salt together in large bowl. Add water; mix well. Add flour; mix well. Knead on lightly floured surface; punch down. Let rise until doubled in bulk. Shape into rolls. Place on greased cookie sheet. Bake for 30 minutes. Yield: 15 rolls.

Juanita B. Chancey, Beta Master
Wilmington, Ohio

OATMEAL DINNER ROLLS

This is an all-time favorite in our family. My husband's 93-year-old grandmother gave it to me.

2 cups boiling water
1 cup oatmeal
3 tablespoons margarine
2/3 cup packed light brown sugar
1 tablespoon sugar
1 1/2 teaspoons salt
2 packages dry yeast
1/3 cup warm water
5 cups all-purpose flour

Pour boiling water over oatmeal and margarine in saucepan; bring to a boil. Cook for 1 minute; let cool to lukewarm. Pour into bowl. Add brown sugar, sugar and salt. Dissolve yeast in water; add to oatmeal mixture. Add flour, 1 cup at a time; knead. Place in greased bowl, turning dough to coat. Let rise in warm place for 1 1/2 to 2 hours. Punch down; let rest for 10 minutes on floured bread board. Shape into rolls; place close together in greased 9-by-13-inch baking pan. Let rise for 45 minutes. Preheat oven to 350 degrees. Bake for 20 to 25 minutes or until lightly browned. Yield: 20 rolls.

Pamela Walker, Zeta Beta
Gentry, Missouri
*Luanna Weimer, Theta Omega
Salisbury, Missouri

Home for the Holidays

From New Year's Day to New Year's Eve, the
year is full of holidays with countless ways and
reasons to celebrate. And there is nothing like
a holiday—any holiday— to bring people home
for fun, feasting, and family togetherness.
In this chapter you'll find menus and recipes for
all the big, traditional holidays, but also some
ideas for lesser observed days of celebration
such as cakes for a Valentine's Day tea, a
traditional Irish feast for St. Patrick's Day,
grilled favorites for a Father's Day cookout,
easy-to-prepare treats for a 4th of July
picnic, fun cookies for a Halloween party, and
more! Don't limit yourself to just Easter,
Thanksgiving, and Christmas. Invite family
and friends home for the holidays
all through the year.

Home Sweet Home

Father's Day Lunch

Barbecued Brisket — Potato Salad
Relish Plate — Strawberry Supreme
See index for similar recipes.

My Dad was very special and I prepared this lunch for him in 1989, not knowing that it was the last Father's Day we would celebrate together. I miss him very much, but I am glad I decided to serve the Strawberry Supreme because he loved it.

Vickie Carruth, Xi Lambda Beta
Waco, Texas

STRAWBERRY SUPREME

1 6-ounce package strawberry gelatin	3 bananas, mashed
2 10-ounce packages frozen strawberries, thawed	1 16-ounce can crushed pineapple, drained 8 ounces sour cream

Prepare gelatin using package directions. Add strawberries, bananas and pineapple; mix well. Spoon half the mixture into 9-by-13-inch dish. Chill until firm. Layer half the sour cream and remaining strawberry mixture over congealed layer. Chill until firm. Top servings with remaining sour cream. Yield: 20 servings.

Bring-a-Dish Holiday Dinner

Foolproof Turkey
Sausage and Sage Dressing
Corn Casserole — Cranberry Salad

I use this during the holiday season for family gatherings where everyone brings a dish. These are the four dishes that everyone always asks for. Of course, it doesn't have to be only for the holidays and is a good basic meal for any potluck dinner and allows the hostess to enjoy a great meal, too.

Pamela S. Jones, Epsilon Alpha
Garland, Texas

FOOLPROOF TURKEY

This easy and foolproof way to prepare a turkey came from a German friend many years ago. The turkey will be moist, tender and delicious.

1 turkey, any size

Preheat oven to 500 degrees. Remove neck, liver and gizzard from turkey. Rinse turkey inside and out and pat dry. Place in large roasting pan. Tent large piece of foil over turkey with shiny side down; seal edges to pan. Roast for 1 hour. Turn off oven. Let turkey stand in closed oven for 2½ hours or until cool. Remove roasting pan from oven. Preheat oven again to 500 degrees. Roast for 1 hour longer. Turn off oven and let turkey stand in closed oven until cool. Yield: variable.

SAUSAGE AND SAGE DRESSING

2 16-ounce packages sage sausage	5 cups chicken broth
1 16-ounce package corn bread stuffing mix	1 cup chopped onion 2 cups chopped celery

Preheat oven to 350 degrees. Brown sausage in skillet, stirring until crumbly; drain. Combine remaining ingredients in large bowl. Add sausage; mix well. Spoon into rectangular baking dish. Bake for 1 hour or until brown. Yield: 8 to 10 servings.

CORN CASSEROLE

1 onion, chopped	1 cup shredded Cheddar cheese
¼ cup margarine	
1 16-ounce can cream-style corn	2 eggs
1 16-ounce can whole kernel corn, drained	1 cup milk 2 tablespoons sugar
1 cup cracker crumbs	Salt and pepper to taste

Preheat oven to 350 degrees. Sauté onion in margarine in skillet. Add remaining ingredients; mix well. Spoon into deep baking dish. Bake for 1 hour or until set and brown on top. Yield: 8 to 10 servings.

CRANBERRY SALAD

1 12-ounce package fresh cranberries	1 cup whipping cream, chilled
1 cup sugar	
1 8-ounce can crushed pineapple, partially drained	1 10-ounce package miniature marshmallows
Chopped walnuts or pecans	

Chop cranberries in several batches in food processor or blender. Combine with sugar, pineapple and walnuts in bowl. Let stand for 2 hours or longer. Whip cream in mixer bowl until soft peaks form. Stir

in marshmallows. Chill until ready to add to cranberries. Combine mixtures in serving bowl. Chill overnight or until serving time.
Yield: 8 to 10 servings.

Family Thanksgiving Dinner

Roast Turkey
Corn Bread and Giblet Dressing
Glazed Sweet Potatoes
Fresh Green Peas
Mixed Green Salad with
Oil and Vinegar Dressing
Pimento Salad
Fruit and Sour Cream Congealed Salad
Black Olives — Sweet Pickles
Yeast Rolls — Butter — Pumpkin Pie
Apple Pie — Lemon Meringue Pie

See index for similar recipes.

This was my father-in-law's traditional Thanksgiving dinner. The only real variation was in what he put in his green salad or in the combination of fruit in the congealed salad. He always made a special production of his dinners as he loved to cook and to have his whole family around. There would be at least 28 of us in addition to visiting cousins, aunts and uncles. I never knew if his Pimento Salad was an old family recipe but I know that it was his specialty and he didn't give it to everyone. My husband and I were married for 15 years before he gave it to me. I suppose that he wanted to be sure that I was really a family member before he shared it with me.

Nadine Rawlins, Xi Pi Nu
Chico, California

PIMENTO SALAD

2 pounds mild Cheddar cheese	2 tablespoons vegetable oil
4 hard-cooked eggs	1/2 cup vinegar
2 or 3 sweet pickles	1/3 cup water
1 4-ounce jar pimento	1 egg, beaten
Salt to taste	1 teaspoon (or more) sugar

Grind cheese, hard-cooked eggs, pickles, pimento and salt together. Combine remaining ingredients in double boiler. Cook over boiling water for 10 minutes or until slightly thickened, stirring constantly. Cool slightly. Add to cheese mixture in large bowl; mix well. Chill until serving time. Yield: 24 servings.

Thanksgiving Dinner

Roast Turkey
Herb Dressing
Butternut Squash Casserole
Tossed Salad
Cranberry Relish
Fresh Home-Baked Bread
Pumpkin or Apple Pie
Coffee

See index for similar recipes.

This is a basic Thanksgiving Dinner menu. It includes variety and all the food groups, but is not so much food that guests are tempted to overeat in order to taste everything.

Alice Fitzgibbon, Laureate Sigma
Scottsbluff, Nebraska

BUTTERNUT SQUASH CASSEROLE

3 eggs	1 teaspoon each lemon and vanilla extract
3/4 cup sugar	Nutmeg to taste
2 tablespoons all-purpose flour	1/4 cup butter or margarine
2 cups mashed cooked squash	

Preheat oven to 300 degrees. Beat eggs in mixer bowl. Add sugar and flour; mix well. Beat in squash. Add flavorings and nutmeg. Melt butter in 8-inch square baking dish. Spoon squash mixture into prepared dish. Bake for 45 minutes. Yield: 6 to 8 servings.

Kay Stankee, Preceptor Beta Epsilon, Cedar Rapids, Iowa, makes a Luscious Chocolate Pie by combining 1 1/3 cups coconut and 3 tablespoons melted margarine in bowl. Press mixture into 8-inch pie plate. Bake in preheated 350-degree oven for 15 minutes. Melt one 8-ounce chocolate bar with almonds in saucepan; let cool slightly. Stir in one 9-ounce carton whipped topping. Pour into pie shell; refrigerate.

Thanksgiving Dinner Tradition

Roast Turkey
Giblet Gravy
Mashed Potatoes
Green Bean Casserole
Relish Tray
Cranberry Relish
Half-Time Spoon Rolls
Pumpkin Pie — Mincemeat Pie
Whipped Cream

See index for similar recipes.

This is our traditional Thanksgiving dinner. With our seven children, their wives and husbands and our grandchildren, we total 20 in number. Daughters and daughters-in-law bring salads and desserts, so there is always plenty to go around.

Arlene Burken, Preceptor Zeta
Carthage, Missouri

HALF-TIME SPOON ROLLS

1 envelope dry yeast	*3/4 cup milk, scalded*
1/4 cup warm water	*1/2 cup cold water*
1/4 cup sugar	*1 egg*
1/4 cup vegetable	*31/2 cups sifted*
* shortening*	* all-purpose flour*
1 teaspoon salt	

Stir yeast into warm water; let stand for 5 minutes. Combine sugar, shortening and salt in large bowl. Stir in scalded milk. Stir in cold water to cool to lukewarm. Beat in egg and yeast mixture. Add flour gradually, mixing well. Let rise, covered, in warm place for 45 minutes to 1 hour or until doubled in bulk. Stir down and fill greased muffin cups half full. Let rise for 45 minutes or until batter has risen to edge of muffin cups and is rounded in center. Preheat oven to 400 degrees. Bake rolls for 15 to 20 minutes or until golden brown. Yield: 1½ dozen.

Carolyn L. Kidwell, Elko, Nevada, makes Hamburger and Tomato Gravy by mixing 1 pound ground beef and 1 chopped onion in bowl; shape into 4-by-1½-inch patties. Roll in flour. Brown in small amount of cooking oil in skillet. Add 1 can condensed tomato soup and 1 soup can water. Simmer, covered, for 45 minutes.

❖ Family Christmas Dinner

Turkey — Gravy — Dressing
Broccoli and Cauliflower with
Cheese Sauce
Stuffed Mushrooms — Corn Casserole
Fried Artichoke Hearts
Cranberry Salad — Garden Salad
Pecan Pie

See index for similar recipes.

This is my family's menu for Christmas and Thanksgiving. It is special because the family enjoys it together. We sometimes vary it a little, but this is what we usually serve.

Fay Scordato, Laureate Kappa
Fort Washington, Maryland

DRESSING

1 cup butter or	*1 cup water*
* margarine*	*Salt and pepper to taste*
2 cups chopped	*1 16-ounce package*
* mushrooms*	* stuffing mix*
1 cup each chopped	
* onion and celery*	

Preheat oven to 325 degrees. Combine first 7 ingredients in saucepan. Cook until celery is tender. Add stuffing mix; mix well. Spoon into baking dish. Bake, covered, for 50 minutes. Yield: 8 servings.

STUFFED MUSHROOMS

8 ounces Italian sweet	*1/2 cup Italian bread*
* or hot sausage,*	* crumbs*
* crumbled*	*24 large mushroom caps*

Brown sausage in skillet; drain. Add bread crumbs; mix well. Spoon into mushroom caps; arrange in glass dish. Microwave on High for 4 minutes. Yield: 24 mushrooms.

CORN CASSEROLE

1 16-ounce can whole	*1 egg*
* kernel corn*	*1 7-ounce package corn*
1 16-ounce can cream-	* muffin mix*
* style corn*	*1/2 teaspoon butter*
1/2 cup melted margarine	* flavoring (optional)*
1 cup sour cream	*Salt and pepper to taste*

Preheat oven to 350 degrees. Combine undrained corn with remaining ingredients in bowl; mix well. Spoon into 8-by-12-inch baking dish. Bake for 45 minutes or until set. Yield: 8 servings.

FRIED ARTICHOKE HEARTS

1 10-ounce package frozen artichoke hearts	Olive oil Italian bread crumbs Vegetable oil for frying

Place artichoke hearts in dish to thaw. Sprinkle with olive oil as they thaw. Coat with bread crumbs. Fry in vegetable oil in skillet until light brown. Yield: 8 servings.

CRANBERRY SALAD

1 6-ounce package red gelatin 2 cups boiling water 2 16-ounce cans whole cranberry sauce	1 cup each chopped celery, chopped nuts and crushed pineapple

Dissolve gelatin in boiling water in medium bowl. Add cranberries; mix well. Stir in remaining ingredients. Spoon into mold or dish. Chill until firm. Unmold onto serving dish. Yield: 8 servings.

PECAN PIE

4 eggs 1 cup sugar 1 cup light corn syrup 1/4 cup butter or margarine, chopped	1/2 teaspoon vanilla extract 2 cups chopped pecans 1 unbaked pie shell

Preheat oven to 350 degrees. Beat eggs and sugar in medium bowl. Add corn syrup, butter and vanilla; mix well. Stir in pecans. Spoon into pie shell. Bake for 50 minutes or until set. Yield: 8 servings.

FRESH APPLE SALAD

1 20-ounce can pineapple chunks 1/4 cup butter or margarine 1/4 cup sugar 1 tablespoon lemon juice 1 tablespoon cornstarch 2 tablespoons water	1 cup mayonnaise 2 cups seedless grapes 8 cups chopped unpeeled red apples 1 to 2 teaspoons poppy seed 11/2 cups toasted pecans

Drain pineapple, reserving juice. Combine butter, sugar, lemon juice and pineapple juice in saucepan; heat to boiling. Mix cornstarch and water in small bowl; stir into hot mixture. Let cool completely. Stir in mayonnaise. Combine pineapple chunks and next 3 ingredients in large bowl. Add dressing; mix well. Chill; stir in pecans just before serving. Yield: 16 servings.

Geneva M. Hiley, Preceptor Delta
Phoenix, Arizona

RED HOT SALAD

2/3 cup red hots 1 cup boiling water 1 small package lemon gelatin 1/2 cup applesauce	1/2 cup mayonnaise 8 ounces cream cheese, softened 1/2 cup chopped pecans

Dissolve red hots in boiling water in large bowl. Stir in gelatin. Add applesauce; mix well. Pour 1/2 mixture in 8-inch square dish; chill until set. Cream mayonnaise and cream cheese in mixer bowl. Add pecans; spread over gelatin layer. Spoon remaining gelatin mixture on top. Refrigerate, covered, until set. Yield: 4 servings.

Cathey Hubenthal
Georgetown, Texas
*Carol Lendman, Laureate Alpha Phi
Loveland, Colorado

APRICOT SALAD

2 small packages orange gelatin 2 cups boiling water 1 large can apricots 1 20-ounce can crushed pineapple 2 cups miniature marshmallows	2 tablespoons all-purpose flour 1 egg, beaten 1 small container whipped topping

Dissolve gelatin in boiling water in bowl. Drain apricots, reserving juice. Add water to juice to equal 2 cups. Stir 1 cup juice mixture into gelatin mixture. Let cool until partially set. Mix in next 3 ingredients. Pour into 9-by-13-inch dish. Refrigerate, covered, until set. Mix flour and 1 cup juice mixture in saucepan. Cook until begins to thicken. Stir small amount of hot mixture into egg; stir egg mixture into hot mixture. Chill until thickened. Stir in whipped topping; spread over gelatin. Yield: 12 servings.

Robin Peoples, Xi Tau
Biloxi, Mississippi

FROZEN SALAD

2 cups whipping cream 4 tablespoons sugar 8 ounces cottage cheese 1 cup grated Cheddar cheese 1 8-ounce can crushed pineapple	1 cup miniature marshmallows 8 maraschino cherries, chopped Maraschino cherry halves

Whip cream in chilled mixer bowl; add sugar. Combine remaining ingredients in bowl. Fold into whipped cream. Pour into 9-by-13-inch pan. Garnish with cherry halves. Freeze overnight. Thaw for 5 minutes before cutting. Yield: 12 to 16 servings.

Melba Parchman, Xi Gamma Sigma
Lubbock, Texas

BLUEBERRY GELATIN SALAD

2 3-ounce packages
   grape or blackberry
   gelatin
2 cups boiling water
1 20-ounce can crushed
   pineapple with juice
1 can blueberry pie
   filling

1 cup sour cream
8 ounces cream cheese,
   softened
1 teaspoon vanilla
   extract
1/2 cup sugar
1 cup chopped pecans

Dissolve gelatin in boiling water in large bowl. Add pineapple and pie filling; mix well. Pour into 9-by-13-inch dish. Refrigerate, covered, until firm. Mix next 4 ingredients in mixer bowl. Spread over gelatin. Top with pecans. Yield: 10 to 12 servings.

Susan D. Gebhardt, Preceptor Iota
Florence, Alabama
*Kathryn Barnett, Xi Lambda Tau
Urich, Missouri

MINCEMEAT HOLIDAY SALAD

1/2 envelope plain
   gelatin
2 tablespoons cold
   water
2 cups orange juice
1 6-ounce package
   lemon gelatin
1 28-ounce jar
   prepared mincemeat

1 cup chopped celery
1 cup chopped walnuts
   or pecans
1 8-ounce can crushed
   pineapple, drained
2 medium red apples,
   cored, diced
Pinch of salt

Soak plain gelatin in water until softened. Heat orange juice in saucepan. Add gelatins; stir until dissolved. Cool slightly; add remaining ingredients. Pour into lightly oiled 9-by-13-inch dish. Chill until set. May serve on lettuce leaf with dollop of mayonnaise if desired. Yield: 12 to 15 servings.

Linda Jackson, Xi Alpha Alpha
Jacksonville, Florida

ORANGE SHERBET SALAD

A very dear sorority sister brought this salad to me often during a difficult time in my life.

1 3-ounce package
   orange gelatin
1/4 cup boiling water
1 9-ounce carton
   whipped topping
1 large can mandarin
   oranges, drained

1 8-ounce can crushed
   pineapple, drained
1/2 cup chopped pecans
1/2 cup shredded coconut
1/2 cup miniature
   marshmallows

Dissolve gelatin in boiling water in large bowl. Add remaining ingredients; mix well. Chill for at least 1 hour. Yield: 8 servings.

Cindy Speiser, Xi Gamma Nu
Allen, Texas

PEPPERMINT SALAD

Crushed graham
   crackers
2 10-ounce cartons
   whipped topping
1 cup chopped nuts

4 cups miniature
   marshmallows
20 peppermint sticks,
   crushed

Line 9-by-13-inch dish with crushed crackers. Mix whipped topping, nuts, marshmallows and peppermint in large bowl; pour over crackers. May sprinkle with additional crushed crackers. Yield: 12 servings.

Tami Muller, Mu Phi
Ness City, Kansas

PINEAPPLE GELATIN DE-"LIGHT" SALAD

It is fun to change the colors of the bottom and top layers for different holidays.

1 8-ounce package
   sugar-free lemon
   gelatin
2 cups boiling water
3 cups miniature
   marshmallows
1 8-ounce package
   sugar-free pineapple
   gelatin
2 cups boiling water
16 ounces fat-free cream
   cheese

1 8-ounce carton lite
   whipped topping
1 20-ounce can crushed
   pineapple, drained
1 8-ounce package
   sugar-free lime gelatin
2 cups boiling water
2 cups canned fruit
   cocktail including
   juice

Dissolve lemon gelatin in 2 cups boiling water in bowl. Add marshmallows; stir until melted. Pour into 9-by-13-inch dish. Chill until set. Dissolve pineapple gelatin in 2 cups boiling water in bowl. Add cream cheese and whipped topping; blend well. Fold in pineapple. Spoon mixture over first layer; chill until set. Dissolve lime gelatin in 2 cups boiling water in bowl. Stir in fruit cocktail; pour over pineapple layer. Refrigerate, covered, until set. Yield: 20 servings.

Constance L. Shifty, Xi Phi
Butte, Montana

RAINBOW GELATIN SALAD

This beautiful salad was served at our Valentine Party and everyone raved about it.

1 3-ounce package
   black raspberry gelatin
9 cups boiling water
1 3-ounce package
   cherry gelatin
11/2 cups evaporated
   milk
1 3-ounce package
   lime gelatin
1 3-ounce package
   lemon gelatin

1 3-ounce package
   orange gelatin
1 3-ounce package
   orange-pineapple
   gelatin
1 3-ounce package
   strawberry gelatin
Lettuce leaves

Dissolve raspberry gelatin in 1½ cups boiling water in bowl; let cool slightly. Dissolve cherry gelatin in 1 cup boiling water and ½ cup evaporated milk in bowl; let cool slightly. Dissolve lime gelatin in 1½ cups boiling water in bowl; let cool slightly. Dissolve lemon gelatin in 1 cup boiling water and ½ cup evaporated milk; let cool slightly. Dissolve orange gelatin in 1½ cups boiling water in bowl; let cool slightly. Dissolve orange-pineapple gelatin in 1 cup boiling water and ½ cup evaporated milk in bowl; let cool slightly. Dissolve strawberry gelatin in 1½ cups boiling water in bowl; let cool slightly. Spray bottom and side of 9-by-13-inch dish with nonstick cooking spray. Pour raspberry gelatin into dish; chill for 20 to 30 minutes or until firm. Spoon cherry gelatin mixture over raspberry layer; chill for 20 to 30 minutes or until firm. Repeat for each layer, chilling for 20 to 30 minutes or until firm. Cut into squares with sharp knife. Serve on lettuce leaf on salad plate. Yield: 28 to 32 servings.

Carol Handler, Iota
Devils Lake, North Dakota

CHERRY CONGEALED SALAD

This family favorite is delicious with any meat.

1 16-ounce can red tart
  pitted cherries
¾ cup sugar
1 3-ounce package
  cherry gelatin
1 8-ounce can crushed
  pineapple with juice

½ cup chopped pecans
  or walnuts
Few drops red food
  coloring (optional)

Combine cherries and sugar in saucepan. Bring to a boil; remove from heat. Add gelatin; stir until dissolved. Let cool; add pineapple, pecans and food coloring. Pour into 1½-quart mold or 8-inch square dish. Chill until set or overnight. Yield: 8 servings.

Marie S. Welch, Preceptor Alpha Kappa
Chattanooga, Tennessee

CHRISTMAS CRANBERRY SALAD

This is my mother Katie Haley's salad and has been on our Christmas table all my life. I helped grind the cranberries in the old hand grinder as a child.

1 14-ounce can crushed
  pineapple
1 quart cranberries,
  ground
2 cups sugar
2 4-ounce packages
  lemon or strawberry
  gelatin

2 cups boiling water
2 oranges, peeled, diced
½ orange rind, grated

Drain pineapple, reserving juice. Combine cranberries and sugar in bowl. Dissolve gelatin in boiling water in large bowl. Add enough water to pineapple juice to equal 1½ cups; stir into gelatin. Add cranberry mixture, pineapple, oranges and orange rind; mix well. Pour into 9-by-13-inch dish. Refrigerate, covered, overnight or for 2 to 3 days, stirring every 30 minutes until set. Yield: 20 servings.

Lela R. Gould, Preceptor Beta Rho
Salem, Indiana
*Gazelle B. Shankle, Laureate Alpha Epsilon
Williamsburg, Virginia

CHERRY-CRANBERRY SALAD

This has always been a favorite holiday salad.

2 3-ounce packages
  cherry gelatin
3 cups boiling water
2 cups cranberries
1 large or 2 small
  apples, pared, cored

Juice of 1 orange
Grated rind of 1 orange
1½ cups sugar
½ cup chopped walnuts
  or pecans

Dissolve gelatin in boiling water in large bowl. Let cool until partially set. Grind cranberries and apples together. Combine with remaining ingredients in large bowl; mix well. Fold into gelatin. Pour into 9-by-13-inch glass dish. Refrigerate, covered, until set. Yield: 10 to 12 servings.

Dixie Buzick, Preceptor Alpha
Carson City, Nevada
*Geneva Williams, Preceptor Alpha Delta
Lexington, North Carolina
*Carol Jean Johnson, Preceptor Gamma Pi
Needmore, Pennsylvania

HEAVENLY SALAD

My mother always served this salad at Christmas. It would not have been Christmas dinner without it.

1 tablespoon all-
  purpose flour
¼ cup sugar
1 tablespoon butter or
  margarine
1 cup pineapple juice
2 eggs, beaten
1 cup whipping cream,
  whipped

1 cup pineapple, cut
  into small pieces
1 cup white grapes,
  seeded, cut into halves
1 cup marshmallows,
  cut into quarters
½ cup broken English
  walnuts

Mix flour, sugar and butter together in saucepan. Add small amount pineapple juice to make a paste. Stir in remaining pineapple juice; cook until thickened. Stir small amount of hot mixture into eggs; stir egg mixture into hot mixture. Cook, stirring, until smooth. Pour into mixer bowl; refrigerate until very cold. Beat in whipped cream; fold in remaining ingredients. Serve on bed of lettuce.
Yield: 8 to 12 servings.

Lavei Rocke, Xi Gamma Iota
Little Rock, Arkansas

MYSTERY SALAD

1 3-ounce package lemon gelatin	1 cup diced celery
1 20-ounce can pineapple with juice	3/4 cup chopped pecans or walnuts
6 to 8 ounces cream cheese, softened	2 cups whipped topping or whipped cream
1 2-ounce jar chopped pimento, drained	

Place gelatin in large bowl. Drain pineapple, reserving juice. Heat pineapple juice in saucepan over medium heat to boiling. Add to gelatin, stirring until gelatin is dissolved. Combine cream cheese and pimento in small bowl; mash well. Add pineapple, pimento mixture, celery and pecans to gelatin; mix well. Fold in whipped topping. Pour into 9-by-13-inch dish. Chill, covered, for several hours. Yield: 16 servings.

Mary Hildebrand, Xi Lambda Mu
Sunrise Beach, Missouri
*Judy Leshovsky, Alpha Epsilon
Minneapolis, Minnesota

RASPBERRY DELIGHT SALAD

1 8-ounce can crushed pineapple in juice	1 6-ounce jar Hawaiian Delight baby food
1 3-ounce package raspberry gelatin	8 ounces cream cheese, softened
2/3 cup sugar	Whipped topping

Combine pineapple and gelatin in saucepan. Heat, stirring, over low heat until gelatin is dissolved. Pour into blender container. Add sugar, baby food and cream cheese; blend until smooth. Pour into 1-quart soufflé dish; chill until firm or overnight. Top with whipped topping. Yield: 6 servings.

Elizabeth Ann Gray, Beta
Rogers, Arkansas

SOUR CREAM-STRAWBERRY SALAD

1 8-ounce package strawberry gelatin	1 cup broken pecans
2 cups boiling water	2 11-ounce cans mandarin oranges
1 10-ounce package frozen strawberries	1 1/2 to 2 cups sour cream, at room temperature
1 20-ounce can crushed pineapple	

Dissolve gelatin in boiling water in large bowl. Add next 4 ingredients. Pour 1/2 mixture into large mold or 8-by-12-inch pan. Chill until firm. Spread sour cream over congealed layer. Spoon remaining gelatin mixture over sour cream. Chill until firm. Yield: 8 to 10 servings.

Monica Farr, Xi Tau
Biloxi, Mississippi

THOUSAND-DOLLAR SALAD

1 3-ounce package orange gelatin	2 bananas, sliced
1 cup boiling water	1 jar maraschino cherries
1 cup 7-Up	1/2 cup chopped pecans
1 8-ounce can crushed pineapple	1 cup flaked coconut
	1 cup whipped cream

Dissolve orange gelatin in boiling water in bowl. Stir in 7-Up; chill for 45 minutes. Add next 5 ingredients; fold in whipped cream. Pour into 1 1/2-quart salad bowl; chill. Yield: 8 servings.

Juanita Padgett, Laureate Psi
Altus, Oklahoma

OYSTER SALAD

This special recipe was brought to the United States from England by my grandmother in 1859.

1 egg, beaten	Cream
1 tablespoon all-purpose flour	1 8-ounce can oysters Crushed saltine crackers
1/2 cup vinegar	Paprika
1/2 cup water	Radishes
Salt and pepper to taste	

Combine first 5 ingredients in saucepan; cook until thickened. Let cool; thin with cream. Add oysters with liquid; mix well. Add enough crackers to make stiff mixture. Garnish with paprika or radishes. May use commercial mayonnaise if desired. Yield: 8 servings.

Gertrude Herda, Laureate Delta
Caldwell, Idaho

SHRIMP AND CRAB CLOUD SALAD

This is a great salad for a crowd. It can be prepared the day before.

1 frozen loaf sandwich bread	2 6-ounce cans shrimp, drained
Butter	2 6-ounce cans crab, drained
4 hard-cooked eggs, chopped	1 cup chopped celery
1 onion, chopped	3 cups mayonnaise

Trim crust from bread. Butter each bread slice; cut in 1-inch cubes. Mix bread, eggs and onion together in bowl. Refrigerate, covered, overnight. Combine shrimp and crab in bowl. Mix in celery and mayonnaise; refrigerate, covered, overnight. Combine bread and shrimp mixtures; mix thoroughly. Chill, covered, for 3 to 4 hours before serving. Yield: 18 to 20 servings.

Barbara Runstadler, Preceptor Alpha Omicron
Roseburg, Oregon

WHITE BEAN SALAD

1/2 cup salad oil	1 1/2 teaspoons dry
1/2 cup white vinegar	mustard
2 tablespoons lemon	1 tablespoon Bouquet
juice	Garni
3 tablespoons chopped	1 tablespoon chopped
onion	parsley
1/4 teaspoon pepper	2 15-ounce cans Great
1 teaspoon salt	Northern beans

Combine first 9 ingredients in jar with tightfitting lid; shake until well blended. Pour over beans in bowl. Refrigerate, covered, for at least 2 hours or overnight. Yield: 4 to 6 servings.

Jo-Ann Kaikkonen, Xi Eta Omicron
Arlington, Texas

BROCCOLI SALAD

"I cannot believe I ate broccoli." Non-broccoli eating men have had their wives call the next day to verify after eating three servings.

2 10-ounce packages	3 hard-cooked eggs,
frozen chopped	chopped
broccoli	2 tablespoons (heaping)
1 cup chopped celery	mayonnaise
1 cup stuffed green	Salt and pepper to taste
olives, chopped	1 hard-cooked egg,
1/2 cup chopped onion	sliced

Cook broccoli according to package directions until tender-crisp; drain. Combine broccoli, celery, olives, onion and chopped eggs in bowl. Add mayonnaise, salt and pepper; toss to mix well. Refrigerate, covered, for 6 hours or overnight. Garnish with egg slices. Yield: 8 servings.

Anna J. Stephan, Delta Chi
West St. Paul, Minnesota

FRESH CAULIFLOWER SALAD

1 cup fine dry bread	2 tablespoons grated
crumbs	Parmesan cheese
3 tablespoons butter	1 small clove of garlic,
or margarine	crushed
9 to 10 cups bite-size	Salt and pepper to taste
pieces romaine lettuce	1/2 head cauliflower,
1 cup mayonnaise	grated
1 tablespoon lemon juice	

Brown bread crumbs in butter in skillet; let cool. Place lettuce in salad bowl. Combine mayonnaise, lemon juice, cheese, garlic, salt and pepper in bowl; mix well. Pour mixture over lettuce; toss to mix well. Top with bread crumbs; do not toss. Sprinkle with cauliflower; do not toss. Serve immediately. Yield: 6 to 8 servings.

Lisa McClure, Alpha Eta
Green River, Wyoming

ONION SALAD

My grandfather always made this salad to go with our turkey and dressing at all family Christmas and Thanksgiving dinners. It is not meant to be eaten by itself and is for those who enjoy a strong onion taste.

6 hard-cooked eggs	3 large onions, cored,
1/2 box saltine crackers,	ground
finely crushed	Vinegar

Separate egg yolks from egg whites. Grind egg whites; crush egg yolks. Mix crackers, onions and egg whites together in bowl. Add enough vinegar to moisten. Spoon into salad bowl. Top with crushed yolks. Yield: variable.

Betty E. Duncan, Preceptor Delta Psi
Downing, Missouri

RICE SALAD

This rice salad was served at a district meeting I attended here in Oklahoma.

1 package white and	1 cup chopped celery
wild rice	1/2 pound fresh
2 chicken bouillon cubes	mushrooms, sliced
1 cup chopped green	1 4-ounce jar diced
onions	pimentos
1 cup chopped green bell	Creamy Italian dressing
pepper	to taste

Cook rice according to package directions using both seasoning and rice packets and bouillon cubes; let cool. Combine rice with next 5 ingredients in large bowl. Add dressing, tossing to coat well. Yield: 8 servings.

Ruth M. Burgess, Preceptor Alpha Nu
Muskogee, Oklahoma

TRY AND GUESS SALAD

I served this salad at one of our church anniversaries. It was a hit, especially with the men. No one has ever guessed what was in it.

3 3-ounce packages	2 cups sour cream
raspberry gelatin	1 tablespoon creamed
1 1/4 cups boiling water	horseradish
3 16-ounce cans	1/4 teaspoon salt
stewed tomatoes	1/2 teaspoon sugar
6 drops Tabasco sauce	Mixed salad greens

Dissolve gelatin in boiling water in large bowl. Stir in tomatoes, breaking with spoon. Add Tabasco sauce. Pour into lightly oiled 3-quart ring mold; chill until firm. Mix next 4 ingredients in bowl; blend well. Unmold gelatin on greens; fill center with sour cream mixture. Yield: 10 to 12 servings.

Lorene Harris, Laureate Delta Kappa
Montoursville, Pennsylvania

LENTIL-WATERCRESS SALAD WITH FETA CHEESE

My friend served this at her new house with crescent rolls and spritzers made of Champagne and white wine.

4¼ cups water	**¼ teaspoon pepper**
1 cup plus 3 tablespoons dried lentils	**½ teaspoon dried oregano**
1 tablespoon plus 1 teaspoon olive oil	**2 small cloves of garlic, minced**
1 tablespoon red wine vinegar	**¾ cup crumbled feta cheese**
½ teaspoon salt	**2 cups trimmed watercress**

Combine 4 cups plus 2 tablespoons water and lentils in saucepan. Bring to a boil; reduce heat to low. Cook, covered, for 30 minutes or until tender; drain. Combine 2 tablespoons water and next 6 ingredients in medium bowl; mix well. Add lentils, cheese and watercress; toss to mix. Serve warm or at room temperature. Yield: 4 servings.

Norma Blaine, Eta Nu
Mountain Home, Arkansas

EVERYTHING BUT THE KIDS SALAD

Five generations of our family go to my grandmother's for Christmas dinner every year. They always ask me to bring this salad. They named it and take great delight in looking to make sure I didn't get the kids in it.

3 cups shell macaroni, cooked, drained, cooled	**½ cup chopped carrot**
	1 cup slivered almonds
1 16-ounce frozen package tiny peas, thawed	**1 cup unsalted sunflower seeds**
	1½ cups mayonnaise-type salad dressing
1½ pounds imitation crab meat, shredded	**1 teaspoon salt**
½ cup chopped green bell pepper	**1 teaspoon pepper**
	1 teaspoon celery salt
½ cup chopped onion	**1 tablespoon vinegar**
1 16-ounce can black olives, cut into halves	**1 tablespoon sugar**
	2 tablespoons milk

Combine first 9 ingredients in large bowl. Combine next 6 ingredients in bowl; mix well. Add milk; blend well. Pour over macaroni mixture; stir gently to mix. Yield: 15 servings.

Vickie B. Helderman, Delta Eta
Arco, Idaho

ROAST BEEF DINNER

1 4- to 6-pound rolled beef roast	**Vegetables To Cook With Roast**

Preheat oven to 325 degrees. Insert roast-meat thermometer into center of roast. Place roast on rack in shallow baking pan. Roast, uncovered, for 2 hours and 45 minutes to 3½ hours or to 140 degrees in center for rare, 3 hours and 15 minutes to 4 hours and 15 minutes or to 160 degrees in center for medium and 3½ to 4 hours and 45 minutes or 170 degrees in center for well done. Let stand for 15 minutes before carving. Serve with Vegetables To Cook With Roast. Yield: 10 to 16 servings.

VEGETABLES TO COOK WITH ROAST

(1½ hours before roast is done)
New potatoes: Place 2 pounds unpeeled new potatoes in ovenproof dish; add 1 tablespoon butter or margarine, ¼ cup water and 2 teaspoons salt. Bake, covered, for 1½ hours; drain. Yield: 12 servings.
Whole green beans: Place 1½ pounds green beans or three 9-ounce packages frozen whole green beans in ovenproof dish. Add 1 tablespoons butter or margarine, ¼ cup water and 2 teaspoons salt. Bake, covered, for 1½ hours; drain. Yield: 12 servings.
Carrots: Slice 1½ pounds carrots into 3-inch chunks; place in ovenproof dish. Add ¼ cup water, 1 tablespoon butter or margarine, 1 teaspoon sugar, 1 teaspoon salt and ½ teaspoon nutmeg. Bake, covered, for 1½ hours; drain. Yield: 8 to 10 servings.
(1 hour before roast is done)
Corn: Cut 6 ears corn into 3-inch chunks. Spread each with butter or margarine; sprinkle with "seasoned salt." Wrap in foil, 2 chunks at a time, twisting foil ends. Bake for 1 hour. Yield: 12 servings.

Dorothy I. Barnd, Laureate Nu
Fresno, California

ROAST TENDERLOIN WITH STUFFING

1 teaspoon dried oregano	**1 whole beef tenderloin**
1 teaspoon dried thyme leaves	**2 finely chopped green onions**
	6 ounces sliced mushrooms
1 teaspoon paprika	**1 clove of garlic, minced**
1 teaspoon salt	**2 tablespoons chopped parsley**
½ teaspoon pepper	
½ teaspoon garlic powder	**4 tablespoons butter or margarine**
½ teaspoon onion powder	**3 tablespoons bleu cheese, crumbled**
½ teaspoon ground red pepper	

Preheat oven to 425 degrees. Mix first 8 ingredients in bowl; rub mixture over surface of tenderloin. Slit tenderloin in half, leaving 1 side attached. Sauté onions, mushrooms, garlic and parsley in butter in skillet until onions are tender. Spread on tenderloin; sprinkle with bleu cheese. Close slit with wooden toothpicks. Place meat on rack in roasting pan. Roast, uncovered, for 1 hour for rare to medium-rare. Let stand for 5 minutes in warm place before carving. Yield: 12 servings.

Shirley L. Ladd, Preceptor Omicron
Germantown, Maryland

STANDING RIB ROAST

I cooked this recipe on Christmas Eve after closing my Cinnamon Roll Shop. It was so easy and so good!

1 standing rib roast,
    any size

Preheat oven to 400 degrees. Place roast on rack in roasting pan; place, uncovered, in preheated oven. Reduce oven temperature to 350 degrees; bake for 1½ hours. Turn off oven; do not open door. Let set in oven for 1 hour; do not open door. Turn oven to 350 degrees; bake for 30 minutes. Yield: variable.

Bonnie Thompson, Preceptor Beta Lambda
Grand Rapids, Michigan

BRISKET OF BEEF

This is a wonderful no fuss meat dish with gravy.

1 3- to 4-pound beef
    brisket
1 package onion soup
    mix
1 can beer
½ cup catsup
1 16-ounce can
    cranberry sauce

Preheat oven to 325 degrees. Place brisket in medium size roasting pan. Add remaining ingredients; mix well. Bake, covered, for 3 hours. Yield: 6 servings.

Sandy Seeler, Alpha Omega
Camarillo, California

CREOLE POT ROAST

1 14-ounce trimmed
    boneless beef
    bottom round
1 tablespoon plus 1
    teaspoon vegetable oil
½ cup fresh or frozen
    small whole onions,
    peeled
½ cup green bell pepper
    strips
½ cup chopped celery
1 ounce chopped
    Canadian bacon
4 cloves of garlic,
    crushed
2 cups low-sodium beef
    broth
1½ cups canned whole
    tomatoes with juice
1 tablespoon Dijon
    mustard
1 teaspoon dried thyme
¼ teaspoon hot pepper
    sauce
Freshly ground black
    pepper to taste
1 cup frozen okra

Preheat broiler. Place beef on broiler rack; broil 4 inches from heat for 5 minutes. Turn; broil for 5 minutes longer. Heat oil in large pot over medium-high heat until hot but not smoking. Sauté onions, bell pepper, celery, bacon and garlic for 5 minutes. Add beef and next 6 ingredients. Bring to a boil; reduce heat to low. Simmer, covered, for 1½ hours, adding water if necessary. Add okra; simmer for 30 minutes. Yield: 4 servings.

Teresa Ledgerwood, Xi Epsilon Iota
Bristow, Oklahoma

HUNGARIAN GOULASH

This is a great dish to serve at a Christmas buffet.

2 pounds stew beef, cut
    into 1-inch cubes
1 cup sliced onion
⅛ teaspoon instant
    garlic
¼ cup vegetable
    shortening
¼ cup catsup
2 tablespoons
    Worcestershire sauce
2 teaspoons paprika
1 tablespoon light
    brown sugar
½ teaspoon dry
    mustard
Dash of cayenne pepper
1¾ cups water
2 tablespoons
    all-purpose flour
Cooked noodles

Cook meat, onion and garlic in shortening in large skillet until meat is brown and onion is tender; drain. Stir in next 6 ingredients and 1½ cups water. Cover tightly; simmer for 2 to 2½ hours. Combine ¼ cup water and flour in jar with tightfitting lid; shake well. Stir into meat mixture. Heat, stirring, until gravy boils for 1 minute. Serve over hot noodles. Yield: 6 to 8 servings.

Mary Skinner, Preceptor Nu Rho
Morro Bay, California

LASAGNA FOR A CROWD

My mother, who was a Beta Sigma Phi, was served this recipe by a sorority sister 40 years ago.

2 29-ounce cans
    tomatoes
4 8-ounce cans tomato
    sauce
2 teaspoons salt
3 teaspoons oregano
¼ teaspoon pepper
2 teaspoons onion salt
2 cups minced onions
2 cloves of garlic, minced
⅓ cup salad oil
2 pounds ground beef
2 teaspoons
    monosodium
    glutamate
2 teaspoons salt
1 pound lasagna noodles
1½ pounds ricotta
    cheese or small curd
    cottage cheese
1 pound mozzarella
    cheese
1 cup grated Parmesan
    cheese

Preheat oven to 350 degrees. Combine tomatoes and next 5 ingredients in large kettle; simmer uncovered. Sauté onion and garlic in oil in skillet until lightly browned. Add ground beef and next 2 ingredients; cook until beef loses red color. Add to tomato sauce. Simmer, uncovered, for 2½ hours or until thickened. Cook lasagna noodles according to package directions, stirring occasionally; drain. Spoon enough sauce into two 9-by-13 inch baking dishes to cover bottom. Top with criss-cross layer of noodles. Layer ½ ricotta cheese, ⅓ mozzarella cheese and ½ Parmesan cheese over sauce. Repeat layers, ending with sauce. Top with remaining ⅓ mozzarella cheese. Bake for 50 minutes or until bubbly. Let stand for 15 minutes before serving. Yield: 12 servings.

Debbie Collins, Kappa Kappa
Meriden, Kansas

RICOTTA LASAGNA SWIRLS

2 10-ounce packages frozen chopped spinach	Dash of pepper
2 tablespoons grated Parmesan cheese	1/4 teaspoon grated nutmeg
1 pound ricotta cheese	1 pound lasagna noodles
1/2 teaspoon salt	Spaghetti sauce with meat

Preheat oven to 350 degrees. Cook spinach according to package directions for 2 to 3 minutes; drain well. Push through colander. Mix spinach, cheeses and seasonings in bowl. Cook noodles according to package directions; drain. Spread spinach mixture on noodles; roll up. Spoon small amount of sauce in bottom of pan; add roll-ups. Spoon remaining sauce over roll-ups. Bake, covered, for 45 minutes. Yield: 8 to 10 servings.

Cindy Rank, Delta Psi
Clare, Michigan

❖ JEWELED BUFFET HAM

This fruit-glazed ham will be the center of attraction of your buffet.

1 8-ounce can whole-berry cranberry sauce	1/2 cup orange juice
1 8-ounce can jellied cranberry sauce	1 teaspoon seasoned salt
1 8-ounce can mandarin orange segments, drained	1/2 teaspoon garlic powder
	2 to 4 dashes Tabasco sauce
	1 5- to 6-pound fully cooked ham

Preheat oven to 350 degrees. Combine first 7 ingredients in medium saucepan. Cook over low heat for 15 to 20 minutes, stirring occasionally. Have butcher slice ham into 1/4-inch slices; tie in original shape. Place in shallow roasting pan; bake for 1 hour. Remove from oven; pour off juices. Spoon enough fruit mixture over ham to coat well, mounding fruit generously on top. Return ham to oven. Bake, uncovered, for 30 minutes, basting occasionally with remaining fruit mixture. Place ham on serving platter. Cut and carefully remove strings. May serve remaining fruit mixture with ham slices if desired. Yield: 10 to 12 servings.

Lynn Parson, Preceptor Beta Sigma
Magalia, California

RON'S HAM

My children beg for this ham at any special occasion. They love it and you will too!

1 sugar cured ham	1 1-pound package dark brown sugar
Ground cloves to taste	
1 can crushed pineapple in heavy syrup	2 teaspoons soy sauce
1 large box dark raisins	1/4 teaspoon ground cloves

Preheat oven to 325 degrees. Remove rind from ham; coat with cloves. Place in deep roaster; tent with aluminum foil. Bake for 20 minutes per pound or until internal temperature reaches 160 degrees. Trim fat; score. Remove drippings; return ham to pan. Mix remaining ingredients in saucepan; simmer for 15 minutes. Baste ham with mixture. Bake, basting every 10 minutes, for 1 hour. Yield: variable.

Ann Gordon, Laureate Theta
Graniteville, South Carolina

HAM BALLS

3 1/2 pounds ground ham	2 10-ounce cans condensed tomato soup, undiluted
1 1/2 pounds ground beef	
3 eggs, beaten	
2 cups milk	2 1/2 cups packed dark brown sugar
3 cups graham cracker crumbs	
3/4 cup vinegar	1 teaspoon prepared mustard

Preheat oven to 350 degrees. Combine first 5 ingredients in bowl. Shape into balls using 1/3-cup measuring cup. Place in two 9-by-13-inch roasting pans. Combine remaining ingredients in bowl; pour over balls. Bake for 1 hour. Yield: 20 to 24 servings.

Cheryl Miller, Xi Zeta Rho
Muncy, Pennsylvania

BURGUNDY LAMB SHANKS

This is great for important company as it leaves you free to entertain them and yet serve an elegant dish.

6 lamb or veal shanks	2 10-ounce soup cans hearty red wine
All-purpose flour	
Olive oil	1/4 cup Worcestershire sauce
1 pound fresh mushrooms, sliced	
1 cup sliced scallions, including tops	1/4 cup soy sauce
2 10-ounce cans condensed tomato soup	1 bay leaf
	Mushroom sauce

Preheat oven to 325 degrees. Coat lamb with flour. Brown in oil in large skillet; drain. Place in roasting pan. Combine next 7 ingredients in large bowl; pour over lamb. Bake, covered, for 2 1/2 to 3 hours. Serve with mushroom sauce. Yield: 6 servings.

Joan Hayn, Beta Master
San Diego, California

ROASTED PORK LOIN

This is a holiday must. Everyone fights for the juicy end pieces!

1 2-pound pork loin	1/4 teaspoon sage
2 teaspoons salt	1/4 teaspoon garlic powder
1/4 teaspoon pepper	
1 teaspoon paprika	

Preheat oven to 350 degrees. Have butcher crack bones to aid in carving. Wipe loin with damp cloth; pat dry. Mix seasonings together in bowl; rub mixture into loin. Insert meat thermometer through fat side into center without touching bone. Place in 9-by-13-inch baking pan. Roast until temperature reaches 185 degrees. Yield: 4 servings.

Linda Katicich, Preceptor Alpha Beta
Harvey, Louisiana

CHICKEN ALOUETTE

2 cans crescent rolls	8 boneless skinned
8 ounces garlic-spiced	chicken breasts
Alouette cheese	Salt and pepper
1/2 cup grated Cheddar	to taste
cheese	

Preheat oven to 350 degrees. Separate rolls into squares, sealing perforations. Spread thin layer Alouette cheese on each square. Sprinkle with grated cheese. Place 1 chicken breast in center of each square. Add salt and pepper. Fold dough around chicken breast, sealing edges. Place, seam side down, in 9-by-13-inch baking pan. Bake, covered, for 30 minutes. Uncover; bake for 15 minutes. Yield: 8 servings.

Lois Kornbrot, Xi Iota Chi
Naperville, Illinois

CHICKEN FANTASIA

This is very impressive when igniting in a dark room.

6 small boneless	1/2 teaspoon dry
skinned chicken breasts	mustard
6 thin slices boiled ham	1 8-ounce can
2 tablespoons butter or	pineapple tidbits
margarine	2 tablespoons
2/3 cup water	cornstarch
1/2 cup apricot preserves	Canned apricots
2 tablespoons vinegar	1/4 cup Brandy
1/2 teaspoon salt	

Place chicken breasts, boned side up, on cutting board. Pound lightly to make cutlets; place ham slice on each cutlet. Tuck in sides; roll up jelly-roll fashion. Tie or skewer. Brown slowly in butter in skillet. Stir in water, preserves, vinegar, salt and dry mustard; cook, covered, for 20 minutes. Drain pineapple, reserving syrup. Blend cornstarch and reserved syrup in bowl. Blend cornstarch mixture and pineapple tidbits into sauce in skillet. Cook, uncovered, for 15 minutes or until chicken is tender. Place chicken in blazing pan of chafing dish. Garnish with canned apricots. Place chafing dish over burner. Pour sauce into heatproof dish. Warm Brandy in small saucepan. Pour Brandy over sauce at table; ignite immediately. Spoon flaming sauce over chicken. Yield: 6 servings.

Nancy Prout, Preceptor Beta Omicron
Oshawa, Ontario, Canada

CHICKEN PARMIGIANA

1/2 cup chopped onion	5 or 6 boneless skinned
1 clove of garlic, crushed	chicken breasts
2 tablespoons olive oil	2 eggs, beaten
1 14-ounce can Italian	1 cup seasoned dry
tomatoes	bread crumbs
1 can tomato paste	1/2 cup olive oil
2 teaspoons sugar	1 8-ounce package
1/2 teaspoon dried	sliced mozzarella
oregano	cheese
1/4 teaspoon dried basil	1/4 cup grated Parmesan
1/4 teaspoon pepper	cheese

Preheat oven to 350 degrees. Sauté onion and garlic in 2 tablespoons hot oil for 5 minutes or until golden. Add next 6 ingredients; mix well, mashing tomatoes with fork. Bring to a boil; reduce heat. Simmer, covered, for 10 minutes. Wipe chicken breasts with damp paper towels. Dip in eggs; roll in bread crumbs, coating lightly. Heat 1/4 cup oil in large skillet. Add chicken; brown on each side, adding remaining oil as needed. Arrange chicken in single layer in 6-by-10-inch baking dish. Add 1/2 the sauce, 1/2 the mozzarella cheese and 1/2 the Parmesan cheese. Repeat layers, ending with Parmesan cheese. Bake, covered, for 30 minutes. Yield: 4 to 6 servings.

Brenda Sparks, Beta Beta Chi
Cedar Hill, Texas

CHICKEN MONTEREY WITH PECAN PILAF

3/4 cup all-purpose flour	1 pound fresh or canned
1 to 2 teaspoons	mushrooms
seasoned salt	3 cups chicken broth
3/4 teaspoon tarragon	1 chicken bouillon cube
2 frying chickens,	6 cups hot cooked rice
cut up	1 cup chopped pecans
6 tablespoons	Mandarin oranges
margarine	Green grapes

Preheat oven to 325 degrees. Mix flour with seasoned salt and tarragon in bowl. Coat chicken with flour mixture; let dry for few minutes. Reserve remaining flour. Sauté chicken on both sides in 3 tablespoons margarine in large skillet until golden brown. Place in 9-by-13-inch baking pan. Add mushrooms to skillet; cook for few minutes or until lightly browned. Spoon over chicken. Add remaining 3 tablespoons margarine to skillet. Stir in 1/4 cup reserved flour; add chicken broth and bouillon. Cook, stirring, until smooth and thickened. Pour sauce over chicken. Cover tightly with foil. Bake for 1 hour. Toss hot rice with pecans in bowl. Arrange chicken on bed of rice mixture. Top with small amount of sauce. Serve remaining sauce in separate bowl. Garnish with mandarin oranges and grapes. Yield: 8 servings.

Tamara S. Appleget, Alpha Kappa
Oskaloosa, Iowa

HOT CHICKEN SALAD CASSEROLE

This is simple to prepare but very elegant. I served it as the main course at a Victorian Tea Luncheon Party.

3 cups cubed cooked
  chicken breasts
1/2 10-ounce can cream
  of chicken soup
1 cup diced celery
1 tablespoon lemon juice
1/4 cup chopped green
  bell pepper
1 tablespoon chopped
  onion
1/2 cup mayonnaise-
  type salad dressing

1 can sliced water
  chestnuts, drained
1/2 cup sliced
  mushrooms, drained
2 chopped tomatoes
1 small can sliced black
  olives
1 small package sliced
  or slivered almonds
1 cup cornflakes,
  crumbled
Grated Cheddar cheese

Preheat oven to 350 degrees. Combine first 7 ingredients in large bowl; mix well. Add water chestnuts and mushrooms; mix well. Spoon into 9-by-13-inch baking pan. Add tomatoes, olives and almonds. Sprinkle with cornflakes; top with cheese. Bake for 40 minutes. Yield: 6 servings.

Vanesa E. Wencl, Xi Zeta Rho
Wichita, Kansas

STUFFED CORNISH GAME HENS

2 Cornish game hens
1 6-ounce can
  Mexicorn, drained
1/2 cup chopped onion
1 1/2 cups cooked white
  rice

1/2 teaspoon poultry
  seasoning
1/2 cup melted butter or
  margarine
1/2 teaspoon garlic
  powder

Preheat oven to 350 degrees. Rinse hens; pat dry. Combine corn, onion, rice and poultry seasoning in bowl; mix well. Stuff hen cavities; truss. Mix butter and garlic powder in bowl. Place hens in 8-inch square baking pan; baste with butter mixture. Bake for 1 hour or until golden brown, basting often. Yield: 2 servings.

Judy Silver, Delta Eta Beta
Sacramento, California

SALMON FLAN

1 8-ounce can salmon,
  undrained
3 eggs, well beaten
1 1/4 cups milk
1/4 teaspoon salt
Dash of pepper

1 cup grated Cheddar
  cheese
1 small onion, chopped
1 10-inch unbaked pie
  shell

Preheat oven to 350 degrees. Combine first 7 ingredients in bowl. Pour into pie shell. Bake for 45 minutes or until knife inserted in center comes out clean. Let stand for 10 minutes. Serve hot or cold. Yield: 4 to 5 servings.

Valerie Leonard, Preceptor Alpha Iota
Campbell River, British Columbia, Canada

COQUILLES ST. JACQUES

I have belonged to a gourmet group in California and Colorado and both have used this recipe. I have served it at many dinner parties with rare reviews. It is well worth the time and dishes.

1 1/2 cups dry white wine
Bouquet garni
2 pounds small bay
  scallops
Salt to taste
8 ounces fresh
  mushrooms, chopped
6 shallots or 1 small
  onion, finely chopped
2 teaspoons butter or
  margarine
2 teaspoons water

1 tablespoon finely
  chopped parsley
1 teaspoon lemon juice
1/4 cup butter or
  margarine
1/4 cup all-purpose flour
2 egg yolks
1/4 cup heavy cream
Salt and pepper to taste
1 cup soft bread crumbs
1 tablespoon butter or
  margarine

Preheat oven to 400 degrees. Bring wine with bouquet garni to a boil in saucepan. Add scallops and salt. Simmer for 3 minutes or until tender; drain, reserving broth. Combine next 6 ingredients in saucepan. Simmer, covered, for 10 minutes. Strain; add liquid to wine broth. Melt 1/4 cup butter in saucepan. Add flour; stir until well blended. Add broth gradually; cook, stirring constantly, until thickened and smooth. Remove from heat. Beat egg yolks with cream in small bowl. Add small amount warm sauce into egg mixture; stir egg mixture into sauce. Add salt and pepper to taste. Stir in scallops, shallots and mushrooms. Fill scallop shells or ramekins with mixture, mounding high in center. Sprinkle with bread crumbs; dot with butter. Bake for 5 to 10 minutes or until browned or brown under broiler. To make a bouquet garni, tie bay leaf, thyme leaf and parsley in cheesecloth or net bag; remove after cooking. Yield: 8 servings.

Sylvia S. Appel, Laureate Alpha Phi
Loveland, Colorado

LUXURIOUS CRAB
AND ARTICHOKE CASSEROLE

3 tablespoons minced
  onion
1/2 cup butter or
  margarine
1/2 cup all-purpose flour
2 cups cream
2 cups half and half
1/2 cup Sherry
2 1/2 cups shell
  macaroni, cooked,
  drained
2 cups grated Swiss
  cheese
3/4 teaspoon salt
1/8 teaspoon pepper

2 tablespoons lemon
  juice
1 package frozen
  crabmeat
2 7-ounce cans
  crabmeat
2 9-ounce cans
  artichoke hearts,
  drained, quartered
2 1/2 cups shell mcaroni,
  cooked, drained
2 cups grated Swiss
  cheese
Paprika

Preheat oven to 350 degrees. Sauté onion in butter in saucepan until transparent; stir in flour. Remove from heat. Combine cream and half and half in saucepan; heat just to boiling, Add to flour mixture, stirring vigorously. Return to moderate heat; bring to a boil, stirring constantly. Remove from heat. Add Sherry, salt and pepper. Pour lemon juice over crabmeat. Combine crabmeat, artichoke hearts, macaroni and sauce in casserole. Sprinkle cheese over top. Garnish with paprika. Bake for 20 to 30 minutes or until lightly browned. Yield: 12 servings.

Susan Hendricks, Epsilon Nu
Parsons, Kansas

ASPARAGUS SUPREME

This dish was a big hit at a dinner of gourmet cooks.

4 cups fresh asparagus	1 teaspoon grated onion
1 teaspoon salt	1/8 teaspoon pepper
1 10-ounce can cream of shrimp soup	1/2 cup herb-seasoned stuffing mix
1/2 cup sour cream	1 tablespoon butter or margarine
2 tablespoons shredded carrots	

Preheat oven to 350 degrees. Cook asparagus in small amount of water and 1 teaspoon salt in saucepan for 5 to 6 minutes; drain. Combine next 5 ingredients in large bowl; fold in asparagus. Pour into greased 5-by-8-inch baking dish. Combine stuffing mix and butter; sprinkle around edge of casserole. Bake, uncovered, for 40 minutes. Yield: 6 servings.

Leona M. Rodwell, Laureate Delta
Caldwell, Idaho

BROCCOLI-CAULIFLOWER-CARROT CASSEROLE

1 bunch broccoli, chopped	2 tablespoons all-purpose flour
1 head cauliflower, chopped	1/2 teaspoon Dijon mustard
1 pound carrots, chopped	1 cup chicken broth
1 8-ounce can whole mushrooms, chopped	2 cups whipping cream
2 tablespoons butter or margarine	1 1/2 cups shredded Swiss cheese
	Green onions, chopped

Parboil vegetables in saucepan until tender-crisp; drain and let cool. Combine butter, flour and Dijon mustard in medium saucepan; cook until bubbly. Add broth, whipping cream and cheese; mix well. Combine vegetables and cheese sauce in large bowl. Pour into 3-quart casserole. Serve warm. Garnish with green onions. Yield: 8 servings.

N. Vicki Lackmanec, Laureate Epsilon
Yorkton, Saskatchewan, Canada

ZITI WITH BROCCOLI

1 8-ounce package ziti pasta	1 cup chopped yellow, red or green pepper
3 cups broccoli flowerets	2 cups cherry tomato halves
2 tablespoons butter or margarine	1/4 cup grated Parmesan cheese
2 tablespoons olive or vegetable oil	1/4 teaspoon salt
5 cloves of garlic, finely chopped	1/4 teaspoon ground black pepper

Cook pasta according to package directions; add broccoli 3 minutes before pasta is done. Drain; return to saucepan. Heat butter and oil over medium-high heat in large skillet. Add garlic and pepper; cook until pepper is just tender. Stir in tomatoes; heat through. Add mixture to pasta, tossing to mix. Season with Parmesan cheese, salt and pepper. Yield: 8 servings.

Rosemary Battaglia, Preceptor Lambda
Monroe, Connecticut

ITALIAN GREEN BEANS

We served this recipe at a bridal luncheon and got rave reviews.

2 medium onions, chopped	1 1/4 teaspoons oregano
2 16-ounce cans green beans	1 tablespoon sugar
	1/4 cup olive oil
1 16-ounce can tomatoes, chopped	Salt and pepper to taste
	Garlic to taste

Layer 1/2 the onions, 1/2 the green beans and 1/2 the tomatoes in 10-inch skillet; repeat layers. Combine remaining ingredients in bowl; pour over layered mixture. Simmer, covered, on low heat for 1 hour. Yield: 8 servings.

Betsy Dozier, Zeta Nu
Monroeville, Alabama

WRAPPED GREEN BEANS

I took this dish to a holiday dinner for a club and it was an instant hit.

2 16-ounce cans whole green beans, drained	3/4 cup butter or margarine
Bacon slices	1/2 cup packed light brown sugar
Salt and pepper to taste	

Preheat oven to 325 degrees. Wrap 5 or 6 beans with 1/2 slice bacon; secure with wooden toothpick. Arrange bundles in 9-by-13-inch baking dish. Sprinkle with salt and pepper. Melt butter in saucepan; stir in brown sugar. Pour mixture over bundles; bake for 30 to 45 minutes or until bacon is thoroughly cooked. Yield: 6 to 8 servings.

Carol Tillman, Chi Alpha
Hayti, Missouri

MUSTARD BRUSSELS SPROUTS

This is a great addition to our Thanksgiving and Christmas menus. Even people who do not care for Brussels sprouts enjoy this.

1 pound fresh Brussels
  sprouts
4 teaspoons butter or
  margarine
4 teaspoons Dijon
  mustard
1/4 cup dry white wine

Cut "X" in stem-end of sprouts to hasten cooking. Steam sprouts for 5 to 8 minutes or until tender; drain well. Sauté sprouts in butter in 12-inch skillet. Mix mustard and wine in bowl; add to sprouts. Cook over high heat for 10 to 12 minutes or until sauce reduces and thickens. Yield: 4 to 6 servings.

Peggy Cebulski, Lambda Delta
Lake Zurich, Illinois

GOLDEN CABBAGE

My Pennsylvania Dutch mother-in-law, who lived in Puerto Rico for 40 years, always served this as a side dish to accompany holiday dinners of roasted turkey or pit roasted pork.

2 1/2 pounds shredded
  cabbage
1 1/2 tablespoons salt
1 tablespoon sugar
1/4 cup cornstarch
2 cups milk
3/4 teaspoon salt
4 tablespoons butter or
  margarine
1/4 pound Swiss cheese,
  shredded

Boil cabbage in water with salt and sugar in covered saucepan for 1 hour; drain. Dissolve cornstarch in 1/2 cup milk in large saucepan. Stir in remaining milk, salt and butter; bring to a boil, stirring constantly. Add cabbage. Reserve 4 tablespoons cheese. Add remaining cheese to cabbage mixture; mix well. Spoon into greased 9-by-13-inch baking dish. Sprinkle reserved cheese on top; broil for few minutes or until golden brown. Yield: 8 servings.

Beth Benavent, Alpha Gamma
El Centro, California

CARROT CASSEROLE

3 cups sliced carrots
1/4 teaspoon salt
3/4 cup bread crumbs
1 tablespoon minced
  onion
2 tablespoons melted
  margarine
1/4 teaspoon pepper
Sliced American or
  Velveeta cheese

Preheat oven to 425 degrees. Boil carrots in salted water in covered saucepan until tender; drain, reserving 1/2 cup liquid. Mash carrots with reserved liquid; stir in crumbs, onion, margarine and pepper. Layer in greased 1 1/2-quart baking dish with sliced cheese. Bake until heated through. Yield: 6 servings.

Debbie L. Hennessy, Preceptor Epsilon Phi
Pleasant Hill, Missouri

CELERY BAKE

My Aunt Jenny made this recipe for Christmas dinner several years ago. We all loved it so much, it has become a family tradition.

3 cups sliced cooked
  celery
1 8-ounce can sliced
  water chestnuts
1 10-ounce can cream
  of chicken soup
1 10-ounce can sliced
  mushrooms
1 bunch green onions,
  chopped
1/4 cup butter or
  margarine, melted
1 1/2 cups dried bread
  crumbs

Preheat oven to 350 degrees. Combine first 5 ingredients in bowl; mix well. Pour into 1-quart greased casserole. Combine butter and crumbs in bowl; mix well. Sprinkle over top. Bake for 30 minutes. Yield: 6 to 8 servings.

Barb Rodrigues, Beta Xi
Calgary, Alberta, Canada

CORN AND PEA CASSEROLE

1 16-ounce can small
  peas, drained
1 11-ounce can Shoe
  Peg corn, drained
1 10-ounce can cream
  of celery soup
1/2 cup chopped celery
1/2 cup chopped green
  bell pepper
1/2 cup chopped onion
1/2 cup sour cream
1/2 cup shredded
  Cheddar cheese
1/2 large box cheese
  crackers, crushed
1/2 cup margarine,
  melted

Preheat oven to 350 degrees. Combine first 8 ingredients in bowl; mix well. Pour into ungreased 2-quart casserole. Bake for 25 minutes. Toss cracker crumbs with melted butter in bowl; sprinkle over casserole. Bake for 5 minutes longer.
Yield: 8 servings.

Janice Lewey, Omega Kappa
Holt, Missouri

SCALLOPED CORN

Mother always made this at Thanksgiving and Easter. She put oysters in one side for Dad.

1 16-ounce can cream-
  style corn
1/4 cup chopped onion
1 cup crushed cracker
  crumbs
1 cup milk
1 egg, slightly beaten
1 tablespoon butter
Dash of salt and pepper
3 tablespoons chopped
  pimentos (optional)
1 cup bread crumbs
1 tablespoon butter
  or margarine

Preheat oven to 350 degrees. Mix first 8 ingredients in bowl. Pour into greased 1 1/2-quart casserole. Top with bread crumbs. Dot with butter. Bake for 1 hour. Yield: 4 to 6 servings.

Steva Kelley, Xi Tau
Biloxi, Mississippi

CORN CASSEROLE

1/2 cup margarine,
  melted
1 16-ounce can cream-
  style corn
1 16-ounce can whole
  kernel corn

1 cup sour cream
1 package Jiffy corn
  bread mix
Salt and pepper to taste

Preheat oven to 350 degrees. Combine all ingredients in large bowl; mix well. Pour into greased 9-by-13-inch baking dish. Bake for 1 hour. Yield: 12 servings.

Claudeen Herrli, Laureate Alpha Gamma
Sarasota, Florida
*Anna Laura Doane, Xi Gamma Lambda
Porter, Indiana

NO-BAKE EGGPLANT

1 20-ounce can
  tomatoes, cut into
  small pieces
1 small eggplant,
  peeled, diced
1 large onion, diced
1/4 cup green bell pepper,
  diced

1/4 cup packed light
  brown sugar
1 tablespoon butter or
  margarine
1 tablespoon cornstarch
1/4 cup water
1 cup grated extra sharp
  Cheddar cheese

Combine tomatoes and eggplant in large saucepan. Add next 4 ingredients; mix well. Simmer, covered, until eggplant is transparent. Dissolve cornstarch in water in small bowl. Add to eggplant mixture, stirring until thickened. Spoon into covered serving dish. Top with grated cheese; cover. Serve when cheese is melted. Yield: 8 to 12 servings.

Mary Lou Bunch, Laureate Pi
Virginia Beach, Virginia

MUSHROOM CASSEROLE

3 pounds fresh
  mushrooms
1/2 cup margarine
1 large onion, chopped
1/2 pound Velveeta
  cheese, shredded

1 6-ounce package
  chicken-flavored
  instant stuffing mix
2 cups half and half

Preheat oven to 350 degrees. Cut large mushrooms into small pieces. Combine mushrooms, margarine and onion in 5-quart saucepan. Cook, covered, over low heat for 30 minutes or until mushrooms are tender. Layer 1/3 the mushrooms, 1/3 the cheese and 1/2 the stuffing mix in greased 2-quart casserole. Repeat layers, ending with remaining mushrooms and cheese. Pour half and half over casserole. Bake, uncovered, for 30 minutes or until set and cheese is melted. Yield: 10 to 12 servings.

Lucy Lutz, Preceptor Eta
Laurel, Delaware

❖ VIDALIA DEEP DISH

1 cup long grain rice
2 cups water
6 large sweet onions,
  sliced
1/2 cup margarine
2 tablespoons fresh
  parsley, minced

1/4 teaspoon salt
1/4 teaspoon pepper
1 cup shredded Swiss
  cheese
1 cup whipping cream
Paprika to taste

Preheat oven to 350 degrees. Cook rice in water in covered saucepan for 10 minutes. Sauté onions in margarine in large saucepan until tender. Add rice and next 5 ingredients; mix well. Pour into greased 9-by-13-inch baking dish; sprinkle with paprika. Bake for 30 minutes. Yield: 12 servings.

Margie Nord, Preceptor Beta Upsilon
Sellersburg, Indiana

GOOBER PEAS

1 10-ounce package
  frozen peas
1 cup salted peanuts
1/2 cup chopped celery

1/4 cup sour cream or
  yogurt
1/4 cup mayonnaise

Combine all ingredients in bowl; mix well. Refrigerate, covered, for 2 to 3 hours before serving. Yield: 6 servings.

Tommie Chellberg, Delta Kappa Psi
Escondido, California

PARTY POTATO PIES

1 1/2 cups all-purpose
  flour
1/2 teaspoon salt
1/4 cup butter or
  margarine
1/4 cup shortening
1 cup shredded Cheddar
  cheese
1/4 cup ice water
8 potatoes
1 teaspoon salt

1/2 cup milk
1/2 cup sour cream
1/4 cup butter or
  margarine, melted
1 cup shredded Cheddar
  cheese
1/4 cup chopped green
  onions
Salt and pepper to taste
2 teaspoons melted
  butter or margarine

Combine flour and 1/2 teaspoon salt in bowl. Cut in 1/4 cup butter and shortening until mixture resembles coarse crumbs; mix in 1 cup cheese. Add enough water, 1 tablespoon at a time, to flour mixture to make dough hold together. Press into ball; wrap and refrigerate for at least 30 minutes. Roll out pastry; cut out rounds. Fit gently into large muffin cups. Cook potatoes in boiling water with 1 teaspoon salt in covered saucepan; drain. Mash with potato masher. Add next 6 ingredients; mix well. Let cool; fill pastry-lined muffin cups. Drizzle with melted butter. Bake for 20 minutes or until golden. Yield: 12 servings.

Nancy Kunsch, Laureate Gamma Delta
Windsor, Ontario, Canada

MASHED POTATO CASSEROLE

This is a great fix-ahead dish and a good way to use leftover mashed potatoes.

5 pounds potatoes, cooked	1/4 teaspoon seasoned pepper
6 ounces cream cheese	2 tablespoons butter or margarine
1 cup sour cream	
2 teaspoons seasoned salt	

Preheat oven to 350 degrees. Mash potatoes in mixer bowl. Add remaining ingredients; beat until light and fluffy. Spoon into greased 9-by-13-inch baking dish. Bake for 30 minutes or until lightly browned around edges. May add 1/4 cup chopped chives and 1 clove of garlic, minced, if desired. Yield: 12 servings.

Gerry Wiche, Preceptor Alpha Zeta
Leavenworth, Kansas
*Ellen Green, Laureate Chi
Manassas, Virginia
*Lynn Farnen, Theta Omega
Salisbury, Missouri

RUTABAGA AND WHITE POTATOES

1 small rutabaga, peeled, cubed	1/2 cup mayonnaise
6 to 8 small white potatoes, peeled, cubed	1/4 cup butter or margarine
	Salt and pepper to taste

Boil rutabaga for 45 minutes in covered saucepan; drain. Boil potatoes for 20 minutes in covered saucepan; drain. Combine rutabaga and potatoes in bowl; mash with potato masher. Add mayonnaise, butter, salt and pepper; mix well. Yield: 4 servings.

Patricia De Bow, Preceptor Theta
Daytona Beach, Florida

SPINACH-CHEESE BAKE

4 10-ounce packages frozen chopped spinach	1 cup grated Parmesan cheese
2 cups chopped onions	4 3-ounce packages cream cheese
1/2 cup butter or margarine	
2 small jars marinated artichoke hearts, drained	

Preheat oven to 350 degrees. Cook spinach according to package directions; drain. Sauté onions in butter in skillet until tender. Add spinach, 1 jar artichoke hearts, Parmesan cheese and cream cheese; mix well. Pour into greased 3-quart casserole. Bake for 30 minutes. Arrange remaining jar artichoke hearts on top. Yield: 8 to 10 servings.

Joan Maddock, Xi Lambda Iota
Lompoc, California

SQUASH WITH PRALINE TOPPING

2 12-ounce packages frozen squash	2 eggs, beaten
4 tablespoons butter or margarine	1/3 cup packed light brown sugar
1 teaspoon salt	1/2 teaspoon cinnamon
Dash of pepper	1/2 cup chopped pecans

Preheat oven to 350 degrees. Combine squash, 4 tablespoons butter, salt and pepper in saucepan. Heat over low heat, stirring frequently, until squash is completely thawed. Add gradually to beaten eggs in large bowl; mix well. Pour into greased 1-quart casserole. Combine remaining ingredients in bowl; sprinkle over squash. Bake for 30 minutes. Yield: 6 servings.

Denise Sheehy, Lambda Mu
Cresco, Iowa
*Cindy Taylor, Delta
Des Moines, Iowa

SWEET POTATO CASSEROLE

4 cups cooked sweet potatoes	1 tablespoon lemon juice
1/2 cup margarine	1/2 cup evaporated milk
3 eggs	1/2 cup chopped pecans
1 teaspoon cinnamon	1/2 cup chopped coconut
	Marshmallows

Preheat oven to 350 degrees. Place sweet potatoes in medium bowl. Add next 7 ingredients; mix well. Pour into greased 3-quart casserole. Top with marshmallows. Bake for 35 to 40 minutes or until browned. Yield: 6 to 8 servings.

Suzanne Sowder, Xi Delta Mu
Johnson City, Tennessee

SWEET POTATO SURPRISE

1 17-ounce can whole sweet potatoes, drained, halved lengthwise	1/8 teaspoon cinnamon
	1 teaspoon shredded orange peel
11/4 cups packed light brown sugar	1 16-ounce can apricot halves
11/2 tablespoons cornstarch	2 tablespoons butter or margarine
1/4 teaspoon salt	1/2 cup pecan halves

Preheat oven to 375 degrees. Place sweet potatoes in greased 6-by-10-inch baking dish. Combine next 5 ingredients in saucepan. Drain apricots, reserving syrup. Stir apricot syrup into sugar mixture. Cook, stirring, over medium heat until boiling; boil for 2 minutes. Add apricots, butter and pecans. Pour over sweet potatoes; bake, uncovered, for 25 minutes. Yield: 6 servings.

Sue Troyer, Preceptor Alpha Zeta
Woodbridge, Virginia

❖ GREEN AND GOLD CASSEROLE

2 8-count cans crescent rolls	1/4 cup all-purpose flour
1/2 cup grated Parmesan cheese	1/4 teaspoon salt
	1/8 teaspoon pepper
3 or 4 medium zucchini	1 6-ounce jar marinated artichoke hearts, drained, chopped
3 cups sliced fresh mushrooms	
1 large onion, sliced	1 cup shredded Monterey Jack cheese
2 cups sour cream	

Preheat oven to 350 degrees. Unroll 1 can rolls; press evenly in lightly greased 9-by-13-inch baking pan to cover bottom, sealing perforations. Sprinkle 1/4 cup Parmesan cheese over dough. Bake for 10 to 15 minutes. Cut zucchini in half lengthwise; slice 1/4 inch thick. Steam zucchini, mushrooms and onion for 8 to 10 minutes or until tender-crisp. Mix sour cream, flour, salt and pepper in large bowl. Add zucchini mixture and artichoke hearts. Spread over baked crust. Sprinkle evenly with cheese. Unroll remaining can rolls; separate into triangles. Arrange over cheese. Sprinkle with 1/4 cup Parmesan cheese. Bake for 30 to 40 minutes or until top is golden and filling is heated through. Yield: 10 to 12 servings.

Kelli Clevenger, Xi Theta Delta
Topeka, Kansas

NO-COOK CRANBERRY RELISH

1 large orange, unpeeled	1 tablespoon grated peeled gingerroot
3 cups cranberries	
1 cup pitted prunes	1 16-ounce can pears in extra light syrup, drained, diced
1/2 cup walnuts	
1/2 cup sugar	

Cut orange into 8 pieces; discard seeds. Blend orange and next 5 ingredients in food processor with knife blade until coarsely chopped. Pour into bowl; stir in pears. Chill, covered, for 1 hour. Yield: 6 cups.

Carolyn Wells, Nu Delta
Clinton, Iowa

BAKED PINEAPPLE

2 20-ounce cans pineapple chunks, drained	2 cups grated medium-sharp Cheddar cheese
	2 cups crushed buttery crackers
1/2 cup all-purpose flour	1/2 cup margarine
1/2 cup sugar	

Preheat oven to 325 degrees. Place pineapple in 9-by-13-inch baking dish. Mix flour, sugar and cheese in bowl; sprinkle over pineapple. Mix crackers and margarine in bowl; sprinkle over top. Bake for 30 minutes or until hot and bubbly. Yield: 12 servings.

Emogene Walters, Zeta Eta
Goshen, Alabama
*Susan George, Xi Beta Iota
Atlanta, Georgia

SPICED FRUIT

1 29-ounce can peach halves	3/4 cup packed light brown sugar
1 29-ounce can pear halves	1 tablespoon cornstarch
1 20-ounce can pineapple chunks	1/2 cup butter or margarine
1 10-ounce jar maraschino cherries	2 teaspoons curry powder

Preheat oven to 325 degrees. Drain fruit thoroughly; mix in bowl. Pour into greased 9-by-13-inch glass baking dish. Mix brown sugar, cornstarch, butter and curry powder in saucepan; heat. Pour over fruit; bake, uncovered, for 1 hour. Serve warm. Yield: 10 servings.

Ruth Haugland, Iota Preceptor
Devils Lake, North Dakota

MY FAVORITE RICE

2 cups cooked wild rice, drained	1/2 cup sliced water chestnuts
1/3 cup butter or margarine	1/2 cup cashews
11/2 cups sliced fresh mushrooms	

Sauté wild rice in 2 tablespoons butter in saucepan. Sauté sliced mushrooms and water chestnuts in remaining butter in separate saucepan. Combine rice and mushroom mixture in large bowl. Add cashews; toss to mix well. Yield: 8 servings.

Charlotte Rutherford, Preceptor Gamma Chi
Elgin, Illinois

CROCK•POT DRESSING

2 cups chopped onion	11/2 teaspoons salt
2 cups chopped celery	11/2 teaspoons sage
1/4 cup chopped parsley	1 teaspoon dried thyme
1 18-ounce jar sliced mushrooms, drained	1/2 teaspoon marjoram
1/2 cup margarine	31/2 to 41/2 cups chicken or turkey broth
12 cups dry bread pieces	2 eggs, well beaten
1 teaspoon poultry seasoning	

Sauté onion, celery, parsley and mushrooms in margarine in saucepan until onion and celery are tender. Pour over bread in large bowl. Add seasonings; toss well. Add broth and beaten eggs; mix well. Pack lightly into Crock•Pot. Cover; cook on High for 45 minutes. Reduce to Low; cook for 4 to 6 hours. Yield: 12 servings.

Diana Marberry, Xi Lambda Gamma
Sesser, Illinois

MUSHROOM-WALNUT DRESSING

Our chapter has an annual Family Thanksgiving Dinner Social. This is the most requested dish for the meal.

3 8-ounce packages
  Jiffy corn muffin mix
10 slices white bread,
  torn into bite-sized
  pieces
1 cup diced onion
2 8-ounce cans sliced
  mushrooms
4 large ribs celery with
  tops, finely chopped

2 cups chopped English
  walnuts
Salt and pepper to taste
Poultry seasoning to
  taste
Sage to taste
Turkey or chicken broth

Preheat oven to 350 degrees. Bake corn muffin mix according to package directions; let cool. Crumble into large bowl. Add bread; mix well. Turn bread mixture to allow it to dry as much as possible. Add next 4 ingredients and seasonings. Add enough broth to make mixture very moist. Pour into greased 10-by-15-inch baking pan. Bake for 45 to 50 minutes or until lightly browned. Yield: 12 to 16 servings.

Sharon K. Crisjohn, Xi Delta Pi
Yale, Oklahoma

SQUASH DRESSING

2 cups chopped cooked
  squash
1 large onion, chopped
1 10-ounce can cream
  of chicken soup

1/4 cup melted butter
2 cups crumbled cooked
  corn bread
Salt to taste
Pepper to taste

Preheat oven to 350 degrees. Combine all ingredients in large bowl; mix well. Pour into greased 2-quart casserole. Bake for 40 to 45 minutes or until lightly browned on top. Yield: 6 to 8 servings.

Dana Allgood, Phi Theta Gamma
Stephenville, Texas

"CRAZY" TURKEY FILLING

3/4 cup butter or
  margarine
1/2 onion, finely chopped
1/2 loaf bread, cubed
2 eggs, well beaten
3 cups milk

1/2 tablespoon salt
1/2 tablespoon celery
  salt
11/4 pounds cooked
  turkey, finely chopped
11/2 ounces parsley

Preheat oven to 325 degrees. Combine first 3 ingredients in large bowl. Combine eggs, milk, salt and celery salt in bowl. Add to butter mixture; mix well. Add turkey and parsley. Place in large roasting pan. Bake, covered, for 11/2 to 2 hours or until lightly browned. Yield: 6 servings.

Shirley J. Lassiter, Laureate Alpha Epsilon
Newport News, Virginia

SAUSAGE STUFFING

2 cups chopped celery
2 cups chopped onion
1/4 cup butter or
  margarine
1 pound pork sausage
12 cups dry broken up
  bread
3/4 cup butter or
  margarine, melted

3 cups chicken broth
2 tablespoons parsley
11/2 teaspoons sage
1 teaspoon poultry
  seasoning
2 teaspoons salt
1 teaspoon black
  pepper

Preheat oven to 350 degrees. Sauté celery and onion in 1/4 cup butter in large saucepan until tender. Brown sausage in skillet, stirring until crumbly; drain. Add sausage to celery and onion. Add remaining ingredients; mix well. Pour into greased 9-by-13-inch baking pan. Bake for 45 minutes or until lightly browned. Yield: 12 to 15 servings.

Kathy Martin, Xi Delta Delta
Indianola, Iowa

SPICED CRANBERRY NUT STUFFING

1 cup whole berry
  cranberry sauce
1 teaspoon grated
  orange peel
1/4 teaspoon cinnamon
2 cups sliced celery
1/2 cup butter or
  margarine

1 16-ounce package
  herb-seasoned stuffing
  mix
1 14-ounce can clear
  ready-to-serve chicken
  broth
1/2 cup coarsely chopped
  toasted nuts

Preheat oven to 375 degrees. Mix first 3 ingredients in small bowl. Sauté celery in butter in 4-quart saucepan until tender. Add cranberry sauce mixture and remaining ingredients. Toss to mix well. Spoon into buttered 2-quart casserole. Bake, covered, for 30 minutes. Yield: 16 servings.

Debbie Meegan, Xi Alpha
Lemont Furnace, Pennsylvania

FAVORITE STUFFING

2 packages corn bread
  stuffing mix
1 package toasted bread
  crumbs
1 cup chopped onions
1 cup chopped celery

2 tablespoons margarine
6 eggs, slightly beaten
Salt and pepper to taste
1 tablespoon sage
6 cans chicken broth,
  heated

Preheat oven to 375 degrees. Mix stuffing mix and crumbs in large bowl. Sauté onions and celery in margarine until soft. Add to stuffing mix. Add eggs, salt, pepper and sage; mix well. Add chicken broth; mix well. Pour into 9-by-13-inch baking pan. Bake for 1 hour. Yield: 16 servings.

Margaret Owen, Preceptor Beta Epsilon
Needles, California

GIBLET GRAVY FOR DRESSING

We always had this gravy for Thanksgiving and Christmas when dressing was served to a house full of people. I was the 13th child of 14 children. Mom never measured anything and cooked much more than the below recipe would serve.

Turkey neck, liver, gizzard	1 cup uncooked corn bread dressing
2 cups water	3 hard-cooked eggs, chopped
1/2 onion, finely chopped	Salt to taste
2 celery stalks, finely chopped	1/4 teaspoon pepper
2 cups chicken broth	

Boil turkey neck, liver and gizzard in 2 cups water until done; let cool. Remove bones and skin; chop turkey. Cook onion and celery in broth in saucepan until celery is tender. Add remaining ingredients. Bring to a boil; simmer until thickened. May use cornstarch or flour to thicken if desired. Yield: 6 to 8 servings.

Geraldine M. Peters, Xi Beta Xi
Dublin, Georgia

YORKSHIRE PUDDING

2 eggs, slightly beaten	1 cup (scant) all-purpose flour
2 cups milk	

Preheat oven to 350 degrees. Combine eggs and milk in bowl. Stir in flour; mix well. Pour into greased 8-inch square pan. Bake for 30 minutes. Yield: 4 to 6 servings.

Annette Gabbert, Xi Iota Omicron
Houston, Texas

CHRISTMAS BREAD

4 cups all-purpose flour	1 teaspoon vanilla extract
1 teaspoon salt	1/2 cup seedless golden raisins
1/2 cup sugar	Sliced maraschino cherries
1/2 cup butter	
1 egg, slightly beaten	1/4 cup blanched slivered almonds
1 cup warm milk	
1 package dry yeast	1 egg, beaten
1/4 cup warm water	1 tablespoon milk
1 tablespoon lemon rind	

Mix flour, salt and sugar in large bowl; cut in butter. Combine egg and milk in bowl. Soften yeast in warm water. Stir softened yeast, lemon rind and vanilla into milk mixture. Add to flour mixture, mixing with wooden spoon until well combined. Turn dough out onto lightly floured board. Knead for 10 minutes or until smooth. Let rise in warm place for 1 1/2 to 2 hours or until doubled in bulk. Add raisins; mix with hands until well distributed. Divide dough into 9 parts. Roll each piece by hand into strips 20 inches long. Make 3 layers of twists. Bottom layer will be 4 strands. Twist 2 together and twist 2 more together and place side by side. Middle layer will be 3 strands braided together. Top layer will be 2 strands, twisted together. Form bread on greased 9-by-13-inch baking sheet, stretching and shaping so the twists fit firmly on top each other. Pinch edges together. Let rise until doubled in bulk. Decorate with maraschino cherry slices and almonds on top. Preheat oven to 350 degrees. Combine egg and milk in small bowl; mix well. Brush bread with egg mixture. Bake for 35 to 40 minutes or until golden brown. Yield: 1 loaf.

Nancy Mandell, Theta Theta
Goshen, Indiana

ALL-SEASON BREAD

3 cups all-purpose flour	3 eggs
2 teaspoons baking soda	2 cups sugar
1 teaspoon salt	3/4 cup vegetable oil
1/2 teaspoon baking powder	2 teaspoons vanilla extract
1 1/2 teaspoons ground cinnamon	1 8-ounce can crushed pineapple
3/4 cup chopped walnuts or pecans	2 cups Prepared Fruit or Vegetable

Preheat oven to 350 degrees. Combine first 6 ingredients in large bowl until well blended. Beat eggs lightly in large mixer bowl. Add sugar, oil and vanilla; beat until creamy. Drain pineapple, reserving juice. Add pineapple and Prepared Fruit or Vegetable to egg mixture; blend well. Add dry ingredients, stirring only until moistened. Spoon batter into 2 well-greased and floured 5-by-9-inch loaf pans. Bake for 1 hour or until wooden toothpick inserted in center comes out clean. Let cool in pans for 10 minutes. Bread may be baked in different size pans as follows: two 6-cup bundt pans, bake for 45 minutes; two 3-pound shortening cans, bake for 1 hour and 15 minutes; two 3 1/2-by-7-inch pans, bake for 45 to 50 minutes; or eight 2 1/2-by-4 1/2-inch pans, bake for 30 to 35 minutes. Yield: 8 servings.

PREPARED FRUIT OR VEGETABLE

Apple Bread: Peel, core and shred 2 medium apples to make 2 cups fruit. Applesauce also works well.

Sweet Potato Bread: Peel and shred 1 medium-sized sweet potato to make 2 cups vegetable. Stir in 1 tablespoon reserved pineapple juice.

Carrot Bread: Peel and shred 2 medium carrots to make 2 cups vegetable. Stir in 1 tablespoon reserved pineapple juice.

Zucchini Bread: Shred 2 medium zucchini to make 2 cups vegetable.

Catherine C. Pottschmidt, Iota Epsilon
Baton Rouge, Louisiana

CHOCOLATE CHERRY KUCHEN

3/4 cup margarine or butter	1/2 teaspoon baking powder
3 squares unsweetened chocolate	1 16-ounce can pitted sour cherries, drained
1 1/2 cups sugar	1 1/2 teaspoons vanilla extract
3 eggs, beaten	
1 1/2 cups sifted all-purpose flour	1 cup whipping cream, whipped
1/2 teaspoon salt	

Preheat oven to 350 degrees. Melt margarine and chocolate in top of double boiler over hot water. Add sugar gradually to beaten eggs in mixer bowl; beat well. Add chocolate mixture to egg mixture; beat for 1 minute. Sift flour, salt and baking powder together into bowl. Add cherries to flour mixture; stir into chocolate mixture. Add vanilla. Pour into 2 greased and floured 9-inch cake pans. Bake for 35 to 40 minutes or until done. Let cool. Frost with whipped cream; chill. Yield: 8 servings.

Virginia Barron, Laureate Delta Lambda
Graham, Texas

APPLE NUT BREAD

1 cup sugar	1/4 teaspoon baking soda
1/2 cup butter or margarine	1/4 teaspoon nutmeg
2 eggs	1/2 teaspoon cinnamon
2 cups all-purpose flour	1 teaspoon vanilla extract
1/2 teaspoon baking powder	1 cup chopped nuts
	1 cup chopped apple

Preheat oven to 350 degrees. Cream sugar, butter and eggs in mixer bowl. Add flour, baking powder, baking soda, nutmeg and cinnamon; mix well. Add vanilla, nuts and apples; mix well. Pour into greased 5-by-9-inch loaf pan. Bake for 1 hour. Let cool for 10 minutes in pan; remove to rack. Yield: 8 servings.

Wanda L. McGuire, Preceptor Beta Epsilon
Kentland, Indiana

WHITE CHOCOLATE BANANA BREAD

Softened butter or margarine	3 tablespoons dark rum
Wheat germ	1 teaspoon vanilla extract
2 3/4 cups unsifted all-purpose flour	2 cups mashed bananas
1 1/4 teaspoons baking soda	6 ounces white chocolate, cut into 1/4-inch squares
1 teaspoon salt	3 1/2 ounces coconut
1 1/2 cups sugar	1 cup chopped walnuts (optional)
1 cup butter or margarine, melted	Sesame seeds (optional)
2 eggs	

Preheat oven to 350 degrees. Butter two 6-cup loaf pans; dust with wheat germ. Stir flour, baking soda and salt together in bowl. Cream sugar and butter in mixer bowl. Add eggs, rum and vanilla; beat for 5 minutes. Mix in bananas. Add dry ingredients gradually until well mixed but still lumpy. Stir in chocolate, coconut and walnuts with spoon. Pour into prepared pans; smooth tops. Sprinkle generously with sesame seeds. Bake for 55 minutes. Cover pans with foil to prevent overbrowning; bake for 20 minutes longer. Cool in pans for 10 minutes; remove to rack. Yield: 24 servings.

Diane Heyman, Xi Eta Iota
Paxton, Illinois

CHERRY NUT ROUND BREAD

2 cups sifted all-purpose flour	1 cup buttermilk
1 teaspoon baking soda	1 teaspoon vanilla extract
1 teaspoon salt	1 cup chopped nuts
1/2 cup margarine	1 cup drained maraschino cherries
3/4 cup sugar	
2 eggs	

Preheat oven to 350 degrees. Combine first 8 ingredients in mixer bowl; blend well. Beat for 1 minute on slow speed. Stir in nuts and cherries. Spoon into 4 well-greased 10-ounce cans. Bake for 45 to 50 minutes. Cool in cans for 10 minutes; remove to rack. Yield: 8 to 12 servings.

LaVerne Burmeister, Laureate Zeta
Sparks, Nevada

EASTER HOLIDAY BREAD

2 cups milk	8 to 8 1/2 cups all-purpose flour
1/2 cup butter or margarine	3/4 cup candied pineapple
1/2 cup sugar	3/4 cup red or green candied cherries
2 teaspoons salt	
2 teaspoons cardamom	3/4 cup candied orange or lemon peel
3 packages granulated yeast	1 cup chopped pecans
3/4 cup warm water	
3 eggs, slightly beaten	

Combine milk, butter, sugar, salt and cardamom in saucepan; scald. Cool slightly; place in large bowl. Dissolve yeast in warm water in bowl; add to milk mixture. Add eggs; mix well. Add 3 to 4 cups flour; mix well. Stir in candied fruits and pecans. Add 4 to 5 cups flour gradually; knead until smooth. Let rise in bowl until doubled in bulk; punch down. Shape into 4 loaves; place in 4 greased 5-by-9-inch loaf pans. Let rise again. Preheat oven to 350 degrees. Bake for 35 to 40 minutes or until loaves test done. Yield: 36 servings.

Bernette M. Romero, Preceptor Epsilon Omicron
Atwater, California

FRANKENMUTH FRUIT BREAD

This sweet bread is a famous favorite made in German restaurants in Frankenmuth, Michigan. It was published in our local newspaper for all to enjoy.

1/4 cup warm water	2 tablespoons
1 package active dry	shortening
yeast	1 cup candied fruit
3/4 cup lukewarm milk	1 cup raisins
1/2 cup sugar	31/4 to 31/2 cups
1/2 teaspoon salt	all-purpose flour
1/2 teaspoon ground	1 egg yolk
cardamom	2 tablespoons cold
1 egg, slightly beaten	water

Sprinkle water over yeast in large bowl; stir to dissolve. Stir in milk, sugar, salt, cardamom and egg. Add shortening, fruit and raisins. Add 1/2 the flour, mixing with wooden spoon. Add remaining flour, mixing by hand. Turn out onto lightly floured board; knead until smooth and elastic. Place in greased bowl; let rise, covered, for about 11/2 hours or until doubled in bulk. Shape into round loaf. Place in greased and floured 9-inch round baking pan; let rise for 45 minutes. Beat egg yolk and cold water together in bowl; brush loaf with mixture. Preheat oven to 350 degrees. Bake for 40 minutes. Yield: 12 to 16 servings.

Cynthia Mason, Preceptor Epsilon
Grand Blanc, Michigan

COUNTRY APPLE GINGERBREAD

5 tablespoons unsalted	1 tablespoon ground
butter	ginger
2 pounds tart green	1 teaspoon cinnamon
apples, peeled, cored,	1/2 teaspoon salt
thinly sliced	1/2 cup unsalted butter
1/4 cup sugar	1 cup boiling water
1/4 cup Bourbon	11/2 cups molasses
2 cups all-purpose flour	2 eggs
1 teaspoon baking soda	Confectioners' sugar in
1 teaspoon baking	shaker
powder	Whipped cream or ice
1/2 teaspoon ground	cream
cloves	

Preheat oven to 400 degrees. Melt butter in 12-inch cast iron skillet over medium heat. Add apples; cook for 10 to 15 minutes or until tender, stirring and tossing often. Add sugar; stir as apples begin to caramelize. Pour in Bourbon; shake pan as alcohol evaporates. Sift next 7 ingredients in large bowl. Add butter to boiling water in bowl; let stand until melted. Stir in molasses; beat in eggs. Add liquid ingredients to flour mixture, beating until smooth. Spread apples over bottom of skillet into smooth layer. Oil side of skillet. Pour in gingerbread batter. Bake for 30 to 35 minutes or until knife inserted in center comes out clean. Cool on rack for 10 minutes; invert onto serving plate. Scrape off any apples sticking to skillet with spatula; spread over gingerbread. May sprinkle few drops bourbon over apples while warm if desired. Dust top with confectioners' sugar; serve warm. Garnish with whipped cream or ice cream if desired. Yield: 8 to 10 servings.

Karen Witzel, Xi Beta Lambda
Randolph, New Jersey

ORANGE SLICE BREAD

2 cups cut-up dates	1 teaspoon baking soda
1 cup boiling coffee	1 teaspoon salt
3/4 cup shortening	1 cup buttermilk
2 eggs	1 package candy orange
2 cups sugar	slices, cut up
4 cups all-purpose flour	1 cup chopped nuts

Preheat oven to 350 degrees. Soak dates in boiling coffee in bowl; let cool. Dates will soak up coffee. Cream shortening in mixer bowl. Beat in eggs and sugar. Combine dry ingredients in bowl. Add to creamed mixture alternately with buttermilk, stirring after each addition. Add dates, orange slices and nuts; stir until blended. Pour into 2 greased 5-by-9-inch loaf pans. Bake for 1 hour and 15 minutes. Cool in pans for 10 minutes; remove to rack.
Yield: 16 servings.

Helen Johnson, Preceptor Gamma Mu
Twenty-Nine Palms, California

DELICIOUS PEAR BREAD

This bread wrapped in plastic wrap and tied with a yarn bow is a beautiful and delicious gift.

1/2 cup butter or	1/8 teaspoon nutmeg
margarine	1/8 teaspoon allspice
1 cup sugar	1/4 cup buttermilk or
2 eggs	yogurt
2 cups sifted all-	11/2 cups fresh pears,
purpose flour	peeled, finely diced
1/2 teaspoon salt	1 teaspoon vanilla
1/2 teaspoon baking soda	extract
1 teaspoon baking	
powder	

Preheat oven to 350 degrees. Cream butter and sugar in mixer bowl. Beat in eggs, 1 at a time. Combine dry ingredients in bowl. Add to egg mixture, alternating with buttermilk. Stir in pears and vanilla. Pour into greased 5-by-9-inch loaf pan. Bake for 1 hour. Cool in pan for 10 minutes; remove to rack.
Yield: 12 to 16 servings.

Sandy Treadwell, Eta Chi
Woodstock, Virginia

Pat Tarpley, Xi Alpha Epsilon, Louisville, Kentucky, makes Beer Muffins by mixing 3 cups baking mix, 3 tablespoons sugar and 1/2 cup beer in bowl. Spoon into greased muffin cups. Bake in preheated 425-degree oven for 25 minutes.

HONEY BREAD

2 cups all-purpose flour
1 teaspoon baking
  powder
1 teaspoon baking soda
1 teaspoon salt
1/2 teaspoon cinnamon
1 teaspoon ginger
1/2 cup strained honey
1 egg, slightly beaten
1 cup milk

Preheat oven to 350 degrees. Sift dry ingredients together in mixer bowl. Add remaining ingredients; beat for 15 minutes. Pour into greased 5-by-9-inch loaf pan. Bake for 50 minutes to 1 hour or until bread tests done. Cool in pan for 10 minutes; remove to rack. May add 1 tablespoon rum to mixture if desired. Yield: 12 to 16 servings.

Nelly T. Caunter, Preceptor Alpha
El Dorado, Panama

PECAN BREAD

2 1/2 cups sifted
  all-purpose flour
1 cup sugar
1 teaspoon salt
2 teaspoons baking
  powder
1 cup instant nonfat dry
  milk
1 cup water
2 eggs, well beaten
1 cup chopped pecans

Preheat oven to 350 degrees. Sift first 5 ingredients together in bowl. Stir water into eggs in bowl. Add eggs and pecans to dry ingredients, mixing just until blended. Grease and line bottom of 5-by-9-inch loaf pan with waxed paper. Spoon batter into loaf pan. Bake for 50 minutes to 1 hour. Let cool in pan for 10 minutes. Invert on rack; remove paper from bottom. Yield: 12 to 15 servings.

Faye Williams, Xi Delta Pi
Kennett, Missouri

PLUM BREAD

This bread is red in color and great to serve at Christmas.

2 cups sugar
2 cups all-purpose flour
2/3 teaspoon baking soda
1/4 teaspoon salt
1 teaspoon cinnamon
3 eggs
1 cup salad oil
2 small jars baby food
  plums with tapioca
1 ounce red food
  coloring
Confectioners' sugar

Preheat oven to 325 degrees. Combine first 5 ingredients in mixer bowl. Add eggs, oil, plums and food coloring; mix for 5 minutes. Pour into 2 greased and floured 4-by-8-inch loaf pans. Bake for 40 to 45 minutes or until bread tests done. Remove from pans while warm; sprinkle with confectioners' sugar. Let cool; wrap in plastic wrap until ready to serve. Yield: 16 servings.

Viola Fern Ward, Beta Eta
Thorntown, Indiana

POPPY SEED BREAD

3 cups all-purpose flour
2 cups sugar
3 eggs
1 1/2 cups milk
3/4 cup vegetable oil
1 1/2 teaspoons baking
  powder
1 1/2 teaspoons salt
1 1/2 tablespoons poppy
  seeds
1 1/2 teaspoons vanilla
  extract
1 1/2 teaspoons almond
  extract
1 cup sifted
  confectioners' sugar
2 tablespoons orange
  juice
1/4 teaspoon vanilla
  extract
1/4 teaspoon almond
  extract

Preheat oven to 350 degrees. Combine first 10 ingredients in large mixer bowl; beat for 2 minutes at medium speed. Spoon batter into 2 greased and floured 4-by-8-inch loaf pans. Bake for 1 hour or until toothpick inserted in center comes out clean. Cool in pans for 10 minutes; remove to rack. Combine remaining ingredients in small mixer bowl; mix well. Drizzle over loaves. Yield: 12 servings.

Lynn Sundholm, Xi Alpha Alpha Phi
League City, Texas
*Beverly Marr, Omega Rho
Kansas City, Missouri

PUMPKIN BREAD

2/3 cup butter or
  margarine
2 2/3 cups sugar
4 eggs
1 16-ounce can
  pumpkin
2/3 cup water
3 1/3 cups all-purpose
  flour
1/2 teaspoon baking
  powder
2 teaspoons baking soda
1 1/2 teaspoons salt
1 teaspoon cinnamon
1 teaspoon ground
  cloves
1 teaspoon nutmeg
2/3 cup broken nuts

Preheat oven to 350 degrees. Cream butter and sugar in mixer bowl until light and fluffy. Add eggs, pumpkin and water; mix well. Sift next 7 ingredients together into bowl; add to pumpkin mixture. Stir in nuts. Pour into 2 greased 5-by-9-inch loaf pans. Bake for 1 hour. Let cool in pans for 10 minutes; remove to rack. Yield: 12 to 16 servings.

Jan Manning, Xi Gamma Theta
Largo, Florida
*Beverley Beashore, Xi Lambda Mu
Sunrise Beach, Missouri

Elayna Benton, Xi Rho Theta, Ennis, Texas, makes Sausage Rolls by separating one 8-count package crescent rolls into rectangles. Roll out to 1/8-inch thickness. Spread 1 pound lean sausage over dough, covering completely. Roll up from longest side. Wrap loosely in waxed paper; chill overnight. Slice into 1/8- to 1/4-inch thick slices. Bake on cookie sheets in preheated 450-degree oven for 10 to 15 minutes or until golden brown. Serve warm.

STRAWBERRY BREAD

This recipe is easy, fast, pretty and delicious.

3 cups all-purpose flour	1¼ cups vegetable oil
1 teaspoon baking soda	2 10-ounce packages
1 teaspoon cinnamon	frozen strawberries,
2 cups sugar	thawed
1 teaspoon salt	1 teaspoon red food
4 eggs, beaten	coloring

Preheat oven to 350 degrees. Mix dry ingredients together in bowl. Make well in center. Mix eggs, oil and strawberries in bowl; stir in food coloring. Pour into well. Mix by hand until well mixed. Pour into 2 greased and floured 5-by-9-inch loaf pans. Bake for 1 hour or until loaves test done. Cool completely in pans. May reserve ½ cup strawberry juice and combine with 8 ounces softened cream cheese for spread if desired. Yield: 12 to 16 servings.

Rosemary Grant, Xi Gamma Alpha
Norfolk, Nebraska

CRANBERRY MUFFINS WITH PECANS

2 eggs, beaten	½ teaspoon salt
1 cup milk	1 cup sugar
1½ cups coarsely	½ cup vegetable
chopped cranberries	shortening
¼ cup sugar	1 cup chopped pecans
3 cups all-purpose flour	2 teaspoons grated
4½ teaspoons baking	lemon rind
powder	

Preheat oven to 400 degrees. Mix eggs and milk in bowl. Combine cranberries and ¼ cup sugar in bowl; let stand. Sift next 4 ingredients in large bowl. Cut in shortening with pastry blender until crumbly. Stir in pecans and lemon rind. Add egg mixture to flour mixture, stirring just until moistened. Fold in cranberry mixture. Spoon into greased medium-sized muffin cups, filling ⅔ full. Bake for 20 minutes. Remove to wire racks; serve warm. Yield: 30 muffins.

Imogene Rodekuhr
Barstow, California

PUMPKIN-APPLE STREUSEL MUFFINS

2½ cups all-purpose	½ cup vegetable oil
flour	2 cups finely chopped
2 cups sugar	peeled apples
1 tablespoon pumpkin	2 tablespoons
pie spice	all-purpose flour
1 teaspoon baking	¼ cup sugar
soda	½ teaspoon ground
½ teaspoon salt	cinnamon
2 eggs, lightly beaten	4 teaspoons butter or
1 cup canned pumpkin	margarine

Preheat oven to 350 degrees. Combine first 5 ingredients in large bowl. Combine eggs, pumpkin and oil in bowl. Add liquid ingredients to dry ingredients, stirring until just moistened. Stir in apples. Spoon batter into greased or paper-lined muffin cups, filling ¾ full. Combine 2 tablespoons flour, ¼ cup sugar and cinnamon in bowl. Cut in 4 teaspoons butter until mixture is crumbly. Sprinkle over batter. Bake for 35 to 40 minutes or until muffins test done. Yield: 24 to 30 muffins.

Emily Whittemore, Psi Upsilon
Orlando, Florida
*Kathryn Machado, Laureate Beta Eta
Elyria Township, Ohio
*Marcy Knotwell, Beta Nu
Encampment, Wyoming

SWEET POTATO MUFFINS

While on a tour of the Jack Daniels Distillery in Leitchfield, Kentucky, we were served these muffins. I requested the recipe to no avail. Later, I got it from a chef in New Orleans, Louisiana.

1¼ cups sugar	1 teaspoon cinnamon
½ cup butter or	¼ teaspoon nutmeg
margarine	¼ teaspoon salt
1¼ cups mashed sweet	1 cup milk
potato	½ cup chopped raisins
2 eggs	¼ cup chopped pecans
1½ cups all-purpose	or walnuts
flour	Cinnamon-sugar
2 teaspoons baking	
powder	

Preheat oven to 400 degrees. Cream sugar, butter and sweet potato in mixer bowl until smooth. Add eggs; blend well. Sift flour, baking powder, spices and salt together into bowl. Add alternately with milk to potato mixture; do not overmix. Fold in raisins and pecans. Partially fill greased or paper-lined muffin cups with batter. Sprinkle with cinnamon-sugar. Bake for 25 minutes. Yield: 24 small muffins.

Faye J. Holborow, Preceptor Beta Epsilon
Needles, California

CLASSIC ITALIAN BISCUITS

2 cups self-rising flour	½ teaspoon dillseed
⅓ cup cooking oil	2 tablespoons melted
¾ cup Italian spaghetti	butter
sauce	

Preheat oven to 450 degrees. Sift flour 3 times into large bowl. Add oil, sauce and dillseed; mix well. Pour onto lightly floured surface. Roll out to about ¼-inch thickness. Cut into biscuits 2¼ inches in diameter. Brush tops with butter. Place on greased cookie sheet. Bake for 12 to 15 minutes or until browned. May put ham or cheese in center of biscuits if desired. Yield: 14 to 16 biscuits.

Lou Gibson, Preceptor Beta Eta
Christiansburg, Virginia

GOUGERE

This bread had a distinct flavor all its own. It is great served as an appetizer.

1/2 cup butter or margarine	1/2 teaspoon salt
11/4 cups all-purpose flour	1/4 teaspoon freshly ground pepper
4 eggs	1 clove of garlic, minced
3 cups grated sharp Cheddar cheese	2 jalapeño peppers, chopped
1 cup grated Swiss cheese	1/4 cup chopped onion
	1/8 teaspoon cayenne pepper

Preheat oven to 375 degrees. Melt butter in medium saucepan over medium heat. Add flour; stir until mixture forms a ball. Remove from heat; continue stirring until mixture cools. Beat in eggs, 1 at a time, stirring until mixture is slightly glossy and smooth. Stir in remaining ingredients. Pour batter into greased 10-inch skillet. Bake for 40 to 45 minutes or until golden brown. Yield: 32 servings.

Cathy Kibler, Xi Delta Omega
Altamont, Kansas

SPICED WALNUTS

1/2 cup water	2 tablespoons cinnamon
1 cup sugar	1/2 teaspoon nutmeg
1 teaspoon salt	2 cups walnut halves

Combine first 5 ingredients in saucepan; cook over medium heat to soft-ball stage. Remove from heat. Add walnuts; stir until creamy. Turn onto waxed paper; separate. Let cool. Yield: 6 to 8 servings.

Kathe L. Ramsey, Preceptor Laureate Alpha Phi
Vacaville, California

BUTTERMILK CANDY

1 cup buttermilk	2 tablespoons butter or margarine
1 teaspoon baking soda	1 teaspoon vanilla extract
2 cups sugar	1 cup chopped pecans
2 teaspoons light corn syrup	

Combine buttermilk and baking soda in 4-quart saucepan; mix well. Let stand for 1 minute. Add sugar, corn syrup and butter. Cook to soft-ball stage, 236 to 238 degrees on candy thermometer. Add vanilla and pecans; beat until mixture begins to thicken. Drop by teaspoonfuls onto buttered cookie sheet. Yield: 36 pieces.

June Avis, Epsilon Xi
Unionville, Ontario, Canada
*Susan Grissom, Xi Gamma Pi
Pocahontas, Arizona
*Kathy Cocks, Xi Delta Sigma
Corpus Christi, Texas

PEANUT BRITTLE

I make this every year for our customers at Wagoner Lumber. I use a 110-pound toe sack of peanuts from November 1 through Christmas each year.

1 cup light corn syrup	4 cups raw peanuts
3 cups sugar	1 tablespoon baking soda
3/4 cup margarine	

Place 18-by-24-inch sheet aluminum foil on flat surface. Place candy thermometer on inside of heavy 4-quart saucepan; do not let touch bottom. Pour syrup and sugar in saucepan; place over high heat. Mix continuously. Stir in margarine when sugar melts, stirring until margarine melts. Add peanuts. Cook to hard-crack stage on candy thermometer; remove from heat. Add baking soda, stirring constantly. Mixture will be foamy. Pour into center of foil. Do not spread. Let cool; break into pieces. Yield: enough to fill 1 gallon plastic food bag.

Betty L. Wofford, Xi Zeta Iota
Wagoner, Oklahoma
*Jean Gretsch, Xi Xi Omicron
Palm Desert, California
*Penny McCurdy, Alpha Alpha Zeta
Independence, Missouri
*Dawn Dillon, Xi Gamma Theta
Pinellas Park, Florida

DATE NUT ROLL

My grandmother made this when I was a child. I'm 81 years old now and make it every Christmas for my children and grandchildren.

3 cups chopped nuts	11/2 cups milk
3 pounds chopped dates	36 graham crackers, crushed
11/2 pounds miniature marshmallows	Whipped cream

Combine nuts, dates and marshmallows in bowl; mix well. Stir in milk; mix well. Add graham crackers; shape into rolls. Wrap in foil; store in freezer. Slice into serving portions to serve. Serve with whipped cream. Yield: 24 to 36 servings.

Elizabeth Kuhlman, Laureate Alpha Nu
Wichita, Kansas

CANDY APPLES

An elderly lady in the neighborhood made candy apples to sell to the neighborhood kids. She gave me her recipe when I became a teenager.

6 apples	2/3 cup light corn syrup
6 Popsicle sticks	Red food coloring
2 cups sugar	1 cinnamon stick, finely chopped
1 cup water	

Prepare apples with sticks inserted to hold. Combine sugar, water and corn syrup in saucepan; cook over medium heat, stirring constantly, until mixture begins to boil. Cook, without stirring, to hard-crack stage, 290 degrees on candy thermometer. Remove from heat; add food coloring and cinnamon. Dip apples into candy syrup and place on waxed paper to harden. Reheat candy syrup to keep dipping consistency, if necessary. Yield: 6 apples.

Clara C. Flores, Alpha Pi Gamma
Edinburg, Texas

ICE CREAM PUMPKIN PIE

My mother created this recipe. It became the family's favorite holiday dessert.

1 cup canned pumpkin	1 package instant
1/2 teaspoon nutmeg	vanilla pudding mix
1/2 teaspoon cinnamon	1 baked 9-inch pie shell
1 pint vanilla ice cream,	Whipped cream
slightly softened	

Combine first 3 ingredients in mixer bowl; mix well. Add ice cream and pudding mix; beat for 1 minute. Pour into pie shell; chill. Serve with whipped cream. Yield: 6 to 8 servings.

Helen Harsaulas Hunt, Iota Eta
Havelock, North Carolina

ITALIAN CREAM PIE

My Italian grandmother handed this recipe down to me. It is baked only during the Easter season.

4 cups all-purpose flour	1 teaspoon butter or
3/4 cup vegetable	margarine
shortening	1 teaspoon vanilla
1/2 cup sugar	extract
1/4 cup milk	4 cups whole milk
3 eggs	1 teaspoon grated
1 1/2 teaspoons baking	lemon rind
powder	2 squares unsweetened
6 egg yolks, beaten	chocolate
2 cups sugar	Confectioners' sugar
1 cup all-purpose flour	

Preheat oven to 375 to 400 degrees. Place 4 cups flour on pastry board; make well in center. Add and work next 5 ingredients into well until well mixed. Divide dough into 2 portions. Roll out 1 portion on lightly floured surface for 10-inch pie crust. Arrange pastry in 10-inch fluted pie dish. Combine next 6 ingredients in mixer bowl; beat well. Cook in top of double boiler until thickened; add lemon rind. Dissolve chocolate in 1/4 hot cream mixture in small bowl; pour into center of pie crust. Pour remaining cream mixture over chocolate mixture. Roll out remaining pastry dough. Place over cream mixture, fluting edges and sealing crusts. Bake for 25 minutes; let cool. Sprinkle confectioners' sugar over top. Store in refrigerator. Yield: 12 servings.

Janice C. Butcher, Xi Alpha Epsilon
Westfield, Massachusetts

DOVE'S DATE PIE

This recipe, handed down from my husband's German relatives, is a must for Thanksgiving and Christmas.

1 cup margarine,	1/4 cup water
softened	1/4 cup light or dark
2 cups sugar	corn syrup
1 tablespoon all-	1 cup chopped dates
purpose flour	1 8-inch baked pie shell
5 eggs, beaten	1/2 cup chopped pecans

Combine margarine and sugar in saucepan. Add next 5 ingredients; mix well. Cook over low heat, stirring constantly, until mixture boils and becomes thickened. Pour into pie shell. Sprinkle with pecans. Yield: 8 servings.

Judy Casey, Xi Rho Beta
Duncanville, Texas

CRANBERRY-RAISIN PIE

2 tablespoons	2 teaspoons grated
all-purpose flour	lemon rind
2 cups sugar	2 tablespoons
1/4 teaspoon salt	margarine or butter
2/3 cup water	2 9-inch unbaked pie
3 cups cranberries	shells
1 cup raisins	

Preheat oven to 425 degrees. Blend first 3 ingredients in saucepan. Add water; bring to a boil. Add next 3 ingredients; cook, stirring, for 2 minutes or until cranberries begin to pop. Stir in margarine; let cool. Pour into pastry shell. Cut remaining pastry shell into strips; place on pie in lattice-fashion. Bake for 20 minutes. Yield: 8 servings.

Faye Williams, Xi Delta Pi
Kennett, Missouri

CAN'T FAIL CHRISTMAS COOKIES

We always went to Grandma Ridley's to help make and decorate these cookies. It just isn't Christmas without making these.

1 cup vegetable	2 teaspoons vanilla
shortening	extract
2/3 cup sugar	3 cups sifted
3/4 teaspoon salt	all-purpose flour
1/3 cup (exactly) eggs	

Combine first 5 ingredients in mixer bowl; beat until smooth and light. Stir in flour until well mixed. Chill dough for at least 2 hours. Preheat oven to 350 degrees. Roll out on lightly floured pastry canvas using covered rolling pin. Press lightly floured cutter into dough evenly; lift and rub cutting edge clean of dough with thumb. Place on cookie sheet. Bake for 12 to 15 minutes; do not brown. May frost and decorate if desired. Yield: 3 to 4 dozen cookies.

Kathy Erickson, Nu
Montrose, Colorado

BAVARIAN MINT TARTS

15 single saltine
  crackers, crushed
3 egg whites, stiffly
  beaten
1 cup chopped nuts
1 cup sugar
1 teaspoon vanilla
  extract
1 1/2 cups softened
  margarine
3 cups confectioners'
  sugar

6 squares semisweet
  chocolate, melted
6 eggs
1 1/2 teaspoons
  peppermint flavoring
1 teaspoon vanilla
  extract
Whipped cream
Cherry candy or candy
  canes, crushed

Preheat oven to 325 degrees. Combine first 5 ingredients in bowl; mix well. Spoon into foil cupcake liners in muffin cups; bake for 14 minutes. Cream margarine in mixer bowl; add confectioners' sugar gradually. Beat for 5 minutes; add cooled chocolate. Beat for 3 minutes; add eggs, 1 at a time, beating after each addition. Add peppermint flavoring and 1 teaspoon vanilla; beat for 5 minutes. Fill cupcake liners to top; freeze. Top with whipped cream and crushed candy before serving. Yield: 24 servings.

Eunice E. Hansen, Preceptor Xi
Hampton, Nebraska

PEPPERNUTS

Having peppernuts in our home at Christmas was an annual tradition. You just let them melt in your mouth.

3 cups packed light
  brown sugar
2 cups vegetable
  shortening
1 cup light corn syrup
1 cup green label
  molasses
4 tablespoons water
4 tablespoons vinegar

3 eggs, beaten
2 teaspoons baking soda
1 teaspoon allspice
1 teaspoon cinnamon
1 teaspoon salt
1 teaspoon ground
  nutmeg
All-purpose flour

Preheat oven to 350 degrees. Cream brown sugar and shortening in mixer bowl. Add next 5 ingredients; mix well. Stir in next 5 ingredients and enough flour to make stiff dough. Roll out on lightly floured table into 1 1/2-inch rope. Cut into 1/2-inch pieces; place on greased cookie sheet. Bake until lightly browned or firm to the touch. Remove immediately.
Yield: 3 to 4 dozen cookies.

Rita M. Ensminger, Laureate Sigma
Garland, Texas

Shari M. Short, Delta Delta Chi, Fontana, California, makes "I Can't Believe It's a Cookie" cookies by mixing 1 cup sugar, 1 well-beaten egg, 1 cup chunky peanut butter and 1 teaspoon vanilla extract in bowl. Drop by teaspoonfuls onto greased cookie sheet. Top with chocolate kiss. Bake in preheated 350-degree oven for 8 to 10 minutes.

NORWEGIAN KRINGLA

2 cups sugar
1/2 teaspoon salt
2 tablespoons lard
  or 3 tablespoons
  vegetable shortening
1 egg
1 1/2 teaspoons baking
  powder
1/2 to 1 teaspoon nutmeg

3 teaspoons anise seed
5 cups all-purpose flour
1 1/2 teaspoons baking
  soda
2 cups rich cream,
  soured
2 teaspoons vanilla
  extract

Cream sugar, salt and shortening in mixer bowl. Add egg; beat well. Sift next 4 ingredients into bowl. Mix baking soda and sour cream in bowl. Add flour mixture alternately with sour cream mixture to sugar mixture. Add vanilla; mix well. Refrigerate for 1 hour or until chilled thoroughly. Preheat oven to 400 degrees. Divide dough into 3 or 4 rolls 2 inches in diameter. Slice rolls into 3/4 inch pieces. Roll out each piece into pencil-like strip; shape into kringla or round pretzel shape with 2 twists in middle and second twist in center of pretzel ring. Place on lightly greased cookie sheet. Bake for 5 to 7 minutes, watching closely not to brown top; bottom will brown slightly. Yield: 4 to 5 dozen.

Helen Sellberg, Beta Iota
Harrisonville, Missouri

CHRISTMAS CHEWY BARS

1 cup sifted all-purpose
  flour
3 tablespoons
  confectioners' sugar
1/2 cup butter or
  margarine, softened
3/4 cup chopped nuts
1/2 cup quartered
  maraschino cherries

1 cup sugar
1/2 teaspoon baking
  powder
1/4 teaspoon salt
1/4 cup all-purpose flour
1 teaspoon vanilla
  extract
1/2 cup coconut
2 eggs, slightly beaten

Preheat oven to 350 degrees. Mix flour, confectioners' sugar and butter in bowl until smooth. Spread into greased 8-inch square baking pan. Bake for 25 minutes. Combine remaining ingredients; mix well. Spread over baked pastry. Bake for 25 minutes or until done. Let cool in pan; cut into squares. Yield: 12 bars.

Jewel Barrett, Zeta Beta
Timberon, New Mexico

TOASTED BUTTER PECAN CAKE

1/4 cup butter
2 2/3 cups broken pecans
1 cup butter or
  margarine
2 cups sugar
4 eggs
3 cups sifted
  all-purpose flour

2 teaspoons baking
  powder
1/2 teaspoon salt
1 cup milk
2 teaspoons vanilla
  extract

Preheat oven to 350 degrees. Melt 1/4 cup butter in large shallow baking pan. Add pecans; toast for about 25 minutes, stirring frequently. Let cool; reserve 2/3 cup pecans for frosting. Cream 1 cup butter and sugar in mixer bowl until light and fluffy. Add eggs, 1 at a time, beating well after each addition. Sift flour, baking powder and salt together in bowl. Combine milk and vanilla in bowl. Add flour mixture alternately with milk mixture to egg mixture; mix well. Stir in toasted pecans. Pour into 2 greased 9-inch cake pans lined with waxed paper. Bake for 30 minutes or until layers test done. Let cool on wire racks. Frost cake with Frosting.
Yield: 20 to 30 servings.

FROSTING

1/4 cup butter or margarine	1 teaspoon vanilla extract
1 pound confectioners' sugar, sifted	4 to 6 tablespoons cream or milk

Cream butter and sugar in mixer bowl; mix in vanilla and cream gradually. Stir in reserved toasted pecans. Yield: enough to frost 2-layer cake.

Dorothy M. Smith, Delta Lambda
Strawberry Plains, Tennessee

YULE CAKE

1 1/2 cups chopped pecans	3/4 cup sugar
1 cup chopped walnuts	1/2 teaspoon baking powder
1/2 cup sunflower seeds	
1 1/2 cups chopped dried apricots	1/2 teaspoon salt
1/2 cup raisins	3 eggs, beaten
3/4 cup all-purpose flour	1 teaspoon vanilla extract

Preheat oven to 300 degrees. Place first 5 ingredients in bowl; sift flour, sugar, baking powder and salt over fruit mixture. Mix eggs and vanilla in small bowl; blend into fruit mixture. Pour into greased 5-by-9-inch loaf pan lined with waxed paper. Bake for 1 hour and 45 minutes; let cool in pan for 10 minutes. Loosen edges; turn onto wire rack. Remove waxed paper. Yield: 8 to 12 servings.

Tamara Randi, Xi Alpha Eta
Grass Valley, California

OLD-FASHIONED FRUITCAKE

24 ounces whole pecans	1 ounce Brandy flavoring
1 1/2 pounds chopped mixed candied fruit	4 cups sifted all-purpose flour
1 pound seedless white raisins	1 teaspoon nutmeg
1 cup butter or margarine	1 1/2 teaspoons cinnamon
2 1/4 cups sugar	1 teaspoon salt
6 eggs	Honey

Preheat oven to 275 degrees. Reserve enough pecans and fruit to decorate top of cake. Mix butter, sugar, eggs and flavoring in large mixer bowl. Sift dry ingredients together into bowl. Add to butter mixture, mixing thoroughly. Stir in pecans and fruit. Fill 2 greased 5-by-9-inch foil-lined loaf pans 2/3 full. Bake for 1 1/2 hours. Brush tops with honey; decorate with reserved pecans and fruit, pressing down firmly. Bake for 30 minutes longer or until loaves test done. Let cool in pans. Remove from pans; peel off foil. Wrap cakes in Brandy-dampened cloth. Store in airtight container in cool place for at least 3 weeks to blend and mellow flavor. Yield: 24 servings.

Mary C. Oglesbee, Pi Master
Cincinnati, Ohio

MINI FRUITCAKES

3 eggs, well beaten	1 cup chopped nuts
1 14-ounce can sweetened condensed milk	2 cups cornflake crumbs
	1/2 cup all-purpose flour
	1 teaspoon baking soda
1 28-ounce jar mincemeat	36 candied cherries, halved

Preheat oven to 300 degrees. Combine first 7 ingredients in large bowl; mix well. Line muffin cups with cupcake liners. Spoon 1 heaping tablespoonful batter into each liner. Top each with cherry half. Bake for 25 to 30 minutes or until done. Yield: 36 servings.

Hazel R. French, Preceptor Alpha Upsilon
Maybeury, West Virginia

EGGNOG CAKE

This is a great Christmas or holiday cake to serve at an open house or a Christmas brunch.

1 package yellow cake mix	1/2 teaspoon nutmeg
	1/3 cup sugar
1 cup whipping cream	1/4 teaspoon nutmeg
1/4 cup vegetable oil	1/3 cup margarine
1/4 cup rum	2 tablespoons water
3 eggs	2 tablespoons rum

Preheat oven to 350 degrees. Blend first 6 ingredients in large mixer bowl until moistened; beat for 2 minutes at high speed. Pour into greased and floured 12-cup bundt pan. Bake for 35 to 45 minutes or until toothpick inserted in center comes out clean. Heat sugar, nutmeg, margarine and water in small saucepan until mixture boils and sugar is melted. Remove from heat; add rum. Pour half the glaze around edges of hot cake in bundt pan. Cool upright in pan for 5 minutes; turn onto serving plate. Pour remaining glaze over top. Serve warm or cold. Yield: 16 servings.

Dorothy Isdell, Epsilon Chi
Bolivar, Missouri

ROYAL ENGLISH CHRISTMAS WEDDING CAKE

2 cups all-purpose flour
1 teaspoon ground cinnamon
1/2 teaspoon baking powder
1/4 teaspoon baking soda
1/4 teaspoon ground nutmeg
1/4 teaspoon ground cloves
1 1/2 cups currants
2 cups dark and/or light raisins
1 1/2 cups diced mixed candied fruits and peels
1 cup red and/or green cherries

1/2 cup ground almonds
4 eggs, beaten
1 cup sugar
3/4 cup melted butter or margarine
3/4 cup Brandy, rum or orange juice
2 teaspoons almond extract
3 tablespoons lemon juice
1 8-ounce can almond paste, softened
Royal Icing

Preheat oven to 300 degrees. Combine first 6 ingredients in large bowl; mix well. Stir in next 5 ingredients. Combine eggs, sugar, butter, 1/2 cup Brandy, almond extract and lemon juice in bowl; mix well. Stir egg mixture into fruit mixture. Pour into 2 greased parchment or waxed-paper lined 9-inch cake pans. Bake for 1 hour. Cover pans loosely with foil to prevent overbrowning; bake for 15 to 30 minutes longer or until tests done. Let cool; remove from pans. Wrap layers separately in cheesecloth moistened in 1/4 cup rum, Brandy or orange juice; overwrap in foil. Store in refrigerator for at least 1 week and up to 2 weeks; remoisten cheesecloth every 3 to 4 days. Place 1 layer, top side down, on serving plate. Shape almond paste into 2 balls. Place 1 ball between 2 sheets waxed paper. Roll out with rolling pin; remove 1 sheet waxed paper. Trim almond paste to fit cake; invert onto cake. Spread Royal Icing over almond paste on first cake layer. Add second cake layer, top side up. Add almond paste, repeating procedure above. Frost with Royal Icing. May decorate wedding cake with roses. Yield: 24 servings.

ROYAL ICING

4 cups sifted confectioners' sugar
1/2 cup water

1/4 cup meringue powder
1 teaspoon almond extract

Combine all ingredients in large mixer bowl. Beat at high speed until very stiff; use immediately.
Yield: 4 cups.

Joan Hayn, Beta Master
San Diego, California

SOME CHRISTMAS CAKE

1 cup butter or margarine
8 ounces cream cheese
1 1/2 cups sugar
2 teaspoons vanilla extract
Lemon rind to taste, finely grated
4 eggs

2 cups all-purpose flour
1 1/2 teaspoons baking powder
1/2 cup seedless raisins
1/2 cup golden raisins
1/2 cup mixed fruit
1/2 cup chopped maraschino cherries
1/2 cup chopped nuts

Preheat oven to 300 degrees. Cream butter and cream cheese in mixer bowl; add sugar, mixing well. Beat in vanilla and lemon rind. Add eggs, 1 at a time, beating well after each addition. Sift 1 3/4 cups flour with baking powder into bowl; add to batter. Dredge fruit and nuts in remaining 1/4 cup flour; stir into batter. Pour batter into greased and floured 10-inch bundt or tube pan. Bake for 1 hour and 10 minutes to 1 hour and 20 minutes. Let cool in pan for 10 minutes; turn onto wire rack to cool completely. Yield: 16 servings.

Pat Pigot, Epsilon Phi
Abbotsford, British Columbia, Canada

CHRISTMAS EGGNOG DESSERT

2 packages unflavored gelatin
1 cup boiling water
2 cups eggnog
2 cups whipping cream
1/4 cup sugar

1 to 2 teaspoons rum or rum extract
Sliced fresh fruit
Lemon juice
1/4 cup sugar

Dissolve gelatin in boiling water in small bowl. Place eggnog in large bowl; add gelatin. Whip cream in mixer bowl until stiff, adding 1/4 cup sugar gradually. Add rum to eggnog; fold in whipped cream. Pour into 2 1/2-quart mold; refrigerate for at least 2 hours. Sprinkle fruit with lemon juice to prevent browning; stir in 1/4 cup sugar. Unmold gelatin onto serving plate; fill center with sweetened fruit.
Yield: 8 servings.

Lorraine Mear, Zeta Sigma
Elkford, British Columbia, Canada

WHIPPED CREAM-COCONUT CAKE

1/2 cup vegetable shortening
1 1/2 cups sugar
2 1/2 teaspoons baking powder
1/2 teaspoon salt
2 1/4 cups sifted all-purpose flour
1 cup milk

1 teaspoon vanilla extract
4 egg whites, stiffly beaten
2 cups whipping cream
2 tablespoons sugar
1 teaspoon vanilla extract
Fresh coconut, grated

Preheat oven to 350 degrees. Cream shortening and sugar in mixer bowl. Combine baking powder, salt and flour in bowl; sift again. Add flour mixture to shortening mixture alternately with milk, beating continuously. Add 1 teaspoon vanilla. Fold in egg whites gently until well mixed. Spoon batter into 2 greased and floured 8-inch cake pans. Bake for 30 minutes or until cake is lightly browned and tests done. Whip cream in mixer bowl until stiff, adding 2 tablespoons sugar and 1 teaspoon vanilla. Spread whipped cream over first layer; sprinkle with coconut. Add top layer; spread with remaining whipped cream. Sprinkle with coconut. Store in refrigerator. Yield: 16 servings.

Susie Wiseman, Sigma Lambda
Burbank, Illinois

DANISH KRINGLE

1 cup all-purpose flour	*1 cup chopped nuts*
1/2 cup sour cream	*3 cups confectioners'*
1/2 cup butter or	*sugar*
margarine	*1 tablespoon milk*
3 egg whites	*1/4 teaspoon lemon juice*
1 cup sugar	

Combine first 3 ingredients in bowl; mix well. Shape into ball. Refrigerate, covered, overnight. Preheat oven to 300 degrees. Roll dough into large thin rectangle on generously floured surface. Beat egg whites in mixer bowl until soft peaks form; add sugar, 1 spoonful at a time, until stiff peaks form. Add nuts. Place 1/2 filling in center of dough. Fold 1/3 dough over filling; place remaining filling on top. Fold remaining dough over filling. Press edges together. Place on greased cookie sheet. Bake for 20 to 30 minutes or until lightly browned. Combine remaining ingredients in bowl, adding additional milk and lemon, if needed, to make of spreading consistency. Pour frosting over hot kringle. Yield: 8 servings.

Suzanne Trieschmann, Gamma Theta
Camp LeJeune, North Carolina

MERINGUE NUT TORTE

I have used this recipe as the centerpiece on the buffet for my holiday parties. My guests were delighted when they tasted it.

1 1/2 cups finely crushed	*1 1/2 tablespoons rum or*
saltines	*almond extract*
2 cups finely chopped	*2 cups whipping cream,*
pecans	*whipped*
2 teaspoons baking	*Sugar to taste*
powder	*Bananas*
6 egg whites	*Slivered almonds*
2 cups sugar	*Maraschino cherries*

Preheat oven to 325 degrees. Combine saltines, pecans and baking powder in bowl; mix well. Beat egg whites in mixer bowl until stiff but not dry. Add sugar 1 tablespoon at a time, beating after each addition. Add rum. Fold into cracker crumb mixture. Spread into 2 greased and floured 9-inch cake pans, rounding mixture up in middle slightly. Bake for 40 minutes; let cool. Remove from pan carefully. Mix whipped cream with sugar to taste in bowl. Slice bananas over torte. Add layer of whipped cream; repeat for second layer. Garnish with almonds and cherries. Refrigerate until ready to serve. Yield: 8 to 10 servings.

Traci McCosh
Columbia, Missouri

CHRISTMAS PUDDING SAUCE

1/4 cup butter or	*1 cup milk*
margarine	*2 egg whites, stiffly*
1/4 cup all-purpose flour	*beaten*
1 cup sugar	*1/4 cup whipping cream,*
2 egg yolks	*stiffly beaten*
Dash of salt	*Rum to taste*

Beat butter, flour, sugar, egg yolks and salt in mixer bowl; add milk. Pour into top of double boiler. Cook over hot water over medium heat, stirring constantly, until thickened. Remove from heat; let cool. Fold in egg whites and whipped cream gently. Add rum. Refrigerate until ready to serve. Yield: 4 cups.

Barbara Scobie, Xi Alpha Pi
Abbotsford, British Columbia, Canada

RICE PUDDING WITH CHERRY SAUCE

We add one whole almond to rice and the person who finds it gets a small prize. We enjoy this dessert after Christmas Eve dinner.

1 1/2 cups milk	*1 17-ounce can pitted*
1/4 cup sugar	*Bing cherries*
1/2 teaspoon salt	*1 tablespoon cornstarch*
2/3 cup minute rice	*Dash of salt*
1/4 cup chopped almonds	*1 teaspoon lemon juice*
1 teaspoon vanilla	*1/2 teaspoon almond*
extract	*extract*
2 cups whipping cream,	
whipped	

Combine first 4 ingredients in saucepan; boil, uncovered, for 8 minutes, fluffing rice occasionally. Remove from heat; let stand, covered tightly, for 10 minutes. Add almonds and vanilla; cover and chill. Fold whipped cream into rice mixture. Drain cherries, reserving juice. Add enough water to cherry juice to make 1 1/2 cups; blend juice, cornstarch and salt in saucepan. Cook, stirring constantly, over medium heat until thickened and clear. Add cherries, lemon juice and almond extract. Spoon over individual servings. Yield: 4 to 6 servings.

Karen Nielsen, Xi Delta Theta
Rock Creek, British Columbia, Canada

DICKENS' PLUM PUDDING

2 tablespoons sugar
4 cups white bread cubes
1 cup all-purpose flour
1/4 cup packed light
  brown sugar
1 teaspoon baking soda
1 teaspoon cinnamon
1/4 teaspoon salt
1/4 teaspoon nutmeg
3/4 cup orange juice

1/2 cup butter or
  margarine
3 tablespoons dark
  molasses
2 eggs
1 teaspoon grated
  lemon peel
3/4 cup raisins
1/2 cup currants
Hard Sauce

Coat bottom and side of generously greased microwave-safe 8-cup ring baking dish with sugar. Place next 14 ingredients in large mixer bowl. Beat at medium speed for 2 minutes or until blended, scraping bowl occasionally. Spoon into prepared dish. Cover with plastic wrap. Place on inverted saucer in microwave oven. Microwave on medium or 50% for 12 to 17 minutes, or until pudding pulls away from edge of dish and wooden toothpick inserted in center comes out clean. Let stand, covered, for 5 minutes. Invert onto serving dish. Serve warm with Hard Sauce. Yield: 12 servings.

HARD SAUCE

1/2 cup butter or
  margarine
2 cups confectioners'
  sugar

2 tablespoon water
2 teaspoons grated
  orange peel

Beat butter in mixer bowl at high speed until fluffy. Mix in remaining ingredients. Yield: 2 cups.

Diana Cozart, Xi Tau Chi
Santee, California

SWEET POTATO PUDDING

1 1/2 cups sugar
3 eggs, beaten
3 cups milk
1 teaspoon cinnamon
1 teaspoon nutmeg
1 teaspoon salt
1/4 teaspoon pepper

4 medium sweet
  potatoes
2 tablespoons butter or
  margarine, melted
1 1/2 teaspoons vanilla
  extract
Marshmallows

Preheat oven to 325 degrees. Combine first 7 ingredients in large bowl; mix well. Grate sweet potatoes directly into mixture, mixing after each potato. Mixture should be firm; potatoes will absorb any milk during cooking. Add butter and vanilla; mix well. Pour into greased 3-quart glass baking dish. Bake for 1 hour and 30 minutes to 2 hours or until pudding is set, stirring every 45 minutes. Top with marshmallows; bake until melted. Yield: 10 to 15 servings.

Catherine Love Allen, Eta Chi
Woodstock, Virginia

SUET PUDDING WITH VANILLA HARD SAUCE

My mother's family brought this recipe from Norway.

1 cup suet or 3/4 cup
  vegetable shortening
1/2 cup sugar
1/2 cup molasses
3 1/2 cups sifted all-
  purpose flour
3 1/2 teaspoons baking
  powder
1/2 teaspoon salt

1 teaspoon cinnamon
3/4 teaspoon cloves
1 egg, beaten
1 cup milk
1/2 cup chopped nuts
1 1/2 cups raisins
1 1/2 cups currants
Vanilla Hard Sauce

Cream first 3 ingredients in mixer bowl. Sift flour, baking powder, salt and spices into bowl. Add egg to creamed mixture; mix well. Add flour mixture alternately with milk. Add nuts, raisins and currants; mix lightly. Spoon mixture into pudding mold. Place mold in steaming pan with water; steam for 3 hours. Serve with Vanilla Hard Sauce. Yield: 12 servings.

VANILLA HARD SAUCE

1 cup sugar
3 tablespoons all-
  purpose flour
2 cups boiling water

2 teaspoons vanilla
  extract
1 to 2 tablespoons
  butter or margarine

Mix sugar and flour in saucepan; add boiling water. Cook over medium heat, stirring constantly, for 5 minutes or until thickened. Remove from heat; stir in vanilla and butter. Yield: 2 cups.

Muriel Brainard, Laureate Xi
Coos Bay, Oregon

CRANBERRY PUDDING

1 1/3 cups all-purpose
  flour
1/2 cup mild molasses
2 cups fresh cranberries
1/4 cup chopped nuts

2 teaspoons baking soda
1/3 cup hot water
Brown Sugar and
  Butter Sauce

Combine flour, molasses, cranberries and nuts in bowl. Mix baking soda and hot water in small bowl; add to cranberry mixture, mixing lightly. Pour into greased 1-quart mold. Cover tightly with foil. Steam over boiling water for 1 1/2 hours. Serve warm with Brown Sugar and Butter Sauce. Yield: 6 servings.

BROWN SUGAR AND BUTTER SAUCE

1/2 cup butter, melted
1/2 cup packed light
  brown sugar

1/2 cup heavy cream
1/2 teaspoon vanilla
  extract

Combine butter, brown sugar and cream in saucepan. Bring to a boil; remove from heat. Add vanilla. Yield: 1 to 1 1/2 cups sauce.

Janet Dougherty, Xi Beta Alpha
Appleton, Wisconsin

Sweet-Tooth Satisfiers

Long before we knew anything about watching
cholesterol, counting fat grams, or cutting back
on sodium, there were sweets—sweet,
satisfying treats that would bring us running
home from school. Nothing satisfied us then
like a glass of cold milk and a big, chewy,
hot-from-the-oven cookie. Chocolate chip,
peanut butter, sugar cookie—it didn't matter
what kind, as long as it was fresh and
homemade. Don't just reminisce—experience!
In this chapter we've included recipes for all the
most luscious, spectacular, and satisfying cakes,
pies, candies, and other delectables we could
come up with. Forget the diet for once and let
yourself go. Your sweet tooth is waiting.

Home Sweet Home

The Creative Cook's Bundt Cakes

Basic Bundt Cake
Fresh Apple Bundt Cake
Piña Colada Bundt Cake
Butterscotch Bundt Cake (page 176)
Decadent Chocolate Bundt Cake
(page 177)
Heath Bar Bundt Cake (page 177)
Tart Lemon Bundt Cake (page 179)
Orange Sunshine Bundt Cake (page 180)

These are my suggestions for creating a variety of easy bundt cakes from the same basic recipe; the creative instincts of the cook are what make it fun.

I always bake 4 or 5 cakes in each session of 3 or 4 hours, using identical bundt pans. I plan each cake with a sense of adventure and fun, assembling all the ingredients and preparing the pans first, aiming either for complementary flavors, contrasting flavors or even an occasional taste surprise. I start with the simplest and most bland cake and work toward the spice or chocolate last because (and this is the best part) I don't wash the bowl or beaters between cakes. I circulate 3 or more pans in and out of the oven, with 1 or 2 baking, one cooling and one cake in the mixer.

I have served the cakes as a Bundt Bar at a luncheon for up to 100 people and enjoyed watching them swap and sample to decide which they like best. I have also assembled contrasting quarters of different cakes to make a whole "sampler bundt" for smaller parties or for Christmas gifts. I always keep several assorted quarters in the freezer for instant dessert whenever needed.

I also have a secret to pass along. I just can't do all that creative work without sampling myself, so I cut a small piece out of each cake and then cut it into quarters, wrap the quarters and pack them for gifting or freezing; the recipients never know that I took my "wages" out first, unless I choose to confess!

Barbara Boatright, Delta Kappa Psi
Escondido, California

BASIC BUNDT CAKE

1 2-layer package white or yellow cake mix	4 eggs
	1/2 cup vegetable oil
	1/2 cup water
1 4-ounce package vanilla instant pudding mix	1/2 cup sour cream

Preheat oven to 350 degrees. Combine basic 6 ingredients in large mixer bowl; beat for 2 minutes. Spoon into greased and floured bundt pan. Bake for 50 to 60 minutes or until cake tests done. Cool in pan for 10 minutes; remove to wire rack to cool completely. Yield: 16 servings.

FRESH APPLE BUNDT CAKE

1 2-layer package spice cake mix	1 cup chopped Rome apples
1 4-ounce package butterscotch instant pudding mix	1/2 cup walnuts
	1/2 cup raisins
4 eggs	Melted butter or margarine
1/2 cup oil	Light brown sugar
1/2 cup water	Vanilla extract to taste
1/2 cup sour cream	Chopped walnuts

Prepare and bake first 6 ingredients as for Basic Bundt Cake (page 174), using spice cake mix and butterscotch pudding mix; fold in apples, 1/2 cup walnuts and raisins. Drizzle with mixture of melted butter, brown sugar and vanilla and top with chopped walnuts. Yield: 16 servings.

PIÑA COLADA BUNDT CAKE

1 2-layer package yellow cake mix	1 16-ounce can crushed pineapple, drained
1 4-ounce package coconut instant pudding mix	1 cup finely chopped coconut
	1 teaspoon rum extract
4 eggs	Pineapple juice
1/2 cup vegetable oil	Confectioners' sugar
1/2 cup pineapple juice	Coconut
1/2 cup sour cream	

Prepare and bake first 6 ingredients as for Basic Bundt Cake (page 174), using yellow cake mix and coconut pudding mix, substituting pineapple juice for water; fold in pineapple, 1 cup coconut and rum extract. Poke holes in warm cake and drizzle with mixture of pineapple juice and confectioners' sugar; sprinkle with additional coconut. Yield: 16 servings.

Glenda Knoth, Lee's Summit, Missouri, makes Whiskey Sauce by melting 1/2 cup butter or margarine and 1 cup confectioners' sugar in top of double boiler until very hot but not boiling. Add 1 well-beaten egg, whisking until smooth. Refrigerate; add whiskey to taste before serving.

Let Them Eat Cake

❖ APPLE DECADENCE

2 cups sugar
1/2 cup margarine
2 eggs
4 cups diced apples
2 1/2 cups all-purpose flour
1 teaspoon nutmeg
1 teaspoon cinnamon
2 teaspoons baking soda
1/2 teaspoon salt
1 cup packed light brown sugar
1 cup sugar
2 tablespoons all-purpose flour
1 cup butter or margarine
1 cup half and half
1 cup chopped pecans (optional)

Preheat oven to 350 degrees. Cream 2 cups sugar and margarine in mixer bowl. Add eggs and apples. Mix in next 5 ingredients. Pour into greased 9-by-13-inch baking pan. Bake for 45 minutes. Combine next 5 ingredients in saucepan. Bring to a boil; cook, stirring, until sauce is thickened. Serve with warm sauce. Sprinkle with pecans. Yield: 16 servings.

Kristine R. Schweitzer, Alpha
Fargo, North Dakota

APPLE CAKE WITH CARAMEL SAUCE

4 cups chopped apples
2 eggs
2 cups sugar
2 teaspoons cinnamon
1/2 cup salad oil
1/2 cup chopped nuts
2 cups all-purpose flour
1 teaspoon salt
2 teaspoons baking soda
Caramel Sauce

Preheat oven to 350 degrees. Place apples in large bowl. Break eggs over apples; mix well. Add next 4 ingredients. Sift flour, salt and baking soda together. Add to apple mixture; beat well. Pour into greased 9-by-13-inch baking pan. Bake for 45 minutes. Serve with warm Caramel Sauce. Yield: 12 servings.

CARAMEL SAUCE

1/2 cup packed light brown sugar
1/2 cup sugar
1/2 cup butter or margarine
1/2 cup whipping cream
1 tablespoon all-purpose flour
1 teaspoon vanilla extract

Combine all ingredients in saucepan. Bring to a boil over medium-low heat; boil, stirring, for 1 to 2 minutes or until thickened. Serve warm. Yield: 1 1/2 cups.

Kim Walerius, Alpha
West Fargo, North Dakota

APPLE BUTTER AND PEAR CAKE

1/2 cup margarine or butter
1 cup packed light brown sugar
1/2 cup chopped pecans
1 29-ounce can pear halves, drained
1 package yellow cake mix
1 teaspoon cinnamon
3/4 cup water
1/2 cup apple butter
1/3 cup cooking oil
3 eggs

Preheat oven to 350 degrees. Melt margarine in small saucepan over medium-low heat. Add brown sugar, stirring until dissolved. Spread mixture into greased and floured 9-by-13-inch baking pan; sprinkle with pecans. Cut pear halves into thin slices; arrange on top mixture. Blend next 6 ingredients in large mixer bowl until moistened; beat for 2 minutes at high speed. Pour over pears. Bake for 40 to 50 minutes or until toothpick inserted in center comes out clean. Invert immediately onto serving plate. Serve warm or cold. Yield: 12 servings.

Karen Hudgins, Delta Nu
Columbia, South Carolina

BANANA WALNUT CAKE

1 package white cake mix	1 teaspoon baking soda
2 eggs	2 cups chopped walnuts
1/4 cup cooking oil	2 whole bananas, mashed

Preheat oven to 325 degrees. Combine cake mix, 1/2 the amount of water on package directions, eggs, oil and baking soda in mixer bowl; beat until mixed well. Add 1 1/2 cups walnuts and bananas; mix until stiff. Pour into 9-by-13-inch baking pan sprayed with nonstick cooking spray and floured. Frost with any cream cheese icing; sprinkle with remaining 1/2 cup walnuts. Yield: 12 to 15 servings.

Bernadine M. Faulconer, Tau Delta
Maywood, Missouri

BLUEBERRY CRUMBLE CAKE

2 1/4 cups all-purpose flour	1/2 cup finely chopped nuts (optional)
3/4 cup sugar	1 egg, slightly beaten
3/4 cup butter or margarine	1 cup plain yogurt
1/2 teaspoon baking powder	2 teaspoons grated lemon rind
1/2 teaspoon baking soda	1 19-ounce can blueberry pie filling

Preheat oven to 350 degrees. Combine flour and sugar in large bowl. Cut in butter until mixture is crumbly; reserve 1/2 cup mixture. Add baking powder, baking soda and nuts to remaining mixture. Combine egg, yogurt and lemon rind in small bowl. Add to dry ingredients; stir just until moistened. Spread 2/3 batter over bottom and part way up side of greased 1 1/4-by-4 1/2-inch tart pan. Spoon pie filling over batter. Drop remaining batter by small spoonfuls over filling; sprinkle with reserved crumb mixture. Bake for 25 to 30 minutes or until cake tests done. Serve warm or cold. Yield: 8 servings.

Sandy Rompf, Laureate
Goderich, Ontario, Canada

BUTTERSCOTCH BUNDT CAKE

1 2-layer package white or yellow cake mix	1/2 cup water
	1/2 cup sour cream
1 4-ounce package butterscotch instant pudding mix	Crushed Werther's butterscotch candies
	Melted butter or margarine
4 eggs	Light brown sugar
1/2 cup vegetable oil	

Prepare and bake first 6 ingredients as for Basic Bundt Cake (page 174), using butterscotch pudding mix; alternate layers of batter and candy in bundt pan. Drizzle cooled cake with mixture of butter and brown sugar. Yield: 16 servings.

Barbara Boatright, Delta Kappa Psi
Escondido, California

CANNOLI CAKES

This recipe is great for a large crowd.

1 package yellow or white cake mix	1 small bag sliced almonds
4 cups half and half	1 large container whipped topping
8 tablespoons (rounded) cornstarch	1 solid milk chocolate bar
1 cup sugar	

Bake cake according to package directions for layer cake. Mix 1/2 cup half and half with cornstarch in small bowl. Mix remaining half and half and sugar in saucepan. Add cornstarch mixture; cook slowly, stirring constantly, over low heat for 30 minutes or until thickened. Let cool completely, stirring occasionally. Slice cake layers in half. Place bottom halves on 2 cake plates. Spread cream mixture on layers. Reserve 2 tablespoons almonds; sprinkle remaining almonds over cakes. Place top halves over almonds. Frost cakes with whipped topping. Sprinkle with reserved almonds. Grate or shave chocolate bar; sprinkle on cakes. Yield: 24 servings.

Connie Hannenberg, Xi Alpha Zeta
Sterling Heights, Michigan

❖ CARROT CAKE BARS

3 eggs	1 4-ounce jar baby food apricots in tapioca
1 1/4 cups corn oil	
2 cups sugar	8 ounces cream cheese
2 cups all-purpose flour	1/2 cup margarine, softened
2 teaspoons baking soda	
2 teaspoons ground cinnamon	1 teaspoon vanilla extract
1 4-ounce jar baby food strained carrots	1 small box confectioners' sugar
1 4-ounce jar baby food applesauce	

Preheat oven to 350 degrees. Beat eggs in mixer bowl. Add oil; mix well. Add next 7 ingredients; stir until thoroughly mixed. Pour into greased 10-by-20-inch baking pan. Bake for 35 to 40 minutes; let cool. Beat cream cheese and margarine thoroughly in small mixer bowl. Add vanilla and confectioners' sugar; beat until of spreading consistency. Spread on cooled cake; cut into bars. Yield: 15 to 20 bars.

Lorene Ashby, Xi Lambda Eta
Cincinnati, Ohio

Carol Smock, Xi Beta Alpha, Bowling Green, Kentucky, makes Lemon Cookies by mixing 1 package lemon cake mix, 1 egg and 2 cups whipped topping together in bowl. Drop by teaspoonfuls into confectioners' sugar; coat and shape into balls. Place 2 inches apart on ungreased cookie sheet. Bake in preheated 350-degree oven for 10 to 12 minutes or until lightly golden brown.

❖ ALMOND JOY CAKE

2 cups sugar
2 cups all-purpose flour
1 cup water
1/2 cup margarine
1/2 cup shortening
3 1/2 tablespoons cocoa
1/2 teaspoon salt
2 eggs
1/2 cup buttermilk
1 teaspoon vanilla
  extract
1 teaspoon baking soda
1 cup sugar
1 cup evaporated milk
24 large marshmallows
1 7-ounce package
  coconut
1/2 cup margarine
1 12-ounce package
  semisweet chocolate
  chips
1 cup sliced almonds

Preheat oven to 350 degrees. Mix 2 cups sugar and 2 cups flour in large bowl. Mix water, 1/2 cup margarine, shortening and cocoa in saucepan; bring to a boil. Pour over sugar-flour mixture; mix well. Add next 5 ingredients; mix well. Pour into greased and floured 9-by-13-inch baking pan. Bake for 40 to 45 minutes or until toothpick inserted in center comes out clean. Mix 1 cup sugar, evaporated milk and marshmallows in saucepan. Cook until marshmallows are melted, stirring constantly. Add coconut; pour over hot cake. Melt 1/2 cup margarine and chocolate chips in saucepan; mix well. Add almonds; spread over filling. Yield: 18 to 24 servings.

Barbara Gale, Theta Phi
Terrell, Texas

CHOCOLATE AMARETTO CAKE

1 package devil's food
  cake mix
1 4-ounce package
  instant chocolate
  pudding mix
3/4 cup sour cream
1/2 cup cooking oil
1/2 cup water
1/4 cup mayonnaise
4 eggs
3 tablespoons Amaretto
  liqueur
1 tablespoon almond
  extract
1 cup chocolate chips

Preheat oven to 350 degrees. Combine cake mix and pudding mix in mixer bowl. Stir in next 7 ingredients. Beat for 2 minutes on medium speed. Stir in chocolate chips. Pour into greased and floured bundt pan. Bake for 50 to 55 minutes or until tests done. Let cool in pan for 10 minutes. Yield: 12 servings.

Pamela A. Pecora, Xi Alpha Beta Tau
New Caney, Texas

DECADENT CHOCOLATE BUNDT CAKE

1 2-layer package dark
  chocolate cake mix
1 4-ounce package
  chocolate instant
  pudding mix
4 eggs
1/2 cup vegetable oil
1/2 cup water
1/2 cup sour cream
1 cup semisweet
  chocolate chips
1/2 cup chopped nuts
1/2 cup butter or
  margarine
1/2 cup semisweet
  chocolate chips
Chopped nuts

Prepare and bake first 6 ingredients as for Basic Bundt Cake (page 174), using dark chocolate cake mix and chocolate pudding mix; fold in 1 cup chocolate chips and 1/2 cup nuts. Drizzle cooled cake with mixture of melted butter and 1/2 cup chocolate chips; sprinkle with chopped nuts. Yield: 16 servings.

Barbara Boatright, Delta Kappa Psi
Escondido, California

HEATH BAR BUNDT CAKE

1 2-layer package
  white cake mix
1 4-ounce package
  vanilla instant
  pudding mix
6 egg whites
1/2 cup vegetable oil
1/2 cup water
1/2 cup sour cream
1/2 cup chopped pecans
1/2 cup crushed Heath bars
1/4 cup butter or
  margarine
1/2 cup semisweet
  chocolate chips
Chopped pecans

Prepare and bake first 6 ingredients as for Basic Bundt Cake (page 174), substituting 6 egg whites for eggs; fold in 1/2 cup pecans and Heath bars. Drizzle cooled cake with mixture of melted butter and chocolate chips; sprinkle with chopped pecans. Yield: 16 servings.

Barbara Boatright, Delta Kappa Psi
Escondido, California

HOLLAND RUSK CHOCOLATE DELIGHT CAKE

6 egg yolks
1 cup sugar
1 cup Holland rusk
  crumbs
1 teaspoon baking
  powder
1 cup chopped pecans or
  hickory nuts
1/4 teaspoon salt
1 teaspoon vanilla
  extract
6 egg whites
2 cups whipping cream
1/3 cup confectioners'
  sugar
2 squares bitter
  chocolate
3 egg whites
1 cup confectioners'
  sugar or 2 packages
  whipped topping mix

Preheat oven to 350 degrees. Beat egg yolks in mixer bowl until frothy. Add sugar, crumbs, baking powder, pecans, salt and vanilla; mix well. Beat 6 egg whites in small mixer bowl until stiff; fold into egg yolk mixture. Bake in greased and lightly floured 9-by-13-inch baking pan for 30 minutes or until tests done. Whip whipping cream in mixer bowl. Add 1/3 cup confectioners' sugar, beating until stiff. Spread over cooled cake; refrigerate. Melt chocolate in top of double boiler over hot water; let cool. Beat 3 egg whites in mixer bowl until stiff; fold in 1 cup confectioners' sugar. Add cooled chocolate; spread on top of whipped cream. Refrigerate. Yield: 12 servings.

Gail Engel, Epsilon Beta
Brookfield, Wisconsin

MAYONNAISE CAKE

I was looking for a recipe for mayonnaise cake that did not use eggs. This cake fits the bill quite easily.

2 cups all-purpose flour	1¹/2 cups sugar
¹/2 teaspoon salt	1 tablespoon light corn
1 teaspoon baking	syrup
powder	2 1-ounce squares
1 teaspoon baking soda	unsweetened or
4 tablespoons cocoa	semisweet baking
1 cup sugar	chocolate
³/4 cup mayonnaise	7 tablespoons milk
1 cup water	2 tablespoons butter or
¹/2 teaspoon vanilla	margarine
extract	¹/8 teaspoon salt
2 tablespoons	1 teaspoon vanilla
shortening	extract

Preheat oven to 350 degrees. Sift first 6 ingredients together 4 times into large bowl. Stir in mayonnaise, water and vanilla. Pour into 2 greased and floured 8- or 9-inch cake pans. Bake for 30 to 40 minutes or until layers test done. Combine next 7 ingredients in large saucepan. Bring to a rolling boil over low heat; boil for 1 minute. Remove from heat; cool to room temperature. Add vanilla; beat until smooth and of spreading consistency. Frost cooled cake. Yield: 12 servings.

Barbara Howe, Xi Omicron Gamma
Sacramento, California

❖ MURDER BY CHOCOLATE

16 1-ounce squares	6 1-ounce squares
semisweet baking	semisweet baking
chocolate, coarsely	chocolate
chopped	3 tablespoons butter
1 cup sugar	2 tablespoons half and
2 cups butter	half
1 tablespoon vanilla	2 tablespoons light corn
extract	syrup
1 cup half and half	Whipped cream
Dash of salt	Fruit
6 eggs	

Preheat oven to 350 degrees. Combine 16 ounces chocolate, sugar, 2 cups butter, vanilla, 1 cup half and half and salt in heavy saucepan. Cook over low heat, stirring occasionally, until melted. Beat eggs slightly with whisk in large bowl. Add warm chocolate mixture slowly to beaten eggs, whisking until smooth. Line bottom of 9-inch springform pan with aluminum foil; butter foil and side of pan. Pour batter into prepared pan. Bake for 40 to 45 minutes or until toothpick inserted in 2-inch area around edge comes out clean. Middle will look loosely set, almost unbaked; cake will set after refrigeration. Remove cake from oven; let cool at room temperature. Center may crack as it cools. Refrigerate in pan until chilled. Combine 6 ounces chocolate and 3 tablespoons butter

in heavy saucepan or top of double boiler over hot water; stir until melted. Add 2 tablespoons half and half and corn syrup; mix well. Remove side of springform pan; pour glaze over top and side of cake. Refrigerate until glaze is set. Garnish with whipped cream or fruit. Yield: 12 servings.

Shirley Welch, Psi Iota
Theodosia, Missouri

SAUERKRAUT CHOCOLATE CAKE

I gave a program on "weird foods" and served this for dessert without telling what it was! Everyone loved it.

1¹/2 cups sugar	1 teaspoon baking soda
²/3 cup butter or	1 teaspoon baking
margarine	powder
3 eggs	¹/4 teaspoon salt
1 teaspoon vanilla	1 cup water
extract	²/3 cup chopped
2¹/4 cups all-purpose	sauerkraut, rinsed,
flour	well drained
¹/2 cup cocoa	

Preheat oven to 350 degrees. Cream sugar and butter in large mixer bowl. Beat in eggs and vanilla. Sift dry ingredients together into bowl. Add dry ingredients alternately with water to creamed mixture. Stir in sauerkraut. Pour into greased and floured 9-by-13-inch baking pan. Bake for 30 minutes or until tests done. Yield: 12 to 15 servings.

JoAnne Thornton, Preceptor Alpha Psi
Kingman, Arizona

CRANBERRY CAKE

1 cup margarine	1 16-ounce can whole
1 cup sugar	berry cranberry sauce
2 eggs	¹/2 cup chopped pecans
2 cups self-rising flour	1 cup confectioners' sugar
8 ounces sour cream	2 tablespoons milk
¹/2 teaspoon almond	¹/2 teaspoon vanilla
extract	extract

Preheat oven to 350 degrees. Cream margarine and sugar in mixer bowl until light and fluffy. Beat in eggs 1 at a time. Add flour to creamed mixture alternately with sour cream, beating well after each addition. Add almond extract; mix well. Spoon ¹/3 of the batter into greased and floured 10-inch tube pan. Spread ¹/3 of the cranberry sauce over batter. Repeat for 2 more layers, ending with cranberry sauce. Sprinkle pecans over top. Bake for 1 hour or until cake tests done. Let cool for 5 minutes; remove from pan. Combine remaining ingredients in mixer bowl; beat until of spreading consistency. Spread glaze over cake. Yield: 10 to 12 servings.

George Ann Jackson, Chi Lambda
Crystal River, Florida
*Doris Nickoles, Preceptor Omicron
Ashton, Maryland

FRUIT COCKTAIL CAKE

2 cups all-purpose flour
1 1/2 cups sugar
1 teaspoon baking soda
1/4 teaspoon salt
1 16-ounce can fruit
    cocktail
2 eggs, beaten
1/2 cup packed light
    brown sugar
1 cup chopped nuts
1/2 cup margarine,
    melted
1 1/4 cups sugar
1/2 teaspoon vanilla
    extract
1 small can evaporated
    milk

Preheat oven to 350 degrees. Combine first 6 ingredients in mixer bowl; mix well. Pour batter into greased 9-by-13-inch baking pan; sprinkle with brown sugar and nuts. Bake for 40 to 45 minutes or until cake tests done. Combine margarine, sugar, vanilla and milk in saucepan; mix well. Boil for 2 minutes, beating well. Pour over warm cake. Yield: 12 servings.

Evelyn F. Whitely, Beta Epsilon Omicron
Brackettville, Texas

GINGERBREAD

I remember the aroma of my mother's gingerbread filling our home during the fall and winter months. She would bring out a jar of Bartlett pears from the pantry that she had canned to make a delicious duo.

1 cup packed dark
    brown sugar
1/2 cup butter or
    margarine
1/2 cup molasses
1 egg
1 1/2 cups all-purpose
    flour
1/2 teaspoon ginger
1 1/2 teaspoons baking
    powder
1/4 teaspoon salt
1 cup boiling water
Home-canned pears
Whipped cream

Preheat oven to 350 degrees. Cream sugar and butter in mixer bowl until light. Add molasses and egg; beat thoroughly. Sift dry ingredients together into bowl. Add to creamed mixture alternately with water, beating after each addition. Pour into greased and lightly floured 8-inch square baking pan. Bake for 35 to 40 minutes or until cake tests done. Serve warm with home-canned pears and topped with whipped cream. Yield: 8 to 10 servings.

Theresa Trunnell, Xi Pi Nu
Chico, California

TART LEMON BUNDT CAKE

1 2-layer package
    lemon cake mix
1 4-ounce package
    instant lemon
    pudding mix
4 eggs
1/2 cup vegetable oil
1/2 cup sour cream
1/4 cup lemon juice
1/4 cup water
Grated rind of 1 lemon
1/2 cup toasted sliced
    almonds
Lemon juice
Confectioners' sugar
Lemon zest

Prepare and bake first 6 ingredients as for Basic Bundt Cake (page 174), using lemon cake mix and lemon pudding mix, substituting 1/4 cup lemon juice for part of the water; fold in grated lemon rind and almonds. Poke holes in warm cake and drizzle with mixture of lemon juice and confectioners' sugar; top with lemon zest. Yield: 16 servings.

Barbara Boatright, Delta Kappa Psi
Escondido, California

MILK DUD CAKE

Everyone who tries this unusual cake cannot stop talking about it. It is so very different.

48 milk duds
1/2 cup milk
1 cup confectioners'
    sugar
2 tablespoons butter or
    margarine
6 egg yolks
1 cup sugar
1 cup Holland rusk
    crumbs
1/2 cup chopped nuts
1 teaspoon baking
    powder
1 teaspoon vanilla
    extract
6 egg whites
1 8-ounce carton
    whipped topping

Preheat oven to 350 degrees. Combine first 4 ingredients in saucepan. Heat until melted; do not boil. Let cool completely. Mix next 6 ingredients in large bowl. Beat egg whites in mixer bowl until stiff; fold gently into egg mixture. Pour batter into greased and floured 9-by-13-inch baking pan. Bake for 30 minutes; let cool completely. Spread whipped topping over cake. Pour caramel sauce over top; let cool. Yield: 12 servings.

Stacey L. Middlecamp, Eta Epsilon
Muskegon, Michigan

MANDARIN ORANGE CAKE

I served this cake the first time I had a chapter meeting at my house. It was a hit!

1 package yellow cake
    mix
1 cup vegetable oil
4 eggs
1 11-ounce can
    mandarin oranges
    with juice, chopped
1 20-ounce can crushed
    pineapple with juice
1 package vanilla
    instant pudding mix
1 8 or 9-ounce carton
    whipped topping

Preheat oven to 350 degrees. Combine cake mix, oil and eggs in mixer bowl; mix for 2 minutes. Stir in oranges. Pour into greased and floured 9-by-13-inch baking pan. Bake for 35 minutes; let cool. Mix pineapple, pudding mix and whipped topping in bowl. Spread on cooled cake. Store in refrigerator. Yield: 12 servings.

Susan Mages, Xi Alpha Epsilon
Durango, Colorado

ORANGE SUNSHINE BUNDT CAKE

1 2-layer white or
   yellow cake mix
1 4-ounce package
   vanilla instant
   pudding mix
4 eggs
1/2 cup vegetable oil
1/2 cup sour cream
1/2 cup orange juice
   Confectioners' sugar
   Orange juice
   Orange zest

Prepare and bake first 6 ingredients as for Basic
Bundt Cake (page 174), substituting 1/2 cup orange
juice for water. Drizzle with mixture of confectioners' sugar and additional orange juice; sprinkle
with orange zest. Yield: 16 servings.

Barbara Boatright, Delta Kappa Psi
Escondido, California

❖ ORANGE NUGGETS

These are wonderful and different.

1 18-ounce package
   orange supreme cake
   mix
3 eggs
1/3 cup vegetable oil
1 cup fresh orange
   juice
1 11-ounce can
   mandarin oranges,
   drained, chopped
2 cups confectioners'
   sugar
1/2 cup fresh orange
   juice

Preheat oven to 350 degrees. Combine cake mix,
eggs, oil and orange juice in mixer bowl; beat for 2
to 3 minutes or until well blended. Fold in oranges.
Pour into greased miniature muffin cups. Bake for 10
to 14 minutes or until muffins test done. Let cool
slightly in pan. Combine confectioners' sugar and
orange juice in mixer bowl; beat until smooth. Dip
each muffin in glaze. Yield: 8 dozen nuggets.

Nancy D. Hunt, Zeta Alpha
Fredonia, Kentucky

PEANUT BUTTER CUPCAKES

1 3/4 cups all-purpose
   flour
1 cup milk
3/4 cup sugar
1/2 cup peanut butter
1/4 cup shortening
1 tablespoon baking
   powder
3/4 teaspoon vanilla
   extract
1/2 teaspoon salt
2 eggs

Preheat oven to 350 degrees. Combine flour, milk,
sugar, peanut butter, shortening, baking powder,
vanilla, salt and eggs into large mixer bowl. Beat at
low speed until well blended; beat at high speed for
2 minutes. Spoon into paper-lined muffin cups. Bake
for 18 to 20 minutes or until toothpick inserted in
center comes out clean. Yield: 24 cupcakes.

Lisa Graff, Theta Xi
Crescent, Oklahoma
*Cindy Rank, Delta Psi
Clare, Michigan

CHOCOLATE CHIP-PEANUT BUTTER CAKE

2 1/4 cups all-purpose
   flour
2 cups packed light
   brown sugar
1 cup peanut butter
1/2 cup butter or
   margarine, softened
1 teaspoon baking
   powder
1/2 teaspoon baking soda
1 cup milk
1 teaspoon vanilla
   extract
3 eggs
1 cup semisweet
   chocolate chips

Preheat oven to 350 degrees. Combine first 4 ingredients in large mixer bowl; blend at low speed
until crumbly. Reserve 1 cup mixture. Add next 5
ingredients. Blend at low speed until moistened; beat
for 3 minutes at medium speed. Pour into greased
and floured 9-by-13-inch baking pan. Sprinkle with
reserved mixture. Sprinkle chocolate chips over top.
Yield: 12 servings.

F. Elizabeth Ennis, Xi Epsilon Eta
Gainesville, Virginia

GOLDEN PINEAPPLE LAYER CAKE

1 20-ounce can crushed
   pineapple with juice
1 8-ounce carton
   whipped topping,
   thawed
1/2 teaspoon almond
   extract
1 small package vanilla
   instant pudding mix
1 16-ounce frozen
   pound cake, thawed
1/3 cup almond-flavored
   liqueur or 1/3 cup
   pineapple juice
   Slivered almonds
   (optional)

Combine pineapple, whipped topping, pudding mix
and almond extract in large bowl; let stand for 5
minutes. Cut cake lengthwise into thirds; drizzle
with liqueur. Spread 1/3 pudding mixture over bottom layer. Top with second layer; repeat layering,
ending with pudding mixture. Chill for 30 minutes.
Sprinkle with almonds. Yield: 12 servings.

Jan Brawdy, Beta Omicron
Petersburg, Indiana

APPLESAUCE POUND CAKE

*This cake contains no eggs and is great for people who
are watching their cholesterol.*

1 large box raisins
1 cup margarine or
   3/4 cup vegetable oil
2 cups sugar
4 cups self-rising flour
1 teaspoon cinnamon
1 teaspoon ground
   cloves
1 teaspoon nutmeg
1 teaspoon baking soda
2 cups applesauce

Preheat oven to 350 degrees. Place raisins in medium
bowl; cover with warm water. Cream margarine and
sugar in mixer bowl. Combine dry ingredients in
bowl. Add dry ingredients to creamed mixture alter-

nately with applesauce. Drain raisins; fold into batter. Pour into greased and floured tube pan; bake for 1 hour and 15 minutes or until cake tests done. Yield: 12 to 16 servings.

Carolyn Hardin, Zeta Theta
Spindale, North Carolina

BLACKBERRY POUND CAKE

1 package yellow cake mix	*2 cups blackberries*
	4 eggs
1 3-ounce package blackberry gelatin	*³⁄4 cup cooking oil*

Preheat oven to 350 degrees. Combine all ingredients in mixer bowl; mix until well blended. Pour into greased and floured tube pan. Bake for 30 to 45 minutes or until cake tests done. May serve warm with whipped topping if desired. Yield: 12 servings.

Shirley Ofsa, Preceptor Alpha Upsilon
Northfork, West Virginia

COCONUT POUND CAKE

1 cup butter or margarine, softened	*¹⁄2 teaspoon baking powder*
¹⁄2 cup shortening	*1 can cream of coconut*
2¹⁄2 cups sugar	*1 teaspoon lemon juice*
5 eggs	*1 teaspoon vanilla*
3 cups all-purpose flour	*extract*

Preheat oven to 350 degrees. Blend butter and shortening in mixer bowl. Add remaining ingredients; mix well. Pour into greased and floured bundt pan. Bake for 1 hour and 15 minutes or until cake tests done. Yield: 12 servings.

Thyra Strate, Xi Zeta Omega
Lewis, Kansas

LEMON POUND CAKE

4 eggs	*1 18-ounce package yellow cake mix*
³⁄4 cup water	
¹⁄2 cup salad oil	*2 cups confectioners' sugar*
1 4-ounce package instant lemon pudding mix	*¹⁄3 cup lemon juice*

Preheat oven to 350 degrees. Beat eggs in mixer bowl until thick and lemon colored. Add water, oil, pudding mix and cake mix; mix well. Pour into greased and floured 10-inch tube pan with bottom lined with brown paper. Bake for 50 minutes or until cake tests done. Combine sugar and lemon juice in saucepan. Bring to a boil; boil until clear. Remove cake from oven; turn onto plate immediately. Remove brown paper; punch holes in cake. Pour glaze over hot cake. Yield: 16 servings.

Billie B. Washburn, Preceptor Delta Sigma
Tampa, Florida

LEMON DELIGHT POUND CAKE

2¹⁄2 cups all-purpose flour	*³⁄4 cup cooking oil*
1¹⁄2 cups sugar	*2 teaspoons lemon extract*
3 teaspoons baking powder	*4 eggs*
¹⁄2 teaspoon salt	*1¹⁄2 cups confectioners' sugar*
³⁄4 cup apricot nectar	*¹⁄2 cup lemon juice*

Preheat oven to 325 degrees. Combine first 8 ingredients in mixer bowl; beat for 3 minutes at medium speed. Pour into greased fluted tube pan. Bake for 40 to 50 minutes or until toothpick inserted in center comes out clean. Prick top deeply at 1-inch intervals with fork. Blend confectioners' sugar and lemon juice in mixer bowl until smooth. Spoon half of glaze over hot cake in pan. Let stand for 10 minutes. Invert onto serving plate. Spoon remaining glaze over cake. Yield: 10 servings.

Gloria Davis Cobb, Alpha Alpha
Decatur, Alabama

RED VELVET POUND CAKE

When featured as "Cook of the Week" in our local paper, this is the recipe that so many people called me or stopped me on the street to let me know how much they enjoyed it. This is also the cake I take to many social functions at special requests.

1¹⁄2 cups vegetable shortening	*1 cup warm milk*
3 cups sugar	*2 teaspoons vanilla extract*
7 eggs	*1 ounce red food coloring*
3 cups sifted all-purpose flour	*Cream Cheese Frosting*
¹⁄2 teaspoon salt	

Preheat oven to 325 degrees. Cream shortening and sugar in mixer bowl. Add eggs, 1 at a time, beating well after each addition. Beat for 3 minutes. Combine flour and salt in bowl; add to creamed mixture alternately with milk, beginning and ending with flour mixture. Add vanilla and food coloring; blend well. Pour into large greased tube pan. Bake for 1 hour and 15 minutes or until cake tests done. Frost with Cream Cheese Frosting. May sprinkle with nuts if desired. Yield: 12 servings.

CREAM CHEESE FROSTING

¹⁄2 cup margarine	*3 ounces cream cheese, softened*
1 teaspoon salt	
1 teaspoon vanilla extract	*1 box confectioners' sugar*

Blend all ingredients in mixer bowl. Yield: 2 to 3 cups.

Eleanor Heath, Laureate Pi
LaGrange, Georgia

SOUR CREAM POUND CAKE

1 cup butter	3 cups sifted
3 cups sugar	all-purpose flour
6 eggs, separated	1 cup sour cream
1/4 teaspoon baking soda	

Preheat oven to 300 degrees. Cream butter and sugar in mixer bowl. Beat in egg yolks 1 at a time. Sift baking soda and flour together 2 times into bowl. Add flour mixture and sour cream alternately to creamed mixture, beating well after each addition. Beat egg whites in mixer bowl until stiff; fold into batter. Pour into greased and floured bundt pan. Bake for 1 1/2 hours or until cake tests done. Remove from pan immediately. Yield: 10 to 12 servings.

Janis Young, Epsilon Tau
Louisville, Kentucky

TEXAS POUND CAKE

1 1/2 cups margarine, at room temperature	1 package frozen strawberries, thawed (optional)
1 box confectioners' sugar	1 8-ounce can pineapple, drained (optional)
6 eggs, at room temperature	
3 1/2 cups all-purpose flour	1 cup applesauce with 1 tablespoon cinnamon (optional)
1 tablespoon vanilla extract	1 cup broken nuts
2 small bananas, mashed (optional)	

Preheat oven to 325 degrees. Cream margarine in mixer bowl until light and fluffy. Add confectioners' sugar; beat until creamy. Add eggs, 1 at a time, beating well after each addition. Sift flour 3 times in bowl; mix into creamed mixture, 3/4 cup at a time. Add vanilla, any optional ingredients and nuts. Pour into greased and floured bundt pan. Bake for 2 hours or until cake tests done. May serve with whipped topping or ice cream if desired. Yield: 16 to 20 servings.

M. Anne Shelton, Preceptor Delta
Phoenix, Arizona

RASPBERRY TEA MUFFINS

1 cup packed light brown sugar	1 teaspoon baking powder
1/2 cup cooking oil	1 teaspoon baking soda
1 egg	1/2 cup chopped pecans
2 teaspoons vanilla extract	1/2 cup packed dark brown sugar
1 cup buttermilk	1/4 cup all-purpose flour
1 1/2 cups frozen chopped raspberries	1 teaspoon cinnamon
1 cup all-purpose flour	2 tablespoons butter or margarine, melted
1 1/2 cups whole wheat flour	

Preheat oven to 400 degrees. Combine brown sugar, oil, egg and vanilla in large mixer bowl; beat until well blended. Stir in buttermilk and raspberries. Combine next 4 ingredients in bowl; add all at once to raspberry mixture. Stir until well blended. Fill greased muffin cups 2/3 full. Combine remaining ingredients in bowl; mix well. Sprinkle evenly over muffins. Bake for 20 minutes. Yield: 24 muffins.

Karen Kretzul, Xi Kappa
Nanaimo, British Columbia, Canada

RHUBARB CRUMB CAKE

Rhubarb is the first thing to grow in our garden every spring, so this cake is our celebration that winter is over and spring is here.

1/2 cup sugar	1/2 cup sour cream
1 teaspoon cinnamon	2 cups sifted all-purpose flour
1 tablespoon butter or margarine	1 1/2 cups rhubarb, cut into 1/2-inch cubes
1/2 cup shortening	1 teaspoon vanilla extract
1 1/2 cups packed light brown sugar	
1 egg	1/2 cup chopped nuts (optional)
1 teaspoon baking soda	

Preheat oven to 350 degrees. Mix sugar, cinnamon and butter in bowl. Cream shortening and brown sugar in mixer bowl. Stir in egg; blend well. Combine baking soda and sour cream in bowl. Add to creamed mixture alternately with flour. Stir in rhubarb and vanilla. Pour into greased 9-by-13-inch baking pan. Sprinkle with cinnamon mixture and nuts. Bake for 35 to 40 minutes or until cake tests done. Yield: 12 to 15 servings.

Mickie Fichtner, Xi Epsilon Alpha
Veradale, Washington

ROOT BEER CAKE

1 cup sugar	1 teaspoon salt
1/2 cup butter or margarine	2 cups all-purpose flour
2 eggs	2/3 cup root beer
1/2 teaspoon vanilla extract	1 package icing mix
1 teaspoon baking powder	1 cup root beer

Preheat oven to 375 degrees. Cream sugar and butter in mixer bowl. Add eggs and vanilla; mix well. Add baking powder and salt; mix well. Add flour and 2/3 cup root beer alternately; mix well. Pour into greased and floured 9-by-13-inch baking pan. Bake for 30 to 35 minutes or until tests done. Blend icing mix and remaining 1 cup root beer in mixer bowl; beat until smooth. Spread on cake. Yield: 12 to 15 servings.

Suzanne Moore, Delta Nu
Columbia, South Carolina

The Cookie Monster

POLBORONES

1¹/₂ cups sugar
3 cups vegetable
  shortening
1 teaspoon anise extract

5 cups all-purpose flour
1 teaspoon baking
  powder
4 cups ground almonds

Preheat oven to 350 degrees. Cream sugar, shortening and anise extract in mixer bowl. Add flour, baking powder and almonds. Knead until all ingredients are mixed. Roll out into ¹/₂-inch thick square. Cut diagonally forming small diamonds. Bake on ungreased cookie sheets for 15 minutes or until lightly browned. Yield: 9 to 10 dozen cookies.

Louise Stith, Preceptor Gamma Psi
Vacaville, California

BEST-EVER BAR COOKIES

1 cup boiling water
¹/₂ cup snipped dried
  apricots
1 cup all-purpose flour
¹/₂ teaspoon baking
  powder
¹/₄ teaspoon baking soda
¹/₄ cup butter or
  margarine
¹/₂ cup packed light
  brown sugar
1 egg
¹/₂ teaspoon finely
  shredded lime peel

1 tablespoon lime juice
¹/₂ cup milk
¹/₂ cup finely chopped
  walnuts
1¹/₂ cups confectioners'
  sugar
1 tablespoon butter or
  margarine
1 tablespoon lime juice
¹/₄ teaspoon lime peel
Milk

Preheat oven to 350 degrees. Pour boiling water over apricots to cover in bowl. Let stand for 5 minutes; drain. Stir flour, baking powder and baking soda together in bowl. Beat ¹/₄ cup butter in mixer bowl for 30 seconds. Add brown sugar; beat until fluffy. Add egg, ¹/₂ teaspoon lime peel and 1 tablespoon lime juice; beat well. Add dry ingredients to mixture alternately with milk. Fold in apricots and walnuts. Spread evenly in greased 7-by-12-inch baking pan. Bake for 20 to 25 minutes or until tests done. Let cool. Combine next 4 ingredients in small mixer bowl. Add enough milk to make of spreading consistency. Beat until well blended. Spread over cake; cut into bars. Yield: 28 bars.

Loy Bressler, Preceptor Sigma
Roswell, New Mexico

BANANA BARS

¹/₄ cup shortening
1 cup packed light
  brown sugar
¹/₂ teaspoon vanilla
  extract
¹/₂ teaspoon lemon
  extract
1 cup mashed ripe
  banana

1¹/₂ cups sifted
  all-purpose flour
1¹/₂ teaspoons baking
  powder
¹/₂ teaspoon salt
¹/₂ cup chopped nuts
¹/₂ cup confectioners'
  sugar
1 teaspoon cinnamon

Preheat oven to 350 degrees. Combine first 5 ingredients in mixer bowl; beat well. Sift next 3 ingredients together in bowl; add to creamed mixture, mixing well. Stir in nuts. Pour into greased 7-by-11-inch baking pan. Bake for 30 to 35 minutes or until tests done. Cut into bars while warm. Mix confectioners' sugar and cinnamon in bowl. Roll bars gently in sugar-cinnamon mixture. Yield: 24 bars.

Ruth M. Fountain, Beta Omega
Savannah, Missouri

BUTTERSCOTCH BROWNIES

1/4 cup butter or margarine	1 teaspoon baking powder
1 cup packed light brown sugar	1/2 teaspoon salt
1 egg	1/2 teaspoon vanilla extract
3/4 cup all-purpose flour	1/2 cup chopped walnuts

Preheat oven to 350 degrees. Melt butter in saucepan over low heat; remove from heat. Stir in brown sugar until blended; let cool. Stir in egg. Sift flour, baking powder and salt together in bowl; add to mixture. Stir in vanilla and walnuts. Spread in well-greased 8-inch square glass baking dish. Bake for 25 minutes or until tests done. Yield: 12 servings.

Cindy Fane, Tau Phi
Sterling, Illinois

EASY BROWNIES

2 3-ounce packages chocolate pudding mix	2/3 cup salad oil
	4 eggs
1 cup sugar	1/2 cup nuts (optional)
1 cup all-purpose flour	

Preheat oven to 350 degrees. Mix all ingredients in mixer bowl. Pour into greased 9-by-13-inch baking pan. Bake for 35 minutes or until tests done. Let cool; cut into squares. Yield: 15 to 20 brownies.

Joyce E. Miller, Xi Zeta Eta
St. John, Kansas

NO-BAKE BROWNIES

1/2 cup butter or margarine	1 teaspoon vanilla extract
1/2 cup sugar	30 arrowroot biscuits, crushed
1/4 cup cocoa	
2 eggs, slightly beaten	Chocolate Velvet Frosting
1 cup chopped walnuts	

Mix butter, sugar, cocoa and eggs in top of double boiler. Cook, stirring, over medium heat until thickened. Remove from heat; add walnuts and vanilla, mixing thoroughly. Add crushed biscuits; spoon into well-greased 8-inch square pan. Chill; ice with Chocolate Velvet Frosting. Yield: 16 brownies.

CHOCOLATE VELVET FROSTING

2 ounces unsweetened chocolate	1 cup plus 2 tablespoons confectioners' sugar
1 tablespoon plus 1 1/2 teaspoons butter or margarine	1/4 cup light cream
	1/2 teaspoon vanilla extract

Melt chocolate and butter in top of double boiler over hot water. Remove from heat; add remaining ingredients. Pour into mixer bowl; beat until of cool and of spreading consistency. Yield: 1 to 1 1/2 cups.

Mary-Frances Lessard, Alpha Zeta
Calgary, Alberta, Canada

ZUCCHINI CAKE-BROWNIES

This recipe was given to me by another Beta Sigma Phi sister. She helped me with ideas when I was overwhelmed with a bumper crop of zucchini!

Milk	1/2 cup cocoa
1 egg	2 cups grated zucchini
1 1/2 cups sugar	2 1/2 cups confectioners' sugar
1/2 cup cooking oil	
2 teaspoons vanilla extract	1/3 cup cocoa
	1/3 cup margarine, melted
2 cups all-purpose flour	2 to 4 tablespoons milk
1 teaspoon salt	
1 1/2 teaspoons baking soda	

Add enough milk to egg to make 1/2 cup liquid. Beat egg mixture, sugar, oil and vanilla in large bowl by hand. Combine flour, salt, baking soda and cocoa in bowl; add to liquid mixture. Stir in zucchini. Pour into greased 9-by-13-inch baking pan. Bake for 30 minutes or until tests done. Let cool. Blend confectioners' sugar, cocoa and margarine in mixer bowl; add milk until of desired consistency. Frost brownies; cut into squares. Yield: 12 to 16 brownies.

Cathy Lynch, Beta Nu
Encampment, Wyoming

CHOCOLATE REVEL BARS

1 cup butter or margarine	3 cups oatmeal
2 cups packed light brown sugar	1 12-ounce package chocolate chips
2 eggs	1 15-ounce can sweetened condensed milk
2 teaspoons vanilla extract	
2 1/2 cups all-purpose flour	2 tablespoons butter or margarine
1 teaspoon baking soda	1/2 teaspoon salt
1 teaspoon salt	1/2 teaspoon vanilla extract

Preheat oven to 350 degrees. Cream 1 cup butter and brown sugar in mixer bowl. Mix in eggs and 2 teaspoons vanilla. Stir in flour, baking soda, 1 teaspoon salt and oatmeal. Combine chocolate chips, condensed milk, 2 tablespoons butter, 1/2 teaspoon salt and 1/2 teaspoon vanilla in microwave-safe bowl; microwave until melted. Beat until smooth. Spread 2/3 batter in greased 10-by-15-inch baking pan. Cover with chocolate filling. Dot with remaining batter. Bake for 25 to 30 minutes or until tests done. Yield: 24 bars.

Teddie Farnsworth, Preceptor Delta Phi
Jefferson City, Missouri
*Karrie Beach, Xi Beta Lambda
Syracuse, Nebraska

CARAMEL APPLE OAT SQUARES

1³/4 cups unsifted all-purpose flour	1 cup cold margarine
1 cup quick-cooking oats	1 cup chopped walnuts
¹/2 cup packed light brown sugar	20 caramels
¹/2 teaspoon baking soda	1 14-ounce can sweetened condensed milk
¹/2 teaspoon salt	1 21-ounce can apple pie filling

Preheat oven to 375 degrees. Combine flour, oats, brown sugar, baking soda and salt in large bowl. Cut in margarine until crumbly; reserve 1¹/2 cups mixture. Press remaining mixture in bottom of 9-by-13-inch baking pan. Bake for 15 minutes. Add walnuts to reserved crumb mixture. Combine caramels and condensed milk in heavy saucepan; cook over low heat until caramels are melted, stirring until smooth. Spoon apple filling over prepared crust. Top with caramel mixture and reserved crumb mixture. Bake for 20 minutes or until set; let cool. Yield: 10 to 12 servings.

Debbie Corbett, Nu Phi Mu
Goodland, Kansas

❖ LEMON COCONUT BARS

1¹/2 cups all-purpose flour	2 tablespoons all-purpose flour
¹/2 cup packed light brown sugar	¹/2 teaspoon baking powder
¹/2 cup margarine	¹/2 teaspoon vanilla extract
2 eggs	1 cup confectioners' sugar
1 cup packed light brown sugar	
1¹/2 cups coconut	1 tablespoon butter or margarine, melted
1 cup chopped nuts	
¹/4 teaspoon salt	Juice of 1 lemon

Preheat oven to 275 degrees. Combine first 3 ingredients in bowl; mix well. Press into greased 9-by-13-inch baking pan. Bake for 10 minutes; remove from oven. Increase oven temperature to 350 degrees. Beat eggs in mixer bowl; add next 7 ingredients, mixing well. Spread over crust; bake for 20 minutes. Combine remaining ingredients in mixer bowl; beat until of spreading consistency. Spread over warm cake; cut into bars. Yield: 24 bars.

Diane Bowren, Preceptor Omega
Waterford, Michigan

PEACH SQUARES

1 cup butter or margarine	2 egg whites
¹/2 cup sugar	¹/2 teaspoon almond extract
¹/2 teaspoon vanilla extract	1 cup powdered fruit sugar
2 cups all-purpose flour	¹/2 cup slivered almonds
1¹/2 cups peach jam	

Preheat oven to 350 degrees. Cream butter, sugar and vanilla in mixer bowl until fluffy. Stir in flour; mix well. Spread in ungreased 9-by-13-inch baking pan. Bake for 15 minutes; let cool. Spread jam over crust. Beat egg whites and almond extract in mixer bowl until soft peaks form. Add fruit sugar; beat until stiff. Spread over jam. Sprinkle with almonds. Bake for 15 to 20 minutes or until tests done. Cut into squares. Yield: 24 squares.

Joann Templeton, Xi Zeta Theta
Pickering, Ontario, Canada

PEANUT BUTTER BARS

¹/2 cup butter or margarine	¹/2 teaspoon vanilla extract
¹/2 cup sugar	1 cup all-purpose flour
¹/2 cup packed light brown sugar	1 cup quick oats
1 egg	1 cup chocolate chips
¹/3 cup peanut butter	¹/2 cup confectioners' sugar
¹/2 teaspoon baking soda	¹/4 cup peanut butter
¹/4 teaspoon salt	4 tablespoons milk

Preheat oven to 350 degrees. Cream first 3 ingredients in mixer bowl. Add next 7 ingredients; mix well. Spread in greased 9-by-13-inch baking pan. Bake for 20 to 25 minutes or until tests done. Sprinkle chocolate chips on top while warm; spread evenly. Combine remaining ingredients in mixer bowl; blend well. Drizzle on top. Cut into squares. Yield: 24 bars.

Connie Brown, Pi Eta
Castalia, Ohio

PECAN PIE SQUARES

3 cups all-purpose flour	1¹/2 cups light or dark corn syrup
¹/4 cup plus 2 tablespoons sugar	3 tablespoons margarine or butter, melted
³/4 cup margarine or butter, softened	
³/4 teaspoon salt	1¹/2 teaspoons vanilla extract
4 eggs, slightly beaten	
1¹/2 cups sugar	2¹/2 cups chopped pecans

Preheat oven to 350 degrees. Beat flour, ¹/4 cup plus 2 tablespoons sugar, ³/4 cup margarine and salt in large mixer bowl at medium speed until crumbly. Press firmly in greased 10-by-15-inch baking pan. Bake for 20 minutes or until light golden brown. Mix eggs, remaining 1¹/2 cups sugar, corn syrup, remaining 3 tablespoons margarine and vanilla in mixer bowl until well blended. Stir in pecans. Spread evenly over baked layer. Bake for 25 minutes or until filling is set; let cool. Cut into 1¹/2-inch squares. Yield: 70 squares.

Jaynece Tekippe, Xi Eta Alpha
Fort Atkinson, Iowa

VACUUM CLEANER COOKIES

1/2 cup margarine, melted	1 1-pound box confectioners' sugar
1 box yellow cake mix	1/2 cup flaked coconut
3 eggs	1/2 cup chopped walnuts or pecans
8 ounces cream cheese, softened	

Preheat oven to 325 degrees. Combine margarine, cake mix and 1 egg in large bowl, stirring until dry ingredients are moistened. Press mixture into bottom of well-greased 10-by-15-inch baking pan. Beat remaining eggs lightly in mixer bowl. Beat in cream cheese and confectioners' sugar. Stir in coconut and walnuts. Spread evenly over mixture in baking pan. Bake for 45 to 50 minutes or until browned. Let cool to room temperature; cut into bars. Yield: 48 bars.

Marilynn Kirchner, Preceptor Beta Epsilon
Needles, California

APRICOT JEWELS

1 1/4 cups all-purpose flour	3 ounces cream cheese
1/4 cup sugar	1/2 cup coconut
1 1/2 teaspoons baking powder	1/2 cup apricot preserves
	1 cup confectioners' sugar
1/4 teaspoon salt	1 tablespoon butter or margarine
1/2 cup butter or margarine	1/4 cup apricot preserves

Preheat oven to 350 degrees. Sift first 4 ingredients together in bowl. Cut in butter and cream cheese. Add coconut and preserves. Drop by teaspoonfuls onto greased cookie sheet. Bake for 15 to 18 minutes or until lightly browned; let cool. Combine remaining ingredients in mixer bowl; blend well. Frost cookies. Yield: 36 to 48 cookies.

Sandy Stubblefield, Beta Omega
Savannah, Missouri

BANANA-CHOCOLATE CHIP COOKIES

2/3 cup shortening	2 1/4 cups all-purpose flour
2/3 cup sugar	
2 eggs	2 teaspoons baking powder
2/3 cup mashed banana	
1/3 cup milk	1/4 teaspoon baking soda
1 teaspoon vanilla extract	1/2 teaspoon salt
	1 cup chocolate chips

Preheat oven to 400 degrees. Cream shortening, sugar and eggs in mixer bowl. Add banana, milk and vanilla; mix well. Combine dry ingredients in bowl. Add to liquid mixture; mix well. Stir in chocolate chips. Drop by teaspoonfuls onto greased cookie sheet. Bake for 10 to 12 minutes or until lightly browned. Yield: 48 cookies.

Catherine Kershaw, Xi Alpha Epsilon
Durango, Colorado

BLACK FOREST COOKIES

1 1/2 cups all-purpose flour	1 egg
1/2 cup cocoa	1 1/2 teaspoons vanilla extract
1/4 teaspoon baking powder	1 10-ounce jar maraschino cherries
1/4 teaspoon baking soda	6 ounces chocolate chipits
1/2 cup soft butter or margarine	1/2 cup sweetened condensed milk
1 cup sugar	

Preheat oven to 350 degrees. Sift dry ingredients together in bowl. Cream butter and sugar in mixer bowl. Add egg and vanilla; beat well. Add dry ingredients; mix until well blended. Shape into 1-inch balls; place on ungreased cookie sheet. Make thumbprint in center of each ball. Drain cherries, reserving juice. Place cherry in center of each cookie. Combine chocolate chipits and condensed milk in heavy saucepan. Heat until chocolate chipits become softened. Stir in 4 teaspoons cherry juice. Spoon 1 teaspoonful of mixture on top each cookie to cover cherry. Yield: 48 cookies.

Yvette Wright, Alpha Rho
Estevan, Saskatchewan, Canada

BROWN SUGAR COOKIES

1/2 cup butter or margarine, melted	1 3/4 cups all-purpose flour
3/4 cup packed light brown sugar	1/2 teaspoon baking soda
	1/2 teaspoon cream of tartar or 2 teaspoons baking powder
1 egg, well beaten	
1/2 teaspoon vanilla extract	1/4 teaspoon salt

Preheat oven to 325 degrees. Combine butter and brown sugar in bowl. Stir in egg and vanilla. Sift remaining ingredients 4 or 5 times into bowl. Add to liquid mixture; mix well. Shape into small balls. Place on cookie sheet; press with fork to flatten. Bake for 10 to 15 minutes or until lightly browned. Yield: 36 to 48 cookies.

Audrey Buffie, Xi Gamma Delta
Surrey, British Columbia, Canada

CHOCOLATE MACAROONS

2 1-ounce squares bitter chocolate	1 teaspoon vanilla extract
1 cup sweetened condensed milk	1 12-ounce package coconut

Preheat oven to 350 degrees. Melt chocolate in top of double boiler over hot water. Add milk and vanilla; mix well. Add coconut; mix well. Drop by teaspoonfuls onto greased cookie sheet. Bake for 10 minutes or until lightly browned. Yield: 36 to 48 cookies.

Jan McGough, Alpha Psi Kappa
Humble, Texas

BROWNIE MOUNDS

1 1/2 cups sugar
2/3 cup margarine
2 eggs
2/3 cup light corn syrup
6 1-ounce squares
   semisweet chocolate,
   melted

3 1/3 cups all-purpose
   flour
1 teaspoon baking
   powder
1 1/2 cups chopped
   walnuts

Preheat oven to 350 degrees. Cream sugar and margarine in mixer bowl. Add eggs, syrup and chocolate; mix until smooth. Add flour and baking powder; stir until blended. Stir in walnuts. Drop by teaspoonfuls onto greased cookie sheet. Bake for 10 to 12 minutes or until test done. Yield: 24 to 36 cookies.

Deb Williams, Zeta Kappa
Emerson, Iowa

CHOCOLATE CHIP
SOUR CREAM COOKIES

1 cup butter or
   margarine
3/4 cup packed light
   brown sugar
3/4 cup sugar
2 eggs
1/2 cup sour cream
1 teaspoon vanilla
   extract

2 1/4 cups all-purpose
   flour
1 teaspoon baking soda
1/2 teaspoon salt
1 package chocolate
   chips
1 1/2 cups chopped
   pecans

Preheat oven to 375 degrees. Cream first 3 ingredients in mixer bowl. Add eggs, sour cream and vanilla; mix well. Add flour, baking soda and salt; mix well. Stir in chocolate chips and pecans. Drop by teaspoonfuls onto nonstick cookie sheets. Bake for 10 to 12 minutes or until lightly browned.
Yield: 24 cookies.

Anna Magoffin, Xi Psi
Douglas, Arizona

❖ CHOCOLATE CHIP SANDIES

1 cup butter or
   margarine
1/3 cup sugar
2 teaspoons water
2 teaspoons vanilla
   extract
2 cups all-purpose flour

1 cup miniature
   semisweet chocolate
   pieces
1/2 cup chopped pecans
1/4 cup sifted
   confectioners' sugar
1 tablespoon shortening

Preheat oven to 325 degrees. Beat butter in large mixer bowl at medium speed for 30 seconds. Add sugar; beat until fluffy. Add water and vanilla; beat well. Stir in flour, 1/2 cup chocolate pieces and pecans. Shape into 1/2-by-1 1/2-inch crescents. Place on ungreased cookie sheet. Bake for 25 minutes or until edges are firm and slightly browned. Let cool completely. Sprinkle with confectioners' sugar. Melt remaining chocolate pieces and shortening in saucepan over very low heat. Dip 1 end of each cookie into melted chocolate mixture. Place on waxed paper-lined cookie sheet; chill until chocolate is set.
Yield: 36 cookies.

Carol Tyrrell, Xi Upsilon Omicron
Altaville, California

VANILLA-CHOCOLATE CHIP COOKIES

2 1/4 cups all-purpose
   flour
1 teaspoon baking soda
1 cup margarine,
   softened
1/4 cup sugar
3/4 cup packed light
   brown sugar
1 teaspoon vanilla
   extract

1 package vanilla
   instant pudding mix
2 eggs
1 12-ounce package
   chocolate chips
1 6-ounce package
   vanilla chips
1 cup chopped nuts

Preheat oven to 375 degrees. Mix flour and baking soda in bowl. Combine next 6 ingredients in mixer bowl; beat well. Add flour mixture. Stir in chips and nuts. Drop by teaspoonfuls onto ungreased cookie sheet. Bake for 8 to 10 minutes or until lightly browned. Yield: 48 to 60 cookies.

Marcia Brown, Iota Delta
New Sharon, Iowa

COLOSSAL COOKIES

This recipe does not use any flour.

1/2 cup butter or
   margarine
1 cup sugar
1 1/2 cups packed light
   brown sugar
4 eggs
1 teaspoon vanilla
   extract

2 cups peanut butter
6 cups oatmeal
2 cups chocolate chips
2 1/2 teaspoons baking
   soda

Preheat oven to 350 degrees. Beat first 3 ingredients in large mixer bowl. Add eggs, vanilla and peanut butter; mix thoroughly. Stir remaining ingredients into peanut butter mixture. Drop by 1/4 cupfuls onto ungreased cookie sheet about 2 1/2 inches apart. Flatten to 2-inch circles. Bake for 10 to 12 minutes or until test done. Yield: 36 to 48 cookies.

Louann Jensen, Laureate Alpha Phi
Loveland, Colorado

Joyce Grove Ellinger, Xi Beta Xi, Huntingdon, Pennsylvania, makes Sugar Brownies by combining 2 packages honey graham crackers, crushed, 12 ounces chocolate chips and two 14-ounce cans sweetened condensed milk in bowl; mix well. Spread into greased and floured 9-by-13-inch baking pan. Sift 2 tablespoons sugar over top. Bake in preheated 350-degree oven for 30 minutes. Cut into pieces.

❖ FIVE-FLAVOR COOKIES

1 cup sugar	1/4 to 1/2 teaspoon black
1 cup packed light	walnut flavoring
brown sugar	3 1/2 cups all-purpose
1 cup butter or	flour
margarine, softened	1 teaspoon cream of
1 cup cooking oil	tartar
1 egg	1 teaspoon baking soda
2 teaspoons vanilla	1 teaspoon salt
extract	1 cup crisp Rice Krispies
1 teaspoon caramel	1 cup chopped pecans
flavoring	1 cup oats
1/2 teaspoon each	1 cup coconut
coconut and butter	Sugar
flavoring	

Preheat oven to 350 degrees. Cream first 3 ingredients in mixer bowl. Add next 7 ingredients; mix well. Combine flour, cream of tartar, baking soda and salt in bowl; add to creamed mixture. Stir in Rice Krispies, pecans, oats and coconut. Shape into balls; place on cookie sheet. Flatten each cookie with fork or glass dipped into sugar. Bake for 10 to 12 minutes or until lightly browned. Yield: 100 cookies.

Estelle Hite, Xi Lambda Sigma
Royalton, Illinois

GINGER CRAKLESNAPS

3/4 cup shortening	1 teaspoon cinnamon
1 cup sugar	1/2 teaspoon salt
1 egg	2 1/4 cups all-purpose
1/4 cup molasses	flour
1 tablespoon ginger	Confectioners' sugar
2 teaspoons baking soda	

Preheat oven to 350 degrees. Cream shortening and sugar in mixer bowl. Add egg and molasses; beat well. Sift remaining ingredients in bowl. Add to creamed mixture; blend well. Form into 1-inch balls; roll balls in sugar. Place 2 inches apart on ungreased cookie sheet. Bake for 12 to 15 minutes or until lightly browned. Let cool on wire racks. Yield: 36 cookies.

Pam Fitzner, Theta
Gillette, Wyoming

GRANNY'S GOOFY GUMMIES

1 cup butter or	4 cups sifted
margarine, softened	all-purpose flour
1 1/2 cups sugar	1/2 teaspoon salt
1 teaspoon vanilla	2 eggs, beaten
extract	1 package large
1/3 cup sour milk, at	gumdrops
room temperature	Sugar
1 teaspoon baking soda	

Preheat oven to 375 degrees. Cream butter and sugar in large mixer bowl. Add vanilla and sour milk; blend well. Sift baking soda, flour and salt together in bowl; add to creamed mixture, mixing well. Add eggs; mix well. Drop by teaspoonful onto greased cookie sheet. Cut gumdrops into quarters; roll in sugar. Place gumdrop slice on each cookie. Flatten each cookie slightly with buttered and sugar-coated bottom of glass. Bake for 7 minutes or until lightly browned. Yield: 60 to 72 cookies.

Lori Towles, Xi Gamma Tau
Mesa, Arizona

HONEY DROPS

2/3 cup margarine	1 teaspoon baking
1 cup honey	powder
2 eggs	1 teaspoon salt
2 1/2 cups all-purpose	1 cup chopped nuts
flour	1 1/2 cups semisweet
1 teaspoon baking soda	chocolate chips

Preheat oven to 350 degrees. Cream margarine in mixer bowl until light and fluffy. Add honey and eggs; mix well. Combine dry ingredients in bowl; add to creamed mixture gradually. Stir in nuts and chocolate chips. Drop by teaspoonfuls onto greased cookie sheet. Bake for 10 to 12 minutes or until lightly browned. Yield: 36 to 48 cookies.

Laurie King, Epsilon Sigma
Toppenish, Washington

LEMONADE COOKIES

1 cup butter or	1 teaspoon baking soda
margarine	1 6-ounce can frozen
1 cup sugar	lemonade, thawed
2 eggs	Sugar
3 cups all-purpose flour	

Preheat oven to 400 degrees. Cream butter and sugar in mixer bowl. Add eggs; beat until fluffy. Combine flour and baking soda in bowl; add to creamed mixture with 1/2 cup lemonade concentrate. Drop by teaspoonfuls 2 inches apart onto ungreased cookie sheet. Bake for 8 minutes or until lightly browned around edges. Brush hot cookies with remaining lemonade concentrate. Sprinkle with sugar. Yield: 48 cookies.

Jean Ann Vincent
Ukiah, California

LUSCIOUS COOKIES

1 cup sugar	1 teaspoon baking soda
1 cup packed light	1 teaspoon salt
brown sugar	1 1/2 teaspoons baking
1 cup butter or	powder
margarine	1 cup coconut
2 eggs	2 cups quick oats
1 teaspoon vanilla	2 cups Rice Krispies
extract	1 cup chopped pecans
2 cups all-purpose flour	1 cup raisins

Preheat oven to 350 degrees. Cream first 3 ingredients in mixer bowl. Mix in eggs and vanilla. Combine next 4 ingredients in bowl; add to creamed mixture. Stir in remaining ingredients. Drop by teaspoonfuls onto greased cookie sheet. Bake for 12 minutes. Yield: 36 to 48 cookies.

Connie Windmiller, Theta Omega
Salisbury, Missouri

MAYONNAISE COOKIES

2 cups self-rising flour	1 or 1¹/₂ teaspoons
1 cup mayonnaise	vanilla extract
1 cup sugar	1 cup chopped pecans

Preheat oven to 350 degrees. Beat flour and mayonnaise in mixer bowl. Add sugar and vanilla; blend well. Fold in pecans. Shape into balls. Place on cookie sheet; flatten with fork. Bake for 10 to 12 minutes or until lightly browned. Yield: 36 to 48 cookies.

Louise H. Sansing, Xi Mu
Bessemer, Alabama

NATURALLY SWEET SOFT COOKIES

¹/₂ cup raisins	¹/₄ cup water
¹/₂ cup packed chopped dates	1 egg
1 medium-sized ripe banana, sliced	1 teaspoon vanilla extract
¹/₃ cup creamy peanut butter	1 cup oatmeal
	¹/₂ cup all-purpose flour
	1 teaspoon baking soda

Preheat oven to 350 degrees. Combine first 7 ingredients in mixer bowl; beat until blended. Add oatmeal, flour and baking soda; mix to blend thoroughly. Drop by teaspoonfuls onto nonstick cookie sheets; flatten slightly. Bake for 10 minutes or until browned on underside. Cool on wire racks. Store in airtight container. Yield: 40 cookies.

J. Susie Crouch, Alpha Beta Psi
Clinton, Missouri

OATMEAL COOKIES

2 eggs, beaten	1 teaspoon baking soda
³/₄ cup salad oil	1 teaspoon salt
1 teaspoon vanilla extract	1 teaspoon nutmeg
	1 teaspoon cinnamon
¹/₂ cup milk	2 cups quick-cooking oats
1 cup sugar	1 cup raisins
2 cups all-purpose flour	¹/₂ cup chopped nuts

Preheat oven to 350 degrees. Mix eggs, oil, vanilla and milk in bowl. Combine remaining ingredients in bowl; mix well. Add dry mixture to liquid mixture; let stand for few minutes. Drop by teaspoonfuls onto greased cookie sheet. Bake for 15 to 17 minutes or until lightly browned. Yield: 30 cookies.

Gladys M. Cook, Laureate Alpha Omega
San Diego, California

PUMPKIN-OAT SPICE COOKIES

¹/₂ cup margarine	2 teaspoons baking
²/₃ cup packed light brown sugar	powder
	¹/₂ teaspoon baking soda
2 eggs, well beaten	1 teaspoon cinnamon
1¹/₃ cups canned or mashed cooked fresh pumpkin	¹/₂ teaspoon nutmeg
	¹/₈ teaspoon allspice
	1¹/₄ cups oats
³/₄ cup all-purpose flour	1 cup raisins
³/₄ cup wheat flour	

Preheat oven to 300 degrees. Cream margarine and sugar in mixer bowl. Add eggs and pumpkin to sugar mixture; mix well. Combine next 7 ingredients in large bowl. Stir in oats and raisins. Add to pumpkin mixture; mix well. Drop by teaspoonfuls onto nonstick cookie sheet. Bake for 15 minutes or until lightly browned. Yield: 72 cookies.

Mary Jo McKee, Preceptor Gamma Zeta
Merrillville, Indiana

YOU'VE WON MY HEART OATMEAL COOKIES

To make his day a little more special, I'd have these cookies waiting for my husband after a hard day at work. He'd always tell me "You've won my heart!"

2 cups sugar	¹/₂ cup creamy peanut
¹/₂ cup milk	butter
¹/₃ cup cocoa	1 teaspoon vanilla extract
¹/₂ cup margarine	3 cups quick-cooking oats

Combine sugar, milk, cocoa and margarine in saucepan; mix well. Bring to a boil; boil for 1 minute, stirring constantly. Add peanut butter, vanilla and oats; mix well. Drop by teaspoonfuls onto waxed paper; let cool. Store in airtight container. Yield: 36 cookies.

Sara Sirovy, Iota Delta
Oskaloosa, Iowa

ORANGE SLICE COOKIES

1 egg	¹/₂ teaspoon baking soda
¹/₂ cup sugar	1 teaspoon vanilla
¹/₂ cup packed light brown sugar	extract
	1 cup quick-cooking oats
¹/₂ cup margarine	
1 cup all-purpose flour	1 cup finely chopped
¹/₂ teaspoon salt	pecans
¹/₂ teaspoon baking powder	2 cups finely chopped orange slice candy

Preheat oven to 350 degrees. Combine first 4 ingredients in mixer bowl; blend well. Add remaining ingredients; mix well. Drop by teaspoonfuls onto greased cookie sheet. Bake for 12 minutes or until lightly browned. Yield: 72 cookies.

Elizabeth Creamer, Pi Master
Texarkana, Arkansas

ORANGE TEA CRISPS

1 cup margarine	1/2 teaspoon baking
2/3 cup sugar	powder
1 egg	1 tablespoon orange
2 1/2 cups all-purpose	juice
flour	1 tablespoon orange rind
Dash of salt	Sprinkles

Preheat oven to 375 degrees. Cream margarine and sugar in mixer bowl. Add egg; mix well. Add sifted dry ingredients to creamed mixture alternately with orange juice and orange rind, beating after each addition. Spoon dough into cookie press. Press cookies onto ungreased cookie sheet. Bake for 10 to 12 minutes or until golden brown. Sprinkle with sprinkles. Yield: 24 to 36 cookies.

Christine Forino Koebke, Eta
Sanford, Florida

SALTED PEANUT COOKIES

1 cup sugar	1 teaspoon baking soda
1 cup packed light	2 cups sifted
brown sugar	all-purpose flour
1 cup margarine	1 teaspoon baking
2 eggs	powder
1 teaspoon vanilla	3 cups quick oatmeal
extract	1 1/2 cups salted peanuts

Preheat oven to 350 degrees. Cream sugar, brown sugar and margarine in mixer bowl. Add eggs and vanilla; mix well. Add baking soda, flour and baking powder; mix until well blended. Add oatmeal; mix until well blended. Stir in peanuts. Shape into balls. Place on cookie sheet; press out with sugared fork. Bake for 10 to 12 minutes or until lightly browned. Yield: 84 cookies.

Velma S. Neleigh, Xi Mu Nu
Dunnellon, Florida

COUNTRY PERSIMMON COOKIES

2 cups ripe persimmon	2 teaspoons ground
pulp	cinnamon
2 teaspoons baking soda	1 teaspoon nutmeg
1 cup butter or	1 teaspoon cloves
margarine, softened	1 teaspoon salt
2 cups sugar	2 cups chopped walnuts
2 eggs	2 cups raisins
4 cups all-purpose flour	

Preheat oven to 350 degrees. Mix persimmon pulp with baking soda in bowl. Cream butter and sugar in mixer bowl. Add eggs, 1 at a time. Sift next 5 ingredients together in bowl; add to creamed mixture. Stir in persimmon mixture. Stir in walnuts and raisins. Drop by teaspoonfuls onto greased cookie sheet. Bake for 15 minutes or until browned. Yield: 96 cookies.

Gloria Church, Preceptor Nu Chi
Corning, California

PINEAPPLE COOKIES

1/2 cup shortening	1 8-ounce can crushed
1 cup sugar	pineapple
1 egg	1/2 cup chopped nuts
2 cups all-purpose flour	2 tablespoons butter or
1 teaspoon baking soda	margarine
1 teaspoon salt	2 cups confectioners'
1 teaspoon baking	sugar
powder	

Preheat oven to 375 degrees. Cream shortening and sugar in mixer bowl. Add egg; mix well. Combine next 4 ingredients in bowl. Drain pineapple, reserving juice. Add pineapple to creamed mixture alternately with flour mixture. Stir in nuts. Drop by teaspoonfuls onto nonstick cookie sheet. Bake for 10 minutes or until lightly browned. Combine butter, confectioners' sugar and reserved pineapple juice in bowl; blend well. Frost warm cookies. Yield: 36 to 40 cookies.

Jean E. Gilborne, Preceptor Gamma Omicron
Geneseo, Illinois
*Cathy Keller, Alpha
Fargo, North Dakota

RAISIN COOKIES

2 cups sugar	2 teaspoons baking soda
1 cup vegetable	2 teaspoons vanilla
shortening	extract
2 eggs	1 15-ounce box raisins
1 cup milk	1 1/2 cups sugar
6 1/2 cups all-purpose	2 cups water
flour	3 tablespoons
4 teaspoons cream of	cornstarch
tartar	

Preheat oven to 350 degrees. Combine first 8 ingredients in mixer bowl; mix well. Roll dough out on cutting board to 1/4-inch thickness; cut with glass. Mix remaining ingredients together in saucepan; bring to a boil. Simmer for 5 minutes; let cool. Place 1 teaspoonful of filling on half the pastry circles. Top with remaining pastry circles; slit tops. Bake for 12 to 15 minutes or until lightly browned. Yield: 96 cookies.

Kathy Bolt, Xi Beta Epsilon
Pineville, West Virginia

SOUTHERN CREAM COOKIES

1 cup margarine	1 teaspoon salt
2 cups sugar	1/2 teaspoon baking soda
3 eggs, well beaten	1 1/2 cups chopped nuts
1 teaspoon vanilla	(optional)
extract	3 tablespoons sugar
1 cup sour cream	1 teaspoon cinnamon
5 cups all-purpose flour	
3 teaspoons baking	
powder	

Preheat oven to 325 degrees. Cream margarine and sugar in mixer bowl until light and fluffy. Add eggs, vanilla and sour cream; mix well. Sift next 4 ingredients together in bowl. Add flour mixture to creamed mixture; mix well. Stir in nuts. Drop by teaspoonfuls onto greased cookie sheet. Mix sugar and cinnamon in bowl. Dip greased bottom of glass into mixture; press cookies to flatten. Bake for 15 minutes or until lightly browned. Yield: 72 cookies.

Janet Hoskins, Preceptor Alpha Mu
Kirksville, Missouri

WHOLE WHEAT SUGAR COOKIES

1/2 cup margarine	1/2 teaspoon baking soda
1 cup packed light	1/2 teaspoon nutmeg
brown sugar	1 tablespoon grated
1 egg	orange rind
1 teaspoon vanilla	2 cups whole wheat
extract	flour
2 tablespoons milk	3 tablespoons sugar
1 teaspoon baking	1/2 teaspoon cinnamon
powder	

Preheat oven to 375 degrees. Combine first 5 ingredients in bowl; beat until light and fluffy. Add next 4 ingredients; mix well. Add flour; mix until smooth. Shape into 1-inch balls. Place 2 inches apart on greased cookie sheets; flatten slightly. Mix sugar and cinnamon in small bowl; sprinkle on cookies. Bake for 8 to 10 minutes or until lightly browned. Yield: 48 cookies.

Teresa W. Penland, Theta Rho
Franklin, North Carolina

STIR 'N DROP SUGAR COOKIES

2 eggs	3/4 cup sugar
2/3 cup cooking oil	2 cups all-purpose flour
2 teaspoons vanilla	2 teaspoons baking
extract	powder
1 teaspoon grated	1/4 teaspoon salt
lemon rind	1/4 cup sugar

Preheat oven to 400 degrees. Beat eggs with fork in bowl until well blended. Stir in oil, vanilla and lemon rind. Blend in 3/4 cup sugar until mixture thickens. Sift remaining ingredients together in bowl. Stir into sugar mixture. Drop by teaspoonfuls 2 inches apart on ungreased cookie sheet. Flatten with greased bottom of glass dipped in 1/4 cup sugar. Bake for 8 to 10 minutes or until lightly browned. May decorate with colored sugar, beads, pecans and "M & M's" Chocolate Candies if desired. Yield: 36 cookies.

Nancy Frerich, Preceptor Theta Sigma
Brackettville, Texas

SUNFLOWER SEED COOKIES

1 cup margarine	2 1/2 cups all-purpose
1 cup packed light	flour
brown sugar	1 teaspoon baking soda
1 cup sugar	3 cups rolled oats
2 eggs	1 cup salted shelled
1 teaspoon vanilla	sunflower seeds
extract	

Preheat oven to 350 degrees. Cream first 3 ingredients in mixer bowl. Beat in eggs and vanilla. Stir in flour, baking soda and oats. Mix in sunflower seeds. Drop by teaspoonfuls on ungreased cookie sheets. Bake for 12 minutes or until lightly browned. Yield: 36 to 48 cookies.

Annette Marie Hoch, Xi Alpha Theta
Topeka, Kansas

THUMBPRINT COOKIES

1 cup shortening	3 1/3 cups all-purpose
1/3 cup sugar	flour
1/2 cup confectioners'	2 teaspoons baking
sugar	powder
1 teaspoon salt	Jam or jelly (optional)
2 teaspoons vanilla	Preserves or marmalade
extract	(optional)
3 eggs	Peanut butter (optional)

Preheat oven to 375 degrees. Blend first 6 ingredients in mixer bowl; beat until creamy. Mix in flour with baking powder. Shape dough into balls; place on greased cookie sheet. Make dent in center with thumb or melon scoop. Fill with jam, preserves or peanut butter. Bake for 8 to 10 minutes or until lightly browned. Yield: 60 cookies.

Les Lee Hill, Rho Lambda
Levelland, Texas

VACATION COOKIES

2 cups butter or	1 tablespoon light or
margarine, softened	dark corn syrup
32 ounces light brown	8 teaspoons baking soda
sugar	48 ounces peanut butter
4 cups sugar	18 cups oatmeal
12 eggs	16 ounces chocolate
1 tablespoon vanilla	chips
extract	

Preheat oven to 350 degrees. Mix all ingredients in large bowl; batter will be stiff. Drop by tablespoonfuls or ice cream scoops onto nonstick cookie sheet. May flatten with greased bottom of glass dipped in additional sugar if desired. Bake for 8 to 12 minutes or until lightly browned. Yield: 18 to 20 dozen cookies.

Linda D. Eidson, Xi Lambda Upsilon
Windsor, Missouri

The Pie's the Limit

CARAMEL APPLE PIE

My mother used to make this pie using apples from the trees on our farm in Iowa.

1 2-crust package pie
    crust mix
6 to 8 tart apples,
    peeled, diced
2 teaspoons cinnamon
1/4 cup sugar

1/3 cup caramel topping
2 tablespoons butter or
    margarine, cut into
    small pieces
1 to 2 tablespoons sugar

Preheat oven to 400 degrees. Prepare pie mix according to package directions. Divide pastry in half; roll out each half on lightly floured surface. Place 1 half in 9-inch pie plate. Combine next 5 ingredients in large bowl. Pour into prepared pie dish. Cover with remaining pastry; flute edges. Sprinkle 1 to 2 tablespoons sugar on top; punch holes in top with fork. Bake for 15 minutes. Reduce oven temperature to 350 degrees; bake for 1 hour. Yield: 6 servings.

Shelby Glunz, Epsilon Rho
Port Orchard, Washington

DUTCH APPLE PIE

I usually make this pie for the Holiday Bazaar. It is always sold before I get it inside!

4 cups sliced tart apples
3/4 to 1 cup sugar
1 teaspoon cinnamon
1 9-inch unbaked pie
    shell
1/3 cup half and half

1/2 cup sugar
3/4 cup all-purpose flour
1/3 cup margarine,
    softened

Preheat oven to 350 degrees. Toss apples with 3/4 cup sugar and cinnamon in bowl. Spoon into pie shell. Pour half and half over mixture. Mix 1/2 cup sugar, flour and margarine in bowl until crumbly; spoon over apple mixture. Bake for 40 to 50 minutes or until bubbly and fork can easily be inserted.
Yield: 6 servings.

Carrie Sullivan, Theta Nu
Batesville, Indiana

BLACK BOTTOM PIE

1/2 cup chopped pecans
1 9-inch unbaked pie
    crust
2/3 cup sugar
1/2 cup butter or
    margarine, softened
2 1-ounce squares
    bitter chocolate,
    melted

1 teaspoon vanilla
    extract
2 eggs
1 3-ounce package
    vanilla instant
    pudding mix
1 cup half and half
3/4 cup milk
1/4 cup rum

Press pecans in bottom of pie crust. Bake according to package directions; let cool. Cream sugar and butter in mixer bowl. Beat in chocolate and vanilla. Add eggs, 1 at a time, beating 1 minute after each addition. Pour into pie crust. Combine remaining ingredients in bowl; mix well. Let set until thickened; spoon over chocolate mixture. Refrigerate until chilled or overnight. Yield: 6 to 8 servings.

LaVerne D. Burt, Xi Alpha
Aledo, Texas

CANADIAN BLUEBERRY PIE

4 cups fresh blueberries, washed, drained	1 tablespoon butter or margarine
1 cup sugar	1 9-inch baked pie shell
3 tablespoons cornstarch	1 cup whipping cream
1/8 teaspoon salt	3 tablespoons confectioners' sugar
1 tablespoon lemon juice	1/2 teaspoon vanilla extract
1 cup water	

Chill 3 cups blueberries. Place remaining blueberries in saucepan. Add next 5 ingredients; mix well. Cook over medium heat until thickened and smooth, stirring constantly. Remove from heat; add butter. Stir in chilled blueberries. Let cool for 30 minutes. Spoon into pie shell; chill. Whip cream in mixer bowl. Add confectioners' sugar and vanilla; blend well. Spoon on top of pie before serving. Yield: 8 to 10 servings.

Carol A. Steele, Delta
Brandon, Manitoba, Canada

CHOCOLATE CHESS PIE

This recipe was given to me at a recipe shower before my marriage 17 years ago by a friend from our Garden Club. Her tips on African violets are just as good as this delicious pie.

1 1/2 cups sugar	1 teaspoon vanilla extract
4 tablespoons melted margarine	1 unbaked 9-inch pie shell
3 1/2 tablespoons cocoa	Sliced almonds (optional)
2 eggs	
2/3 cup evaporated milk	

Preheat oven to 350 degrees. Combine first 6 ingredients in mixer bowl; mix well. Pour into pie shell. Top with almonds. Bake for 50 minutes to 1 hour or until knife inserted near center comes out clean. May serve warm with vanilla ice cream. Yield: 6 to 8 servings.

Rebecca Kay Hicks, Preceptor Nu
Salina, Kansas

LEMON CHESS PIE

Grandma Char always helped me make this pie for our country fair. It never failed to get a blue ribbon in the 4-H section.

1/4 cup butter or margarine	Juice of 2 lemons
1 1/2 cups sugar	1/2 cup evaporated milk
4 eggs	1 9-inch unbaked deep dish pie shell
1 tablespoon cornmeal	

Preheat oven to 350 degrees. Combine first 6 ingredients in bowl; mix well. Pour into pie shell. Bake in center of oven for 45 minutes or until center is set. Yield: 8 servings.

Jane Baker
Strasburg, Virginia

❖ HEAVENLY CHOCOLATE PIE

2 egg whites	2 egg yolks
1/2 teaspoon vinegar	1/4 cup water
1/4 teaspoon cinnamon	1 cup heavy cream
1/4 teaspoon salt	1/4 cup sugar
1/2 cup sugar	1/4 teaspoon cinnamon
1 9-inch baked pie shell	
1 6-ounce package semisweet chocolate chips	

Preheat oven to 325 degrees. Beat egg whites, vinegar, 1/4 teaspoon cinnamon and salt together in mixer bowl until stiff but not dry. Add 1/2 cup sugar gradually, beating until very stiff. Spread over bottom and up side of pie shell. Bake for 15 to 18 minutes or until lightly browned; let cool. Melt chocolate chips in top of double boiler over hot water. Blend in egg yolks and water until smooth. Spread 3 tablespoons chocolate mixture over cooled meringue. Chill remaining mixture until begins to thicken. Beat cream, 1/4 cup sugar and 1/4 teaspoon cinnamon in mixer bowl until thickened. Spread 1/2 cream mixture over chocolate layer. Fold chilled chocolate mixture into remaining cream mixture. Spread over cream mixture. Chill for at least 4 hours. Yield: 6 to 8 servings.

Agnes C. Scannell, Laureate Alpha Phi
Dubuque, Iowa

❖ CLOUD NINE PIE

4 egg whites	4 tablespoons lemon rind
1/4 teaspoon cream of tartar	1 cup sugar
1 cup sugar	1 1/2 cups whipping cream
8 egg yolks	
1/2 cup lemon juice	

Preheat oven to 275 degrees. Beat egg whites until foamy. Add cream of tartar; beat until stiff. Beat in 1 cup sugar gradually. Arrange in 9-inch greased pie plate. Bake for 45 minutes. Open oven; let cool. Beat egg yolks in mixer bowl. Add lemon juice and lemon rind. Add 1 cup sugar gradually. Pour into saucepan. Cook over low heat, stirring constantly, until thickened; let cool. Whip cream in mixer bowl; add to lemon mixture. Spoon into meringue crust. Refrigerate overnight. Yield: 8 servings.

Susan Anderson, Alpha Eta
Tucson, Arizona

Pamela Brooks, Xi Theta Sigma, Farmington, Missouri, makes a Strawberry Pie by combining 1 cup water, 1 cup sugar, 4 tablespoons cornstarch and 3 tablespoons strawberry gelatin in saucepan. Cook until mixture boils and is thickened; let cool. Pour over 1 quart sliced strawberries in 9-inch baked pie shell. Serve with whipped cream.

COCONUT CUSTARD PIE

1 cup flaked coconut	1¼ cups hot water
1 9-inch unbaked pie shell	1 teaspoon vanilla extract
3 eggs	¼ teaspoon salt
1 14-ounce can sweetened condensed milk	⅛ teaspoon ground nutmeg

Preheat oven to 425 degrees. Toast ½ cup coconut to use as topping. Bake pie shell for 8 minutes; cool slightly. Beat eggs in mixer bowl; add next 5 ingredients; mix well. Stir in remaining ½ cup coconut. Pour into pie shell. Sprinkle with toasted coconut. Bake for 10 minutes. Reduce oven temperature to 350 degrees. Bake for 25 to 30 minutes longer or until knife inserted near center comes out clean; let cool. Yield: 6 to 8 servings.

Terry Fohn, Xi Lambda Tau
Urich, Missouri

FRUIT COCKTAIL PIE

25 marshmallows	1 8-ounce can fruit cocktail, drained
½ cup milk	
1 cup whipping cream, whipped	1 9-inch graham cracker crust, chilled

Combine marshmallows and milk in saucepan. Heat until marshmallows are melted; let cool. Add whipped cream and fruit cocktail; mix well. Pour into crust; chill until firm. Yield: 8 servings.

Mary Eison, Xi Psi Upsilon
Bridgeport, Texas

ICE CREAM PIE

½ cup peanut butter	½ cup whipping cream
½ cup light corn syrup	4 tablespoons butter or margarine
2¼ cups rice cereal	
2 cups vanilla ice cream, softened	1 teaspoon vanilla extract
¾ cup sugar	2 cups vanilla ice cream, softened
½ cup cocoa	

Mix peanut butter and corn syrup in large bowl. Add cereal; stir until well coated. Press cereal mixture into 9-inch pie plate. Spread 2 cups softened ice cream over cereal; freeze until firm. Combine sugar, cocoa, whipping cream and butter in saucepan. Cook over medium heat until smooth and boiling; remove from heat. Stir in vanilla. Let cool slightly. Pour 1¼ cups sauce over ice cream; return to freezer for 20 minutes. Spread remaining 2 cups softened ice cream over fudge sauce. Drizzle remaining sauce over ice cream. Freeze for 3 hours. Let stand for 15 minutes at room temperature before slicing. Yield: 8 to 10 servings.

Donna Parker
Port Hope, Ontario, Canada

JEFF DAVIS PIE

⅓ cup butter or margarine	1 teaspoon vanilla extract
2 cups sugar	4 eggs
1 tablespoon all-purpose flour	1 cup milk
¼ teaspoon salt	1 9-inch unbaked pie shell

Preheat oven to 450 degrees. Cream butter and sugar together in mixer bowl until light and fluffy. Add flour, salt and vanilla; beat well. Add eggs, 1 at a time, beating well. Stir in milk slowly. Pour into pie shell. Bake for 10 minutes. Reduce oven temperature to 350 degrees; bake for 30 minutes longer or until firm. Yield: 6 servings.

Lana Thompson, Xi Alpha Nu
San Angelo, Texas

GREEN TOMATO MINCEMEAT FOR PIES

This mincemeat won a blue ribbon at the York Interstate Fair a few years ago.

8 quarts quartered green tomatoes	1 teaspoon ground ginger
2 lemons, cut into pieces	2 pounds raisins
	2 teaspoons ground cloves
4 pounds light brown sugar	
	1 tablespoon ground cinnamon
1 cup cider vinegar	
1 teaspoon ground allspice	½ teaspoon ground mace

Put tomatoes and lemons through food chopper or food processor. Place in large saucepan; stir in remaining ingredients. Cook for 45 minutes, stirring occasionally. Pour into sterilized jars; seal. Use 1 quart for mincemeat pie. Yield: 8 to 10 quarts.

Judy Eisenhart, Laureate Kappa
York, Pennsylvania

AFTER DINNER MINT PIE

2 cups crushed Oreo cookies	Few drops of peppermint extract
¼ cup margarine, melted	Few drops of green food coloring
¼ cup milk	2 cups whipping cream, whipped
1 7-ounce jar marshmallow creme	Mint leaf

Combine crushed cookies and margarine in bowl; mix well. Press mixture onto bottom of 9-inch pie plate or springform pan; chill. Add milk gradually to marshmallow creme in mixer bowl; mix until well blended. Add peppermint extract and food coloring. Fold in whipped cream. Pour over crumb mixture. Freeze until firm. Garnish with mint leaf in center. Yield: 8 servings.

Rebecca E. Wolverton, Eta Chi
Edinburg, Virginia

NO-YOLK LEMON MERINGUE PIE

1¹/2 cups sugar
7 tablespoons
  cornstarch
1¹/2 cups hot water
1 tablespoon margarine
1¹/2 teaspoons grated
  lemon peel
¹/2 cup lemon juice
1 9-inch baked pie shell
3 egg whites
6 tablespoons sugar
1 teaspoon vanilla
  extract

Preheat oven to 350 degrees. Mix 1¹/2 cups sugar and cornstarch in medium saucepan. Stir in water until smooth. Bring to a low boil; cook for 15 minutes, stirring constantly. Stir in margarine, lemon peel and lemon juice; mix well. Pour into pie shell; let stand until cool. Beat egg whites in mixer bowl until stiff. Add 6 tablespoons sugar, 1 tablespoon at a time, beating constantly. Add vanilla, beating until stiff peaks form. Spoon meringue onto pie, sealing to edge of crust. Bake for 10 minutes or until lightly browned. Yield: 6 servings.

Shelia Remick, Beta Nu
Encampment, Wyoming

NEOPOLITAN ICE CREAM PIES

1³/4 cups crushed
  graham crackers
¹/2 cup melted margarine
6 tablespoons sugar
1 teaspoon cinnamon
¹/4 cup finely chopped
  pecans
1 quart vanilla ice
  cream, softened
1 teaspoon vanilla
  extract
1 teaspoon almond
  extract
¹/4 teaspoon green food
  coloring
¹/2 cup chopped
  maraschino cherries
1 can sweetened
  condensed milk
¹/4 cup water
2 1-ounce squares
  unsweetened baking
  chocolate
1 teaspoon vanilla
  extract
1 quart vanilla ice
  cream, softened
1 teaspoon vanilla
  extract
¹/4 teaspoon red food
  coloring
¹/2 cup chopped nuts
1¹/2 1-ounce square
  baking chocolate,
  grated
1 cup whipping cream
3 tablespoons sugar
1 teaspoon vanilla
  extract
Grated chocolate

Combine first 5 ingredients in bowl. Press into two 9-inch pie pans; freeze. Mix next 5 ingredients in bowl. Spread ¹/2 mixture over each crust; freeze. Combine next 4 ingredients in saucepan. Cook over medium-low heat until thickened; let cool. Spread ¹/2 mixture over second layer of each pie; freeze. Mix next 5 ingredients in bowl. Spread ¹/2 mixture over each pie; freeze. Whip cream in mixer bowl. Add 3 tablespoons sugar and 1 teaspoon vanilla; mix well. Spread on top. Garnish with grated chocolate. Freeze until serving time. Yield: 12 to 16 servings.

Jean Keown, Xi Epsilon Beta
Marshalltown, Iowa

OATMEAL PIE

2 eggs
¹/2 cup margarine
¹/2 cup sugar
¹/2 cup packed light
  brown sugar
³/4 cup dark corn syrup
³/4 cup milk
Pinch of salt
³/4 cup coconut
³/4 cup quick oatmeal
1 9-inch unbaked
  pastry shell

Preheat oven to 350 degrees. Beat eggs in mixer bowl until light. Add next 6 ingredients. Beat until thoroughly mixed and light. Add coconut and oatmeal; mix lightly. Pour into pie shell. Bake for 40 minutes or until set. Yield: 6 to 8 servings.

Shirley Workman, Alpha Kappa
Mount Vernon, Ohio

ORANGE PIE

1¹/4 cups all-purpose
  flour
¹/2 cup margarine
¹/2 cup finely chopped
  nuts
¹/2 cup Tang
8 ounces sour cream
1 14-ounce can
  sweetened condensed
  milk
1 8-ounce carton
  whipped topping
2 tablespoons grated
  orange rind

Preheat oven to 400 degrees. Blend flour and margarine into pea-sized pieces. Add nuts; mix well. Press into 9-inch pie plate, covering bottom and side. Bake for 12 to 13 minutes or until lightly browned; let cool. Mix Tang, sour cream and condensed milk together in bowl. Pour into pie shell. Top with whipped topping. Sprinkle with orange rind. Chill. Yield: 8 servings.

Marjorie Vonderlage, Gamma Psi
Paris, Illinois

PEACH CARAMEL PIE

³/4 cup packed light
  brown sugar
¹/4 cup light corn syrup
¹/4 cup butter or
  margarine
3 tablespoons
  all-purpose flour
2 tablespoons water
Pinch of salt
5 cups sliced fresh
  peaches
1 9-inch unbaked pie
  shell
1 unbaked 9-inch lattice
  pie crust

Preheat oven to 400 degrees. Combine first 6 ingredients in saucepan. Cook over low or medium heat until sugar is completely dissolved. Place sliced peaches in pie shell. Pour caramel mixture over peaches; place lattice crust on top. Bake for 10 to 15 minutes. Reduce oven temperature to 350 degrees; bake for 35 minutes longer. Yield: 6 to 8 servings.

Donna Pierson, Laureate Gamma
Spencer, Iowa

SOUR CREAM PEACH PIE

4 cups sliced fresh
  peaches
1 9-inch unbaked pie
  shell
1 cup sugar
1/2 cup sour cream
1/4 cup all-purpose flour

Preheat oven to 350 degrees. Place peaches in pie shell. Mix sugar, sour cream and flour in small bowl. Spread over fruit. Bake for 1 hour or until browned on top. Let cool at room temperature.
Yield: 8 servings.

Kathy L. Robertson, Xi Iota Zeta
San Jose, California

PEANUT BUTTER-BANANA PIE

3/4 cup confectioners'
  sugar
1/2 cup peanut butter
1 9-inch baked pie shell
1 banana, sliced
1 3-ounce package
  vanilla instant
  pudding mix
1 8-ounce carton
  whipped topping

Blend confectioners' sugar and peanut butter with fork until crumbly. Sprinkle 1/2 mixture over bottom of pie shell. Layer banana slices on crumb mixture. Prepare pudding mix using to package directions. Pour over banana layer. Spread whipped topping over pudding. Sprinkle remaining 1/2 crumb mixture over topping. Chill for 1 hour. Yield: 8 servings.

Debbie Corbett, Nu Phi Mu
Goodland, Kansas

PEANUT BUTTER PIE

1 cup confectioners'
  sugar
1/2 cup peanut butter
1 9-inch baked pie shell
2 cups milk
1/4 cup cornstarch
2/3 cup sugar
1/4 teaspoon salt
3 egg yolks, beaten
2 tablespoons butter or
  margarine
1/4 teaspoon vanilla
  extract
3 egg whites
2 tablespoons (rounded)
  sugar
Few drops of vanilla
  extract

Preheat oven to 325 degrees. Combine sugar and peanut butter in bowl; blend until of biscuit mix texture. Spread 3/4 mixture in pie shell. Scald milk in top of double boiler. Combine cornstarch, sugar and salt in bowl; add slowly to scalded milk, mixing well. Beat egg yolks in mixer bowl. Add small amount of hot milk mixture to eggs; pour egg mixture into hot mixture, mixing well. Cook until mixture thickens. Remove from heat. Add butter and vanilla; mix well. Pour into pie shell. Beat egg whites in mixer bowl until stiff, adding sugar gradually. Mix in vanilla. Spread on pie, sealing edges. Sprinkle remaining peanut butter mixture over meringue. Bake until meringue is golden. Yield: 6 to 8 servings.

Patty Welch, Xi Kappa Mu
Keystone Heights, Florida

❖ REESE'S PEANUT BUTTER PIE

1/2 cup peanut butter
1/3 cup milk
3 ounces cream cheese
1 cup confectioners'
  sugar
8 ounces whipped
  topping
1 9-inch graham
  cracker pie crust
1 10-ounce jar fudge
  chocolate sauce

Mix first 4 ingredients in mixer bowl for 3 minutes. Fold in whipped topping. Pour into pie crust. Freeze for 4 hours. Spread chocolate sauce over pie. Freeze for 4 hours longer. Yield: 6 to 8 servings.

Helen H. Quinn, Xi Gamma Psi
St. Marys, Georgia

LEMON PECAN PIE

3 eggs, slightly beaten
1 1/2 cups sugar
1/4 cup margarine or
  butter, melted
Juice of 1/2 lemon
1 teaspoon lemon
  extract
3/4 to 1 cup chopped
  pecans
1 teaspoon grated
  lemon rind
1 9-inch unbaked pie
  shell

Preheat oven to 350 degrees. Combine first 7 ingredients in large bowl; mix well. Pour into pie shell. Bake for 35 to 40 minutes or until center is set. Yield: 6 servings.

Liz Hausserman, Preceptor Alpha Gamma
Fenwick, Michigan

NO-BAKE PECAN PIE

8 ounces vanilla
  caramels
3/4 cup milk
1 envelope unflavored
  gelatin
1/4 cup cold water
Pinch of salt
1/2 cup whipped topping
1/2 cup chopped pecans
1 9-inch baked pie shell

Combine caramels and milk in saucepan; heat until caramels are melted. Soften gelatin in water. Add gelatin and salt to caramel mixture; mix well. Chill until thickened. Fold in whipped topping and pecans. Pour into pie shell. May top with additional whipped topping if desired. Yield: 6 to 8 servings.

Betty McCord, Iota Eta
Ennis, Texas

PRALINE PUMPKIN PIE

1/2 cup ground pecans
1 cup packed light
  brown sugar
2 tablespoons butter or
  margarine, softened
1 9-inch unbaked pie
  shell, chilled
2 eggs
1 cup cooked pumpkin
1 tablespoon
  all-purpose flour
1/4 teaspoon ground
  cloves
1/8 teaspoon mace
1/2 teaspoon cinnamon
1/2 teaspoon ginger
1 cup half and half or
  evaporated milk

Preheat oven to 400 degrees. Combine pecans, 1/2 cup brown sugar and butter in bowl; mix well. Press mixture gently into bottom of pie shell. Beat eggs in mixer bowl until frothy. Add remaining 1/2 cup brown sugar, pumpkin, flour, cloves, mace, cinnamon, ginger and half and half, beating only until well mixed. Pour into pie shell. Bake for 50 to 55 minutes or until knife inserted in center comes out clean. Let cool. Yield: 6 to 8 servings.

Jeannie Erwin, Xi Lambda Tau
Urich, Missouri

SOUR CREAM RAISIN PIE

1 cup raisins	1 tablespoon
1 9-inch unbaked pie	all-purpose flour
shell	1/2 teaspoon cinnamon
1 cup whipping cream	1/4 teaspoon cloves
1/2 teaspoon vinegar	1/4 teaspoon nutmeg
1 cup sugar	2 eggs, beaten

Preheat oven to 425 degrees. Layer raisins in pie shell. Mix whipping cream and vinegar in large bowl. Mix sugar, flour and spices in small bowl. Add eggs to cream mixture. Add dry ingredients; mix well. Pour over raisins. Bake until pie starts to brown. Reduce oven temperature to 375 degrees; bake until knife inserted in center comes out clean. Total baking time is approximately 1 hour.
Yield: 6 servings.

Annora Bentley, Xi Gamma Iota
Alliance, Nebraska

❖ SWEET STRAWBERRITY PIE

1 cup all-purpose flour	1/2 teaspoon almond
1/2 to 1 cup finely	extract
chopped nuts	1 cup confectioners'
1/4 cup packed light	sugar
brown sugar	1 21-ounce can
1/2 cup butter or	strawberru pie filling
margarine, softened	1 cup whipping cream,
8 ounces cream cheese,	whipped
softened	Sugar

Preheat oven to 375 degrees. Combine flour, nuts, brown sugar and butter in 9-by-13-inch baking pan. Bake for 15 to 20 minutes or until golden brown, stirring once. Reserve 1/2 cup crumbs. Press remaining warm crumb mixture into ungreased 10-inch pie plate; chill. Blend cream cheese, almond extract and confectioners' sugar in mixer bowl until smooth. Spread over pie crust. Fold pie filling into whipped cream; add sugar to taste. Spoon over cream cheese layer. Sprinkle with reserved crumb mixture. Chill for 1 to 2 hours before serving. Store in refrigerator. Yield: 6 to 8 servings.

Marty Hards, Xi Eta Theta
Findlay, Ohio

SUGAR-FREE PIE

1 1/2 cups Rice Krispies	1 package any flavor
1 tablespoon honey	sugar-free instant
1/4 cup peanut butter	pudding mix
1 banana, sliced	

Combine first 3 ingredients in bowl; mix well. Press mixture into 8-inch pie plate. Layer banana slices over crust. Prepare pudding mix according to package directions. Pour pudding over banana slices. Chill until serving time. May top with whipped topping, nuts or banana slices if desired.
Yield: 6 servings.

Ruth North, Preceptor Alpha Gamma
Ionia, Michigan

SWEET POTATO PASTRIES

I have had this recipe for 20 years. These were (and may still be) served in the St. Augustine Restoration area and are great eating.

1 package pie crust mix	1/2 cup blanched
1 teaspoon grated	almonds, ground
lemon peel	1/4 cup white rum
1 16-ounce can candied	1/2 teaspoon cinnamon
yams	Confectioners' sugar

Preheat oven to 400 degrees. Prepare pie crust mix according to package directions. Add lemon peel; mix well. Roll out very thin on lightly floured surface. Cut into 3-inch circles. Heat yams in saucepan. Add almonds, rum and cinnamon, blending well. Pour into blender container; purée. Place 1 teaspoonful mixture on each pastry circle. Fold over; press edges together to seal. Prick top. Place on nonstick cookie sheet. Bake for 25 minutes or until golden brown. Sprinkle hot pastries with confectioners' sugar. Yield: 12 to 16 pastries.

Irene M. Greer, Preceptor Eta Lambda
St. Augustine, Florida

TAFFY TARTS

1/4 cup butter or	2 eggs, beaten
margarine	1 teaspoon vanilla
3/4 cup packed light	extract
brown sugar	1/2 teaspoon salt
1 cup light corn syrup	6 to 8 tart shells

Preheat oven to 400 degrees. Combine first 3 ingredients in heavy saucepan. Bring to a low boil; cook until sugar is dissolved. Refrigerate until completely cooled. Add eggs, vanilla and salt; mix well. Spoon into tart shells. Bake for 12 to 15 minutes or until set. Yield: 6 to 8 servings.

Bonnie McKeown, Kappa Pi
Carleton Place, Ontario, Canada

Sweet Somethings

HOMEMADE ALMOND ROCA

*1/2 cup coarsely chopped
  almonds*
*1 cup plus 1 tablespoon
  butter*
1 cup sugar
*1 tablespoon light corn
  syrup*
3 tablespoons water
*3/4 cup semisweet
  chocolate bits*
*1/2 cup finely chopped
  almonds*

Line 9-by-13-inch baking pan with foil, extending over edges. Sprinkle coarsely chopped almonds in bottom of pan. Butter side of 2-quart saucepan with 1 tablespoon butter. Melt 1 cup butter in saucepan. Add sugar, syrup and water; bring to a boil, stirring constantly. Cook, stirring constantly, for 15 minutes or to soft-crack stage or 290 degrees on candy thermometer. Remove from heat; pour into pan over almonds. Spread evenly. Let stand for 5 minutes or until firm. Sprinkle with chocolate bits; let stand for 1 to 2 minutes or until melted. Smooth with spatula. Sprinkle with finely chopped almonds. Chill until firm. Lift out of pan; break into pieces. Store in covered container. Yield: 1 1/2 pounds.

*Kathryn A. Coverston, Xi Iota Zeta
San Jose, California*

MICROWAVE CANDY

2 cups sugar
1 teaspoon baking soda
1 cup buttermilk
*3/4 cup butter or
  margarine*
*1 teaspoon vanilla
  extract*
2 cups pecans

Combine sugar, baking soda, buttermilk and butter in 4-quart microwave-safe dish. Cover with plastic wrap; punch holes in wrap. Microwave on High for 2 1/2 minutes; stir and turn dish. Continue cooking for 15 minutes, stirring every 5 minutes. Microwave for 2 minutes longer or until mixture reaches soft-ball stage or 236 degrees on candy thermometer. Add vanilla. Pour into mixer bowl; beat until soft peaks form. Stir in pecans. Spread in buttered 7-by-12-inch dish. Yield: 1 1/2 pounds.

*Nadine L. McFall, Preceptor Theta
Frederick, Oklahoma*

CHOCOLATE PIZZA

*16 ounces milk
  chocolate or
  chocolate chip wafers*
2 cups Rice Krispies
*1 12-ounce jar dry
  roasted peanuts*
*1 small jar maraschino
  cherries, halved*
*4 ounces white
  chocolate wafers*

Melt milk chocolate wafers in top of double boiler over hot water. Stir in Rice Krispies. Spread on waxed paper in medium pizza pan. Refrigerate for 20 minutes or until set. Sprinkle with peanuts and maraschino cherries. Melt white chocolate wafers in top of double boiler over hot water; drizzle over pizza. Store in refrigerator. Yield: 12 to 16 servings.

*Janet Weaver
Dayton, Ohio*

Gwen Cook, Xi Alpha Epsilon, Durango, Colorado, makes Snacks by boiling 1 cup light corn syrup and 1 cup sugar in saucepan until clear. Remove from heat; mix in 1 1/2 cups crunchy peanut butter. Add 4 cups Crisp Rice cereal; mix to coat completely. Drop by teaspoonfuls onto waxed paper.

FANNIE MAE FUDGE

1 cup milk
4 cups sugar
1 cup butter
1 teaspoon vanilla
  extract
25 large marshmallows,
  cut up or 2 1/2 cups
  miniature
  marshmallows

4 1/2 ounces real milk
  chocolate
2 ounces unsweetened
  chocolate
12 ounces semisweet
  chocolate chips
1 cup chopped nuts
  (optional)

Mix first 4 ingredients in saucepan. Bring to a boil; boil for 2 minutes. Remove from heat; add marshmallows. Add chocolate, a small amount at a time, stirring until melted. Stir in nuts. Pour into greased 9-by-13-inch pan. Let set for 4 hours before cutting. Yield: 36 pieces.

Carol Morse, Laureate Beta Zeta
Decatur, Illinois

FIVE-MINUTE FUDGE

2 tablespoons margarine
2/3 cup evaporated milk
1 2/3 cups sugar
1/2 teaspoon salt
2 cups miniature
  marshmallows

1 1/2 cups semisweet
  chocolate chips
1 teaspoon vanilla
  extract
1/2 cup chopped walnuts
  (optional)

Mix first 4 ingredients in saucepan. Bring to a boil over medium heat, stirring constantly. Cook, stirring, for 5 minutes after first bubble appears. Remove from heat; stir in remaining ingredients. Stir until marshmallows and chocolate chips are melted. Pour into greased 8-inch square pan. Let set; cut into squares. Yield: 36 pieces.

Bev Webber, Preceptor Gamma
Souris, Manitoba, Canada

FOOLPROOF MICROWAVE FUDGE

1 can sweetened
  condensed milk
3 cups chocolate chips
Dash of salt

1 cup chopped nuts
1 teaspoon vanilla
  extract

Combine milk, chocolate chips and salt in microwave-safe bowl. Microwave for 1 minute; stir. Microwave for 45 seconds; stir until smooth. Stir in nuts and vanilla. Spread in 9-by-13-inch greased pan. Chill for 2 hours; cut into pieces. Yield: 36 pieces.

Sylvia Miller, Preceptor Nu
Oklahoma City, Oklahoma

Tammy Brown, Xi Omicron Exemplar, Ottawa, Kansas, makes Date Dessert by mixing 16 ounces crushed graham crackers, 8 ounces chopped walnuts, 16 ounces cut-up marshmallows, 16 ounces chopped dates and 1 cup cream in bowl. Shape into loaf; roll in graham cracker crumbs. Refrigerate; slice and serve with whipped cream.

GRANNY'S MAPLE CREAM FUDGE

2 cups sugar
3 cups packed light
  brown sugar
1 cup evaporated milk
3/4 cup light corn syrup

1/4 teaspoon cream of
  tartar
1 teaspoon vanilla
  extract

Combine first 4 ingredients in saucepan. Bring to a boil on medium-high heat. Boil for 5 minutes or until soft-ball stage. Remove from heat; pour into mixer bowl. Add remaining ingredients; beat for 8 minutes or until starts to thicken. Pour into greased 9-by-13-inch pan. Let cool; cut into squares. Yield: 36 pieces.

Leah Flatt, Gamma Phi
Maple Ridge, British Columbia, Canada

OLD-FASHIONED MICROWAVE PEANUT BRITTLE

This peanut brittle tastes so old-fashioned that most people find it hard to believe it is made in the microwave.

1 cup raw peanuts
1 cup sugar
1/2 cup light corn syrup
1 teaspoon vanilla
  extract

1 teaspoon butter or
  margarine
1 teaspoon baking soda

Combine peanuts, sugar and syrup in 8-cup measuring cup; mix with wooden spoon. Leave spoon in cup; microwave on High for 4 minutes. Stir; microwave on High for 4 more minutes. Add vanilla and butter;. stir. Microwave on High for 2 minutes. Add baking soda; stir until foamy. Spread quickly on cookie sheet sprayed with nonstick cooking spray. Cool completely. Break into pieces. Store in airtight container. Yield: 2 pounds.

Linda Makelki, Preceptor Kappa Lambda
Portland, Texas

TEXAS PEANUT PATTIES

I've made this candy recipe for parties for 30 years.

2 cups sugar
1/2 cup evaporated milk
4 tablespoons margarine
2 tablespoons light corn
  syrup
2 teaspoons vanilla
  extract

2 cups roasted and
  salted peanuts
10 drops of red food
  coloring

Combine sugar, milk, margarine and syrup in saucepan. Cook over medium heat, stirring constantly, to soft-ball stage. Add vanilla, peanuts and food coloring; stir for few minutes. Drop by teaspoonfuls onto buttered foil when patties hold their shape. Yield: 40 pieces.

Audrey D. Porter, Theta Phi
Terrell, Texas

PECAN BRITTLE

1 cup butter or margarine	1 cup sugar
1 tablespoon light corn syrup	3 tablespoons water
	2 cups whole pecans

Combine butter, syrup, sugar and water in heavy 3-quart saucepan. Cook on high heat, stirring rapidly, until color of brown paper bag. Add pecans; mix. Pour onto greased 9-by-13-inch baking sheet; spread thin. Let cool; break into pieces. Yield: 36 pieces.

Ruth C. Matthews, Preceptor Sigma
Grantsville, Utah

PINEAPPLE FUDGE

3 cups sugar	2 tablespoons butter or margarine
1 tablespoon light corn syrup	1/2 teaspoon vanilla extract
1 8-ounce can crushed pineapple, drained	1 cup chopped nuts (optional)
1/2 cup whipping cream	

Combine sugar, syrup, pineapple and whipping cream in saucepan. Bring to a boil, stirring constantly. Boil until mixture reaches soft-ball stage or to 236 degrees on candy thermometer. Remove from heat; stir in butter. Let cool in pan until lukewarm without stirring. Add vanilla; beat until thickened. Add nuts; pour into well-buttered 8-inch square pan. Yield: 16 to 24 pieces.

Lisa Graff, Theta Xi
Crescent, Oklahoma

REECE CUP BALLS

20 ounces confectioners' sugar	7 ounces marshmallow creme
1 cup margarine	1/2 block paraffin
1 cup creamy peanut butter	1 6-ounce package chocolate chips

Mix 1/2 confectioners' sugar with margarine in large bowl. Add peanut butter and marshmallow creme; mix well. Add remaining confectioners' sugar; mix well. Shape into balls; place on waxed paper. Refrigerate until thoroughly chilled. Melt paraffin and chocolate chips in top of double boiler over hot water. Insert toothpick in balls; dip in chocolate. Spoon chocolate over toothpick holes. Yield: 80 balls.

Clara L. Montgomery, Laureate Alpha Phi
Loveland, Colorado

TEXAS MILLIONAIRES

1 cup packed light brown sugar	1 teaspoon vanilla extract
1 cup sugar	3 1/2 cups pecan halves
1 cup light corn syrup	12 ounces milk chocolate chips
1 cup margarine	4 ounces paraffin
2 cups evaporated milk	

Combine sugar, syrup, margarine and 1 cup evaporated milk in saucepan; mix well. Bring to a boil, stirring constantly. Add remaining milk gradually. Do not allow to stop boiling. Cook until mixture reaches soft-ball stage. Add vanilla and pecans. Spoon by teaspoonfuls onto buttered 9-by-13-inch pan. Refrigerate overnight or place in freezer for few minutes or until firm. Melt chocolate chips and paraffin in top of double boiler over hot water. Dip candy into chocolate. Yield: 36 pieces.

Jennie Potter, Preceptor Nu
Oklahoma City, Oklahoma

VANILLA NUT ROLL

1 can sweetened condensed milk	1/2 package vanilla wafers, crushed
1 cup coconut	Confectioners' sugar
2 cups chopped pecans	

Combine all ingredients in large bowl; mix well. Divide into portions; roll into logs or press into 8-inch square pan. Roll logs in confectioners' sugar or sprinkle confectioners' sugar on pan mixture. Chill and slice. Yield: 12 servings.

Ruth Sterns, Xi Tau
Tuscaloosa, Alabama

ORANGE BAKED ALASKA

I was first served this in Bruxelles, Belgium, and it became a family favorite.

8 large oranges	1 tablespoon (about) grated orange rind
1/2 gallon vanilla ice cream	1 tablespoon (about) orange juice
2 egg whites	1/2 cup flaked coconut
1/4 cup sugar	

Slice top off oranges; scoop out pulp. Cut saw tooth pattern around edge of oranges. Fill centers with ice cream. Place in muffin cups; freeze. Beat egg whites until stiff, adding sugar gradually. Add orange rind and orange juice. Spoon on top of oranges; seal edges completely. Sprinkle with coconut. Store in freezer for 2 or 3 days or until needed. Preheat oven to 500 degrees. Bake for 1 to 2 minutes or until meringue is lightly browned. Serve immediately. Slice thin piece from bottom of oranges to set on plate. Yield: 8 servings.

Patricia Cruger, Laureate Beta Alpha
Desert Hot Springs, California

BROWN BETTY

3 cups peeled, cored sliced apples	1 1/2 cups soft bread crumbs
1/3 cup packed light brown sugar	1/2 teaspoon nutmeg
1 teaspoon cinnamon	1/4 cup melted butter
	3/4 cup water

Preheat oven to 350 degrees. Toss first 5 ingredients together in bowl. Pour into greased 2-quart baking dish. Pour butter and water over top. Bake for 45 minutes or until apples are tender. May serve warm with vanilla ice cream, hard sauce or custard sauce if desired. Yield: 6 servings.

Jackie Gitthens, Preceptor Alpha Nu
Havelock, North Carolina

ALL SEASONAL DESSERT

I use this fat-free gelatin dessert for all holiday occasions with napkins for the holiday or to match the color of gelatin. I use raspberry for Christmas; lime for St. Patrick's Day; orange, lime and peach for Easter; and lemon and Hawaiian pineapple for summer.

3/4 cup boiling water	1 carton vanilla or
1 package sugar-free	plain low-fat yogurt
gelatin	Whipped topping
1/2 cup cold water	
1/2 teaspoon vanilla	
extract	

Pour boiling water into blender container. Add gelatin; blend for 1 minute or until dissolved. Combine cold water and enough ice cubes to make 1 cup; add to gelatin. Stir with spoon until ice is almost melted. Blend in vanilla and vanilla yogurt; pour into dessert or tall stem glasses. Chill for 30 minutes or overnight. Top with whipped topping. Yield: 5 to 6 servings.

Janet A. Davis, Omega Xi
Haines City, Florida

BAVARIAN APPLE TORTE

1/2 cup margarine	1 egg
1/3 cup sugar	1/2 teaspoon vanilla
1/4 teaspoon vanilla	extract
extract	1/3 cup sugar
1 cup all-purpose flour	1/2 teaspoon cinnamon
8 ounces cream cheese,	4 cups sliced peeled
softened	apples
1/4 cup sugar	1/4 cup sliced almonds

Preheat oven to 450 degrees. Cream margarine, 1/3 cup sugar and 1/4 teaspoon vanilla in mixer bowl; blend in flour. Spread dough on bottom of 9-inch springform pan. Combine cream cheese and 1/4 cup sugar in bowl; mix well. Add egg and 1/2 teaspoon vanilla. Spread over dough. Combine 1/3 cup sugar and cinnamon in bowl. Add apples; toss together. Spoon apple mixture over cream cheese; sprinkle with almonds. Bake for 10 minutes. Reduce oven temperature to 400; bake for 25 minutes longer. Loosen torte from rim of pan; let cool before removing from pan. Yield: 8 to 10 servings.

Julie Teichert, Xi Epsilon Iota
Port McNeill, British Columbia, Canada

FRIED APPLE SUNDAE

1 Azteca salad shell	1 1/2 cups French vanilla
5 medium apples,	ice cream
peeled	1/2 cup whipped cream
3 tablespoons cooking	1 green cherry
oil	Chopped nuts
3 tablespoons cinnamon	(optional)

Cook Azteca salad shell according to package directions; let cool. Core and slice apples; place in heavy saucepan. Pour oil evenly over apples. Sprinkle evenly with cinnamon. Cook over medium-low heat until apples are soft but firm. Place ice cream in Azteca shell. Spoon hot apple mixture over ice cream. Top with whipped cream and cherry. Sprinkle with nuts. Yield: 2 servings.

Terri Wonsetler, Omega Kappa
Holt, Missouri

"PHILLY" APPLE PIZZA

1 20-ounce roll sugar	4 cups thinly sliced
cookie dough	apples
8 ounces cream cheese,	1/3 cup sugar
softened	1/2 teaspoon cinnamon
1/4 cup sugar	1/4 cup coarsely chopped
1 egg	nuts
1/2 teaspoon vanilla	
extract	

Preheat oven to 375 degrees. Place dough in well-greased 12-inch pizza pan; press over bottom and up side. Bake for 15 to 18 minutes or until lightly browned. Mix cream cheese and 1/4 cup sugar in mixer bowl on medium speed until well blended. Add egg and vanilla; mix well. Spread over baked crust. Toss apples with 1/3 cup sugar and cinnamon in bowl; arrange over cream cheese layer. Sprinkle with nuts. Bake for 20 minutes. Serve warm or at room temperature. Yield: 8 to 10 servings.

Nicolynn Cook, Beta Zeta Alpha
Canyon, Texas

BANANA SURPRISE

1 box vanilla wafers	1 can sweetened
3 or 4 medium ripe	condensed milk
bananas, sliced	8 ounces sour cream
1 small package vanilla	1 medium carton
instant pudding mix	whipped topping
1 cup milk	Chocolate syrup

Layer wafers and banana slices in 2-quart casserole. Stir pudding mix and milk in bowl; mix well. Fold in condensed milk. Chill for 15 minutes. Fold in sour cream and whipped topping. Pour over layered mixture. Drizzle with chocolate syrup. Refrigerate overnight. Yield: 6 to 8 servings.

Mary Rich, Delta Kappa
Albany, Georgia

CARAMEL DUMPLIN'S

1/2 cup sugar	2 tablespoons butter or
2 cups boiling water	margarine
1 cup sugar	1 teaspoon baking
1 tablespoon butter or	powder
margarine	1 teaspoon vanilla
Pinch of salt	extract
1/2 cup sugar	2 cups (or more) all-
3/4 cup milk	purpose flour
Pinch of salt	Whipped cream

Preheat oven to 375 degrees. Heat 1/2 cup sugar in cast iron skillet over medium heat, stirring constantly, until sugar is brown and melted. Add next 4 ingredients; boil for 10 minutes. Mix next 6 ingredients in bowl. Add enough flour to make stiff dough. Drop by tablespoonfuls into boiling caramel mixture. Bake for 15 minutes. Serve warm with whipped cream. Yield: 6 servings.

Marie Coleman, Preceptor Beta Sigma
Magalia, California
*Elaine Murdy, Eta
Prospect, Ohio

CHERRY TORTILLAS

1 20-ounce can cherry	1 cup sugar
pie filling	1 cup water
6 flour tortillas	Ice cream
1/2 cup margarine,	
melted	

Preheat oven to 350 degrees. Spoon pie filling on tortillas. Fold sides and ends to enclose filling. Arrange, fold side down, in lightly greased 9-inch square baking dish. Mix margarine, sugar and water together in bowl. Pour over tortillas. Bake for 40 to 45 minutes or until lightly browned. Serve warm with scoop of favorite ice cream on top. Yield: 6 servings.

Pam Bevel, Xi Alpha Beta Omega
Jasper, Texas

❖ CHOCOLATE BAKLAVA

This was served as a dessert at my dinner club's Greek dinner last year. It is easy, elegant and scrumptious.

41/2 cups sugar	1 pound phyllo sheets
3 cups water	11/2 cups unsalted
2 3-inch sticks	butter, melted
cinnamon	1/3 cup butter
1 tablespoon fresh	21/2 squares
lemon juice	unsweetened chocolate
21/2 pounds finely	1 cup confectioners'
chopped walnuts	sugar
1 teaspoon almond	1/3 cup milk
extract	

Preheat oven to 350 degrees. Combine first 4 ingredients in large heavy saucepan. Cook over low heat, swirling until sugar is dissolved. Increase heat; boil gently for 20 minutes. Let syrup cool; discard cinnamon. Combine walnuts, almond extract and 2 cups syrup in large bowl. Add more syrup if needed to make mixture moist enough to stick together; reserve remaining syrup. Cut phyllo sheets in half crosswise. Brush 1 sheet with unsalted butter; keep remaining sheets under moist towel. Place 2 tablespoons filling on short end. Fold long edges over filling. Roll up like jelly roll. Put seam-side down, 2 inches apart, on ungreased cookie sheet. Brush top with unsalted butter. Repeat with remaining filling and phyllo sheets. May be frozen for up to 1 month on parchment sheets tightly covered. Bake for 20 minutes or until golden and crisp. Bake for 30 minutes if frozen. Let cool for 5 minutes; brush tops with reserved syrup to glaze. Melt 1/3 cup butter and chocolate in top of double boiler over simmering water. Mix in confectioners' sugar slowly alternately with milk. Cook for 20 minutes, stirring frequently. May be refrigerated, covered, for up to 1 week and reheated in double boiler. Place pastry on serving plate; spoon fudge sauce on top. May sprinkle with additional chopped walnuts if desired. Yield: 40 pastry rolls.

Amy Cullis, Theta Beta
Troy, Ohio

CHOCOLATE ECLAIRS AND CREME PUFFS

1/2 cup butter or	1 cup milk
margarine	1 small carton
1 cup boiling water	whipping cream,
1 cup all-purpose flour	whipped
1/4 teaspoon salt	1/4 cup confectioners'
4 eggs	sugar
1 large package vanilla	1 can milk chocolate
instant pudding mix	frosting

Preheat oven to 400 degrees. Melt butter in boiling water in saucepan. Add flour and salt all at once; stir vigorously. Cook and stir until mixture forms a ball that does not separate. Remove from heat; cool slightly. Place in mixer bowl. Add eggs, 1 at a time, beating after each addition until smooth. Shape with tablespoon into oblong or round shapes on greased 9-by-13-inch baking pan. Bake for 30 to 35 minutes or until golden brown and puffy. Split in half; cool on rack. Combine pudding mix and milk in mixer bowl; mix well. Combine whipping cream and confectioners' sugar in bowl; mix well. Add to pudding mixture; blend with whisk. Spoon mixture into creme puffs. Melt chocolate frosting in microwave-safe dish in microwave; drizzle over top of cream puffs. Yield: 10 to 12 servings.

Deena Gordon, Xi Iota
Artesia, New Mexico

❖ CHOCOLATE PARFAIT DESSERT

My sorority sisters love this dessert.

1 package devil's food
   cake mix
1/2 cup margarine,
   melted
1/4 cup milk
1 egg
3/4 cup finely chopped
   peanuts
3/4 cup peanut butter
1 1/2 cups confectioners'
   sugar
8 ounces cream cheese,
   softened

2 1/2 cups milk
8 ounces frozen whipped
   topping, thawed
1 5-ounce package
   vanilla instant
   pudding mix
1/2 cup chopped peanuts
1 1 1/2-ounce bar milk
   chocolate, chilled,
   grated

Preheat oven to 350 degrees. Combine first 5 ingredients in mixer bowl; beat at medium speed until well blended. Spread evenly into 9-by-13-inch baking pan with bottom greased and floured. Bake for 20 to 25 minutes or until tests done; do not overbake. Let cool. Combine peanut butter and confectioners' sugar in mixer bowl; beat at low speed until crumbly. Beat cream cheese in large mixer bowl until smooth. Add milk, whipped topping and pudding mix; beat for 2 minutes at low speed until well blended. Pour 1/2 cream cheese mixture over baked layer. Sprinkle with 1/2 peanut butter mixture. Repeat with remaining cream cheese and peanut butter mixtures. Sprinkle with 1/2 cup chopped peanuts; gently press into filling. Sprinkle with grated chocolate. Refrigerate or freeze, covered, until serving time. Yield: 12 servings.

Agnes Ann Hanson, Xi Eta
Newcastle, Wyoming

DUMP CAKE

1 20-ounce can
   crushed pineapple
1 20-ounce can cherry
   pie filling
1 18-ounce package
   white or yellow
   cake mix

3/4 cup margarine,
   thinly sliced
1/2 cup chopped nuts
   (optional)
1 8-ounce carton
   whipped topping

Preheat oven to 350 degrees. Dump pineapple in greased 9-by-13-inch baking pan; spread evenly. Dump cherry pie filling over pineapple. Shake dry cake mix evenly over pie filling. Arrange margarine evenly over top. Sprinkle with nuts. Bake for 1 hour. Serve with whipped topping.
Yield: 12 to 15 servings.

Rene Chavez, Epsilon Chi
Kingman, Arizona
*Beverly Schwan, Xi Lambda Beta
Waco, Texas
*Sue Catoe, Preceptor Eta Chi
Orlando, Florida

DIRT CAKE

My kids love helping prepare "dirt cake" each Easter. They add a few gummy worms to the artificial flowers and serve up their cake with a small garden spade.

1 16-ounce bag Oreo
   cookies
1/2 cup butter or
   margarine, softened
8 ounces cream cheese,
   softened
1 cup confectioners'
   sugar
1 teaspoon vanilla
   extract
2 4-ounce packages
   chocolate instant
   pudding mix

3 cups milk
12 ounces whipped
   topping
1 silk plant (yellow
   roses)
1 8-inch clay flower
   pot, lined with
   plastic wrap or
   aluminum foil
1 small garden spade

Chill cookies in freezer for 2 hours. Crush in food processor until texture resembles potting soil. Combine next 4 ingredients in mixer bowl; cream until fluffy. Combine pudding mix and milk in large bowl; mix until well blended. Fold in whipped topping. Fold in cream cheese mixture. Place 1/3 crushed cookies in bottom of prepared flower pot. Add 1/2 pudding mixture. Repeat, ending with crushed cookies. Chill overnight. Place silk plant in pot; use spade to serve. Yield: 10 to 12 servings.

Minda Walters, Xi Gamma Rho
Anadarko, Oklahoma
*Rebecca Hahn, Preceptor Psi
Pembroke Pines, Florida
*Kris Hiers, Kappa Theta
Shreveport, Louisiana

FRESH FRUIT COOKIE-CRUST PIZZA

1 18-ounce roll sugar
   cookie dough
8 ounces cream cheese,
   softened
1/4 cup sugar
2 teaspoons lemon juice

1/2 cup whipping cream
Assorted fresh fruit,
   sliced
1/4 cup apricot preserves
   or orange marmalade
1 tablespoon water

Preheat oven to 375 degrees. Press cookie dough into round pizza pan, covering bottom and side. Bake for 10 to 12 minutes or until golden brown; let cool. Combine next 3 ingredients in mixer bowl; mix well. Add whipping cream; mix at high speed until light and fluffy. Spread over cooled crust; chill. Arrange fruit on cream layer. Mix preserves and water in small bowl; brush on top. Chill until serving time. Cut into pie wedges. Yield: 20 slices.

Lorna Ream, Laureate Chi
Hayden Lake, Idaho
*Jonnie Johnson, Theta
Salt Lake City, Utah

BUTTER BRICKLE ICE CREAM

2 small packages butter
  pecan instant pudding
  mix
2 cups milk
8 ounces whipped
  topping

1 can sweetened
  condensed milk
3 large cans Milnot
1 package Bits of Brickle
  Milk

Combine pudding mix and 2 cups milk in mixer bowl; mix well. Add next 4 ingredients; mix until well blended. Pour into 1-gallon ice cream freezer container. Add enough additional milk to equal 1 gallon. Follow manufacturer's directions for freezing ice cream. Yield: 1 gallon.

Lana Harlan, Theta Omega
Salisbury, Missouri

RICE KRISPIE-BUTTER BRICKLE ICE CREAM SANDWICHES

I have served these to my sorority sisters several times.

1/2 cup melted butter
  or margarine
1/2 cup packed light
  brown sugar
1 teaspoon vanilla
  extract

Dash of salt
2 cups flaked coconut
1 cup chopped nuts
3 cups Rice Krispies
1/2 gallon butter brickle
  ice cream

Combine butter and brown sugar in skillet; heat until melted. Add next 5 ingredients; mix well. Press 1/2 mixture into bottom of 9-by-13-inch baking pan. Slice ice cream; arrange in even layer over mixture. Top with remaining mixture. Freeze; cut into squares to serve. Yield: 12 servings.

Sue Hood, Xi Alpha
Omaha, Nebraska

GRANDMOTHER'S HOMEMADE ICE CREAM

2 quarts milk
3 eggs, slightly beaten
2 cups sugar
2 tablespoons (heaping)
  cornstarch

2 teaspoons vanilla
  extract
1 can evaporated milk
  or Milnot

Scald 1 quart milk in saucepan over medium heat. Combine eggs, sugar and cornstarch in bowl; mix well. Add egg mixture slowly to warm milk. Add vanilla; mix well. Cook, stirring, until slightly thickened. Let cool; pour into freezer container. Add evaporated milk and remaining 1 quart milk to fill container within 6 inches of top. Follow freezer instructions for freezing ice cream. Yield: 1 gallon.

Phyllis Everly, Xi Lambda Mu
Camdenton, Missouri

BUSTER BAR DESSERT

12 ounces Oreo cookies,
  crushed
1/4 cup butter or
  margarine, melted
2/3 cup chocolate chips
2 cups confectioners'
  sugar
1 1/2 cups evaporated
  milk
1/2 cup butter or
  margarine

1 teaspoon vanilla
  extract
1/2 gallon vanilla ice
  cream
1 cup chopped Spanish
  peanuts
Whipped cream or
  whipped topping
  (optional)

Mix cookies and 1/4 cup melted butter together in bowl. Press mixture into 9-by-13-inch baking pan. Combine next 4 ingredients in saucepan. Bring to a boil over medium heat; cook for 8 minutes, stirring frequently. Remove from heat; let cool completely. Add vanilla. Slice ice cream onto cookie crust. Sprinkle with peanuts. Pour chocolate mixture over peanuts; freeze. Serve with whipped cream. Yield: 15 servings.

Iva Parelius, Preceptor Alpha Phi
South Bend, Indiana

FROZEN MINT MALLOW

20 Oreo cookies, finely
  crushed
1/4 cup butter or
  margarine, melted

1/2 cup milk
32 large marshmallows
1/2 cup Crème de Menthe
2 cups whipping cream

Combine crushed cookies and butter in bowl; mix well. Reserve 1/2 mixture for topping. Press remaining mixture in bottom of 9-inch springform pan. Heat milk in top of double boiler over hot water; add marshmallows, stirring until melted. Cool slightly; stir in Crème de Menthe. Chill until slightly thickened. Whip cream in mixer bowl until begins to thicken. Beat in marshmallow mixture until thickened. Pour into prepared pan; sprinkle with reserved crumb mixture. Freeze for 6 to 8 hours. Yield: 8 servings.

Brenda Richardson, Gamma Phi
Maple Ridge, British Columbia, Canada

KAHLUA SPICED PEACHES

2 29-ounce cans cling
  peaches
1/2 cup Kahlua
1/2 cup packed light
  brown sugar
1/4 cup tarragon white
  wine vinegar

2 sticks cinnamon
3 4-inch thin strips
  orange peel
3 4-inch thin strips
  lemon peel

Drain peaches, reserving 1½ cups syrup. Combine reserved syrup and remaining ingredients in saucepan. Simmer for 5 minutes. Pour over peaches in bowl; let cool. Store, covered, in refrigerator for up to 4 weeks. Yield: 12 to 14 peaches.

Suzanne Lambertson, Delta Gamma Iota
Moreno Valley, California

PEACHES AND CREAM CAKE DESSERT

I was having a Xi Beta Beta sister and her husband for dinner and made this dessert from the pantry. They loved it.

1 package yellow butter cake mix	1 teaspoon almond extract
3/4 cup margarine, softened	1 teaspoon vanilla extract
4 eggs, at room temperature	1/2 cup sugar
1 teaspoon almond extract	1 8-ounce carton whipped topping
1 29-ounce can freestone peaches	Mint sprigs

Preheat oven to 350 degrees. Combine first 4 ingredients in mixer bowl; mix for 2 minutes or until well mixed. Pour into greased 9-by-13-inch baking pan. Bake for 45 minutes or until tests done. Drain peaches, reserving syrup. Combine ½ can peaches, 2 tablespoons reserved syrup and next 4 ingredients in blender container; blend until smooth. Pour into bowl. Chop remaining peaches into small pieces; stir into mixture with large spoon until ingredients are well distributed. Cut cake into small squares; spoon peach mixture on top. Garnish with mint sprig. Yield: 12 to 16 servings.

Kay Johnston, Xi Beta Beta
Birmingham, Alabama

HASTY PEACH DESSERT

I made this dessert 25 years ago for my sorority sisters when I lived in Belmond, Iowa.

1 29-ounce can sliced peaches	Crushed walnuts to taste
1 package butter brickle or yellow cake mix	1 carton whipped topping
1 cup butter or margarine, melted	

Preheat oven to 350 degrees. Place peaches with syrup in bottom of 9-by-13-inch baking pan. Sprinkle dry cake mix over peaches. Drizzle butter over cake mix. Sprinkle with walnuts. Bake for 1 hour. Serve with whipped topping. Yield: 12 servings.

Charlene Johnson, Epsilon Beta
Truman, Minnesota

PEANUT BUTTER-CREAM CHEESE DELIGHT

I first tasted this dessert at our local Bed and Breakfast Inn. We were having a social for our rushees and were treated to many gourmet desserts and a tour of the Inn.

1½ cups vanilla wafers, crushed	1/2 cup sugar
1/2 cup peanuts, chopped	1/2 cup peanut butter
1/4 cup butter or margarine, melted	2 teaspoons vanilla extract
2 tablespoons peanut butter	4 eggs
16 ounces cream cheese, softened	4 cups frozen whipped topping, thawed
	3/4 cup chocolate fudge ice cream topping

Combine wafer crumbs, peanuts, butter and 2 tablespoons peanut butter in bowl; blend until crumbly. Press 1 cup crumb mixture into bottom of 9-inch springform pan; chill. Combine cream cheese, sugar, peanut butter and vanilla in mixer bowl; beat at high for 3 minutes. Add eggs, 1 at a time, beating after each addition. Fold in whipped topping. Spoon ½ cream cheese mixture over crust. Drop fudge topping by tablespoonfuls over cream cheese mixture. Add remaining cream cheese mixture. Marble by cutting through almost to bottom with table knife in an over-and-under fashion. Smooth top. Sprinkle with remaining crumb mixture; press lightly. Freeze for several hours or overnight. Yield: 16 servings.

Lorrie Stickney, Phi Alpha Epsilon
Great Bend, Kansas

PEAR-PINEAPPLE CRISP

2 cups uncooked quick-cooking oats	1/2 teaspoon cloves
1 cup all-purpose flour	2 cups sliced fresh pears
2 cups packed light brown sugar	1 8-ounce can crushed pineapple
3/4 cup butter or margarine	Whipped cream (optional)
1 teaspoon cinnamon	Vanilla ice cream (optional)
1/2 teaspoon nutmeg	

Preheat oven to 350 degrees. Combine first 3 ingredients in bowl; mix well. Cut in butter until mixture is crumbly. Place ½ mixture in greased 9-inch square glass baking dish. Combine next 5 ingredients in bowl. Spoon over oats mixture. Top with remaining oats mixture. Bake for 45 minutes or until lightly browned. Cut into squares. Serve warm topped with whipped cream or vanilla ice cream. Yield: 12 servings.

Helen Marcheschi, Laureate Zeta Epsilon
Ukiah, California

QUICK AND EASY PINEAPPLE DESSERT

1 3-ounce can flaked coconut
1 angel food cake, torn into small pieces
1 15-ounce can crushed pineapple
1 6-ounce jar maraschino cherries, drained, chopped
1 12-ounce carton whipped topping

Preheat oven to 350 degrees. Spread coconut on cookie sheet; bake for 6 minutes or until toasted. Let cool. Arrange cake evenly in 9-by-13-inch glass dish. Pour 1/2 pineapple with juice over cake. Sprinkle with 1/2 cherries. Spoon 1/2 whipped topping over fruit. Sprinkle with 1/2 toasted coconut. Repeat layers. Refrigerate, covered, overnight.
Yield: 8 to 10 servings.

Lola Keating, Zeta Master
Colorado Springs, Colorado

FROZEN PISTACHIO CREAM DESSERT WITH RASPBERRY SAUCE

1 cup crushed vanilla wafers
1/2 cup finely chopped red pistachio nuts
1/4 cup margarine, melted
6 ounces cream cheese, softened
1 3-ounce package pistachio instant pudding and pie filling mix
1 1/4 cups milk
1 8-ounce carton frozen whipped topping, thawed
1 10-ounce package frozen raspberries, partially thawed
2 tablespoons sugar
2 tablespoons orange-flavored liqueur
2 tablespoons chopped red pistachios

Combine first 3 ingredients in medium bowl; blend well. Press firmly in bottom of ungreased 8-inch springform pan. Beat cream cheese in mixer bowl until light and fluffy. Add pudding mix and milk; beat until smooth. Reserve 3/4 cup whipped topping, covered, in refrigerator. Fold remaining whipped topping into cream cheese mixture; spoon into prepared pan. Freeze for 5 hours or overnight. Let thaw in refrigerator for 1 hour before serving. Combine raspberries, sugar and liqueur in blender container; blend until smooth. Strain to remove seeds. Top servings with reserved whipped topping, raspberry sauce and 2 tablespoons pistachios.
Yield: 9 servings.

LaVonne Craig, Laureate Alpha Upsilon
Garden City, Kansas

Karen Brice, Laureate Epsilon, Yorkton, Saskatchewan, Canada, makes Lemon Butter by combining 6 well-beaten eggs, 2 cups sugar and juice of 3 lemons in top of double boiler. Cook, stirring, until thickened. Remove from heat; stir in 1/2 cup butter. Store in sterilized jars in refrigerator for up to 6 weeks. Serve in baked tart shells with topping.

BREAD PUDDING WITH LEMON SAUCE

1 16-ounce loaf French bread, cut into 1-inch cubes
4 cups milk
3 eggs, beaten
2 cups sugar
3 tablespoons margarine, melted
2 tablespoons vanilla extract
1 cup raisins (optional)
Lemon Sauce

Preheat oven to 325 degrees. Combine bread and milk in large bowl; let stand for 5 minutes. Add next 5 ingredients; stir well. Spoon mixture into greased 9-by-13-inch glass baking dish. Bake, uncovered, for 1 hour or until firm. Let cool in pan for 20 minutes. Cut into squares; serve with Lemon Sauce.
Yield: 12 servings.

LEMON SAUCE

1 cup sugar
2 tablespoons (heaping) cornstarch
2 cups water
1/4 cup lemon juice
1 teaspoon vanilla extract
Yellow food coloring

Mix sugar and cornstarch in saucepan. Add water; mix well. Cook over medium-low heat until thickened, stirring constantly. Remove from heat; stir in lemon juice, vanilla and drop of food coloring.
Yield: 2 to 3 cups.

Pat Nutter, Laureate Nu
Conway, Arkansas

STOVE-TOP BREAD PUDDING

1 cup packed dark brown sugar
1 tablespoon butter
3 slices buttered bread, cubed
2 eggs, beaten
1 teaspoon vanilla extract
2 cups milk
1/4 teaspoon nutmeg
1/2 cup raisins

Combine sugar and butter in top of double boiler. Place bread cubes on top. Combine remaining ingredients in bowl; pour over bread. Do not stir. Cook for 1 hour over simmering water. May serve warm with ice cream, whipped cream or hard sauce if desired. Yield: 4 to 6 servings.

Maureen K. Hadley, Phi
Peterborough, New Hampshire

GRAPE NUT PUDDING

1/2 cup Grape Nuts
2 cups milk
1/4 cup sugar
1 egg, beaten
Whipped cream, ice cream or hard sauce

Preheat oven to 350 degrees. Soak Grape Nuts in milk in 1-quart casserole for 25 minutes or until soft. Add sugar and egg; mix well. Bake for 1 hour. Serve warm with whipped cream. Yield: 6 servings.

Christine Greenleaf, Xi Alpha Theta
Limestone, Maine

EGG CUSTARD

4 cups milk	1 teaspoon vanilla
4 eggs, beaten	extract
2/3 cup sugar	Cinnamon to taste
1/2 teaspoon salt	

Preheat oven to 325 degrees. Scald milk in saucepan. Mix next 4 ingredients in bowl. Pour milk slowly into egg mixture, stirring constantly until well blended. Pour into custard cups; sprinkle with cinnamon. Place cups in pan of hot water. Bake for 1 hour or until firm. Yield: 8 servings.

Carrie Jo Henshaw, Mu Omega
Tahlequah, Oklahoma

HOT FUDGE PUDDING

1 cup all-purpose flour	2 tablespoons melted
2 teaspoons baking	shortening
powder	1 cup packed light
1/4 teaspoon salt	brown sugar
3/4 cup sugar	4 tablespoons cocoa
2 tablespoons cocoa	3/4 cup boiling water
1/2 cup milk	

Preheat oven to 350 degrees. Blend first 5 ingredients in 1-quart casserole. Add milk and shortening; mix well. Bake for 10 minutes. Combine remaining ingredients in bowl; blend well. Spoon over casserole. Bake for 40 to 50 minutes longer or until tests done. Yield: 6 servings.

Susanna Marie Davis, Laureate Alpha Tau
Chillicothe, Ohio

LEMON SPONGE PUDDING

1 cup sugar	2 egg yolks
2 tablespoons butter or	1 cup milk
margarine	Juice and grated rind of
2 tablespoons	1 lemon
all-purpose flour	2 egg whites, stiffly
1/4 teaspoon salt	beaten

Preheat oven to 350 degrees. Cream sugar and butter together in mixer bowl. Add flour and salt. Combine egg yolks, milk, lemon juice and lemon rind in bowl; mix well. Add to creamed mixture. Fold in egg whites. Pour into 9-by-13-inch baking dish. Set dish in pan of hot water. Bake for 45 minutes or until tests done. Yield: 8 to 10 servings.

Gloria Golder, Laureate Xi
Coos Bay, Oregon

BAKED RICE PUDDING

1 quart milk	1/8 teaspoon salt
1/2 cup sugar	1/4 teaspoon nutmeg
4 tablespoons uncooked	2 tablespoons margarine
white rice	

Preheat oven to 325 degrees. Mix all ingredients together in large bowl. Pour into 2-quart baking dish sprayed with nonstick cooking spray. Bake for 2 to 2 1/2 hours, stirring every 20 to 30 minutes, or until thickened. Yield: 4 to 6 servings.

Mary L. Huber, Theta Theta
Goshen, Indiana

OLD-FASHIONED MOLASSES PUDDING

1/2 cup melted butter	8 ounces raisins
1/2 cup sugar	3 tablespoons butter,
1 teaspoon baking soda	melted
1 cup molasses	2 teaspoons all-purpose
3 1/4 cups all-purpose	flour
flour	2/3 cup packed light
1 teaspoon cinnamon	brown sugar
1 teaspoon cloves	1 cup boiling water
1 teaspoon allspice	1 teaspoon vanilla
1/2 teaspoon salt	extract
1/2 cup hot water	

Preheat oven to 350 degrees. Cream 1/2 cup butter and 1/2 cup sugar in mixer bowl. Mix baking soda with molasses in bowl; add to creamed mixture. Sift 3 cups flour, cinnamon, cloves, allspice and salt together into bowl. Add to creamed mixture alternately with water. Dredge raisins lightly in 1/4 cup flour; stir into batter. Pour batter into greased 9-inch square baking pan. Bake for 50 minutes or until knife inserted in center comes out clean. Combine 3 tablespoons butter, 2 teaspoons flour and brown sugar in bowl. Add boiling water; stir until smooth and thickened. Stir in vanilla; mix well. Serve with pudding. Yield: 6 to 8 servings.

Helen Pollock, Xi Xi
Lewisporte, Newfoundland, Canada

PUMPKIN UPSIDE-DOWN CAKE

1 29-ounce can	1 teaspoon vanilla
pumpkin	extract
1 12-ounce can	1 18-ounce package
evaporated milk	yellow cake mix
3 eggs	18 ounces butter or
1 1/4 cups packed light	margarine, melted
brown sugar	Whipped cream
2 teaspoons nutmeg	(optional)
2 teaspoons cinnamon	Chopped nuts (optional)
1/2 teaspoon ginger	

Preheat oven to 325 degrees. Mix first 8 ingredients together in large bowl. Pour into 9-by-13-inch baking pan sprayed with nonstick cooking spray. Sprinkle dry cake mix on top. Drizzle with melted margarine. Bake for 40 minutes to 1 hour or until tests done. Serve with whipped cream and nuts. Yield: 12 to 15 servings.

Sharon Van Winkle, Xi Alpha Omega
Story, Wyoming

RAISIN CRISP

2 cups raisins	1³/4 cups oats
3/4 cup sugar	1 teaspoon baking soda
3 tablespoons all-purpose flour	1 cup packed light brown sugar
1¹/4 cups hot water	1¹/2 cups all-purpose flour
2 tablespoons lemon juice	
1 cup butter or margarine, softened	

Preheat oven to 350 degrees. Combine first 5 ingredients in saucepan. Cook over medium heat until thickened; let cool. Mix remaining ingredients in large bowl. Press 1/2 oats mixture in greased 9-by-13-inch baking pan. Add raisin mixture. Sprinkle remaining oats mixture over raisin mixture. Press down lightly. Bake for 40 minutes or until tests done. Yield: 12 servings.

Joy Andorfer, Eta
Marion, Ohio

TASTY TIRAMISU

2 egg yolks	1/4 cup whipping cream
3 tablespoons sugar	10 ladyfingers
1 teaspoon vanilla extract	3 tablespoons coffee, cooled
8 ounces cream cheese	1 chocolate bar, grated

Beat egg yolks with sugar in mixer bowl. Add vanilla, cream cheese and whipping cream; beat until mixture is fluffy and smooth. Line bottom of 8-inch square glass baking dish with 1/2 the ladyfingers. Sprinkle coffee on top. Spoon 1/2 cream cheese mixture over ladyfingers. Sprinkle 1/2 grated chocolate on top. Repeat layers, ending with grated chocolate. Refrigerate for 2 hours. Cut into 6 to 8 pieces. Yield: 6 to 8 servings.

Margaret Lawrence, Laureate Phi
Montgomery, New York

RASPBERRY DELIGHT

2 10-ounce packages frozen red raspberries in syrup	50 large marshmallows
1 cup water	1 cup milk
1/2 cup sugar	2 cups heavy cream, whipped
2 teaspoons lemon juice	1¹/4 cups graham cracker crumbs
4 tablespoons cornstarch	1/4 cup chopped nuts
1/4 cup cold water	1/4 cup butter or margarine, melted
Few drops of red food coloring	

Heat raspberries with water, sugar and lemon juice in saucepan. Dissolve cornstarch in 1/4 cup cold water in bowl; stir into raspberry mixture. Cook over medium-low heat until thickened and clear. Stir in food coloring; let cool. Melt marshmallows in milk in top of double boiler over boiling water; let cool thoroughly. Fold whipped cream into marshmallow mixture. Mix remaining ingredients in bowl. Press firmly into bottom of greased 9-by-13-inch baking pan. Spread marshmallow-cream mixture over crumbs. Spread raspberry mixture over top. Refrigerate until firm. Cut into squares. Yield: 15 servings.

Patricia Reece, Xi Tau Iota
Ripon, California

RASPBERRY PRETZEL DESSERT

1¹/2 cups margarine	2 cups boiling water
1/2 cup sugar	1 6-ounce package raspberry gelatin
3 cups crushed pretzels	1/2 cup sugar
8 ounces cream cheese, softened	1 quart fresh or frozen raspberries
1 cup confectioners' sugar	
1 12-ounce carton whipped topping	

Preheat oven to 400 degrees. Melt margarine in 9-by-13-inch glass baking dish. Add 1/2 cup sugar and pretzels; mix well. Press into bottom of dish. Bake for 6 minutes; let cool. Beat cream cheese in mixer bowl. Add confectioners' sugar; mix well. Add whipped topping; blend well. Spread mixture over crust. Add boiling water to gelatin and 1/2 cup sugar in bowl; stir until dissolved. Chill until slightly thickened; add raspberries. Pour over cream cheese mixture. Refrigerate until serving time. Yield: 15 servings.

Angela Black, Epsilon Lambda
Jackson, Michigan

FROSTY STRAWBERRY SQUARES

1 cup all-purpose flour	2 cups sliced strawberries
1/2 cup chopped walnuts	1 cup sugar
1/2 cup margarine or butter, melted	2 tablespoons lemon juice
1/2 cup packed light brown sugar	1 cup whipping cream
2 egg whites	

Preheat oven to 350 degrees. Combine first 4 ingredients in bowl; mix well. Spread in 9-by-13-inch baking pan. Bake for 20 minutes, stirring occasionally. Sprinkle 2/3 crumbs into 9-by-13-inch glass ovenproof dish. Combine egg whites, strawberries, sugar and lemon juice in large mixer bowl. Beat on high speed for 10 minutes or until stiff peaks form. Beat whipping cream in small mixer bowl until soft peaks form. Fold into strawberry mixture. Spoon evenly over crumbs in dish. Sprinkle with remaining crumbs. Cover; freeze. Yield: 12 to 16 servings.

Shellie M. Heath, Beta Omega
Gering, Nebraska

BROWNIE TRIFLE

1 8-ounce package fudge brownie mix	8 Heath bars, crushed
2 3-ounce packages chocolate instant pudding mix	1 12-ounce package frozen whipped topping

Prepare and bake brownie mix according to package directions. Let cool; crumble. Prepare pudding mix according to package directions, omitting chilling. Place 1/2 crumbled brownies in bottom of 3-quart trifle dish. Top with 1/2 pudding, 1/2 candy and 1/2 whipped topping. Repeat layers ending with whipped topping. Chill for 8 hours. Yield: 16 to 18 servings.

Sharon Devolder, Omega Rho
Kansas City, Missouri
*Kathy Massey, Beta Gamma Kappa
Markham, Texas
*Stacy Kays, Zeta Upsilon
Miami, Oklahoma

BUTTERFINGER TRIFLE

3 egg yolks	1 8-ounce carton whipped topping
1/3 cup butter or margarine	1 angel food cake, torn into pieces
1 1/2 cups confectioners' sugar	4 Butterfinger candy bars, crushed
1 teaspoon vanilla extract	

Mix egg yolks, butter, confectioners' sugar and vanilla together in bowl. Add whipped topping; mix well. Layer 1/2 cake pieces in bottom of 9-by-13-inch pan. Spread 1/2 whipped topping mixture over cake. Sprinkle 1/2 candy on top. Repeat layers, ending with candy. Refrigerate until serving time. Yield: 12 servings.

Linda Schmitt, Beta Delta
Calmar, Iowa

❖ NATIONAL FRUIT TRIFLE

2 cups frozen blueberries, thawed	1/2 cup toasted slivered almonds
4 cups frozen strawberries, thawed	1 cup whipping cream
2 cups frozen peaches, thawed, sliced	2 tablespoons sifted icing sugar
1 1-pound cake, cubed	1/4 teaspoon vanilla extract
1/2 cup sherry (optional)	Fresh blueberries or strawberries
1/4 cup sugar	
2 1/2 to 3 cups vanilla custard	

Drain blueberries, strawberries and peaches. Line 3-quart glass dish with 1/2 pound cake cubes. Sprinkle with 1/2 sherry. Place 1 cups strawberries and 1/4 cup sugar in blender container; purée. Pour 1/2 purée over soaked cake; sprinkle 1 cup each strawberries, blueberries and peaches on top. Spread with 1/2 custard sauce; sprinkle 1/2 toasted almonds on top. Repeat layers. Refrigerate, covered with plastic wrap, for several hours or overnight. Whip cream, icing sugar and vanilla in mixer bowl until stiff peaks form. Spread over trifle. Garnish with fresh berries. Yield: 10 to 12 servings.

Shirley Gallant, Laureate Beta Delta
Scarborough, Ontario, Canada

ORANGE TRIFLE

1 11-ounce can mandarin oranges	4 cups milk
2 3-ounce packages vanilla instant pudding mix	1 cup heavy cream
	2 packages ladyfingers
	1 teaspoon almond extract
1 2-envelope box whipped topping mix	1/4 cup sugar

Drain oranges, reserving liquid. Arrange oranges on paper towel on plate; place in freezer. Mix pudding mix, whipped topping mix, milk, cream and almond extract in large mixer bowl; mix at low speed until blended. Beat on high speed for 5 minutes or until thickened and fluffy. Line bottom and side of 2-quart glass bowl with ladyfingers. Drizzle with reserved orange liquid. Spoon 1/2 pudding into bowl. Arrange remaining ladyfingers on pudding. Spoon remaining pudding over ladyfingers. Arrange orange slices in pretty design on top. Melt sugar in saucepan over high heat until amber in color; stir for 2 minutes. Drizzle over oranges for beautiful effect. Yield: 6 to 8 servings.

Joan Giunta, Xi Eta Upsilon
West Chester, Pennsylvania

STRAWBERRY PUDDING TRIFLE

1/2 large angel food cake	1 3-ounce package strawberry gelatin
1 3-ounce package vanilla instant pudding mix	1 cup hot water
	1 8-ounce package frozen strawberries
1 cup milk	
1 pint vanilla ice cream, softened	1 8-ounce carton whipped topping

Break cake into 1-inch pieces. Place in large deep clear bowl. Beat pudding with milk in mixer bowl until thickened. Stir in ice cream. Pour mixture over cake. Refrigerate for 10 minutes or until firm. Mix gelatin with hot water in bowl. Add strawberries; pour over cake mixture. Refrigerate until firm. Frost with whipped topping. Yield: 6 to 8 servings.

Twila Wolf, Alpha Beta Rho
Windsor, Missouri

TWINKIE DESSERT

2 10-count packages Twinkies	1 can strawberry pie filling
1 large box strawberry gelatin	1 medium carton whipped topping
1 large package vanilla instant pudding mix	1/2 cup chopped pecans

Place Twinkies in 9-by-13-inch pan. Prepare gelatin according to package directions; pour over Twinkies. Prepare pudding mix according to package directions; spread over gelatin. Spread pie filling over pudding. Spread whipped topping on pie filling. Sprinkle with pecans. Refrigerate until serving time. Yield: 20 servings.

Catherine Raye, Laureate Alpha Zeta Trinidad, Colorado

BLUEBERRY MANDARIN PIE

1 11-ounce can mandarin oranges, drained	1/8 teaspoon nutmeg
1 quart fresh blueberries	1 package pie crust mix
1 cup sugar	2 tablespoons butter or margarine
1/4 teaspoon salt	2 tablespoons cream
3 tablespoons quick-cooking tapioca	

Preheat oven to 400 degrees. Reserve several orange sections and blueberries for garnish. Combine remaining oranges and blueberries in large bowl. Sprinkle with sugar, salt, tapioca and nutmeg; toss lightly. Prepare pie crust mix using package directions. Roll half the pastry into 13-inch circle on lightly floured surface; fit into deep 9-inch pie plate. Spoon fruit mixture into pastry; dot with butter. Top with remaining pastry, sealing and fluting edge and cutting vents. Brush with cream. Bake for 45 minutes or until golden brown. Cool on wire rack for 2 hours. Garnish with reserved fruit. Yield: 6 servings.

Photograph for this recipe is on the Cover.

GOLDEN CAULIFLOWER SOUP

2 10-ounce packages frozen cauliflower or 4 cups fresh cauliflowerets	1 cup water
	2 cups milk
1 cup water	1 tablespoon instant chicken bouillon
1/2 cup chopped onion	2 cups shredded mild Cheddar cheese
1/3 cup margarine	Nutmeg to taste
1/3 to 1/2 cup all-purpose flour	Chopped green onions

Cook cauliflower in 1 cup water in medium saucepan until tender. Reserve 1 cup cauliflower. Process remaining cauliflower with cooking liquid in food processor until smooth; set aside. Sauté onion in margarine in large heavy saucepan. Stir in flour.

Add 1 cup water, milk and bouillon. Cook until slightly thickened, stirring constantly. Stir in cheese, puréed cauliflower, reserved cauliflower and nutmeg; mix well. Cook until heated through, stirring to melt cheese; do not boil. Serve from chafing dish; garnish servings with green onions. Yield: 12 servings.

Photograph for this recipe is on the title page.

COCONUT-GLAZED HAM

1 10-to 12-pound ham	2 tablespoons prepared mustard
Whole cloves	
3/4 cup Coco Lopez® cream of coconut	1 1/2 teaspoons cornstarch

Prepare and bake ham using directions on wrapper, removing ham from oven 30 minutes before end of baking time. Score top of ham and stud with cloves. Bring cream of coconut, mustard and cornstarch to a boil in small saucepan. Cook for 2 to 3 minutes or until thickened, stirring constantly. Brush over ham. Bake for 30 minutes longer. May microwave glaze in glass dish on Medium-High for 4 to 6 minutes or until thickened, stirring every 2 minutes and let stand for 5 minutes. Yield: 24 servings.

Photograph for this recipe of on the title page.

WINTER SALAD WITH LEMON VINAIGRETTE

1/2 cup vegetable oil	1/2 teaspoon salt
1/3 cup bottled lemon juice	1 head Bibb lettuce, torn
	8 ounces spinach, torn
1/4 cup sliced green onions	8 ounces mushrooms, sliced
1 tablespoon Dijon mustard	1 cucumber, sliced
	1 small red onion, sliced into rings
1 teaspoon sugar	

Combine first 6 ingredients in 1-pint jar with tight-fitting lid; shake to mix well. Chill until serving time. Combine lettuce, spinach, mushrooms, cucumber and onion in salad bowl. Chill, covered, until serving time. Drizzle desired amount of dressing over salad; toss gently. May use dressing as marinade for asparagus, broccoli, poultry or seafood. Yield: 12 servings

Photograph for this recipe is on the title page.

Pauline Oslanski, Xi Alpha Psi, Airdrie, Alberto, Canada, makes Fruit Kabobs with Strawberry Dip by placing 12 fresh strawberries and 12 fresh pineapple chunks on picks. Combine 1/2 cup fresh strawberries, 1/2 cup plain low-fat yogurt and 1 teaspoon honey in blender container; blend until smooth. Pour into honeydew melon half. Place fruit kabobs around cut edge.

MERRY CHERRY PIE

8 ounces cream cheese,
  softened
1 14-ounce can Eagle®
  Brand sweetened
  condensed milk
1/3 cup bottled lemon
  juice

1 teaspoon vanilla
  extract
1 9-inch graham
  cracker pie shell
1 21-ounce can cherry
  pie filling, chilled

Beat cream cheese in mixer bowl until light. Add condensed milk, beating constantly until smooth. Stir in lemon juice and vanilla. Spoon into pie shell. Chill for 3 hours or until set. Top with pie filling. Chill until serving time. Yield: 8 servings.

Photograph for this recipe is on the title page.

SOUTHERN SUNSHINE

2 cups orange juice
1/2 cup bottled lemon
  juice
1/4 cup sugar

3/4 cup Southern Comfort
1 32-ounce bottle of
  lemon-lime soda,
  chilled

Combine juices and sugar in pitcher, stirring to dissolve sugar. Chill until serving time. Add Southern Comfort and chilled soda at serving time; mix gently. Serve over ice. Yield: 7 cups.

Photograph for this recipe is on title page.

CHEESY BEEF ENCHILADAS

1 pound ground beef
1 10-ounce can
  enchilada sauce
2 envelopes taco
  seasoning mix
12 corn tortillas
Vegetable oil
4 cups shredded
  Monterey Jack cheese

1 medium onion,
  chopped
1 10-ounce can
  enchilada sauce
Parsley sprigs, chopped
  green onions and
  sliced radishes

Preheat oven to 350 degrees. Brown ground beef in skillet, stirring until crumbly; drain. Add 1 can enchilada sauce and taco seasoning mix with water called for in package directions. Simmer for 20 minutes. Soften tortillas in 1/2 inch oil in skillet for several seconds; drain. Spoon meat sauce, 3/4 of the cheese and onion onto tortillas; roll to enclose filling. Place seam side down in baking dish. Heat remaining can enchilada sauce in saucepan. Pour over enchiladas; top with remaining cheese. Bake for 15 to 20 minutes or until heated through. Garnish with parsley sprigs, chopped green onions and sliced radishes. Yield: 4 to 6 servings.

Photograph for this recipe is on page 2.

MEXICAN STACK-UPS

1 pound sirloin steak
1/2 cup soy sauce
2 to 4 tablespoons
  Tabasco sauce
Juice of 1 lime
4 cloves of garlic,
  minced
Salt and pepper to taste

4 large flour tortillas
Vegetable oil
4 cups shredded lettuce
4 to 6 red cherry
  peppers, coarsely
  chopped
1/2 cup sour cream
1 avocado, peeled, sliced

Add steak to mixture of soy sauce, Tabasco sauce, lime juice, garlic, salt and pepper in bowl. Marinate in refrigerator for several hours to overnight; drain. Grill or broil steak until done to taste. Cut into bite-sized pieces. Fry tortillas in oil in skillet until crisp and brown; drain. Place tortillas on plates. Layer lettuce, steak, peppers, sour cream and avocado on tortillas. Serve immediately. Yield: 4 servings.

Photograph for this recipe is on page 2.

PICANTE SAUCE

3 tablespoons chopped
  green onions
1 16-ounce can
  tomatoes
2 or 3 jalapeño peppers
1 1/2 tablespoons vinegar
1 clove of garlic

1 tablespoon chopped
  cilantro
1/8 teaspoon cumin
Sugar to taste
3/4 teaspoon salt
Tostados and corn chips

Combine first 9 ingredients in blender or food processor container; process until vegetables are coarsely chopped. Serve with tostados or corn chips. May substitute 3 large fresh tomatoes for canned tomatoes. Yield: 6 servings.

Photograph for this recipe is on page 2.

PINTO BEANS CALIENTE

2 cups dried pinto beans
1 11-ounce jar picante
  sauce
1 tablespoon extra-hot
  chili powder
1/4 teaspoon garlic
  powder
1 medium onion,
  chopped

Seasoned salt and
  pepper to taste
1 each green and red bell
  pepper, coarsely
  chopped
Shredded Monterey Jack
  cheese

Bring beans to a boil in water to cover in saucepan; remove from heat. Let stand for several hours. Rinse well. Combine with picante sauce, chili powder, garlic powder, onion, salt and pepper in slow cooker; mix well. Cook on Low for 6 hours. Add bell peppers and additional water if needed for desired consistency. Cook until heated through. Serve with cheese. Yield: 10 servings.

Photograph for this recipe is on page 2.

Metric Equivalents

*A*lthough the United States has opted to postpone converting to metric measurements, most other countries, including England and Canada, use the metric system. The following chart provides convenient approximate equivalents for allowing use of regular kitchen measures when cooking from foreign recipes.

Volume

These metric measures are approximate benchmarks for purposes of home food preparation.
1 milliliter = 1 cubic centimeter = 1 gram

Liquid	Dry
1 teaspoon = 5 milliliters	1 quart = 1 liter
1 tablespoon = 15 milliliters	1 ounce = 30 grams
1 fluid ounce = 30 milliliters	1 pound = 450 grams
1 cup = 250 milliliters	2.2 pounds = 1 kilogram
1 pint = 500 milliliters	

Weight   Length

Weight	Length
1 ounce = 28 grams	1 inch = 2½ centimeters
1 pound = 450 grams	¹/₁₆ inch = 1 millimeter

Formulas Using Conversion Factors

When approximate conversions are not accurate enough, use these formulas to convert measures from one system to another.

Measurements	Formulas
ounces to grams:	# ounces x 28.3 = # grams
grams to ounces:	# grams x 0.035 = # ounces
pounds to grams:	# pounds x 453.6 = # grams
pounds to kilograms:	# pounds x 0.45 = # kilograms
ounces to milliliters:	# ounces x 30 = # milliliters
cups to liters:	# cups x 0.24 = # liters
inches to centimeters:	# inches x 2.54 = # centimeters
centimeters to inches:	# centimeters x 0.39 = # inches

Approximate Weight to Volume

Some ingredients which we commonly measure by volume are measured by weight in foreign recipes. Here are a few examples for easy reference.

flour, all-purpose, unsifted	1 pound = 450 grams = 3½ cups
flour, all-purpose, sifted	1 pound = 450 grams = 4 cups
sugar, granulated	1 pound = 450 grams = 2 cups
sugar, brown, packed	1 pound = 450 grams = 2¼ cups
sugar, confectioners'	1 pound = 450 grams = 4 cups
sugar, confectioners', sifted	1 pound = 450 grams = 4½ cups
butter	1 pound = 450 grams = 2 cups

Temperature

Remember that foreign recipes frequently express temperatures in Centigrade rather than Fahrenheit.

Temperatures	Fahrenheit	Centigrade
room temperature	68°	20°
water boils	212°	100°
baking temperature	350°	177°
baking temperature	375°	190.5°
baking temperature	400°	204.4°
baking temperature	425°	218.3°
baking temperature	450°	232°

Use the following formulas when temperature conversions are necessary.

$$\text{Centigrade degrees} \times 9/5 + 32 = \text{Fahrenheit degrees}$$
$$\text{Fahrenheit degrees} - 32 \times 5/9 = \text{Centigrade degrees}$$

American Measurement Equivalents

1 tablespoon = 3 teaspoons	12 tablespoons = ¾ cup
2 tablespoons = 1 ounce	16 tablespoons = 1 cup
4 tablespoons = ¼ cup	1 cup = 8 ounces
5 tablespoons + 1 teaspoon = ⅓ cup	2 cups = 1 pint
8 tablespoons = ½ cup	4 cups = 1 quart
	4 quarts = 1 gallon

Merit Winners

Index

Beta Sigma Phi Cookbooks

available from *Favorite Recipes® Press* are chock-full of home-tested recipes from Beta Sigma Phi members that earn you the best compliment of all... "More Please!"

Every cookbook includes:

☆ color photos or black-and-white photos

☆ delicious, family-pleasing recipes

☆ lay-flat binding

☆ wipe-clean color covers

☆ easy-to-read format

☆ comprehensive index

To place your order, call our **toll free** number **1-800-251-1520** or clip and mail the convenient form below.

BETA SIGMA PHI COOKBOOKS	Item #	Qty.	U.S. Retail Price	Canadian Retail Price	Total
The Best of Beta Sigma Phi Cookbook	88285		$9.95	$12.95	
Home Sweet Home Cooking: Company's Coming	01260		$9.95	$12.95	
Home Sweet Home Cooking: Family Favorites	01252		$9.95	$12.95	
Food In The Fast Lane	94323		$9.95	$12.95	
Shipping and Handling		1	$1.95	$2.95	
TOTAL AMOUNT					

☐ Payment Enclosed
☐ Please Charge My ☐ MasterCard ☐ Visa ☐ Discover

Signature_____
Account Number_____
Name _____
Address _____
City_____State ____ Zip_____

No COD orders please.
Call our toll free number for faster ordering.
Prices subject to change.
Books offered subject to availability.
Please allow 30 days for delivery.

Mail completed order form to:

Favorite Recipes® Press
P.O. Box 305141
Nashville, TN 37230